"Ron Swift understands the key issues facing businesses and governments in servicing their customers and increasing positive relationships. You'll enjoy learning more and more of Swift's insightfulness and vision on the ways and methods to achieve your own success."

—Barbara Haley Wixom, Assistant Professor at the University of Virginia's McIntire School of Commerce and an Editor of "The Journal of Data Warehousing"

"Ron's work of over a decade of customer focused data warehousing has provided a clear view of what companies must do in order to achieve concrete successes in customer centric business initiatives. Ron's book encapsulates this learning and provides a clear roadmap to successfully implementing this."

—John McKean, Author, *Information Masters—Secrets of the Customer Race*
(Wiley, 1999)

"This book gives you essential knowledge for competing in the Networked Economy. How? By providing the competitive edge of knowing what your customers want and how to serve them better."

—Gail Rigler, Vice President of Global Marketing,
EDS Corporation—Plano, Texas

"CRM. It's not a device or a project, it's a process. And *Accelerating Customer Relationships* gives you the architecture for making it happen in your company. Ron Swift shows the way again with his insight, experience, and practical advice."

—Claudia Imhoff, Ph.D., Co-Author of *The Information Factory*,
Senior Vice President of Braun Consulting (www.BraunConsult.com)

"Ron Swift's book is designed to help you tie the loyalty knot with your customers. It has the tools, the framework, and the know-how to deliver customers and profits."

—Martha Rogers, Ph.D., Peppers and Rogers Group—and Co-Author of the books: *The One-to-One Future*, *The One to One Fieldbook*, and *One to One B2B*

"Who really knows their customers? Many companies think they do. In his dynamic book, Ron Swift presents a plan that all businesses want in their customer relationships—providing greater profitability and longstanding loyalty. Swift's more than two decades of consulting, educating, and writing make this a must read book for all managers."

—Victor Sassone, Executive Director
Hogan Center for Performance Excellence

"When your customers know you know them, your business is bound for success. Ron provides insight on how we build a complete data warehouse solution in 100 days...with room to expand as your company grows."

—Marcel Bhend, Founder and CEO
DW and Internet GmbH—Dietzenbach, Germany

Accelerating Customer Relationships
Using CRM and Relationship Technologies

Ronald S. Swift

Prentice Hall PTR, Upper Saddle River, NJ 07458
www.phptr.com

Cataloging-in-Publication Data Available

Editorial/Production Supervision: Kathleen M. Caren
Acquisitions Editor: Miles Williams
Editorial Assistant: Julie Okulicz
Marketing Manager: Kate Hargett
Manufacturing Manager: Alexis R. Heydt
Cover Design Director: Jerry Votta
Cover Designer: Talar Agasyan
Series Designer: Gail Cocker-Bogusz

© 2001 Prentice Hall PTR
Prentice-Hall, Inc.
A Pearson Education Company
Upper Saddle River, NJ 07458

Prentice Hall books are widely used by corporations and government agencies for training, marketing, and resale.

The publisher offers discounts on this book when ordered in bulk quantities.
For more information, contact Corporate Sales Department, Phone: 800-382-3419; fax: 201-236-7141; email: corpsales@prenhall.com or write Corporate Sales Department, Prentice Hall PTR, One Lake Street, Upper Saddle River, NJ 07458.

Printed in the United States of America

10 9 8 7 6 5 4 3 2 1

ISBN 0-13-088984-9

Prentice-Hall International (UK) Limited, *London*
Prentice-Hall of Australia Pty. Limited, *Sydney*
Prentice-Hall Canada Inc., *Toronto*
Prentice-Hall Hispanoamericana, S.A., *Mexico*
Prentice-Hall of India Private Limited, *New Delhi*
Prentice-Hall of Japan, Inc., *Tokyo*
Pearson Education Asia Pte. Ltd.
Editora Prentice-Hall do Brasil, Ltda., *Rio de Janeiro*

This book is dedicated to the many colleagues who made this all possible throughout the world and, especially to that special woman who provided insight and support for the author to complete this journey.

Contents

Preface   xvii

Chapter 1

Managing Customer Relationships 1:1   1

Foundations of the *Past* Drive Our Future   1
The Major Types of Customers   3
Who Really Knows Their Customers?   5
Keeping the Customers You Have   9
How You Serve Your Customers Is a Major Competitive Differentiator   11
Defining Customer Relationship Management   12
Some Companies Do CRM Naturally   16
Targeting Profitable Customers   17
Positioning Is the Key to Success in Business   18
Who Owns the Customer?   19
Changes in Customer Positioning   23
Using Data Better Enables You to Manage Relationships
    with Your Customers   25
CRM Is Easy for Small Companies   26

Large Companies Must Succeed at CRM   26

CRM Is Not Easy for Many Companies   27

Costs and Benefits of Relationship Management   28

Who Is Responsible for CRM?   29

Why this Book Is for You!   29

Are You Ready for CRM?   30

Marketing Communications Strategies   33

The Power of Relationship Optimization   35

Management Considerations   36

Chapter 2

Defining Your CRM Process   37

Why Create a Process for CRM?   39

CRM As a "Process"—Not a Project   39

Major Objectives and Benefits of a CRM Process   42

From Product Focus to Customer Focus   43

The Business View of a Marketing Process   44

The CRM Organization's Structure   51

Integration of Business, Information, People, Process, and Technology   57

Successful Excellence: Israel's Pele-Phone   58

Data Warehouse Requirements Definition   63

Management Considerations   64

Chapter 3

The Role of Information Technology   65

The Change from Data to Relationships   65

Six Key Enterprise Priorities   69

Four Stages of Knowledge Maturity   69

Integrating the Business Functions and Info-Structure
    Provides the Foundation   71

The Enterprise Opportunity 71

Preparing for Cultural and Idea Interchanges 72

The Role of Technology in Driving Customer
    Retention and Profitability 74

Enabling Customer Retention and Higher Profits 74

Who Are Your Customers? 75

CRM Enables Customer Segmentation 75

Data Data Everywhere 76

Enabling the New Marketing Litany: The Four Cs 77

Customer Retention 78

Knowing the Customer and Using Cross-selling 80

Enabling Target Marketing 81

The Importance of Enabling Technologies 82

The Emergence of Relationship Technologies 82

Excellence in Business Transformation: Hallmark Cards 88

Management Considerations 91

Chapter 4

Learning from Information: Data Mining 93

The World of Learning from Information Itself 93

The Role of Data Mining 98

Electronic Commerce 99

Operationalizing the Customer-Centric Data Warehouse 100

The Data Mining Process 112

Using Data Mining and Modeling for Business Problems 114

Selection Criteria for Data Mining Technologies 120

Management Considerations 122

Chapter 5

The Stages of Growth for CRM and Data Warehouse   123

The Six Stages of Growth   125

Categorizing Analytical Approaches   126

The Types of Decision Support   127

Managing the "Stages of Growth" in Customer-Centric
    Enterprise Info-Structure Environment   140

The Info-Structure or Framework   145

DW Successes from Long-Term Detailed Historical Enterprise Data   148

Any Question—At Anytime—of Any Data—
    from Any Level of Business   150

Mature Data Warehousing and CRM Decision Support   151

CRM and the Stages of Growth for Customer-Centricity   153

Management Considerations   156

Chapter 6

Data Warehouse Methodology   157

The Proof Is in the Experience   157

The Planning Phase   158

The Design and Implementation Phase   159

Usage, Support and Enhancement Phase   162

How to Achieve a High Degree of Scalability   166

Management Considerations   166

Chapter 7

Building the CRM Data Warehouse and Info-Structure 169

Defining Your Timeframes and Objectives	169
Defining a DW Framework and Building a Data Warehouse	170
Managing Operational Data into the Warehouse	172
Transforming Data into Information	172
Architectural Strategies—Centralized Versus Distributed	173
Independent Data Marts Versus Enterprise Data Warehouse	173
Data Replication and Propagation	174
Middleware Requirements	174
Data Modeling and Design of the Data Warehouse	175
Building a Data Warehouse in 100 Days	175
Phase 1: Analysis & Design	182
Demand Analysis	182
Data Quality Test	183
Business Data Model (BDM)	184
Logical Data Model (LDM)	185
Validation of Results	186
Phase 2: Implementation	187
Physical Data Model (PDM)	187
Interface Programs	188
Data Loading	189
Concept of Operations	190
Aggregations (into Data Marts)	191
System and Integration Test	192
Phase 3: Reports, Queries, and Analytical Uses	193
Set Up OLAP Tool	194
Designing Report Types	194
Developing Report Templates	195
Supporting Activities	195
Conclusion—100 Days to Success !!!	195

Chapter 8

Critical Success Factors for CRM and DW 197

Strategic "IT and Business" Enterprise CSFs 199
Information Infra-Structure CSFs 204
Guidelines for Success—Knowing Your Providers 205
Seven Rules for Discussions with CRM Solution Providers 206
Business Questions and Issues 208
Information Technology Questions 211
Business Users' Questions 220
Red Flags 221
Management Considerations 223

Chapter 9

Data Privacy: Ensuring Confidence 225

The Need for Data Privacy 225
Alert: Recent Alarms in the U.S. 227
Guidelines—The OECD Principles 228
Web Commerce and Privacy 230
Beginning Resolutions—U.S. Self-Regulation Policy 231
Study of Web Sites by the U.S. Federal Trade Commission 231
Online Privacy Alliance 232
The Emerging "P3P Standard" 233
P3P Standards—Applicability to Data Warehousing 234
European Legislation 235
The Impact on Companies Operating in Europe 237
U.S. "Safe Harbor" Principles 238
The Approach to Privacy in Data Warehousing 239
Threat and Opportunity 239
General Privacy Requirements 240
Global Privacy Requirements 240
Privacy Impact on Data Warehousing, Data Mining and
Database Marketing 245
Opt-Out of Direct Marketing 245

Disclosure to Third Parties   247
Opt-Out of Automated Decisions with Significant Effects
    (Example: Customer Creditworthiness)   247
Notice of "Logic Involved in Automatic Processing"   248
"Special Categories" of Data   248
"Erasure or Blocking" of Certain Data   249
Opportunity for Enhanced Customer Relationship Management   250
Building Privacy into the Data Warehouse   251
Enhancing the Logical Data Model   251
Using Privacy Views to Support Restricted Access, Opt-Outs
    and Anonymity   252
Providing an Interactive Customer Service Interface
    for Personal Data Administration   254
Providing Reports to Verify Privacy Compliance   255
Management Considerations   256

Chapter 10

Implementing Privacy and Customer Views   257

Applying the Privacy Policies to a Data Warehouse for CRM   257
Why the Platform for Privacy Preferences (P3P)?   257
Application of Privacy Policies to a Data Warehouse   258
Can Companies with a Data Warehouse Ignore the Privacy Issue?   260
Opportunities for Managing Your Customers   262
P3P Adoption Scenario: Retail Data Warehouse   263
Enhanced Personal Data   264
Potential Marketing Initiatives   264
Using Privacy Views to Implement Privacy in a CRM Environment   265
Reasons for Using Views   266
The Concept of "Views"   267

Chapter 11

The @ctive Data Warehouse   273

A New Breed of Decision Support   273
Knowing Differences—Old World Versus Active Info-Structures   274

First Generation Implementations—The Refreshment Cycle 275

Current Generation Data Warehouse Implementations 277
Example: Transportation/Airline Customer Sensitivity 278

Learn by Having Very Detailed CRM Data About Customers 279
Example: Health Care CRM Before the Doctor's Services 279
Examples in Banking, Insurance, and Other Industries 280

The @ctive Data Warehouse Strategy 281

Web-Based Business Opportunities 283

Paving the Future for Knowledge Commerce 284

Coming of Age in the New Age of E-Commerce 285

E-commerce and E-business 286
Click-Stream Analysis Opportunities 287
@ctive Data Warehousing for E-business on the Internet 287
Privacy and The Internet 289

Excellence in Business Transformation: Delta Air Lines
Takes Off Using Advanced @ctive Data Warehousing for CRM 289

Management Considerations 293

Chapter 12

The Economic Value of CRM 295

One-to-One Marketing 295

Anticipated Results of CRM—Key Assumptions and Verifications 301

How to Get Your Economics Around CRM 303

The Payback from Detailed Information...
and the Cost of Not Having It 308
High Returns 308
Payback Performance 309
Nimble Response 309
Guarding Against Competition 310
Accurate Direct Marketing 310
Better Portfolio Management 311
Service Versus Profits 311
Measuring Success 312
Identify Profitable Customers 312
Smarter Marketing 312

Driving Propensity Models for New Profits   313
Channel Analysis   313
Keep the Satisfied Customers   314
Increasing Productivity   314
Retaining (and Gaining) Customers   314
Rapid Application Development   315
Competitive Speed   315
Investment Payback Results   316

Advancing Toward Strategic Economics of CRM   316

Management Considerations   318

Chapter 13

The Strategic View of Data Warehousing and CRM   319

Sustainable Competitive Advantage (SCA)   320

The Eternal Struggle of Business   321

Strategic Thinking   323

Data Warehousing and Strategic Thinking   325

A Rising-Tide Strategy   326

Data Warehousing and the Strategic Paradox   330

Data Warehousing and Maneuverability   332
    Data Warehousing and CRM Are Prerequisites to
      a Maneuver Strategy   333
    How Strategic Executives Think of CRM and DW   334

Management Considerations   335

Chapter 14

How Companies Succeed Using CRM, Data Warehousing, and Relationship Technologies   337

The Financial Services Industry   340
    Bank of America (US)   340
    Barclays Bank (UK)   342
    Royal Bank (Canada)   347
    Union Bank (Norway)   348

The Manufacturing and Distribution Industries   351
    Western Digital (US)   *351*

The Retail Industry   354
    Migros (Europe)   *354*
    The Warehouse (NZ)   *359*
    Sears, Roebuck (US)   *361*
    Wal-Mart Stores (US)   *365*

The Airline and Tourism Industries   369
    Continental Airlines   *369*
    Travel Unie (Netherlands)   *372*
    Kinki Nippon Tourist (Japan)   *375*
    "One World"—British Airways, American Airlines, and Qantas   *378*

The Ground Transportation Industry   381
    Burlington Northern Santa Fe Railway (US)   *381*

The Telecommunications Industry   384
    Pele-Phone (Israel)   *384*

The Health Insurance Industry   388
    DCB Actuaries and Consultants (Czech Republic)   *388*
    Anthem Blue Cross/Blue Shield (US)   *390*

The Entertainment Industry   395
    Harrah's Entertainment (US)   *395*

Management Considerations   398

Chapter 15

Studies of Communications Industry Implementations   401

The Oshita Research Project—Focus on Knowledge   401
Four-Phase Technique for Research in CRM   402
The Communications Industry—A Review   403

Research Findings   404
    Strategic Impact   407
    Technology Integration   408
    Strategic Partnership   410
    Technology Assimilation   411
    Technology   412
    Customer Project   413

Understanding Strategic Horizons   420

Management Considerations   422

Appendix A

Author's End Notes and Acknowledgments   423

Appendix B

Bibliography/References   431

Index   457

Preface

Corporations that achieve high customer retention and high customer profitability aim for:

**The right product (or service), to the right customer,
at the right price, at the right time, through the right channel,
to satisfy the customer's need or desire.**

Information Technology—in the form of sophisticated databases fed by electronic commerce, point-of-sale devices, ATMs, and other customer touch points—is changing the roles of marketing and managing customers. Information and knowledge bases abound and are being leveraged to drive new profitability and manage changing relationships with customers.

The creation of knowledge bases, sometimes called data warehouses or *Info-Structures*, provides profitable opportunities for business managers to define and analyze their customers' behavior to develop and better manage short- and long-term relationships.

Relationship Technology will become the new norm for the use of information and customer knowledge bases to forge more meaningful relationships. This will be accomplished through advanced technology, processes centered on the customers and channels, as well as methodologies and software combined to affect the behaviors of organizations (internally) and their customers/channels (externally).

We are quickly moving from Information Technology to Relationship Technology. The positive effect will be astounding and highly profitable for those that also foster CRM.

At the turn of the century, merchants and bankers knew their customers; they lived in the same neighborhoods and understood the individual shopping and banking needs of each of their customers. They practiced the purest form of Customer Relationship Management (CRM). With mass merchandising and franchising, customer relationships became distant. As the new millennium begins, companies are beginning to leverage IT to return to the CRM principles of the neighbor store and bank.

The customer should be the primary focus for most organizations. Yet customer information in a form suitable for marketing or management purposes either is not available, or becomes available long after a market opportunity passes, therefore CRM opportunities are lost.

Understanding customers today is accomplished by maintaining and acting on historical and very detailed data, obtained from numerous computing and point-of-contact devices. The data is merged, enriched, and *transformed into meaningful information* in a specialized database. In a world of powerful computers, personal software applications, and easy-to-use analytical end-user software tools, managers have the power to segment and directly address marketing opportunities through well managed processes and marketing strategies.

This book is **written for business executives and managers** interested in gaining advantage by using advanced customer information and marketing process techniques. Managers charged with managing and enhancing relationships with their customers will find this book a profitable guide for many years. Many of today's managers are also charged with cutting the cost of sales to increase profitability.

All managers **need to identify and focus on those customers** who are the most profitable, while, possibly, withdrawing from supporting customers who are unprofitable.

The goal of this book is to help you:

1. identify actions to categorize and address your customers much more effectively through the use of information and technology,
2. define the benefits of knowing customers more intimately, and
3. show how you can use information to increase turnover/revenues, satisfaction, and profitability.

The level of detailed information that companies can build about a single customer now enables them to market through knowledge-based relationships. By defining processes and providing activities, this book will accelerate your CRM "learning curve," and provide an effective framework that will enable your organization to tap into the best practices and experiences of CRM-driven companies (in Chapter 14).

In Chapter 6, you will have the opportunity to learn how to (in less than 100 days) start or advance, your customer database or data warehouse environment.

This book also provides a wider managerial perspective on the implications of obtaining better information about the whole business. The customer-centric knowledge-based info-structure changes the way that companies do business, and it is likely to alter the structure of the organization, the way it is staffed, and, even, how its management and employees behave.

Organizational changes affect the way the marketing department works and the way that it is perceived within the organization. Effective communications with prospects, customers, alliance partners, competitors, the media, and through individualized feedback mechanisms creates a whole new image for marketing and new opportunities for marketing successes.

Chapter 14 provides examples of companies that have transformed their marketing principles into CRM practices and are engaging more and more customers in long-term satisfaction and higher per-customer profitability.

I would like to take this opportunity to thank the many talented people who have contributed to this book in the form of superlative ideas, sharing of their experiences, and their continuing encouragement. They are recognized throughout the book within the areas of their contributions, as well as in the special acknowledgment section that follows.

The following friends, mentors, and collegues helped to make this book possible:

Heather Anderson	Dean Kelly
Robert Armstrong	Sean Kelly
Tracy Austin	Gabriel T. Kerekes
Carolyn Beauregard-Shinkle	BethAnn Konves
Marcel Bhend	Katherine Kramer
Monty Bieber	Randy Lea
Bernard Boar	John McKean

Peter Boulter
Stephen Brobst
Curt Bynum
Kathleen Caren
Richard Carlson
Elizabeth Corley
Mike DeBrosse
Douglas Ebel
John Eggerding
Clive Evans
Erin Fagan
Christopher Field
Ruth Fornell
Harry Gault
Sam Gragg
Paul Gray
Don Groesser
Sharon Hamilton
Barbara Haley-Wixom
Peter Hand
Dan Harrington
Jerry Hill
Mark Hurd
Lin Hutaff
Claudia Imhoff
Bill Inmon
Mark Jahnke
Jeanene R. Jenkins
Kirk D. Johnsen
Jeffrey M. Jones
Edward Karthaus

Regis McKenna
Michael Meltzer
Holly Michael
Jeanne Nolan
Richard Nolan
Lars Nyberg
Ken O'Flaherty
Yancy Oshita
Sharon Owens
Don Peppers
Rozsi Pogany
Ronald Powell
Fred Reichheld
Martha Rogers
Gregory Sannik
Victor Sassone
William Saylor
Joan Monica Schultz
Rick Schultz
G. Miles Stephenson
Garrett Stolle
Donna Cobb Swift
Marc Teerlink
Dian Terry
Susana Thompson
Chris Twogood
Scarlett Van Der Muellen
Eugene Verdu
Hugh Watson
Joseph Wenig
Chris Yannik

In the title of this book and throughout its pages I have used the phrase "Relationship Technologies" to describe the increasingly sophisticated data warehousing and business intelligence technologies that are helping companies create lasting customer relationships, therefore improving business performance. I want to acknowledge that this phrase was created and protected by NCR Corporation and I use this trademark throughout this book with the company's permission. Special thanks and credit for developing the Relationship Technologies concept goes to Dr. Stephen Emmott of NCR's acclaimed Knowledge Lab in London.

As time marches on, there is an ever-increasing velocity with which we communicate, interact, position, and involve our selves and our customers in relationships.

To increase your Return on Investment (ROI), the right information and relationship technologies are critical for effective Customer Relationship Management. It is now possible to:

1. know who your customers are and who your best customers are
2. stimulate what they buy or know what they won't buy
3. time when and how they buy
4. learn customers' preferences and make them loyal customers
5. define characteristics that make up a great/profitable customer
6. model channels are best to address a customer's needs
7. predict what they may or will buy in the future
8. keep your best customers for many years

This book features many companies using CRM, decision-support, marketing databases, and data-warehousing techniques to achieve a positive ROI, using customer-centric knowledge-bases.

Success begins with understanding the scope and processes involved in true CRM and then initiating appropriate actions to create and move forward into the future. Walking the talk differentiates the perennial ongoing winners. Reinvestment in success generates growth and opportunity.

Success is in our ability to learn from the past, adopt new ideas and actions in the present, and to challenge the future.

Respectfully,

Ronald S. Swift
Dallas, Texas
June 2000

Managing Customer Relationships 1:1

The genius of free-market competition is that the customer...
gets to decide who wins and who loses.
And ultimately, the customer is the biggest winner.

Donald J. Carty, CEO AMR/American Airlines (1999)

▶ Foundations of the *Past* Drive Our Future

The customer is the focal point of marketing, sales, contacts, products, services, time, resource allocations, profitability, and long-term growth and strength of enterprising organizations.

The term *customer* was first coined at the beginning of the twentieth century, and yet it took nearly 100 years for companies to really understand what the term means. As the customer role of the relationship expands, suppliers or service providers are inspired to serve them and to cater to their needs in exchange for (profitable) value in the form of money and repeat business. There is overwhelming evidence of the magnitude of opportunity and strong sense of need for management and marketers to achieve success.

In the 1990s, the roles of the buyer and provider/supplier were reversing: Customers changed from being "the hunted" to being treated as special and "cultivated." Previously, suppliers played the part of the "hunter." Global brand leaders decided who the customer was and into what category that customer best fit. Marketing techniques, it seems, were built around the demands of the product rather than the consumer. In the words of the pop culture phrase, "The public wants what the public gets." But the days of Henry Ford's concept of everyone being able to have any color automobile that he or she wants "as long as it is black" expired long ago. That expired the day someone decided to listen to customers by offering the second color in an automobile.

Today, customers require flexibility, availability, creativity, and price advantage from the supplier or service provider. Therefore, new techniques to discover these attributes are required for organizations to succeed in a forever-changing world of customer wishes, customer preferences, customer behaviors, and customer loyalties.

How can a customer be loyal to a company, such as an airline or a purchasing point, with multiple loyalty accounts/cards in the same marketplace? The professional marketing people at American Airlines—who created a major marketing advantage through their American Airlines AAdvantage Frequent Flyer Program—have created special loyalties through special programs to ignite or accelerate loyalty of their best customers (knowing who they are, what they do, what they prefer, and when they travel), who they contact of these special customers, how they interact with these customers, how they measure these customers, and how they sometimes provide special considerations and services to their best customers. American Airlines continues to lead the way in customer loyalty!

Some of the members of the "One World" Airline Alliance (joined together in 1999 by American Airlines, British Airways, Qantas, Cathay Pacific, Finnair, and Iberia) not only document customer complaints, but telephone customers to discuss their difficulties and suggestions within a specified period of time after their trip itinerary has completed. To determine "retention," they measure when the customer returns to fly on their airline following complaints or problems with their services.

**The high-value, loyal, returning, satisfied, profitable customer
is the key focal point for profitable and growth organizations
throughout the world.**

This change in outbound customer interaction has created a doubling of customer "loyalty" and "retention," along with understanding the issues and concerns of their best customers. This important learning process comes from detailed measuring of the postinteraction return-sales-tickets versus the timings of the calls. One airline does this by comparing precomplaint travel and postcomplaint travel and scores the responses.

Using information and historical patterns to understand buying patterns, behaviors, and ticketing characteristics is important. Using the *info-structure* to manage and measure relationships is new to most companies. This is much more than just using a call center to contact customers to discuss complaints; it is now a management system that listens to the customers, documents the problems and solutions, and changes the behavior of employees and the call center interactions to truly build the relationship.

Customers vote with their purchases and denials of purchases. Knowing their wishes and knowing their history can provide more benefit than ever achieved before. Information transformed into knowledge is the differentiator for success.

▶ The Major Types of Customers

Many companies tend to think of customers as the retail customer or the business customer. This is due to the company's heritage or their industry focus on the major high-volume or big-order customers. As technology changes the terrain of customer accessibility and the ability of the customer to contact your organization directly, it may be better to clearly define your customer groups. This will give your organization a wealth of perspective and also begin the redefinition of the information required for you to succeed in these groupings (or what is known as "segments"). Competition and the birth of a new kind of consumerism have enabled the customer to regain an important position in the actions of a company.

There are hundreds of definitions of a customer. In fact, one of the most challenging aspects to manage customers through information and technology is to define your customers (within the context of data). (We will cover more on this issue in Chapters 6, 7, and 11).

When we define "customers," we are speaking of multiple types or groups of customers (Figure 1-1). The following definitions fall under "customer":

1. **Consumer**—The retail customer who buys the final product or service. Usually an individual or a family.
2. **Business to Business**—The customer who purchases your product (or service) and adds it to its product for sale to another customer or a business using your product within its own organization to increase profitability or services.
3. **Channel/Distributor/Franchisee**—A person or organization that does not work directly for you and is (usually) not on your payroll, which buys your product to sell or utilize it as your representative/location in that area.
4. **Internal Customer**—A person or business unit within your enterprise (or associated companies) that requires your product or service to succeed in their business goals. This is usually the most ignored customer of an organization and (potentially) the most profitable over time.

Products and services are sold to all of these types of customers. The question you might ask is, What marketing and communications strategies do you have for each type of customer?

Consumer

Internal

Business

Channel

Figure 1-1. Types of customers.

In addition, you will need to address the information and knowledge needs of these customers (and also the combinations of them) in order to know what their preferences, nonpreferences, and high-profitability sales may be or could become in the future. Think of businesses as households of units of people whom you wish to do business with. Think of these households as present businesses and also future opportunities.

Householding *Householding* is created in many banking and financial services systems to ensure that the institution maintains a positive relationship and understands the transactions or balances in more than the individual accounts of the individuals (Figure 1-2). In addition, the preferences of the home-based family member(s) or the children are in contrast with the leaders of businesses that you may do business with. You will need to plan carefully for your effective marketing and sales communications with different characteristics and profiles of your customers and households (whether they are business households or family households or both).

Therefore, please keep in mind the multiple types of customer that are addressed in this book when we use the word *customer*.

▶ Who Really Knows Their Customers?

Competition and the birth of a new kind of consumer has enabled the customer to regain an important position in the actions of a company. Companies have begun to realize that they know little or nothing about their customers. From a distance, they all have something in common; get closer and they start to divide into groups—each with different characteristics, requirements, and behaviors. Get *even* closer, and the definitions for each group start to fade, until one is left with many segments. Closeness is not an end in itself—the requirements of each customer will change from day to day, so flexibility in how customers are defined is required.

Figure 1-2. Households are made up of multiple types of customers.

This is the crossroads that many companies reach today. Without the age-old privilege of being exclusive providers of goods to a handful of people, companies are competing with a rash of rivals, all targeting the same customer. Even the cozy cartel arrangements that existed for years to maintain prices in some sectors are crumbling, and competitors using new channels are winning large market share in a matter of months, often without making a significant investment.

Customers Expect You to Know Them

The customer—who was sometimes treated badly to adequately (at best)—was quick to catch onto the market revolution of the 1990s. Initially flattered by being treated less as a number and more as an individual with distinct requirements, consumers are now communicating their demands back to their suppliers. Where once they would not consider the idea of bargaining, they now tell the managers of brand retail chains what they are prepared to pay and specify how they want products sourced, designed, styled, combined, assembled, delivered, and maintained.

Customers also look closely at suppliers and want to know what their credentials are—social, environmental, and economic. Consumers use technology to do this quickly and easily. The letter of complaint has turned into a tide of email, the quiet suggestion to the store manager has turned into a global consumer group. And, the armchair disapproval of poor wages paid to Third World workers now occupies an Internet lobby site with the power to change share prices overnight.

It Could Be Bad News If...

Too many companies have not really embraced *customer relationship management* (CRM). They try to guess what will entice the customer instead of finding out in advance. Today, as ever, it may be their survival that is at stake if they do not institute it appropriately or correctly for their markets and customers. Companies that competed effectively for 100 years can vanish. Equally, an undergraduate with a good idea for an Internet-based company can be valued at $3 billion within a few years, even while profits remain elusive.

In many countries, long-distance telephone carriers are experiencing the phenomenon of **churn**—customers are switching back and forth among competing suppliers, baited by special offers of cash back or free calls. Churn is a key issue for many industries and many competitors.

In competitive markets, if you don't maintain your customers' loyalty, someone else will engage/steal them away. In the mobile phone industry, between 20 and 30% of customers change their provider yearly (known as *churn rate*), and service providers need to know not just who has churned but what will stop them before they decide to go to a competitor. A small reduction in churn can generate millions in maintained revenues or additional profits to a company.

In manufacturing, companies need to look at the long-term profitability of each customer to determine where their development and marketing resources are best spent. In the utilities industry, companies must look at churn as supply becomes deregulated and they must consider who their best customers are. Do *you* really know who your best customers are?

In many cases, it may be easier and more profitable to keep existing customers than to find new ones. Using CRM or 1:1 techniques for acquiring new customers sparks new opportunities. CRM may catapult an organization into a marketplace previously unknown or unavailable to the enterprise. Companies need to look at how they can keep profitable customers, increase customers' spending over time, and only then attract new profitable customers. In fact, sometimes, winning new customers is relatively easy. Using classic price promotion techniques, a company can soon achieve new business, but real profit lies in delineating which customers are likely to be profitable in the long term, long before they become a burden to the profit line.

In some organizations, there may even be benefit in stimulating some customers to go to the competition—especially if they are not profitable and the estimated cost of making them profitable is too high.

But each marketing group must be very careful when performing this type of marketing or sales stimulus to customers. Errors of omission or errors of not knowing the correct or detailed information about relationships with other customers, suppliers, potential customers, or alliance members may create a terribly fractured situation with a customer or a household.

Information infrastructures that allow for householding are required to be successful in marketing and changing policies, prices, accounts, locations, costs, campaign management, and customer communications. Householding refers to understanding the key relationships with two or more parties (or customers) to know the potential opportunities and increased satisfaction (or dissatisfaction) based on communicating with individual or multiple customers.

This reminds me of an 80-year-old woman in Florida who received a letter from her bank saying, "Dear Mrs. Pogany, We appreciate your business. (She had a 50-year relationship with the bank.) We wish to inform you of our new policy of requiring a minimum monthly balance in your accounts of "n" hundreds of dollars, in order to avoid the new minimum monthly charge of $25.00 in each account."

This bank did not have correlated data on the accounts, used segmentation for marketing (without detailed knowledge of the customers), and mailed letters in mass to customers without knowing the possible consequences. A data warehouse would have provided intelligent decisions to produce a better mailing list of appropriately delineated and evaluated customers.

Why is this important? This bank didn't know that the woman's son had two other accounts with over $100,000 in value, that the son paid most of her bills each month, that the son was a gold credit card holder in another state with the same banking institution, and that the son kept her balances low based on some bad experiences with checks written to someone named: "Cash." **This bank needed householding information on its customers.**

What is really appalling is that the bank didn't know that the family had a 50-year relationship in two or three states, that the son was a known successful executive with a major corporation, and that the woman told many people about this bank's total disregard for customers. The truth is in the mind of the beholder and in the voice of the customer, not in the administration of the bank's policies.

What is the value of a customer? What is the value of the household? What is the value of a customer's children and family over a lifetime? How do we avoid communicating incorrectly with our customers?

Keeping the Customers You Have

Customer relationship management is based on the now well-established premise that it costs less to keep the customers that you have than try to win new ones—five times less expensive in fact. If you can keep customers, they are also typically more profitable in the long term. New customers are often attracted by cut price deals or other incentives; however, these people move on as soon as another incentive is dangled in front of them by your competitors.

For this reason, competing on price alone is a zero sum game—anyone can do it. However, there may be strategic reasons to compete mainly on price in a market that is perceived to be overcharging and where service is largely absent.

Price may sometimes be the stimulus to draw in the customers, but it is not the way to keep them for the long term. Traditional insurance companies are battling to offer the best savings rates, currently topped by an insurer at 3% higher than the prime rate on deposits. This offer is probably unsustainable if the company hopes to make money, but it is gambling that it can attract a large customer base that will be willing to purchase other personal finance products over the years. Price is a powerful competitive weapon; but, if used alone, both old players and new entrants will not survive.

Cross selling becomes *the* new opportunity, after acquiring new customers and learning their habits, actions, and desires.

In the United States, **Sam's Direct,** a division of Wal-Mart Stores based in Arkansas, instituted a direct-contact force of 200 people, who directly contact key small- and medium-sized businesses to foster greater customer orientation in its discount club stores. This approach grew sales of this division to approximately $16 billion in the membership wholesale store in a $40 billion industry. This remarkable achievement resulted from the use of an interactive set of analytical and very-detailed queries, using data warehousing and data mining processes and applications. Sam's uses a very effective technique called Market-basket analysis.

Market-basket analysis (MBA) is the capability to correlate multiple products within a customer's purchase to understand what products are bought with what other products. Then a company can also use MBA to understand multiple customer habits by comparing similar customers with similar purchasing patterns. This type of data was provided directly by

Sam's Club merchandising people to their new outbound sales people for marketing and direct sales activities. Wal-Mart Stores and Sam's Stores were traditionally inbound retailers. In the retail industry, using MBA techniques drives acceleration of customer revenues.

Swift's Reasons for "Why Wal-Mart Continually Succeeds"

1. Wide-usage and open access to their "knowledge colony"
2. Advanced analytical tools and asking very complex queries
3. Learning by doing and relearning when success is questionable
4. Massive amounts of detailed historical data on everything in the business
5. Advancing info-structure of operational and DSS (Decision Support Systems) environments
6. Runs every location as if it were a local store—designed to succeed
7. Transforms transactions into information then into knowledge
8. $uperior investment and integration of hundreds of technologies
9. Upper management support and continually questioning strategies
10. Customer-oriented processes, data, info-structures, and people
11. Changed supply chain and integrated suppliers in a value chain
12. Exceptional management of risk and opportunities
13. Striving for creative new thinking through information
14. Scalability for handling growth and new business opportunities
15. Using the power of information and economics

The underlying info-structure at Wal-Mart, used throughout their enterprise, is their enterprise data warehouse (the largest in the world). Although capturing massive amounts of transaction and product flow management data is important, the ever-changing needs of customers and the marketplace requires an active data warehouse environment. Wal-Mart brings together the use of operational, analytical, transaction, interaction, modeling, historical data, and predictive knowledge processes. In Chapter 11, you'll have the opportunity to read about the active warehouse concept and its direction.

Figure 1-3. Customers vary by numerous characteristics.

How You Serve Your Customers Is a Major Competitive Differentiator

There is one major differentiator in business today and that is service. Price is only an attraction differentiator, since many competitors match each other's prices or will equal a price shown in an advertisement.

Already, the "management" in CRM is implied—customers are not simply being sold to; they are being serviced as well. They are being offered something extra, which is broadly and often defined as that little extra that makes dealing with you a pleasant, rewarding, and welcome experience. Service adds value to your basic product or service in ways that your competitors cannot or will not provide.

The customer service industry is vast and unstructured. The basics are most times adhered to: deal with customers promptly, professionally, and courteously; listen to what they have to say, try always to meet or exceed their needs, and give them compelling reasons to keep coming back. On these basics, any number of companies built their business and a reputation for great service. Nordstrom's stores (Seattle, WA), Saks Fifth Avenue or Tiffany's (real exceptions from New York), Blackwells Bookstores (England), Blanquart's Jewelers (Belleville, IL), and Ted Drews Ice Cream Stores (St. Louis, MO) are great examples of these types of success.

In reality, most companies take the parts of the complex service equation that they understand or know they can apply and implement just those parts. Only a proportion of the company's employees are actually equipped to deal with customers with the result that a single customer is treated royally when in direct contact (face-to-face) but then handled roughly on the phone by the telemarketing sales department. Shared information could provide both departments with better information in handling the right customers the right way at the right time for the right products or services.

Consistency of Service: Royalty Becomes Loyalty

If customers are considered "royalty," then they must be treated as such; and consistency of service through multiple channels is critical. For example, a good customer may be given access to bank accounts through the branch, over the telephone, through a kiosk, via a personal home computer, a wireless phone, or personal device.

The high net worth individual is given access to these remote telephone or PC banking services, because he/she is a valued customer, and only the most valued customers can use the service. The bank also has its own agenda in addition to offering high levels of service options; it prefers that the customer use the telephone or PC because it is less expensive for the provider and makes for quicker processing of transactions. However, at times, the same valued customer will want to use a branch and is immediately relegated to the poor service levels that the bank hopes to save him from in introducing the special remote computer service.

Typically, each channel will offer a different level of service (or lack of it) and there is little consistency among them. This behavior may be acceptable up to a point, where the branch is not geared up to offer financial advice, but the branch must be able to refer the inquiry to someone who can, which requires seamless links with all the other channels. For example, a bank's local branch employees could arrange for the customer to be sent an email with the information he/she is seeking so that it is available the next time the customer goes online.

▶ Defining Customer Relationship Management

Customer Relationship Management **is an enterprise approach to understanding and influencing customer behavior through meaningful communications in order to improve customer acquisition, customer retention, customer loyalty, and customer profitability.**

CRM is an iterative process that turns customer information into positive customer relationships.

Technology in the form of advanced techniques of data transformation and graphical presentation accelerates the usefulness and speed of management decision making. It empowers many more customer contact personnel, information workers, marketing and sales functions, and management employees with significantly better and more informative business intelligence about their customers and prospects.

CRM should be integrated into everything a company does, everyone it employs (even suppliers), and everywhere it transacts. When a company says its goal is excellent customer service, it must mean the *entire* company. This approach is mandatory and is a key hallmark in the work by Don Peppers and Martha Rogers in *Enterprise One-to-One Marketing—Tools for Competing in the Interactive Age* (Doubleday, 1997). You must think and strategize on how to actualize "enterprise" in the CRM definition and process.

Ultimately, each company must decide what CRM means to the organization and to the future of its success in the marketplace.

The most useful definition is contained within the CRM term itself: the management of relationships with customers. The key word is *relationship*. While most companies claim to have relationships with their customers, in fact no such connection exists. The extent of their contact with a customer is transactional—a request to buy is fulfilled with a product or service at an agreed price. Further contact is made in anticipation of continued consumption of the product or service or further purchase.

Using incentives to generate further purchases and various "thank you's" is important for long-term growth and customer retention. Furthermore, once the customer initiates a contact with your organization, this contact is generally treated as entirely separate from other marketing activities. In order for a relationship to be in place, communications must be two-way, integrated, recorded, and managed. Without customer historical data, detailed transactions, focused and categorized communications, a relationship cannot be effectively maintained.

Some companies perform CRM well, but because it is inseparable from everything else they do, it is hard to spot the CRM elements. Some of the successful companies focusing on CRM appear on the pages of management magazines or business guides. Some companies, frankly, are not very well informed on what CRM really is; they say they are embracing CRM, but are not really customer-driven organizations.

Strategic and Tactical Goals of CRM

As organizations move closer to their customers and their extended enterprise business units (channels/franchises/suppliers/partners/Internet linkages), the leading organizations specifically communicate their objectives and goals. CRM requires the establishment of an information info-structure to support an environment so that:

CRM's goal is to increase the opportunity by improving the process to communicate with the *right customer*, providing the *right offer* (product and price), through the *right channel*, at the *right time*.

In addition, organizations need to be more specific on the benefits of the goals, which could be characterized as follows:

Right Customer

- Manage customer relationships throughout their life cycles
- Realize customer potential by increasing "share of wallet"

Right Offer

- Efficiently introduce customers and prospects to your company and its products and services
- Customize your offering for each customer

Right Channel(s)

- Coordinate communications across every customer touch point
- Ability to communicate to customer's channel *preference*
- Capture and analyze channel information for continuous learning

Right Time

- Efficiently communicate to customers based on time "relevance"
- Ability to communicate with real/near-real time or traditional marketing

CRM—All Activities that Turn Casual Consumers into Loyal Customers

A broader definition of CRM would include all activities that turn casual consumers into loyal customers by satisfying or exceeding their requirements to the extent that they will buy again. This goal is achieved not just from the core offering, but from product and service extensions or business partners (the channel).

"All activities" can mean everything that a company does that impacts on customers. It means more than training all of the people who have direct contact with customers.

In retailing, it may mean the merchandisers who decide how products should be displayed in stores. In financial services, it could be the system administrators responsible for the timely production of statements or product offers. In manufacturing, it could the inventory controllers using faster replenishment and higher product availability. In airlines, it might be the baggage handlers, who do not work for the airline, but nevertheless play a key customer service role. In any business, it may start with something seemingly unimportant—the receptionist who takes the first telephone call through to the service or a repair person.

Even employees who have no customer management responsibilities at all may be involved in activities that are critical to the quality of customer service. For example, one airline has determined that it can save money if it only stocks alcohol that it knows passengers want, by looking at their previous orders. The customer is impressed at being offered a cocktail that an airline may not normally carry; while the airline saves money by not having to stock expensive vintage liquors for which there is little or no demand. This same airline is now taking the savings made on beverage inventory and redirecting them into a customer telemarketing service to frequent customers.

Some Companies Do CRM Naturally

Some companies know next to nothing about their customers in that they have no name and address files or details of their purchasing habits. Yet they are able to meet their customers' needs precisely by managing product development, stock replenishment, channel delivery, and customer service. Profitability in these companies has been shown to outperform all other companies in their sector (e.g., Wal-Mart).

Surely, these are companies that understand CRM even where active management is not present. In these companies, the marketing manager is not the only key player, as everyone will take some responsibility for managing relationships with customers. Many activities are customer facing and must contain a marketing element because someone has concerned themselves with presentation as well as content of the product or service and of the delivery channel and method. As a result, although roles may be clearly defined, they are bound to cross traditional barriers, effectively raising the visibility of marketing, even where the operations do not take place within a traditional marketing department.

CRM effectively encompasses an organization's ability to:

- Find customers
- Get to know them
- Keep in communication with them
- Ensure that they get what they want from the organization—not just in the product but in every aspect of the organization's dealings with them.
- Check that they receive what they were promised—subject, of course, to it being profitable
- Ensure that the customer is retained—even if the customer is unprofitable today, the goal is long-term profitability

CRM is not about price. It is not about sending higher volumes of mail or making higher volumes of annoying phone calls to prospects. It is definitely not about using channels to drive customers to competitors.

CRM provides the capabilities to generate products, services, responsiveness, individualization, mass customization, and customer happiness.

CRM can focus on obtaining new customers. Generally, marketing programs set objectives to define prospect acquisition. Unfortunately, these are too many one-time customers, since the sale is facilitated through ill-informed market actions without detailed knowledge of the customers or prospects.

Subsequently, organizations build processes to acquire "prequalified" buyers of their products or services, without regard to the longer term future. Marketing management excels at communicating these short-term results, and enterprise management is elated.

To do so, define a customer-centric information infrastructure (info-structure) for marketing, services, distribution, and satisfaction. This approach assists the organization in targeting profitable customers and measuring results.

▶ Targeting Profitable Customers

Targeting profitable customers is a worthy objective. Efficiency is a way of saving financial and human resources but also of providing your organization with the right customers to be addressed for the right products or services.

Targeting is not new, but specialized campaign management is. Specialized campaign management can be subdivided into relatively small customer segments or even one-to-one marketing approaches. Dozens of campaigns can be achieved in a year, in a month, in a week, or even one evening—if you have the right info-structure and effective process experience.

As you will note from Figure 1-4, there are relative aspects to the creation of *return-on-investment* (ROI) and the level of customer focus.

The ROI curve does not truly accelerate until an organization achieves the capabilities to "retain present profitable customers" *and* migrate "preferred customers" to new products, services, channels, or relationships.

The ultimate marketing and ROI opportunity is to facilitate customer loyalty through repetitive purchases of your products and services, and then generate customer referrals to create new business opportunities and new customers. Nothing is more reassuring than a referral from a happy and/or loyal customer to a customer who desires to achieve/receive the same benefit from the customer relationship.

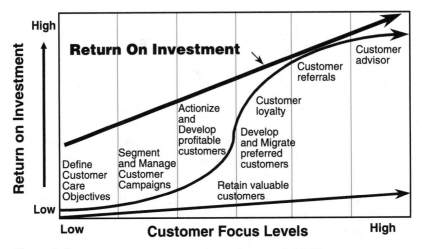

Figure 1-4. Customer focus levels and potential ROI.

Notice that the highest levels of profitability are achieved in the last stages of customer marketing and customer relationship: working together to obtain continuing *and* new relationships. When you become the "customer's advisor," you have the customer's understanding, belief, loyalty, and potentially increasing wallet-share. As an advisor in your product or service arena, CRM becomes your success opportunity. A good example is Travel Unie in Chapter 14.

The knowledge base, or data warehouse environment, provides the means to define individual customer characteristic's, capabilities, requirements, propensities, historical behaviors, and purchase timing opportunities. Mature marketing is developed by knowledge-based marketing planning with development of effective customer communications and interactions to achieve satisfaction for both sides of the relationship.

▶ Positioning Is the Key to Success in Business

The secrets of business success fill whole libraries, yet there is really only one secret. It is not just about having the best products or services, the best advertising, the best brand, or the best supply chain—although all these things play their part—but about having the best customers. If you know who they are, and what they want and can over-satisfy their requirements again and again at the right price, they will remain your customers and reward you for your loyalty.

Bear in mind, though, that the best customers are being chased by everyone else; not just your immediate competitors, but also companies in other sectors.

Customer referrals are the most rewarding and profitable of all sales actions, and it requires few resources or little effort on the part of the direct sales force. The customer does the work, and the prospect buys the product or service (in a very large percentage of cases).

Being an "advisor" to your customers is the highest of all levels of customer happiness, engaging the customer in an ongoing relationship of high value.

Everyone Is After Everyone Else's Customers

Numerous supermarkets and retail stores have mini-banks on their premises, open during major business hours, and also ATMs or kiosks provided for customer transactions during regular *and* off-hours.

Rather than build their own infrastructure, many of these companies chose to work with a partner. While these partnerships work for both parties most of the time, one or the other is likely to dominate. One would argue that the retailers dominate in the relationship with banks because the latter own the customer interface. The latter may handle the processing and customer service, but the opportunities for cross-selling may be limited.

In the United Kingdom, for example, the retail chains Tesco and Sainsbury's introduced financial services in their stores to provide customers with bank loans. Co-op, another U.K. retailer, is looking into selling utilities, such as gas and electricity, through its stores. Safeway has its own in-store pharmacy, dry cleaner, and cafe. And grocery stores, such as Kwik-Fit, Carrefour, and Migros, sell financial services. New partner relationships and opportunities are occurring every month.

▶ Who Owns the Customer?

The issue then becomes who owns the customer? New market dynamics are redefining who partners, competitors, and customers are. Banks are positioning themselves to handle all the financial transactions for electronic commerce, while retailers are reserving the right to use their own banking partners.

Some alliances formed between supermarkets and banks to reach customers have dismantled due to the cost of the alliance and the potential product overlap. Does the customer belong to the bank or to the supermarket? To whom does the customer feel allegiance when a bank account is being administered by a bank but the product was sold to him by the supermarket?

Leading manufacturers for many years built databases of customers and distributors and invested in consumer magazine publishing as a way to promote brands.

Manufacturers May Go Directly to Your Customers

When reviewing the breadth of products offered by leading manufacturers, you could build a case for targeting customers directly. The number of transactions may be small, but the value of those transactions could be quite high. And the probability of repeat business would be very high by creating a linkage process between consumer and supplier, which could be recurring and flexible.

Recently, a major supermarket chain in the United States provided a manufacturer with detailed information regarding customers. This allowed the manufacturer to change the relationship with the final customers and at the same time create differing relationships with retail stores. As a result, both organizations will profit by holding the customers away from the competition.

The estimated *Life-Time Value* (LTV) for a supermarket/grocery store of a customer with a family of four is *approximately $250,000*. And this amount appears to be only half of the expenditures that the family will make on food-related purchases.

The implications of this will be for stores to become much more knowledgeable of a customer/family needs and changes over time, then to address these needs through meaningful interactions (in the store) and communications (through automated and mail delivery mechanisms) correlated with the similar desires and actions of other similar customers in the same quadrants of demographics or purchasing patterns. Therefore, equipped with this knowledge and taking appropriate actions, organizations will not only retain their best customers, but also have opportunity for greater loyalty and higher margins (and therefore, profitability).

Nestlé launched a home-shopping service in Switzerland as part of a trial, which eventually may see a European-wide roll out. Nestlé Easy Shop can be accessed by cable subscribers equipped with modems who click on any one of 264 Nestlé products displayed on screen. All items are delivered within 48 hours. Nestlé is looking at partnerships with other manufacturers and even retailers, so that delivery times can be cut by sourcing the goods from local shops.

Nestlé says the aim of the experiment is to see what allegiance there is to the Nestlé name and what products are in the typical basket of goods. Although no one suggests at present that this pilot program indicates that the company is planning to go direct, such activities will certainly be part of any future direct-selling strategy.

Some manufacturers may even decide to partner with other manufacturers to create a market basket of goods that will be attractive to the customer, for example, all household cleaning products. They can also take advantage of economies of scale in sharing their respective logistics systems and processes. Under this scenario, once two manufacturers get together, they are effectively re-creating themselves as retailers or perhaps wholesalers. If the logistics can be worked out and the consumer is offered a compelling solution, and one or more of the names in the pool are well-known brand names, there will become a competitive advantage. This scenario is enabled by information and technology through a very detailed and long-term historical database of customer transactions and interactions.

Technology makes manufacturers and retailers think differently. The success of Wal-Mart Stores, accelerated by the access and usefulness of the info-structure (see Chapter 5), provides enterprise-wide shared information to management. The Wal-Mart Data Warehouses maintain 65 weeks of detailed data of every sale, at every register, at each of their more than 3,000 stores, for every product, in every size/shape/color. The data warehouse therefore allows them to "know their customers" through purchases. Wal-Mart also gave access to their primary manufacturing suppliers through their "Retail Link" system to generate new just-in-time manufacturing, supply, delivery, stocking, and inventory management. This same type of information infrastructure info-structure) is utilized at Sam's Club and Sam's Direct as discussed earlier.

Through the end of the twentieth century, Wal-Mart Stores did not actually know the names and addresses of each individual customer shopping in their stores, but they knew (better than anyone else in their competitive realm) their customers through the detailed purchasing information for every store in every locale. Wal-Mart also uses market-basket and data mining techniques to discover many facts about their stores, their customers, the products they sell, and meaningful management information for decision-making on many levels.

In August 1999, Wal-Mart Stores announced surpassing the 100 terabyte data storage range for their data warehouse. That is 100,000,000,000,000 of data space available for analytical and business management action-oriented uses in their information infrastructure.

This did not include Wal-Mart's mainframe transaction processing, local servers for in-store systems, and networking computers. The data warehouse, based on the analytical abilities and modeling techniques has become a key competitive info-structure to drive decisions.

Randy Mott, former Senior Vice-President (and CIO) of Wal-Mart, often stated that very detailed data, not summary data alone, is the key to their success. That, along with the ability of hundreds of people to access the detailed data in the data warehouse, to develop market basket models, to create complex questions (e.g., queries) that are extremely useful and in discovering what the customers buy, and will buy and then use marketing stimuli.

Wal-Mart uses the entire value chain of information and process to drive costs lower before the product gets to each store. The wholesale purchase price is lowered through effective sharing of inventory and sales data plus production requirements (products, volume, sizes, colors, features, price range) so that the manufacturer can produce and deliver at a lower cost to the retailer. Wal-Mart Stores also uses linkages, velocity and time, customer and product sales knowledge, and the power of purchasing in quantity to drive down prices and maintain competitiveness (see Figure 1-5). The process is ingrained into the fabric of the company and its relationships with suppliers.

Also, Wal-Mart operates its stores as if every store were "a local store," with specialized products and design of placement of products to meet the local demands of the customers. This approach creates customer loyalty.

Many companies could learn a great deal from Wal-Mart about basic principles of customer orientation and effective use of information to drive profitability and growth.

Wal*Mart Stores

Data warehousing allowed Wal*Mart to shift the costly process of inventory replenishment to their suppliers, reinventing the supply chain and saving millions.

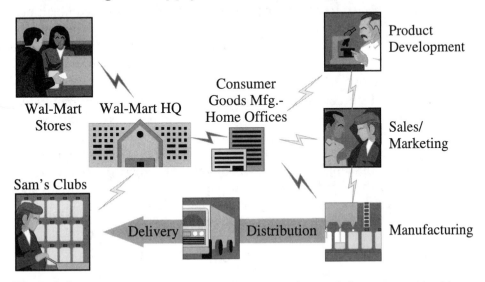

Figure 1-5. Wal-Mart's process for success, using an info-structure to drive the supply value chain and velocity of replenishment.

▶ Changes in Customer Positioning

Working in partnership with other providers as just one link in the customer relationship chain may be the order of the day in the future. It will certainly seem preferable to companies discovering that their competitors are having relationships with their customers. In the supply of services, technology is often the medium—the telephone, multimedia kiosks, personal computers, the Internet, and cable television—and it is knocking down the traditional barriers to entry, letting in companies that are able to make enormous inroads into markets in a few short years.

Exclusivity of supply is a privilege, not a right, and it is becoming rare.

Consumers will increasingly source their products and services from a variety of providers, loyal to some, but disloyal to most.

Even when a customer appears to be locked into the perfect relationship where they use a single supplier for a variety of services, that relationship can be broken at any time. While your company must discover why customers are moving on, management may have to accept that customers sometimes move on for their own reasons that are entirely unconnected to how they have been handled by the incumbent provider. However, as a provider, you will still want to know that some relationships with customers are sufficiently close that you can predict the likelihood of other customers reacting in the same way. A certain level of disloyalty is predictable.

Where companies can together satisfy the wider requirements of groups of customers, they can all profit and perhaps lock customers into a management process. They can also achieve economies of scale in distribution, marketing, data gathering, and product development. While some companies traditionally take over others in order to do this, partnerships enable the separate parties to retain their strengths and avoid the risks inherent in merging or being taken over.

Use Old Information to Create New Actions

Companies strive to keep quality customers. The problem is that defining "quality" customers is difficult for many organizations. Customers are too numerous, too different, and too widely distributed to be personally well known.

Number crunching manually is not possible. While some companies have always wanted to know more about their customers, it was only with the advent of massively parallel decision support computing systems combined with analytical techniques that has enabled them to do anything about it. The way ahead may not always be clear, as no amount of computing resource can make up for a lack of good information, and many companies are still struggling with an infrastructure that simply does not gather, store, and distribute good data. Fortunately, the payoff (as we shall see) is huge.

Knowing Your Customers Boosts Profitability

Organizations that place customer information at the core of their information infrastructure exceed their competitors' business profitability. Competitors who drive competition through manufacturing cost reductions rarely succeed in the long run, unless the organization directly addresses what the market requires and provides a specific solution to a customer's individuals needs.

Using Data Better Enables You to Manage Relationships with Your Customers

The uses to which shared enterprise-wide information infrastructures or data warehouses can and have already been put are many and varied. However, any deployment that does not focus firmly on the customer is only likely to bring modest improvements. CRM has been identified as the most valuable of all uses to date for obvious reasons—it focuses on the most important player in any business, whether the deployment is in the *back office* (e.g., using customers' data to improve store replenishment) or in *operational activities* (e.g., using data to personalize marketing propositions).

The leading corporations in the United States and Europe, which have driven their management teams through shared enterprise-wide information infrastructures (i.e., data warehouse environment), have clearly surpassed their competitors in increasing the value of their stock equity over the first 3–5 years of the investment in such an infrastructure.

High ROI has been the case in retailing, airlines, financial institutions, and emerging marketing organizations within telecommunications companies. While not all increases in share price can be attributed to the installation of a data warehouse, the quality of thinking that specifies a data warehouse is likely to imbue everything the retailer does. In other words, the data warehouse comes second. First is the understanding that knowledge about markets and customers is a resource at least as valuable as the products or services it provides.

According to a study by the International Data Corporation, completed in the summer of 1996 and published from IDC's Toronto Office by Stephen Graham, "The average return-on-investment, from a study of 62 data warehouses implemented in North America, is approximately 401% return on investment (ROI) in the first 2–3 years after implementation."

In another study, conducted by The NCR Corporation, more than 20 data warehouses in the retail industry discovered that approximately 300–1000% ROI was realized in less than 2 years.

Managing customer relationships successfully means learning about the habits and needs of your customers, anticipating future buying patterns, and finding new opportunities to do business.

▶ CRM Is Easy for Small Companies

Small companies have performed CRM effortlessly. They have only to keep close to a small number of people and continue to look for ways to impress them, market to them, sell to them, and service them for a long time afterward. In the division of labor that has ensued, as companies have grown larger, these guiding principles have been lost.

Arguably, the entire history of customer service, customer care, and relationship management is an attempt to get back to the intimacy enjoyed by small traders whose entire clientele lived close to them and who were linked not just by commerce, but also by family and community ties.

Most of the guiding principles that were simple common sense to companies until the 1950s still apply—find your market and know your customers. Both of these tasks have landed almost entirely on the desk of the marketing manager. The same person who is generally the first to see a budget slip away in hard times is now arguably the most important in the organization.

▶ Large Companies Must Succeed at CRM

Most companies talk in purely marketing terms about who their customers are and how many customers they have, which belie the fact that they don't really know. A store will say that it has one million customers a week. It can't say how many are different customers, how many are regular customers, when any of them last shopped or what they bought. They deal in generalities.

These companies are so big that they have fallen in love with their own reflections. They forgot they are in business to serve the customer. Many customers who feel that they are being put second, despite all the corporate slogans about the customer being Number One.

The structure of many companies limits their ability to be close to their customers. Companies are now owned and managed not simply by the traditional names within their own sectors but by players from other sectors. Retailers have become manufacturers and vice versa; software, telecommunications, and transportation companies and financial institutions are usually divisional and do not share information about their customers. Gas companies are selling electricity and vice versa, rarely marketing to a customer's known needs. Automotive accessory companies are selling personal loans. Software companies are selling stock purchasing data. These are not simply holding organizations, but mainstream blue chip companies. And relatively few use direct marketing knowledge-based systems, but instead use mailing lists and much telemarketing or sales force contact systems to track the customers.

▶ CRM Is Not Easy for Many Companies

The old belief that only a handful of companies can ever play at this level has been destroyed by the emergence of new channels to market with a low cost of entry. Tiny start-up companies are taking the stock market by storm and achieving multibillion dollar valuations within a year, based on their seemingly unlimited potential. Operating entirely on line, these start-ups require no physical infrastructure in terms of stores or branches. They can even avoid the cost of setting up their own fulfillment infrastructure by outsourcing to third parties.

Customers do not require the intimacy with their suppliers (normally provided by stores and branches) to establish close relationships.

**Consumers are able to put their relationships with suppliers
on a more open, democratic, and dynamic footing through the
Internet and two-way cable television.**

While still insisting that some level of personal contact is essential, companies are seeing that many high net worth individuals require even less contact with their suppliers than the mass market. This is because they are sophisticated users of remote channels or simply need less hand holding when dealing with what would be regarded as complex products to other customers.

▶ Costs and Benefits of Relationship Management

The benefits of customer relationship management are usually to be found in one or more of these areas:

1. **Lower costs of recruiting customers**—savings on marketing, mailing, contact, follow-up, fulfillment, and services, and so on.

2. **No need to recruit so many customers** to maintain a steady volume of business (especially in business-to-business marketing environments).

3. **Reduced cost of sales**—Usually existing customers are more responsive customers. Better knowledge of your channels or distributors drives more effectiveness in the relationship. CRM will also reduce marketing campaign costs and provide higher ROI in marketing and customer communications.

4. **Higher customer profitability**—larger wallet-share; more follow-up sales; more referrals from higher customer satisfaction and services; ability to cross-sell or up-sell from present purchases.

5. **Increased customer retention and loyalty**—customers stay longer, buy more, contact you for their requirements (which increases the bonding relationship), and customers buy more often. CRM, therefore, increases the opportunity and accomplishment of real lifetime value.

6. **Evaluation of customer profitability**—knowing which customers are truly profitable, which customers should be changed from low/no profit through cross-selling/up selling; which customers might not ever become profitable; which customers should be managed by external channels; and which customers drive future business.

> **CRM is measurable and can be utilized to increase a value chain's profitability.**

CRM equates to things that accountants and business managers relish far more than excellent customer service: turnover and profit.

Figure 1-6 shows how the integrated value chain is enabled through information sharing about customers.

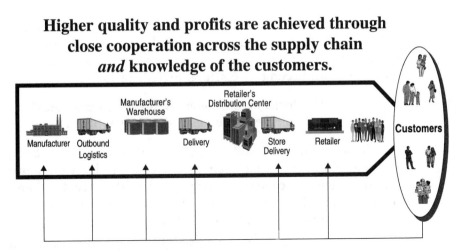

Higher quality and profits are achieved through close cooperation across the supply chain *and* knowledge of the customers.

Figure 1-6. The value chain.

 ## Who Is Responsible for CRM?

The immediate consequence of CRM will be campaign management aimed at customers for whom the marketing manager has intimate details. In the wider sense, the marketing manager is one of a number of managers in every area of a business who carries customer management responsibilities. But to be successful, "everybody always sells."

The marketing manager may start to play a key role in new activities and processes to achieve new objectives and higher results. For example, once the marketing department starts to use data warehousing systems to discover more about customers, this data will not only inform marketing campaigns but also new product development, production scheduling, replenishment, and distribution.

Why this Book Is for You!

This book is designed to assist all enterprise managers as well as marketing managers, but it recognizes that CRM begins to truly change and expand many customer-touching roles. CRM is happening in some sectors; the marketing manager is assuming a high profile and, of course, taking on more responsibility. These managers will need the tools to do the job.

Managers defining, developing, creating, distributing, and servicing customers will require much more detailed information on customers to achieve their objectives. As change comes faster and faster, knowing the customers will become as essential ingredient for success.

**The focus on customers is already putting most
marketing managers in the spotlight.**

Some companies have successfully used their brand and presence with customers to extend their portfolio of products into entirely new industries. It is marketing around the core brand that enabled companies to diversify, and the marketing manager is turning into less of a product manager and more of a corporate strategist.

Business process re-engineering (BPR) may be required to implement to build the business around customers who can never be seen. The marketing manager in turn needs to recognize a new role in this revolution. BPR failed to have a profound impact the first time around except on the consultants and technology vendors whose livelihoods depended on it. Today, the way that knowledge is used will have a profound effect on the structure, operation, and profitability of organizations.

As always when major changes are afoot, nothing less than total commitment from the very top management will enable the changes to have an impact across the organization. Most major data exploitation programs have senior management backing, partly because of the level of initial investment, but also because change simply cannot be brought about only at departmental levels.

▶ Are You Ready for CRM?

Many companies are not structured to meet the demands of a changing commercial environment, let alone exploit CRM. The entire culture and organization of the company is geared to business as we used to know it, not as we are expounding here. Once the idea of CRM has gripped a senior manager, it is often handed to one part of the enterprise as if it were a stand-alone exercise that did not depend on how the rest of the organization worked. However, all employees in a company are customer relationship managers, from the receptionist who first answers the phone to the salesperson, the customer service operator, and all the employees who handle customers in the channels.

This insight effectively creates two tiers of CRM—one aims to make data available to all groups of users as cheaply as possible through desktop packages with a limited or unspecified view of the returns that can be achieved. The other, active CRM, makes data available to a chosen set of users dedicated to managing relationships with selected customers, aiming to increase profit/spend and decrease churn/disloyalty.

In the first tier, the company may not have an active relationship with the customer but needs to ensure that they are handled courteously and efficiently whenever they make contact. In the second tier, the company feels that it is actively and regularly handling the customer's needs and taking full advantage of each contact between them.

Given the ambitious nature of CRM, companies will want to know if they are ready to embrace CRM.

With future expansion of electronic commerce, even greater flexibility will be required. Companies, like most organizations, are organized by departments, although this is an area where "teaming" has had an impact. Although most companies are creating enterprise-wide networks that will enable teams to share data, it is the very departmental structure that perhaps needs to be questioned further.

These questions will prompt the following behavior: some retailers will talk about cross-functional teams drawn from various departments and tasked with handling peripheral activities such as the development of an Internet site or mail order. Generally, once a project is underway or complete, its ownership then reverts to a particular department and the team disperses. Forward-thinking retailers need to look very closely at the contribution of these cross-functional teams because in the future, these teams may become the new departments. Retailers are already engaging in activities that fit within two or more departments. For example, should electronic point-of-sale data be analyzed by the IT department, by the marketing department, or by a separate department that focuses solely on data analysis?

Creating specialist groups to handle particular tasks, whether they are outsourced or kept in-house, is likely to lead to a fragmentation of the retail business. Employees who specialize in a particular area are less likely to make a career in retailing than in their particular field of expertise. For example, a marketing specialist who has brought success to a particular retailer will no doubt be most welcome within the financial services sector, which now regards itself as a retail business.

Companies Will Need to Be Flexible

Consuming will change, the customer will change, the channels will change, and that change will be a constant. There is a need to analyze the impact of future channels. So pervasive is the discussion of nonstore shopping that it is easy to leave traditional channels such as branches and stores out of the equation. Yet no one can see the demise of traditional channels anytime in the future.

Consumers may be fed up with aspects of shopping and banking but they are as enthusiastic as ever about the process as a whole. Equally, companies have built businesses around bricks and mortar, a limited element of nonphysical consumption can be complementary to bricks and mortar, but beyond 10% of business, it starts to erode the need for physical retail space.

Research shows that certain retail formats may disappear, others will be completely transformed—few will be untouched. Only by operating in the context of customer reach and customer value can retailers hope to develop their businesses at the same rate as changes in the market. It is possible up to a point to recognize a growing number of segments within the customer base and to fragment the retail offer accordingly.

The challenge will be to understand which segments require which kind of offer and service and to maintain margins through each channel. Annoying as it must be to watch new players enter the market and cherry-pick the best segments, store-based retailers must continue to focus on their core business and take a measured approach to new channels. History shows that most knee-jerk responses by traditional companies to the rise of players outside their sector are doomed to fail.

The call for a quick change in direction may often seem to come from customers, but customers as a whole are generally conservative; they are more comfortable with gradual than sudden changes in direction or style. Only a handful of companies can ever take a more radical approach, and sometimes these companies totally capture an industry or its customers through the use of nonregular channel creations.

Therefore, preparing their info-structures with detailed historical customer and product turnover data and being able to respond to marketplace change will be the hallmark of successful companies in the future.

▶ Marketing Communications Strategies

For many centuries, enterprises have maintained personal or 1:1 relationships with their customers whenever possible. In today's quick moving world of high volumes of people and businesses, it becomes an ever-increasing challenge to "know" the customers.

Marketing to customers, whether they be individuals or businesses, is expensive and also wide-ranging in activities. The traditional twentieth century methods of mass marketing may still be utilized for "image" and high-volume (low-margin) marketing/sales, but the actualization of the Internet and online individual communications will sure bring forth faster requirements for very tailored or 1:1 specific marketing.

Illustrated in Figure 1-7 are four major marketing communications strategies utilized throughout the world.

The four major marketing communications shown in the figure strategies are separated by two distinct characteristics. The first characteristic is whether the individual customer or prospect generates the "inbound" marketing communications activities or whether it is pushed from the "outbound" enterprise/company. Generally, the outbound company marketing is heard by much more people, but may be very expensive and has (possibly) more sale conversions than inquiry inbound activities.

The second characteristic is whether the communications is passive (one-way) or whether is it interactive (two-way with responses to stimuli). In most cases, passive marketing generates much fewer sales (or conversions) than sales for interactive marketing.

If we move from bottom to top, left to right, a significant change occurs in the sales conversion rates and also in the opportunity for closing a sale and for cross-selling (selling other products).

Based on presentations at The National Council of DataBase Marketing (NCDM), Direct Marketing Association, and numerous U.S. CRM conferences, there appears to be some astounding differences in the marketing/sales conversion rates from bottom to top and left to right shown in Figures 1-7 and 1-8.

As illustrated in Figure 1-8, there is *a tripling of responses* and conversions to sales based on changing from inbound to outbound and a tripling from interactive-outbound to interactive-inbound.

	Company Initiated (Outbound)	Customer Initiated (Inbound)
Interactive	**Differential Marketing** • Direct contact • Telemarketing • Channel Contacting • Electronic Marketing	**Relationship (1:1) Mktg.** • Face to Face • Call Center • Internet / Email • ATM / Kiosks
Passive	**Traditional Marketing** • Mass media • Direct Mail • Seminars / Expos • Catalogs / Faxes	**Informational Marketing** • Voice requests • Mail requests • Email requests • Web browsing

Figure 1-7. Marketing communications strategies.

	Company Initiated (Outbound)	Customer Initiated (Inbound)
Interactive	**Differential Marketing** 6-15% range depending on quality of marketing lists / segments defined	**Relationship (1:1) Mktg.** 18-30% range when using highly targeted, 'one-to-one' type marketing campaigns
Passive	**Traditional Marketing** 2-5% range for traditional types of mass media type campaigns	**Informational Marketing** 1-3% range for customer passively collecting information

Figure 1-8. Response rates for marketing communications.

Although no published research studies have surfaced through 1999 (that we know of), these numbers seem to prove out in numerous cases of CRM with Data Warehousing that we have witnessed in recent years. This is true for a multiplicity of industries that have a high volume of customers in many subsegments. See Chapter 14 for examples and case studies of marketing and customer-centric data warehouse experiences.

▶ The Power of Relationship Optimization

If an enterprise combines the best of three strategies by reducing the expenditures for the bottom left box (the strategy for mass marketing) and performs the inherent positives of each of the other three boxes, the returns or conversions may become continually outstanding.

The combination of differential marketing, interactive inbound informational marketing, and relationship marketing becomes the ultimate ROI for marketing: Relationship Optimization (or 1:1).

They may achieve greater than 35–40% conversions and have much less individual marketing costs per contact with each customer. What this does for a company can change the entire way it markets, the methods and connectivity it facilitates, and the products/services it renders.

It is important to note, using the CRM process illustrated in Figure 1-9, that enterprises set a major objective of becoming a management team that learns and, at the same time, coverts its strategies, processes, interactions, measurements, knowledge, and communications into real actions. The CRM process, shown in Figure 1-9, becomes the cycle for long-term success and cohesive management teamwork. Chapter 2 will provide insight on how this process can and will work for you.

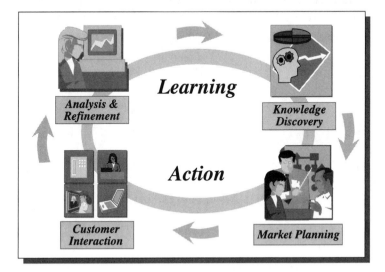

Figure 1-9. The CRM management process.

▶ Management Considerations

- CRM creates a management process of marketing and operational activity. The process can start at any point, depending on how developed the company activities are. Analysis and refinement of data is designed to generate market and customer information (knowledge discovery) that can be put to immediate use by operational and marketing employees.

- The business case (market planning) is contained within the process (e.g., that marketing to a given segment of customers stops a percentage of them from going to another supplier), and therefore the cost benefit is worked out in advance. The strategy is then executed through customer interaction, which immediately generates new data for analysis and refinement—and so the process continues.

The most significant aspect of the CRM process is the continuous *learning* and creating *knowledge* of customers to achieve your objectives and gain higher profitability for the long term.

- The learning organization builds opportunities by feeding on its new knowledge about itself and about its customers or suppliers and therefore positions itself for success. We'll visit this "learning organization" concept in CRM and the CRM process flow as we progress through the following chapters.

2

Defining Your CRM Process

In this chapter, we will define more clearly the elements and benefits of the CRM process and point out the changes and identify the requirements these elements of the process put on the underlying Information Technology and supporting systems.

But before we begin to define and describe the CRM process, it may be of value to discuss the major phases of marketing that have occurred in the past 50 years and will occur for some decades to come. Let's review the illustration on marketing evolution from our experiences (Figure 2-1).

Mass Marketing evolved from the post–First World War era and continues today. The characteristics and technologies clearly show that the use of advanced information technologies enable positive change, reduction or elimination of constraints in marketing, and dynamically changes the scope of marketing to your customers. If your organization is planning for one-to-one marketing, effective campaign management, or online Internet customer relationships, you will require a Data Warehouse or customer-centric info-structure that is defined by customer information. This means that you will have to transform your transaction, accounting, or product-based thinking and planning to a customer-centric approach. You will not, initially, have to change your accounting systems or your customer sales systems, but you will have to extract and transform the data within those transactional systems (on its way into the Data Warehouse environment).

Mass Marketing	Target Marketing	Customer Marketing	1 to 1 Marketing
Characteristics • Market Share • Individual Sales • Limited Segmentation • Huge Campaigns • Not Cost-effective • Single Treatments • Focus on Transactions • # of Relationships	**Characteristics** • Segmented Campaigns • Small Mass Marketing • Focus on Products	**Characteristics** • Customer Share • Life Time Value • Model Distribution • On-going Refinement • Multiple Treatments • Focus on Customer • Breadth of Relationships • Event-Driven	**Characteristics** • Interactive Segmentation • Real-Time Matching • Interactive TV • Active Web Pages • Customer Interaction • One-to-One Relationships • Real-Time Marketing • Prediction-Driven
Technology • In-House • Outsourced Mailings • Flat Files / Mailing Lists • Some Packaged Appl's	**Technology** • Individual Database(s) • Application for Projects • Proprietary Solutions • Limited Analysis	**Technology** • Data Warehouse • Integrated Data & Appl's • Customer Knowledge • Modeling, Analysis & Refinement Process	**Technology** • Integrated Data Warehouse • Internet Enabled • Many Touch Points Integrated • Cross Organization Process • Management by Interaction

Figure 2-1. Marketing evolution with characteristics and technology attributes.

Performing analytics on traditional twentieth-century application-oriented, legacy accounting and reporting (computer) systems is very difficult. That is why it is so difficult for your team to access and use your customer data without major effort or without using very technical resources (in your IT department) to copy or extract the data. Building customer mailings lists and customer sales lists is relatively easy. But building a Data Warehouse can also become easy with the right methodology and a plan that is scaleable and changeable over time. Knowing what is possible, rather than continually attempting to overcome personal or technological roadblocks (of others), provides better advancement of your business. You'll see more of this approach throughout this book in all of the chapters. Roadblocks have been overcome, and it is important that it is shared with you here.

Moving from Mass Marketing to Target Marketing may be a big jump for some enterprises. And some organizations have tried to do this without an extended info-structure. But moving from Target Marketing to Customer Marketing requires much more customer understanding and key cultural changes. Finally, moving from Customer Marketing to Relationship Marketing requires not only knowledge of the customer but the ability to capture information, quickly analyze it, and react to customer immediacy demands.

Why Create a Process for CRM?

Marketing organizations are significantly behind their organizational counterparts in providing bottom-line business benefits. In the high-stakes game of business, understanding the impact of marketing investments can have a dramatic impact on a company's performance. Consider the following statistics:

- Up to 98% of all promotional coupons are thrown away.
- It is up to 10 times more costly to generate revenue from a new customer than from an existing customer.
- A 5% increase in retention rate can increase company profits by 60–100%.
- It is six times more costly to service a customer through a Call Center than via the Internet.
- Loyal customers who refer another customer generate business at a very low (or no) cost.
- Referred customers generally stay longer, use more products, and become profitable customers (faster).

CRM As a "Process"—Not a Project

CRM is an iterative process that turns customer information into customer relationships through active use of and learning from the information. CRM begins with building customer knowledge and results in high-impact customer interactions that enable a business or government agency to establish long-term, resource-manageable, and profitable customer relationships. Let's review the process cycle illustrated in Figure 2-2.

CRM is a process cycle for encompassing major process elements or groups of actions:

- *Knowledge Discovery.* This is the process of analyzing customer information to identify specific market opportunities and investment strategies. This is done through a process of customer identification, customer segmentation, and customer prediction. Knowledge Discovery empowers marketing personnel with access to detailed customer information for better analysis of the historical information and customer characteristics for better decision making.

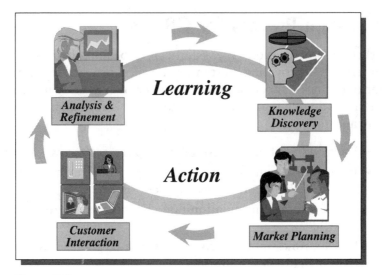

Figure 2-2. The CRM process cycle.

A customer-centric Data Warehouse environment, with very detailed historical internal and external information, organized by subject-group (not by application or accounting systems), helps enterprises through open access and the ability to ask very detailed and very complex questions. Many of these questions are generated by answers to previous questions and therefore provide thoughtful approaches to utilization of the Data Warehouse.

The system needs to collect detailed data from a variety of customer interaction and transactions sources throughout your business locations and transform it into information and knowledge that is usable for management and planners. These sources could be a variety of point-of-sale systems, automatic teller machines, Internet accesses, customer care applications, Call Center files and call records, complaint files, direct marketing contacts and denials, and third-party prospect information. Additionally, many enterprises are including government and/or industry analysis (competitive) information to perform correlations and modeling approaches.

By centralizing detailed customer information, businesses and governments can analyze the complex relationships among all of the different data elements and create specific marketing messages precisely calibrated and targeted to an individual customer's needs.

Chapter **2** I Defining Your CRM Process

The Data Warehouse offers you the opportunity to combine the massive amounts of information, with campaign management, along with data mining tools to improve your response rates. You should plan to facilitate customizing offers, reduce cost by deploying a very targeted campaign, and integrate multiple marketing activities. You have the opportunity to reduce the time it takes to execute new campaigns, your business becomes more agile and proactive, and your customers will appreciate your contacting them with the right message at the right time. CRM must also use knowledge discovery to understand the subtleties of your customer's buying behaviors.

- *Market Planning* (and Offer Planning, Marketing Planning, and Communications Planning). This process group defines specific customer offers, delivery channels, schedules, and dependencies. This empowers your marketing personnel, service management team, manufacturing planners and distribution chain, investment opportunities in your customer interactions and locations/ channels, treatment plans, and products and services.

  Market Planning enables the development of strategic communications plans or programs; predefines specific campaign types, channel preferences, and treatment plans; and selects or develops event and threshold triggers (to put into action your plans from the knowledge gained).

- *Customer Interaction*. This is the key action phase of executing and managing customer/prospect communications with relevant, timely information and offers using a variety of interaction channels and front office applications, including customer care applications, sales applications, customer contact applications, and interactive applications. This phase is the action in the plans and messages created from Knowledge Discovery and in Market Planning.

  Customer Interaction must map the connections to your customers, the potential sites for extended enterprise interactions, and your strategies for sales and customer buying actions (see Figure 2-3). Through advanced technologies and ongoing introductions of technology change in the marketplace, your channels will collect information about your customers. Through these channels, you have the opportunity to deliver marketing messages and sales opportunities, and to handle service issues.

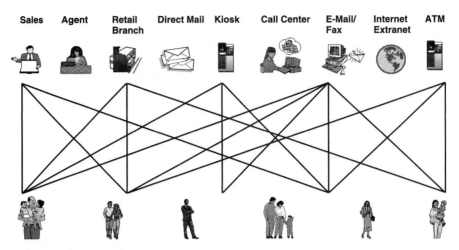

| Sales | Agent | Retail Branch | Direct Mail | Kiosk | Call Center | E-Mail/ Fax | Internet Extranet | ATM |

Figure 2-3. Knowing where your customers interact and the types of technologies and transactions they prefer to utilize is important.

Increasingly, sales and customer care functions may be shifted to less costly automated means of interaction. You will need to estimate and categorize all costs of sales or interactions in marketing activities. It is known that the movement to electronic mechanisms of contact and interaction can create enormous bottom-line returns.

- *Analysis and Refinement.* This is the process phase of continuous learning from customer dialogs by capturing and analyzing data from customer interactions and refining messages, communications, prices, volumes, locations, approaches, and timings, and understanding specific responses to your customer (marketing or sales) stimulus.

▶ Major Objectives and Benefits of a CRM Process

- **Customer Retention**—ability to retain loyal and profitable customers and channels to growth the business (profitably)
- **Customer Acquisition**—acquiring the right customers, based on known or learned characteristics, which drives growth and increased margins
- **Customer Profitability**—increasing individual customer margins, while offering the right products at the right time

Higher Returns on Investments over Time

In Fredrick Reichheld's *The Loyalty Effect*, he cites various excellent case study examples that foster the loyalty of the customers. In his chart, shown in Figure 2-4, he summarizes investment returns over time, which I agree with wholeheartedly from my experience. Notice the additional items that make up new profitability. These include customers paying **premium prices** for great service and confidence; **referrals**, which provide almost zero cost of direct marketing to new customers; and **revenue growth,** which is driven by cross-selling, up-selling or customers just using more and more of your products or services.

▶ From Product Focus to Customer Focus

Marketing and sales management requires a definitive set of offerings and messages to achieve their objectives. In many organizations, unfortunately, the customer comes last in the thought process of what is to be sold or provided. An excellent example of this is the old style of sales at an automobile dealership, where the salesperson welcomes the customer and asks what they desire (then doesn't really listen) and tries to offer the customer what the salesperson "feels" is the appropriate sale.

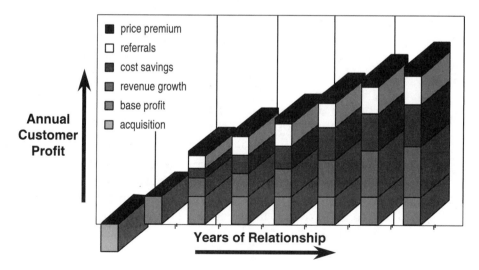

Figure 2-4. CRM returns on investment over time (adapted from Fredrick Reichheld, *The Loyalty Effect*).

In many cases, these types of "relationships" are not based on knowledge of the two parties, but on price or location of the service or product offered. In most cases, even if the customer buys the product (especially in the case of autos), there is a feeling of being "taken." In many product-focused sales situations, the salesperson "moves" the buyer to the product that the salesperson or the organization needs to sell them (for the selling organization's benefits, not for that of the customer).

In Mass Marketing, or even in Target Marketing or multidivisional enterprise marketing, there continues to be multiple offers made to customers (since the customer is a target, not part of a relationship of understanding). Most selling organizations really don't understand their customers and their needs. So they develop a process for targeting the customer, and the customer receives multiple confusing sales communications.

Figure 2-5 illustrates the process for product-centric marketing. Customers do not appreciate this type of marketing and generally reject the multiple offers, especially in business-to-business relationships, that come from processes that are product-centric.

The basic premise of CRM: The customer always comes first.

▶ The Business View of a Marketing Process

Let us take the example of a mobile or cellular telephone company, competing fiercely with other mobile companies, television cable companies, and with the established national telephone company. It will not be difficult to translate this example into the world of retail banking, retail shopping, airline travel, insurance, manufacturing and distribution, energy, utilities, and services—in fact, to most any market.

Suppose the mobile phone company desires to market the ability of their communications system to handle a second line. The traditional plan would be to enclose a special offer to all existing customers, encouraging them to try a second line, **free of charge**, for a month, then to monitor results and decide what changes to make to the campaign.

The expectation would be that perhaps 1% of existing customers would respond, and half of them would accept the offer.

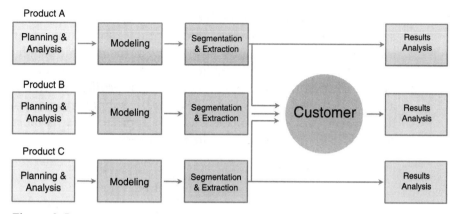

Figure 2-5. Product-focused marketing.

Such a campaign would also do some damage: Customers who already have a second line will feel irritated to be offered something they already have and further irritated that they are having to pay for something being offered to others for free.

In the world of CRM, the **marketing operation** is handled very differently. Supported by the necessary historical data, the first question is, "Who is most likely to buy a second line?" Clearly those who already have a second line are excluded from the **sales campaign**. But also, the profiles (and billing records of calls, known as the Call Detail Records or CDRs) of the customers who already have one line offer the clues about who might buy more services in the future.

The process of **predicting future sales** by looking at previous sales is one of the important benefits of the CRM approach. It uses data mining techniques, which simply look for patterns among existing customers. It is usually done in conjunction with the marketing department, who can offer some guidance to the likely market, for example, people under the age of 30 who are running their own businesses. However, there may be a school of thought that data mining should be a matter of purely statistical analysis, unconstrained by any prejudices held by the marketing department.

Whichever belief is followed, the result is a targeted set of customers who are most likely to buy the new service, which is perhaps 30% of all existing customers. And however the data mining is accomplished, it is based on detailed information about existing customers, including their usage of the service and other characteristics from previous successful sales of additional services.

Having decided on the target customers, the next question is how to approach them. Some people automatically discard the advertisements included with bills without even glancing at them, some people use email extensively, and others would be happy to receive a call on their mobile phone. Clearly, this type of (characteristic or profile) information should also be included in the Data Warehouse supporting your marketing department, and they can then use the approach that is most likely to succeed. It might well be a multistep process, such as:

- First, send an email.
- If there is no response, send a letter.
- If there is still no response, call the mobile phone (or send a short offer message).
- If the customer tells the telemarketer that they do not want calls, it must be maintained in the profile/customer data in the data warehouse.

This is more complicated and expensive than stuffing brochures into envelopes with the bills, but it is only used on people who are likely to buy, and it uses the approach most likely to succeed. But this is not always the best way to communicate with prospects or customers.

The approach can be made yet more attractive by tailoring it to the individual. For example, a likely purchaser is one who receives many telephone calls and is therefore often engaged in one call when another comes in. Instead of merely pointing out the merits of a second line in general terms, the offer letter can include details about how often this customer has failed to receive incoming calls.

The campaign, when executed, achieves two things: First, it brings the offer to the attention of **the *right people*, using the *right channels*, and *tailored to the individual*.**

Second, it brings ***more experience about communicating*** with this set of customers. At the end of the campaign, information about how the target audience responded will be recorded into the Data Warehouse, enriching the data, and helping the next campaign to be even more effective. This ***continual learning about customers***, as recorded within the central Data Warehouse, is at the heart of the CRM process (see Figure 2-6).

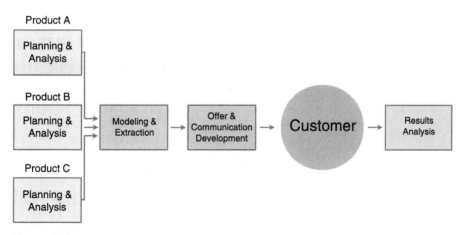

Figure 2-6. Customer-focused marketing.

This same data can also be used to design products in the first place: Once a company has a detailed profile of its customers and the ways they use the existing service, it can use that data to enhance the existing service. Then it can use the data to design new services tailored to their customers and even look for other products, which could be offered to the same audience—thus increasing wallet-share. Our mobile phone company could, for example, offer a book-buying service, specializing in business books, over the mobile network, if it determined that most of its customers were young business people.

Tactical Integration of the CRM Process

During the early stages of CRM introductions and implementations, there will be learning and nurturing experiences. To facilitate growth and actualization of the goals of CRM, your team may desire to refocus on the four key elements of the original CRM process. In this case, "refocusing" may not mean massive change; it may mean learning and utilizing advanced experiences from others before you (or experimenting with academic or theoretical ideas). Illustrated in Figure 2-7 is another view of the CRM process, which provides for terrain and contact point thinking and inclusion in your tactics and strategies.

Figure 2-7. Tactical strategies for the CRM process.

The four elements of the tactical strategies for the CRM process include:

1. **Interact**—A series of transactions and interactions that make up a dialog between a consumer/customer/channel and an organization or enterprise. This is THE data that is collected from all contact points and communications with outside points of contact.
2. **Connect**—The mapping and management of interaction points between a consumer/customer/channel and an organization or enterprise.
3. **Know**—The insight gained through capture and analysis of detailed information to create continuous learning (about customers, products, channels, markets, and competitors) from the data warehouse and/or knowledge bases created, interrogated, and analyzed.
4. **Relate**—The application of insight to create relevant interactions or communications with consumers, customers, channels, suppliers, and partners that builds value relationships.

Throughout this book, you will have the opportunity to map these four activities to each of the relevant subjects and therefore build a tactical plan for implementation and activation of the extended CRM process.

Preparing for Change

Britton Manasco and Bill Hopkins of The Knowledge Capital Group in Austin, Texas shared their thoughts with me about the evolution that is occurring and the managerial and organizational changes that are required. The following is from their excellent book, *Marketing Optimization Solutions*:

No change effort is more important than the one that companies have now embarked on in an effort to build dynamic, profitable and enduring relationships with their customers. What they must realize is that customer relationships cannot be built in a vacuum. They must be managed within the context of the enterprise's larger set of relationships. All organizations must embrace change—perpetual and pervasive change—if they are to meet the objectives that are commonly discussed by advocates of customer relationship management.

As we see it, the punishment for failing to become relationship-driven is becoming increasingly immediate and severe. At the same time, we see long-term relationships being torn apart by hypercompetitiveness on the Internet and elsewhere. Travel agents, car dealerships, and stockbrokers are under assault by an array of e-businesses. By making it easy to defect, Web-based businesses are forcing established consumer businesses of all types to reassess and reinvent. Business-to-business relationships are similarly imperiled as companies realize they can more cost-effectively purchase products and services through Internet auctions and other forms of dynamic trade.

Survival in such a turbulent environment ultimately will hinge on the ability of organizations to build lasting relationships. This is the only way they can remain profitable and competitive in a marketplace of widespread customer infidelity.

If companies are to develop powerful new approaches to relationship management, they must first establish the foundations for change. They must identify the pain points and make those widely evident. They must, as management theorist John Kotter explains, "create a sense of urgency. Change will never be embraced unless compelling reasons for it are presented. The problems that may stand out may be anything from plunging stock values to slipping profits to a recognizable rise in a competitor's position relative to your own. If change advocates can demonstrate that such factors can be traced to inadequate customer relationships, they are in a strong position to help launch a customer-focused initiative. They need to look for indicators—such as falling rates of customer retention, high levels of customer dissatisfaction, or merely declining sales—showing that customers are being poorly managed. Such data points and telling anecdotes can be invaluable tools in the efforts of change leaders to make things happen.

"Of course, it's impossible to effect large-scale changes without dynamic leadership. Relationship management initiatives must draw on the talent and energy of individuals from a variety of places in the organization. There must be leaders who are engaged in customer management activities as well as other leaders involved in capability management efforts. Ideally, change initiatives of this sort will bring together leaders who have deep expertise in the management of customer relationships as well as in supplier and partner relationships."

Change management and increasing measurements to understand the movement and messaging from customers and suppliers will be a prerequisite for success in relationship management. Acceleration, as in the title of this book, is not intended to mean speed and fracturing of trust or confidence along the way. We must take a short-term operational view *and* a have long-term strategic vision for engaging ourselves and our companies in customer relationship management. In addition, we will examine and provide direction on the info-structure and economics of CRM in Chapters 5, 11, 12, 13, and 14.

In Chapter 12, you will have the opportunity to analyze a strategic CRM maturity view and process matrix. This will also bring together the economic benefits and the three levels of maturity to combine with the three key actions (above) that must be integrated into a full-flow CRM process: Know, Relate, Interact. (The "Connect" is important, but it is part of the info-structure where you decide on tactics and strategies for "touch points" with your customers and suppliers and the immediacy of responsiveness.)

Relating to the customer **is the essential result of gathering data from** *interactions and transactions,* **combined with** *knowing customers* **through using relationship technologies.**

The Emerging CRM Organization

Throughout this book, you will find hints and suggestions on how to forge a new relationship with your customers and also how to build an information infrastructure that will redefine the abilities and velocity of marketing and selling and servicing your customers. None is more important than reevaluating your organization's individual responsibilities to ensure that your business processes are supported and also that the people who interact with your customers have what they require to succeed. Dean Kelly and Peter Hand, from Sydney, Australia, provided me with some discussions and development of significant thinking on organizational responsibilities. This could be a subject for a whole book in itself, but in these next few pages, you will gain some insight and direction for you to utilize in your management discussions on "**The Emerging CRM Organization.**"

It is increasingly important to define the requirements for roles and skill sets in positions within any marketing organization. While not always an obvious concern in today's marketing organization, there are fundamental skill changes and capabilities required in the emerging "one-to-one" marketing organization. The requirements for 1:1 Marketing, Real-Time Marketing, Differential Marketing, and finally the extreme necessities for Event-Driven Marketing make today's marketing organization, which is generally organized around products, archaic or stifled. The CRM evolution requires a customer-centric orientation, information, process, activities, and organization.

▶ The CRM Organization's Structure

The basic structure of the CRM organization should align around the key communication process we have already discussed earlier in the CRM process. In order to recognize the Right Customer, relate the Right Offer, schedule the interaction or communication of the offer at the Right Time, with the connection across the Right Channel(s), people will have to share a process and activate their skills to complete the activities and tasks required for success.

For ease of understanding and to map to the CRM process, the marketing organization may follow along the lines of know, relate, interact, and connect (see Figure 2-7). As illustrated in Figure 2-8, each person's job role would include the skills required in executing this role.

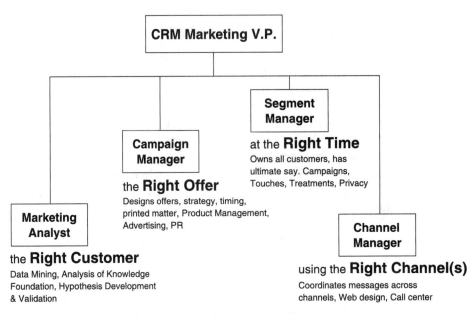

Figure 2-8. The marketing organization with roles.

The CRM Marketing VP

The Marketing VP (or Director) is perhaps more accurately titled the Relationship and Communications VP, for that is what this individual must concentrate resources on and achieve ongoing results for the entire management team. This function emphasizes, manages, and coordinates the entire CRM customer communication process to the betterment of enterprise performance through customer acquisition, retention, and profitability. As illustrated in Figure 2-9, the role is an important cornerstone in the potential success of CRM.

The CRM Marketing Analyst(s)

To identify the right customers, you will need to call on the expertise of the Marketing Analyst(s). They are the miners, the ones responsible for identifying the customers or "discovering" the investment opportunities that are worthy of exploitation. They are intimate with the knowledge foundation (enterprise database or data warehouse) that forms the central core of the knowledge within the CRM process. Review the role and skills for the Marketing Analyst in Figure 2-10. Note that the Marketing Analyst will interact with the IT Department to ensure that the requisite data is being added in accordance with growing business needs; likewise, that new data is being added as the requirements grow and evolve.

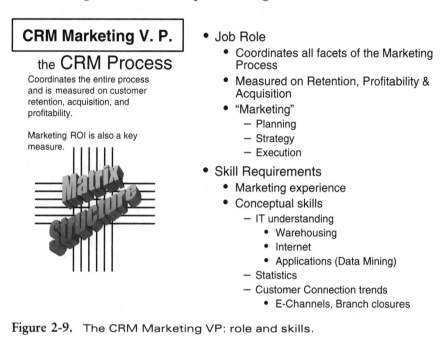

CRM Marketing V. P.

the **CRM Process**

Coordinates the entire process and is measured on customer retention, acquisition, and profitability.

Marketing ROI is also a key measure.

- Job Role
  - Coordinates all facets of the Marketing Process
  - Measured on Retention, Profitability & Acquisition
  - "Marketing"
    - Planning
    - Strategy
    - Execution
- Skill Requirements
  - Marketing experience
  - Conceptual skills
    - IT understanding
      - Warehousing
      - Internet
      - Applications (Data Mining)
    - Statistics
    - Customer Connection trends
      - E-Channels, Branch closures

Figure 2-9. The CRM Marketing VP: role and skills.

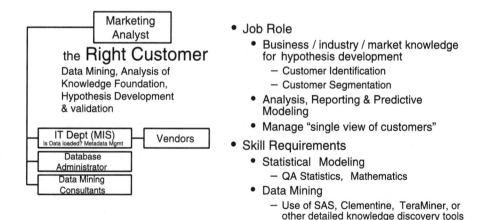

Marketing Analyst

the **Right Customer**

Data Mining, Analysis of Knowledge Foundation, Hypothesis Development & validation

IT Dept (MIS)
Is Data loaded? Metadata Mgmt — Vendors

Database Administrator

Data Mining Consultants

- Job Role
  - Business / industry / market knowledge for hypothesis development
    - Customer Identification
    - Customer Segmentation
  - Analysis, Reporting & Predictive Modeling
  - Manage "single view of customers"
- Skill Requirements
  - Statistical Modeling
    - QA Statistics, Mathematics
  - Data Mining
    - Use of SAS, Clementine, TeraMiner, or other detailed knowledge discovery tools

Figure 2-10. The CRM Marketing Analyst: role and skills.

This individual or group of analysts will need to work closely with a Database Administrator who will be modifying the logical data model to meet and support the changing business needs. There will also be the Data Mining Consultants, who are able to inject new "world views" into the customer segmentation or can identify different "events" that are worthy of analysis in Right Customer decisions.

The CRM Campaign Manager

Having identified the opportunities, the Campaign Manager then creates the right offers that will ultimately be made to the right customers. It is important to align the various campaign "ownership" groups to ensure that the campaign process is fully integrated with the offers. The different messages that are being communicated are aligned, and the Campaign Manager(s) accomplishes the planning. Review Figure 2-11 for the role and skills of the Campaign Manager.

In this role, the other "input" teams make their "cases." IT is also involved, as we know that any offer that is made must be supported in the billing, CIF, or ERP system should the customer buy or transact in response to the offer stimulus. Likewise, to fully coordinate the relationship optimization process, there will be a campaign automation tool that will support this creative process and establish the rules of engagement for each discrete offer within the context of the organizational marketing and communications process.

The CRM Segment Manager

A most important player in the CRM process is perhaps the Segment Manager. This person owns the business problem or the business (marketing) opportunities such as: 1) Customer Retention, 2) Customer Acquisition, and 3) Customer Profitability.

Someone will have to have the final authority and responsibility to decide whether the customer gets touched by the relationship marketing and communications process as the Right Time for the offer is determined. This is an obvious responsibility in the launch of a new product, but as launches and other offer communications are made, they establish the rules governing the touch frequency, multitreatment rules, recency, frequency, monetary segmentations, and other marketing techniques. The Segment Managers are the glue of the team and form the linchpin for the CRM process. To give you a view of the role and its skills, please review Figure 2-12.

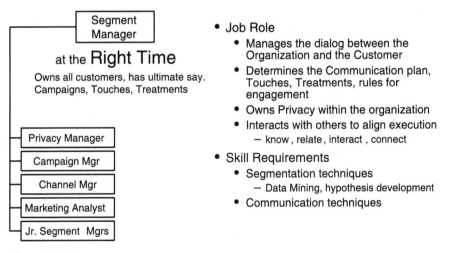

the Right Offer

Campaign
Manager

Designs offers, strategy, timing,
printed matter, Product Management,
Advertising, Public Relations messaging,
interactions, plans, and measurements

Advertising
Public Relations
Agencies & Media

Product Manager

Fulfilment
Mail Houses

IT Dept (ERP Sys)
Can Sys. Deliver? Changes made?
Vendors

IT Dept (MA apps)
Campaign Apps
Vendors

- Job Role
  - Links with Product Managers, Advertising Managers, and Public Relations departments and outside firms
  - Designs "Offers"
  - Determines campaign strategy
  - Test marketing
  - Relationships with Mail houses
  - Relationships with Telemarketing firm(s)
- Skill Requirements
  - "Vector Management"
  - Marketing Automation tools
  - Campaign / Marketing Experience
  - Understand Value and Use of Campaign management tools and databases
  - Work with IT to ensure flow is accurate

Figure 2-11. The CRM Campaign Manager: role and skills.

Segment
Manager

at the Right Time

Owns all customers, has ultimate say.
Campaigns, Touches, Treatments

Privacy Manager

Campaign Mgr

Channel Mgr

Marketing Analyst

Jr. Segment Mgrs

- Job Role
  - Manages the dialog between the Organization and the Customer
  - Determines the Communication plan, Touches, Treatments, rules for engagement
  - Owns Privacy within the organization
  - Interacts with others to align execution
    - know , relate, interact , connect
- Skill Requirements
  - Segmentation techniques
    - Data Mining, hypothesis development
  - Communication techniques

Figure 2-12. Segment Manager—roles and skills.

The Channel Manager(s)

As we continue through the CRM process, we are at the point where the Right Customer is identified, the Right Offers have been created, the Right Time has now come, and the critical transition from single view of customer to single company image is reached. As shown in Figure 2–13, the

Channel Manager coordinates the customer, offer, and timing into the channel decisions, and ensures that the same offer is communicated and then reinforced across all of the enterprises' many "touch points."

The Channel Manager must interact with the Call Center, the Internet, the Web, and the direct or indirect sales force groups (other internal customers who are affected by the process). It must be known/ planned who and where are the external channels of resellers, distributors, franchisees, and the advertising and public relations teams to make sure the process hits the front lines in parallel. This means having the script ready to go, the telephone or email operators trained, the sales force aligned, the Web pages created, the print ads purchased and scheduled, and the TV slots confirmed (in the case of a large campaign). It may also (in the case of an incremental campaign) not require such a high degree of coordination, in which case some of these interest groups may not be required each and every time.

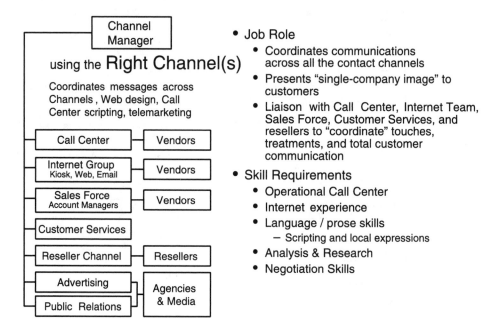

Figure 2-13. The Channel Manager: role and skills.

Title / Role	CRM Objective	CRM Process Step
Marketing Analyst	Right Customer	Know
Campaign Manager	Right Offer	Relate
Segment Manager	Right Time	Interact
Channel Manager	Right Channel(s)	Connect

Figure 2-14. The emerging CRM organization's roles, objectives, and process steps.

The emerging organization completes the CRM objectives, as illustrated in Figure 2-14, for specific process steps with the following assignments in the CRM process (Figure 2-7).

▶ Integration of Business, Information, People, Process, and Technology

Data mining can be used to predict all sorts of customer behavior with considerable success. For example, if a customer of a mobile service is being tempted by a competitor to leave, they will probably send signals through the use of the service. The service usage will perhaps decline sharply as he takes advantage of a free trial offer. Or the customer may begin to use the new cable-connected phone for international calls. If the customer is also near the end of his contract period, he is very likely to reduce his usage and then not renew.

You can clearly see this in very detailed data warehouses of leading telephone companies who have built an info-structure to plan marketing and competitive analysis of their products and services.

The past few years have been characterized mostly by investigation into the potential of data mining. Some companies have moved ahead and have gotten as far as identifying the types of findings they wish to make. The next few years will see companies acting on these discoveries, and the true potential of data mining will come to the fore. It will have a dramatic impact on the business.

There are excellent examples of "customer calling analysis" that have been accomplished by the four surviving major US local telecommunications providers (formerly Regional Bell Operating Companies or RBOCs) and others throughout the world, such as Belgacom in Brussels, France Telecom, Telefonica of Spain, Telefonica de Argentina, Vodaphone in Australia, Bell Canada, Sweden's Telia, Telecom Italia, and smaller companies such as Far East Tone in Taiwan and Pele-Phone in Israel. Pele-

Phone is a good example of a relatively small communications company in a smaller country (of population size), in a highly competitive situation, which has utilized the data warehouse and CRM analytical models for great success in the last two years of the twentieth century.

▶ Successful Excellence: Israel's Pele-Phone

A New Market Entrant = Gaining Competitive Advantage

Pele-Phone Communications, Ltd., pioneered cellular network services in Israel and is so closely identified with the technology that today many Israelis refer to any cellular phone as a Pele-Phone. The company, which is the largest of Israel's three cellular providers, was established in 1986 as a joint venture of Motorola and Bezeq, the Israeli Telecommunications Corporation.

With close to one million business and consumer cellular subscribers, Pele-Phone commands approximately 50% of the market share and is well positioned to continue growing its cellular subscriber base. Among other favorable factors for the company, Israel ranks as one of the world's fastest growing wireless markets. The country's penetration rate of cellular services is over 40%, the fifth highest rate in the world. Another advantage in providing cellular services in the Israeli market is the length of the average cellular phone call, which exceeds that of most other countries.

Pele-Phone, with corporate headquarters in Tel Aviv, maintains 14 service centers in Israel to meet local customer needs. Its highly technical and service-oriented work force of over 1,000 employees continues to expand its portfolio of cellular services.

Pele-Phone's Business Challenges

Only two cellular service providers have operated in Israel over many years, and they have developed a fierce rivalry. In 1998, the Ministry of Telecommunications announced the formation of a third provider, resulting in renewed attention for the country's wireless customers. Deregulation of the telecommunications industry further intensified the competition.

In the face of this new and increasingly aggressive competition, Pele-Phone sought ways to launch its own aggressive marketing initiatives. Pele-Phone's marketing executives wanted a solution that would help them build customer loyalty and reduce churn (customers switching to the competition), while increasing product-line profitability. They also wanted a system in place that would help them use customer data to effectively cross-sell evolving service offerings.

Pele-Phone determined it needed to mine the wealth of customer information it collected each day to increase its competitive advantage.

Pele-Phone's Data Warehousing Solution

Pele-Phone decided to build a Data Warehouse to meet its decision-support needs. The cellular provider was interested in marketing initiatives that would require a very large data repository to build customer history.

During my interview with Avshalom Rov, the Director of Applications (and Data Warehouse leader) at Pele-Phone, he stated: "We used traditional database technologies for billing and operational systems, but none was capable of handling the enormous volumes of consumer data we needed to store and interrogate in order to identify potential customer needs or determine the profitability of individual products." Pele-Phone sought and implemented a highly flexible enterprise data warehouse database solution with high performance.

An enterprise-wide Data Warehouse Strategy was chosen after a 7-month selection process. The process included a Business and Information Discovery analysis that projected a ROI for about US$6 million, based solely on the system's capability to help reduce churn. After weighing the impact of the raw data needed for its marketing initiatives, Pele-Phone analyzed the capabilities of the various systems, focusing on installations with similar usage requirements. The implementation moved from development to production in 6 months.

Pele-Phone conducted thorough research, conferring with industry analysts, Data Warehouse experts, and Data Warehouse users.

"What we needed was real-world experience of delivering successful solutions tailored to the needs of the telecommunications market," said Rov. "We decided to check on reference sites where we could actually see data warehouses in excess of a terabyte running and working. Another important element was Professional Services, which had the expertise and methodology to help us build the application we wanted that met our quality and schedule requirements."

Two classes of users rely on the Data Warehouse's capabilities. A very sophisticated group of users, which may range from five to ten people, depending on the project, includes market analysts, statisticians, or economists. These users understand how data is structured in the Data Warehouse and have the ability to write queries to leverage the data for marketing advantage. Another group of up to 100 users, having far less knowledge of the system, performs predefined queries on call records from the billing system.

Pele-Phone is turning its customer data into a strategic advantage. Mr. Rov attributes the success to the performance and maintenance capabilities of the system. Why is it different than a complex database?

"The Data Warehouse allows us to do complex queries with multiple joins of very large tables," he explained. "And it provides good performance even with a large number of concurrent users. It's also a low maintenance platform, which is a big advantage. We only have one DBA to support the system. You don't need that much DBA time to reorganize the data and you can add capacity simply by adding more disks to the system without worrying about how the data is physically distributed."

Pele-Phone began exploring new marketing capabilities shortly after implementation by building a central repository of enterprise information. The first initiatives focused on customer relationship management, marketing segmentation, and call behavior analysis (for customer retention applications).

Based on the customer profile information stored in the Data Warehouse, Pele-Phone now identifies subscriber's specific needs and targets them with tailored offerings. Customer requirements are also tracked through the Data Warehouse and used in the development of new products and services. For example, the ability to mine customer data allows Pele-Phone to closely monitor mobile phone usage and the profitability of individual customers. This not only helps to focus marketing efforts, but it also helps to develop profitable pricing strategies and evaluate the potential of new marketing initiatives.

"We were considering the idea of promoting car phones with the assumption that they give you better connections and less dropped calls," Rov said. "With the Data Warehouse we were able to go through all the call records and compare the number of dropped calls on car phones to the average number of dropped calls for the handset population. And that told us whether we could justify subsidizing those phones with a big promotion to boost car phone sales, and by how much."

Reducing churn is another benefit resulting from the ability to analyze customer data on a daily basis. By analyzing historical usage patterns, along with other changing market factors, Pele-Phone can pinpoint with greater accuracy customers who may be considering switching to a competitor. These customers then can be quickly targeted with special promotions or tailored services designed to maintain their interest and loyalty.

Being able to spot this likelihood enables the company to do something about it. First, it can determine whether this is a very profitable customer. If he is, then it should make every effort to keep him. Is he on the best tariff for his usage? Isn't it a better business decision to reduce profitability a little than lose it altogether? When sending out the renewal notice, some special inducement could be offered—such as a second line for half price, if he is likely to be interested.

For sure, it is better to have some notice of a profitable customer leaving, so that efforts can be made to retain him. Once he has decided to leave, it is unlikely that he will be persuaded to change his mind because the new contract will already be in place.

One of the calling plans developed with the help of the Data Warehouse focuses on lower rates for calls made within a specific geographic or home region. According to Rov, the Data Warehouse was instrumental in defining the borders of the different regions and determining optimum pricing. The system's advanced analysis capabilities allowed the service to be priced so that it would be attractive to customers and at the same time ensure that it did not cannibalize the regular service.

"We're now able to be a much more customer-focused company," Rov said. "We're segmenting the market and providing each segment with the kind of service and attention that is in line with their needs, and also with their profitability to us. We're able to provide data on customer profitability, including price plan profitability or the profitability of a certain promotion. These are things that we were not able to do in the past."

While many of the initial efforts concentrated on marketing, Pele-Phone is investigating several other promising applications for the Data Warehouse. Work has already begun in the area of fraud management, which is a growing problem for the cellular business. By detecting changes in calling patterns and performing other sophisticated analyses, the Data Warehouse helps identify potential areas of fraudulent use. Pele-Phone also intends to use the Data Warehouse to support engineering applications and to monitor the usage and capacity load of its network infrastructure. This is a significant advantage for any communications supplier anywhere in the world. Significant efficiency gains are expected in this area as well as further increases in overall profitability. This also drives lower costs and lower prices to customers.

Quite simple monitoring can be used to spot fraud: A new customer who starts to make large numbers of international calls may plan to avoid paying his bill. On the other hand, he may be doing genuine overseas business. He may be either your best or your worst customer.

Notice that if a sharp change in usage can be identified as an important indicator, the warehouse itself can continually monitor call history and automatically flag any customers whose usage crosses a certain threshold. At the least, this would alert the marketing department and could conceivably trigger an automatic response, such as a phone call. We are beginning to approach the notion of "one-to-one" marketing.

Pele-Phone has gained a clear strategic advantage through the capabilities of its Data Warehouse. The company now has the ability to operate more competitively and effectively analyze market conditions and potential opportunities.

"I don't think anybody can speculate what the industry will look like three or five years from now," Rov said, "but it's obvious it will be very different than what it is now. Our Data Warehouse will help us adjust to the change by giving us a better understanding of what our customers want and how they're changing. And it will also help us to change ourselves to satisfy these customer needs in a timely manner and with an unmatched advantage in Israel's cellular market."

Reviewing all the activities of the CRM-enabled marketing department, it is clear that their lives have changed dramatically. No longer are they concerned with the design and execution of a few, large-scale marketing campaigns every year. They are now involved in large numbers of small, focused campaigns, some of which are triggered automatically by the system. This would be difficult to manage without some degree of automation, which is exactly what campaign management systems provide: They keep track of all the campaigns and monitor the results; of course, feeding those results back into the Data Warehouse as part of the continual learning process.

It is also clear that the central Data Warehouse plays the crucial part in all of this activity. It contains all the detailed history about every customer, not only the history of his usage of the product and his record of paying bills, but also his preferences about being contacted and his reactions to previous marketing campaigns. From his address, something about his social status can be readily deduced. From credit agencies, his financial status can be gleaned.

▶ Data Warehouse Requirements Definition

So what sort of system is the Data Warehouse? Let's look at what a Data Warehouse is required to do:

1. It must hold vast amounts of detailed data: Every business transaction, every phone call, every call to the help desk, every purchase, every bill, every complaint needs to be logged. It is tempting to compromise by holding averages or by retaining detail for only 30 days. You need to focus in all of your marketing campaigns and thus their effectiveness through detailed measurements. Marketing is an unpredictable process—new opportunities and competitive threats appear overnight: Detailed data allows immediate reaction.

2. The warehouse is continually being updated with business and marketing transactions. Not long ago, monthly updates were seen as adequate; now even a daily update is too slow, and continuous trickle feeding is used.

3. It is used by a large number of people within marketing and management and many other departments. As has been noted elsewhere, CRM is not just about marketing; it is about how the whole company treats its customers.

4. Some of those people want to be able to scan and query the *entire* database looking for new patterns, and they want to do it immediately: Designing a warehouse around a set of expected patterns of use is doomed to failure.

5. The system must be available for use at all times: It is the operational heart of the marketing and management of the company.

6. It must scale. It must be able to grow with the success of the company and with the demands of the increasingly sophisticated marketing department. It is not unusual to find Data Warehouses doubling in volume every 18 months.

7. It must provide appropriate protection for this sensitive data. The general public is increasingly worried by the notion of details of their private lives being made available without their consent. Legislation is increasingly demanding that people explicitly asked about the uses to which this data may be put: The warehouse must also record and implement these preferences and implement them automatically (see Chapters 9 and 10).

In short, the Data Warehouse is a gold mine of information, used not only for the kind of predictions discussed previously, but also for the management of the business: How did last month compare with the same month in previous years? How did the southern region compare with the north? Who are my top 10 most profitable customers? What would happen if I dropped the tariff for local calls by 50% as my competitors are doing?

We shall discuss the design and installation of such a warehouse in Chapters 5 through 8. What should already be clear is that it is not just another use for the existing operational database systems. The customer knowledge Data Warehouse will become the decision info-structure of the entire organization.

▶ Management Considerations

- CRM replaces Mass Marketing with frequent, smaller, and highly focused campaigns. This increases effectiveness and reduces waste and customer irritation. It transforms the life of the marketing department. CRM allows high velocity actions.

- CRM is a process of continual learning—every contact with a customer tells the company something about him, even if he fails to respond.

- CRM is wholly dependent on a central store of detailed data about customers, their behavior, and their preferences, including the preferences and specifics about data privacy: the Data Warehouse.

The Role of Information Technology

Less than five percent of the world's firms achieve the full potential of their customer relationship initiatives. The rest are caught in its paradox.

John McKean, Author,
"Information Masters—Secrets of the Customer Race",
John Wiley, 1999

▶ The Change from Data to Relationships

Harrah's Entertainment (U.S. Casinos), AT&T Consumer Markets Division, SBC Communications, GTE, Sprint, Hallmark Cards, Tesco (U.K.), American Airlines, Continental Airlines, Sam's Clubs (Wal-Mart), Qantas (Australia), Travel Unie (Netherlands), Pele-Phone (Israel), National Australia Bank (Australia), St. George Bank (Australia), and Barclays Bank (U.K.) have all excelled, primarily because they have placed customer information at the center of their information infrastructure.

Detailed customer knowledge, not just raw data about transactions and financial payments, is what successful enterprises use to win and maintain profitable customers. Transforming raw data into actionable information is mandatory to create an environment for shared and breakthrough business decision making. Knowledge of everything, as much as can be managed and integrated for "understanding," will create wisdom in marketing, sales, services, administration, resource management, and all levels of decision making and planning.

As each enterprise defines its business objectives and business units, it typically defines supporting processes, functions, and the actions required to succeed. However, many business units focus on their products and/or services without regard to the interactions and resource consumption by the other business units required for managing a relationship with a specific customer or groups of customers.

The major functions—such as Marketing, Customer Communications, Customer Service, Sales Planning, Product Development, Distribution Management, Financial Analysis and Costing, Risk Assessment, and Channel Management—need to be interlinked through information resources and analytical processes in order to have an accurate, timely and complete view of the customer.

Data Warehouses, not just large "marketing databases," have been built for many managerial decision-making, marketing analysis, and customer-relationship purposes. Examples include a few of the many airline frequent-flyer mileage programs designed to gather and store valuable information that determines customer segmentation, customers' propensity to buy services, customer entry and exit points to the business, flight loading factors compared with volume of loyal customers on selected flights, volume of business by sales channels, customer complaints, frequency and monetary statistics, and other pertinent new knowledge gained from the centralization and reconciliation of detailed historical customer information.

The power of new (or learned) knowledge of the customer relationship drives higher responsiveness and profitability for the business. The resources expended and the opportunities to manage the customer and the channels will grow if information systems and the decision-support capabilities are driven by a multidepartmental or multibusiness unit view. This means an enterprise approach to extracting and transforming information systems into a customer-centric info-structure.

The role of *Information Technology* (IT) organizations traditionally has been to provide the strategy, landscape/network, technology, information, and processes to facilitate the enterprise in collecting, managing, protecting, and providing access to data. IT's new role now includes the objective of gaining knowledge from all appropriate sources of information and driving customers to utilize the latest in relationship technologies.

The most successful IT organizations have teamed up with the business units to forge a Data Warehouse environment that extends the information into knowledge and provides wide access to very detailed historical data.

The goal of building knowledge bases, through data warehousing or other means, is similar to retaining all of the experiences and interactions that you have had with someone, or an institution, or a business throughout your life. You have good and bad feelings, good and bad memories, and good and bad knowledge related to the experience.

Having this knowledge and being able to act on it in a timely manner is what makes today's businesses successful.

It is very important to know your customers in order to achieve long-term growth and strength. Not having a collective knowledge of the multiple touch points has clouded the view of the whole customer.

The **relationship value chain** (Figure 3-1) shows the key processes required for a business to succeed. Many of the functions touch the customers.

Enterprise information systems are redefined to gather transactional data from multiple disparate sources throughout your organization, to a central point for reconciliation, redefinition, and coordination of the information gained by placing the data into *subject areas*. These subject areas can be anything of key value defined within your enterprise or industry, such as customer, product, financial, sales, marketing, and distribution points/franchises/channels.

The IT organization uses an info-structure to provide greater value and contribution to the enterprise. The task of a company's IT group can become easier by leveraging a proven framework and methodology. (A framework for data warehousing is discussed in Chapter 5 and a methodology is discussed in Chapter 6.)

Building and maintaining a *Corporate Historical Memory* and *Knowledge Library* should be a key goal of today's IT organization.

Figure 3-1. Customer information is the core of the info-structure.

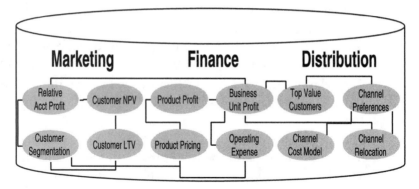

Figure 3-2. Subject areas in a CRM process.

Knowledge bases help companies better understand:

- Revenues and sales
- Asset utilization
- The margin each customer generates
- The costs of doing business with each customer
- Transaction mapping and stimulus to utilize new information technologies in the marketplace
- Costs of and uses of channels
- Producer evaluations

- Customer satisfaction levels
- The present and future earnings potential of customers

Six Key Enterprise Priorities

Leadership organizations focus on six key priorities (or strategies) to forge a management team and philosophy. These include but are not limited to:

1. **Relationships and Marketing**
2. **Technology and Communications Integration**
3. **Services (to and for the customer and suppliers)**
4. **Channel Management**
5. **Financial Management**
6. **Risk Management**

Organizations need to determine the focused priorities and then list key questions that must be answered by the management team to compete successfully in each of these areas.

By defining these (million- or billion-dollar) questions, organizations are identifying the need for knowledge bases and potential ROI opportunities. Organizations without successful data warehouses have *not* really identified the questions that *must* be answered to succeed and grow their business to support their strategies.

Four Stages of Knowledge Maturity

Once the questions are determined, how do you get the answers? To get to the truth you need to understand the sources of information and their value. In business knowledge there are four major stages: Reporting, Analysis, Prediction, and Wisdom.

Reporting, so tools do not make the manager. Reporting in some enterprises is totally focused on the business unit or the products. Summarized reporting is provided to upper management and the details are left to lower level employees to define, use, manage, and visualize.

This is sometimes acceptable, but leading organizations allow all levels of employees and management to view detailed data, query the detailed data, and/or use graphical comparisons to gain knowledge.

Maintaining reporting systems can be cumbersome and also are resource consuming. In effective management systems, managers have standard reporting measurements, can add or delete reports of interest or noninterest, and also can immediately define and create new reporting charts and graphical visualizations to discover and learn new information. Sometimes, in more useful systems and with the aid of experienced power-users, management can gain knowledge from reporting. But this is rare. The whole concept of limiting access to data is a role that IT should reverse. With obvious security protections and procedures for privacy implemented, IT should give very wide access and foster the use of incrementally important data to all business users.

Analysis is a great advisor to the inquisitive but is not the total answer. Ad hoc query and easy access to detailed data is important in stage two. The fostering of comparisons, models, clarity of understanding through questions (and the subsequent answers and more questions) catapults the business user to new heights of knowledge and also enthusiasm. In industries that previously were laden with boring data, business users find answers to questions not previously thought of, therefore bringing forth more questions, which define new knowledge. An example of this is at Anthem Blue Cross Blue Shield (Indiana, Ohio, Kentucky, and Connecticut). At Anthem, users ask open queries of the data warehouse and even build models to learn from very detailed data captured from every line of every claim bill received from every doctor and service supplier. They find out information and abuses never before seen or even remotely available because business units or geographical boundaries (and/or laws) previously separated the claims systems.

Prediction, especially of behaviors, is closer to world-class success. And this will require new thinking regarding your customers and your own organization's capabilities. *Modeling* helps to know the present and see the future. Prediction will be covered in Chapters 4 and 5.

Wisdom (knowledge) of your enterprise, your customers, your competitors, and your marketplace is the highest of all opportunities. Leadership organizations foster relationships and knowledge to create Wisdom. Wisdom drives confidence in taking action and vice versa.

Integrating the Business Functions and Info-Structure Provides the Foundation

The development of a strategy for encompassing the multitudes of information systems investments in your organization requires a clear vision of the potential ("house" of the future) infrastructure. There you will need to identify and categorize your operational, analytical, and strategic processes or applications. In Figure 3-3, there is a leading viewpoint of defining the groupings to more clearly understand and decide which functions may be defined and enhanced together (within the groups). Leadership organizations understand that there is a need to cross-pollinate and cross-integrate the data between these business functions, therefore the need for a data warehouse environment.

The Enterprise Opportunity

Enterprises need to anticipate their customers' needs and have ready the products and services they want before they know they want them—and ahead of your competition. The call is for *customer knowledge* to enable you to understand existing customers and acquire new ones. *Customer Knowledge Systems*, also known as a *Data Warehouses*, with detailed historical customer-centric information, enable companies to be agile, responsive players in the marketplace and to make sound marketing and resource allocation decisions.

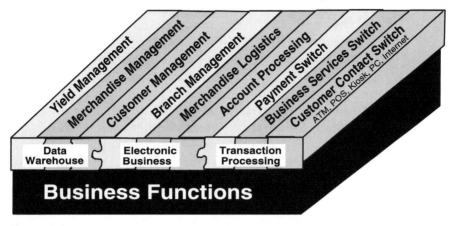

Figure 3-3. Business functions and integrated platforms.

Sometimes, customer knowledge systems require a fundamental shift in business philosophy, cooperation of the management participants, and inclusion of ideas and information that have been rarely utilized before in the organization. As an example, business units agree to share extractions of data, measurement systems, management reporting, analytical processes, marketing techniques, customer service management, and channel facilitation.

The consequences of this strategy have been astounding in a most positive way: customers realize that you are addressing their needs and also have historical views that save them and you enormous amounts of time and resources to deliver what they desire. Being flexible and responsive can win much business even at a price premium to the customer. Imagine what can happen if you have a price advantage *and* deliver what the customer desires in a B2B or B2C environment.

The transformation of data can be accomplished through long-practiced techniques and processes involving data warehousing skills. But the organization desiring to increase their effectiveness through the newer information and knowledge bases may require counseling on the changing role of IT.

▶ Preparing for Cultural and Idea Interchanges

One of the most difficult elements of planning and implementing a new info-structure is the cultural and organizational change required to integrate and absorb the new information availability, flexibility, accessibility, and usefulness.

Peppers and Rogers (1997) provide an open letter to CEOs on how and why to make the investments in CRM and the Relationship Technologies to support their enterprises' new approaches to the marketplace and their customers. "One suggestion is to create a cadre of missionary executives within your organization to serve as change agents. Start with a small group of bright, high-achieving executives, inculcate them in the 1:1 strategies of interactivity, customization, learning relationships, and collaborative marketing. The more knowledgeable they become, the more convinced (and convincing) they will be."

Peppers and Rogers continue with four basic factors the make missionary work successful:

1. Missionaries are well trained.
2. Missionaries rely on a "bible."
3. Missionaries are supported by the "church" (i.e., CEO/Board).
4. Missionaries must be able to rely on the fear of "God" (CEO).

My recommendation is to first read Chapter 14 in Peppers and Rogers, after understanding what it is you desire to achieve and implement, then go forth to the masses and use the missionaries to create the new truth.

Oh, these missionaries and their brethren will need a strong infostructure to purposefully initiate and implement true CRM and 1:1 marketing techniques and philosophies. Therefore, you will need at least 100 days to define your marketing changes, define CRM, allocate resources, and build your initial customer-centric knowledge base (see Chapter 7 in this book).

The key to implementing a sound decision-support infrastructure (DSS), which is an extension of your previous IT investments (not a substitute), is to allow an enterprise to analyze market and customer behavior while rapidly responding to competitive pressures. This is not a simple task, but we will show you that you can build this foundation in about 100 days (see Chapter 7).

Generally speaking, you have the data you need, but it is difficult and time consuming to access and place into formats that are usable by the nontechnical people in your enterprise. This situation is not a new one, but today you must accelerate the investment in usability and accessibility more than ever to provide organizations with high ROI capabilities.

There are a number of successful customers with on-going world-class processes and knowledge-based data warehouses. (Many of these companies are featured in Chapter 14, and Hallmark Cards is featured near the end of this chapter.) Customer-centric data warehouses are being used in most industries, whether a business needs to understand the purchase decision making of each individual customer by name or the market-basket trends by store.

The Role of Technology in Driving Customer Retention and Profitability

The marketing dilemma that many enterprises face is whether to focus on increasing market share, customer share, or both. Which is more profitable? Which has greater long-term payoff?

For traditional service-oriented enterprises, it is becoming increasingly difficult to capture competitors' customers, especially since competitors are becoming larger and more diverse in offering services and products. A steady flow of new, innovative services and delivery channels is usually necessary to build market share. Of course, these can be costly to develop and execute.

With a greater customer focus, you may discover greater profitability within your existing customer base.

The following section discusses how IT should enable the building of customer loyalty and retention, cross-selling opportunities, improved direct marketing campaigns, and marketing to a segment of one.

Enabling Customer Retention and Higher Profits

In the past, it was always easier to attempt to "poach" your competitors' customers. However, studies have shown that companies spend five times the amount of money on acquiring new customers as they do on retaining those they already have. Further studies by Reichheld and Sasser (1990) demonstrated that: "As a customer relationship with a company lengthens, profits rise. And not just a little. Companies can boost profits by 100 percent by retaining just 5 percent more of their customers." (Reichheld 1997.)

Companies can boost profits by 100% by retaining just 5% more of their customers.

Who Are Your Customers?

The key to marketing success is the ability to ask the right questions that relate to a well-thought-out and actionable strategy. These are usually fundamental questions, and should be answerable with available data. Unfortunately, finding that data and getting the answers you need are typically impossible with the way information systems are structured.

The key to marketing success is the ability to ask the right questions that relate to a well thought out and actionable strategy.

The customer-centered data warehouse provides an opportunity to ask those questions with a good chance that most of them will be answered. For example, with better information about who your customers are, you become better able to serve and keep them.

A bank in the United Kingdom attempted to find out just how many customers it had. It derived a number from a range of disparate computer systems that provided different bank services. That number was 25 million. When the data was finally cleaned up and used with matching software to eliminate duplicates, the bank found it actually had 7 million customers. There were customers in different databases that were not stored by name but by account number, and incomplete records existed in many systems that focused on products. To make specific offers to your customer base, you *have* to know who your customers are.

Without a clear picture of who your customers are, it is probably easier to pursue your competitors' customers.

CRM Enables Customer Segmentation

To be able to do even rudimentary segmentation, you need to know at least your customers' names, addresses, ages, and sex. Yet traditional marketing segmentation methods—demographics, psychographics, geodemographics, and behavioral clusters—are just coming into play in some organizations—and is not enough.

If you are utilizing traditional segmentation methods, the data does not reflect household-by-household detailed customer-specific information. Also, profiles taken of particular types of households don't represent the individuals and their likely propensities to act in particular ways.

A reliable predictor of future behavior is actual past behavior.

Transaction data plus interaction information is mandatory. A culture must be fostered that continuously gathers customer-specific information that enhances your customer information database. Every encounter must be seen as another opportunity to find out additional information. This information forms the basis of a company's real assets, its relationships with its customers.

▶ Data Data Everywhere

The sheer amount of data in the multiplicity of systems (in most large organizations) cannot be turned into answers because of duplications of inaccurate information, the lack of focused customer-centric data, and the use of differing information technologies. For example, you have accounting systems, order entry systems, MRP or ERP systems, inventory or asset management systems, distribution systems, financial reporting systems, human resource systems, and customer services systems that are all different in their accesses, uses, applications, and operational data structures.

The data warehouse has become the basis upon which specific business aims can be achieved.

To overcome this, leading enterprises now use data warehouses with a customer focus that sets them apart from their traditional operational databases. The data warehouse has become the basis on which specific business aims can be achieved and predictive models can be built. Data warehouses are much more than repositories for storing data.

Today, banks such as Bank of America, Lloyds/TSB, First American Bank of Tennessee, and Frost Bank of Texas have been able to consolidate names and addresses using matching and deduplication software, clean their data, and then put it all into data warehouses and data marts. With this "single version of the truth" they are now able to identify customers as individuals. How long has that customer been with the bank? Are there any other accounts in the same family? Are they a one-, two-, or many-product family?

The "single version of the truth" is a key strategy for companies desiring to forge ahead of competition by using customer information.

The questions continue to be evoked toward the composite customer data warehouse. One question generates another ten, which, in turn, generates another hundred. The difference is that the answers are at hand. Through data mining, predictive models can be built for database marketing as opposed to limiting the questioners to queries and responsive reports or charts used only for decision support.

Enabling the New Marketing Litany: The Four Cs

When you can see who the customers actually are and what they do with the institution, then there is an opportunity to more effectively market to them. This approach has even changed the traditional description of marketing—"The Four Ps"—to demonstrate a move toward a greater customer focus—"The Four Cs (Table 3-1).

Table 3-1.

Four Ps	Four Cs
Product	Customer needs and wants
Price	Cost to the customer
Place	Convenience
Promotion	Communication

"New Marketing Litany: The Four Ps Passé; C-Words Take Over." Robert Lauterborn

The move to a greater customer focus is an attempt to see things from a customer perspective. Always keep in mind that the purpose of marketing is to profitably generate customer-perceived value. When looking at retention programs, you must appreciate whom you want to retain and why to retain them. What would you plan for the marginal customer, and what would you plan (differently) for those customers that are unprofitable to your company? Customer retention planning is where it begins, and its implementation is where you add to bottom-line profitability.

When creating retention programs you must appreciate whom you want to retain and why to retain them.

Customer Retention

Loyal customers are typically more-profitable customers.

For loyal customer marketing there are no additional acquisition costs. Loyal customers tend to buy more services and try out new ones. Their growing number becomes an annuity. You can manage the costs of servicing their needs. And, they act as word-of-mouth marketers for you.

Customer retention management is achieved by building a deep insight into who your customers are, then developing and using models that will predict which customers are likely to defect. By using these models, along with profitability potential models, you are able to make informed decisions about which customers to attempt to retain. You could also look at their individual profit improvement potential and make decisions about how you can meet their needs.

There is a major difference in the characteristics and requirements of customer retention versus customer acquisition. As you can see in Table 3-2, the characteristics can be guidelines on your strategy of how to plan for inclusion of information as well as its uses.

Table 3-2. Characteristics of Retention and Acquisition. (Source: J. M. McIntyre)

Retention	Acquisition
Nurturing relationships	Acquiring potential relationships
Internal analysis	External research
Demographics and transactional history	Demographic profiles
Actual needs driven	Projected needs driven
Contacts must be personal	Contacts can be less personal
Accuracy required	Inaccuracy tolerated
Offer relationship-driven	Offer driven
Offers must be integrated	Offers can be events
Relatively high response	Relatively low response
Supports reactivating	Supports assimilation
Synergistic with acquisition	Synergistic with retention

Experience has shown that companies with retention focus have achieved significant improvement in retention levels, retaining up to 35% of the customers who would ordinarily have defected. The key is to identify the changes in customers' behavior that could indicate a potential defection—change of address, regular credit lines canceled, complaints made, account balances decline—and then to take some action to prevent potential attrition.

However, key to the profitable success of this action is to be able to assess which customers are worth retaining, from a current or potential profitability standpoint. Knowledge databases have shown through modeling techniques that customers decide to defect many months before they actually leave, so it is important to recognize their behaviors and their profitability potential at the point of their decision, not necessarily at the point of attrition (see Figure 3-3).

There is also strong evidence that retention increases in line with the number of products held by a customer.

Nearly 75% of all defectors hold only one product a full year before leaving.

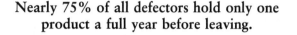

Dynamic Models Look at Behavioral
"Hot Spots" to Trigger Retention Efforts

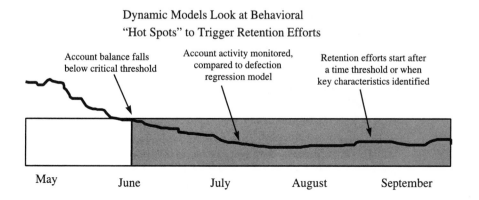

Static models used to identify "high-risk" profiles

Personal	Account Status
Under age 30	Single product held
Not married	First year of relationship
Student/blue-collar worker	No credit relationship
Renter	

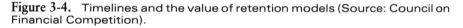

Figure 3-4. Timelines and the value of retention models (Source: Council on Financial Competition).

It is partly for this reason that many companies have introduced "loyalty" programs where customers gain value through discounts on their own products (e.g., Bank of America's secondary mortgages) or on goods and services from third parties (e.g., Canada's Air Miles Program). These programs are intended to lengthen the relationship by making it broader, either through more products being acquired or through greater expenditure on a revolving credit facility.

However, to be successful in this arena, it is essential to understand which customers are to be targeted and to measure how they react to the offer. Giving more of your marketing budget away to already unprofitable or marginal customers is simply not good business. By leveraging information assets, you can become attuned to customers needs, which translates into more responsive services, which leads to improved customer satisfaction.

Information Technology enables your marketing efforts to a "Segment of One."

Predictive modeling technology enables you to pursue new customers by differentiating your offerings dependent on customer needs. An example quoted in the Harvard Business Review in September-October 1995 relates the story of First USA, a fast-growing financial services company (40% annual growth over 10 years) in Dallas, Texas. First USA focuses on hundreds of different customer segments simultaneously. They almost get down to a segment of one by offering 750 (and growing) different credit card offerings of combinations of annual interest rates, annual fees, credit limits, and add-on features such as specific types of insurance. In this case, customers only pay for the range of benefits they require. Technology and a well-thought-out marketing strategy represent First USA's competitive weapons.

▶ Knowing the Customer and Using Cross-selling

By better understanding the customer, the company with a strong customer-centric data warehouse is able to more effectively target the right promotion to the right prospects at the right time through the right channels. By using combinations of internally created information and external (government- or industry-available) information, the cost of customer acquisition can be reduced by more effective target marketing. The adoption of a data warehouse to enable this approach to marketing drives much higher successes, grows your business, and increases income, while reducing costs. The tangible benefits can be clearly measured, as can the spin-off benefits relating to enhanced customer service and employee morale.

The typical results of data warehouse-based marketing activity shows up to 400 percent improvement in converted response rates.

The actual results vary by product, but as a "rule-of-thumb," expect the rate of response before this approach to be multiplied two to four times.

In Australia, the United States, and the United Kingdom, IT and business teams in banks have developed a complete array of models that enable the capability to predict each customer's propensity to buy each product in the consumer range. Each bank was able to prescore all customers for each of four lines of credit—overdraft, credit card, unsecured loan, and debit card. They considered recent behavioral patterns and cross-sell propensity models and also considered preapproving applications. This combined approach to marketing and risk management enabled them to start thinking about new ways of planning to capture a greater customer wallet-share and to deliver a more focused way of achieving its revenue targets.

On the planning side, the models are used to predict the mix of products that could be sold over the early part of the plan, say, the first year of a three-year forecast. This same exercise helps identify gaps in product range as well as customers with little potential. A more intelligent set of targets can then be built into the plan for sales and marketing.

▶ Enabling Target Marketing

On the target marketing side, customers are more likely to respond and buy whenever a "new" or "improved" product or service is offered, due to the more timely and relevant contact.

Two specific campaigns can be cited as examples of the successes. The typical response rate to a bank's campaign designed to attract checking account holders to take out a personal loan had been 1%. This usually cost-justified the campaign. Using target marketing in segments, a second bank, utilizing customer behavior, knowledge and historical detailed transaction and interaction information optimized their investments by targeting specific messages to specific customers on specific products and services, the campaign generated 3–4% converted response.

Now using data warehousing for target marketing generates responses between 20 and 25%, compared with previous bests of around 8%.

Given the increasing success of these database approaches in creating better quality and higher response rates, these banks expect to spend more on direct marketing than on above-the-line TV advertising, and these techniques will be utilized on the Internet in the near future.

▶ The Importance of Enabling Technologies

It becomes clear that IT and business units working together to create, build, extend, and use a data warehouse is highly productive and drives large numbers of marketing and customer-centric activities with high ROI. As you have read, this section has covered some of the ground regarding the benefits of using information as a truly competitive marketing weapon.

To get from where you are now to where you could be is, of course, not a trivial undertaking. It is, however, a step you will have to make to remain competitive. You have a large amount of customer data. Data warehousing is the process that will foster and manage its transformation into marketing information and then into new wisdom.

You need to clearly define the business problems you hope to solve.

An effective data warehouse is not an off-the-shelf solution. You need to clearly define the business problems you hope to solve and work with a vendor that can provide the technology infrastructure, the services, and the experience that is so critical to success.

Furthermore, building a data warehouse is not a destination, but rather a journey. It requires a long-term commitment to be truly effective. But once you have started the journey, you will find a wealth of information that will help you drive customer retention and profitability.

▶ The Emergence of Relationship Technologies

Relationship technologies (RTs) enable companies to initiate and cultivate more advanced relationships and interactions with their customers and suppliers. These technologies will be designed specifically for businesses to move far beyond processing data (or transactions) in their information systems.

Relationship Technologies is the term that describes the critical strategic direction of technologies for the management and development of relationships in a networked economy.

Characteristics and Drivers for Relationship Technology™

- The emerging networked economy will require companies to find new ways to build and maintain relationships with their customers. This is particularly true for business-to business e-commerce as well as business-to-consumer e-commerce.
- An important consequence of the Internet explosion is that it raises the bar on what people expect from businesses. What they expect is a relationship. Increasingly, the ability to form relationships with customers, and to nurture and grow those relationships is what differentiates leaders from the rest.
- A key difference from ITs is that RTs turn information into action. Businesses now have to be prepared to respond to customers in different ways—on demand. A key characteristic RTs is that the ongoing collection and interpretation of customer data is turned into actionable information.

How an "Active" Data Warehouse Is the Relationship Engine

At the heart of relationship technologies is a cross-organizational data warehouse. Industry analysts find that a company with a superior data warehousing platform and surrounding environment enables effective CRM. As time and maturity in this environment grows, the CRM aspects and business processes grow also. RTs are *the* drivers and enablers for customer relationship management. They will specifically detect and analyze patterns and uncover opportunities so that businesses can actively offer personalized products and services to their customers.

The Use and Value of Relationship Technologies

RTs will expand and enhance relationships with their customers and suppliers through speed, flexibility, creativity, specialization, customization, and information-rich interactions. Many leading enterprises have a mission of *transforming transactions into relationships*. RTs are the foundation of the connectivity and gathering of all transactions and interactions at the information sources. The transformation of transactions into knowledge will require highly intelligent software or agents or sophisticated modeling.

RTs will enable enterprises to foresee and drive the opportunities with customers and channels to address *wholly new forefronts*. RTs will encompass all of the advanced hand-held devices (PDA), massive databases (DW), analytical software (BI/DSS/CRM), and action-oriented event-based triggers to immediately communicate with customers (CRM) and subsequently will observe the actions and interactions between offers and buyers.

The Emergence of Relationship Optimization

The acceleration of the value of RTs is embodied in the process of **Relationship Optimization (RO)**. Relationship optimization enables an enterprise to combine the forces of customer interactions, whether they be "customer pull" or enterprise "product push," based on event discovery and cross-organizational communications management with customers.

As illustrated in Figure 3-5, there is **accelerated value** in moving a customer from the marketing "push zone" (or box) upwards, managing the relationship through understanding more and more of the events and also interaction or dialog observances plus analytical knowledge-based decision making. The decision making pertains to the changes, with greater velocity and sophistication of the (sales or offering) messages plus appropriate timing and channel delivery.

As shown in Figure 3-6, there are four major management activities within Relationship Optimization. They are:

1. Event management
2. Communication management
3. Interaction management
4. Analysis management

As shown in Figure 3-7, the integration of all four **management** activities, with Relationship Optimization, is essential to ensure achieving the goals of CRM.

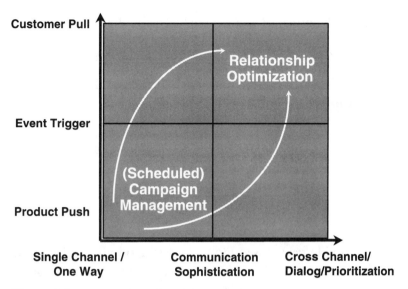

Figure 3-5. Push versus pull for Relationship Optimization.

Figure 3-6. Defining relationship optimization.

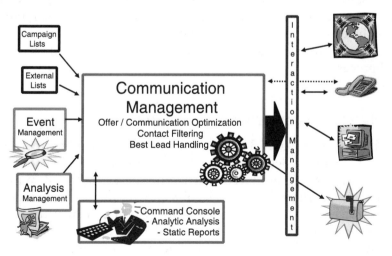

Figure 3-7. Defining effective relationship optimization and technologies.

To take advantage of the advancing technologies and also to institute appropriate inclusion of these processes and technologies, an enterprise must strive to complete a strategy that encompasses:

- **Globally define the business logic across the enterprise**
- **Automating customer communications**
    - **Strategy and planning**
    - **Discovery, classification, and design**
    - **Execution and delivery**
    - **Interaction collection and flow**
    - **Measurement and reporting**
    - **Analysis and refinement**
- **Provide true closed-loop processing on all opportunities**
- **Empower all channels with information from RO processes**
- **Prioritize customer offers and channel selection(s)**
- **Eliminate conflict management and integrate touch points**
- **Generate the right messaging at the right time via the right channel**

Creating Value Through Relationship Optimization

As the "customer focus" increases for external actions, higher business value is achieved. As illustrated in Figure 3-8, the actions and behaviors internally and externally change in customer focus activities. There should be a direct correlation with the amount of historical detailed transactions (combined with analytical interrogation of interactions) to provide instant knowledge discovered within the CRM process and also the RO subprocess.

Shifting to "Event-driven" Marketing

As illustrated in Figure 3-9, "Campaign Management" normally is driven from a company-defined proposition or product-oriented sales/offering process. In RO, the product or service offering is "triggered" by a customer or external event, followed by significance, evaluation, and then meeting or exceeding a "service need." This is a highly powerful action in marketing and services that drives accelerated customer satisfaction and retention as well as higher opportunity for profitability.

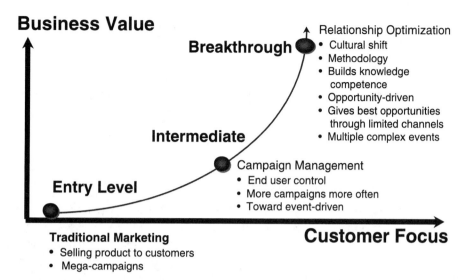

Figure 3-8. Creating business value through customer focus.

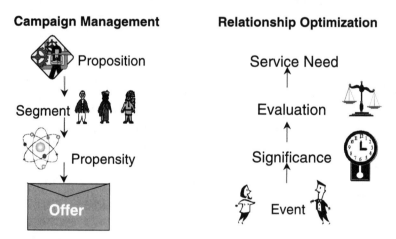

Figure 3-9. Moving from campaign to event-driven marketing.

"Sticky Relationships" and the Internet   As the calendar turned to
the new century, there were numerous new offerings that enticed and
engaged the online customer in seeking new information and being
communicated with in ways not previously exploited by information
providers.

In an interview, Lin Hutaff of MicroStrategy, a leading provider of Intelligent E-Business software highlighted the purpose as follows: "to allow consumers to receive highly insightful, personalized, actionable messages via any device that they may have access to, whether that's their E-Mail, Pagers, PDA, Fax Machine, or via telephone." Clearly, this has catapulted people into the Internet age.

MicroStrategy has created Strategy.com™, a Personal Intelligence Network™, which provides stock market information defined by the user and also provides alerts and action-oriented data to request the users to do something. This accelerates the era of "sticky relationships."

Why Is Creating "Sticky Relationships" Important? Lin Hutaff went on to say: "By providing Strategy.com to businesses, it enhances the value of their brand and creates customer loyalty through personal and proactive information services. It's a valuable differentiation, and enables the sticky relationship to become of high value in the CRM model."

Software and databases combined with an instant customer-driven or information-driven info-structure is emerging to provide services to individuals and businesses that *engage* the customer and provide instant value. Through the use of electronic connections, the sticky relationship becomes integrated into the behaviors of users/people.

Are Enterprises Changing to Utilize CRM/RT/RO Solutions? Hallmark Cards is a great example of bringing together product inventory data and store sales data to develop a data warehouse for planning and decision making around product development and manufacturing. Hallmark also is utilizing in-store technologies to more clearly understand its customers, even before instituting a specific customer loyalty/identification system in their stores and franchises.

▶ Excellence in Business Transformation: Hallmark Cards

Tony Marshall of Hallmark Cards, Kansas City, MO, has written several articles on Hallmark's use of customer and product sales information from their Data Warehouse. Here are excerpts.

Hallmark Cards is the leader in the personal expression industry and has become consumers' preferred brand of greeting cards. Founded in 1910, Hallmark has grown to annual sales of over $3.8 billion and is ranked 36 on Forbes Magazine's list of privately held U.S. companies. The company offers more than 40,000 products through nearly 45,600 retail outlets. Hallmark products are manufactured in more than 30 languages and distributed in more than 100 countries.

But, despite its obvious leadership position, Hallmark knew it had to learn more about what was happening in each store and at the cash registers. The company that helped millions of people to stay in touch wanted to get in better touch with its own customers.*

The goal for us was to move from a wholesale-driven company to a customer-driven company that understands our retailers and customers and that knows how to meet their needs.

This goal meant understanding what products customers are buying, where they are buying and when they are buying. In addition to cards, Hallmark produces albums, calendars, Christmas ornaments, gift wrap, party goods, personal expression software, stickers, writing paper, and other personal expression products.

Hallmark recognized that it needed to leverage the vast amounts of data generated at the point of sale, find a way to analyze it and turn it into a competitive advantage. The emergence of superstores as a major retail distributor of greeting cards gave Hallmark a new opportunity and a new challenge. Since greeting cards are not typically a destination product in many of these stores, locations, and outlets, Hallmark wanted to better understand how to draw these consumers into the card department.

Hallmark implemented a data warehouse to understand its manufacturing supply and distribution requirements and subsequently has matured its use of the data warehouse into applications surrounding complex market basket analysis for its card shops. By knowing what sells with what, Hallmark is able to strategically position items in the store to make it more convenient for consumers to buy what they desire or need.

*In this case, the "customer" may be all four of the definitions in Chapter 1: retailers, businesses (that resell), franchises, and owned sales locations. Hallmark is an excellent example of handling consumers, manufacturing, distribution, inventory, channels/distributors/franchises, automated card creators (or standalone interactive) devices, and internal customers/owned stores.

For example, hot-selling items can be strategically positioned throughout the store, while items that sell well together can be placed in an integrated display. Groups of seasonal items that often sell together can be placed in end-of-aisle displays or put in other areas of the stores.

We want to get to the point that when somebody walks into the store, they look at a display and think that it was actually made for them.

As managers and analysts at Hallmark became more skilled at using the Data Warehouse, they also became more demanding. Reporting requirements became daily demands for queries and detailed information based on slicing and dicing data, in order to make decisions in shorter and shorter time frames to meet customers needs. Hallmark has very creative people. So various decision-support systems were cropping up around the company to meet their individual (team/local/departmental) needs. Hallmark realized the power of working together and integrating the various systems into an enterprise DSS strategy in the data warehouse.

Hallmark learned that a massively parallel decision support data warehouse system was better suited for DSS than a symmetrical multiprocessing system provided. This is due primarily to the volume of concurrent queries from hundreds of business users and mathematical models/statisticians that use such systems, and the requirement to run complex queries (more than one at a time, which is a restriction of many DSS systems running on a mainframe or standard accounting/transaction system).

The Hallmark Executive Information System (EIS) provides management with a high-level view of the business across all brands and channels of distribution. The "Chain-Level Management System" gives analysts the information necessary for managing departments and reporting back to retailers. The data warehouse ad hoc query capabilities provide flexible access to data across all dimensions of the business.

By merging the functionality of these three systems into a single data warehouse environment, Hallmark made it possible for business users and management to execute 85 per cent of all traditional types of ad hoc queries in real time. Productivity across the business accelerated.

Hallmark also built special "home-pages" by working with seasoned analysts to automate their most common analysis. As a result, sophisticated analyses became available to all users and helped promote increased data sharing and knowledge transfer across business areas. This ongoing management process, using the data warehouse, expands geometrically, as the requirements, queries, decisions, ideas, and people change over time.

Market Basket data is also being used to customize displays to meet the needs of specific groups of shoppers. Research has proven, for example, that seasonal customers who shop early have different shopping patterns than those who buy closer to the end of the season. So, it may make sense for Hallmark to create special displays late in the season for last-minute shoppers.

Hallmark also is able to track sales of items on a more timely basis, allowing it to predict just-in-time manufacturing and distribution/replenishment of products as stocks are expiring. The data warehouse also has allowed Hallmark to closely align itself with its large superstore retailers. By knowing which Hallmark products are selling in these stores, Hallmark is better able to meet the stores' needs by providing the right products at the right time and in the correct quantities.

With the amount of data generated from the sales of thousands of greeting cards and other Hallmark products every day, Hallmark needed a scalable data warehouse with room to grow.

Hallmark began the data warehouse journey in 1990, using NCR's Teradata Data Warehouse, and has continually reinvested in their DW "info-structure" for enhancing their decision support and managerial measurements of thousands of elements of their business. In the many years that Hallmark has utilized data warehousing, they have tripled the amount of data they have been collecting and transforming into DW/DSS information and knowledge about their business.

Hallmark continues using their product and customer information, now through loyalty marketing and sales programs, and to new competitive advantages while advancing their business by remaining at the top of the relationship business.

▶ Management Considerations

- New applications are being built using data from data warehouses to provide management and business users with information on almost every area of the business. Governments have also implemented data warehouses to foster better information and service to the citizens, save budgets and resources for providing more effective services, and plan for future taxation and regulations.

- The demand for timely CRM using decision-support information continues to grow rapidly. The role of information technology is changing daily in organizations that have considered IT as an investment in their customers, stakeholders, their suppliers, their partners, and their industry.

- In Chapter 14, you will find dozens of successful organizations fostering new relationships and using decision-support with data warehousing to exceed their expectations. You will also have the opportunity to learn about the Stages of Growth in Chapter 5, which begins with Reporting, moves onto Ad Hoc Queries and analysis, and then onto Prediction. But gaining wisdom, the highest level of maturity in the Stages of Growth, you'll require more of an integrated and time-sensitive solution for your management team. And the changes in thinking and acting will become more accelerated as management teams gain confidence in the customer-centric info-structure value-chain environment.

- As the role of information technology matures and changes in any organization, the power and usefulness of the information itself increases. As management adopts and learns from the use of the technology, the people involved accelerate the thinking of the group. As information transforms into knowledge, the leap to wisdom is generated by the integration of the processes and assumptions developed, which become a reality in life.

- Leading organizations on five continents have experienced success that can be tied back to the teaming of business management and the information technology organizations to build a new info-structure. The elements that make up these successes require understanding of knowledge-based customer-centric investments that drive new thinking and new relationships.

Learning from Information: Data Mining

▶ The World of Learning from Information Itself

Data Mining and Knowledge Discovery are receiving increasing attention in the business and technological press, among industry analysts, and among corporate management.

> ***Data mining*** **is the process of extracting and presenting new knowledge, previously undetectable, selected from databases for actionable decisions.**

More and more managers are using data mining to help solve their most critical business problems—for example, to increase market share, to improve internal productivity, or to gain a competitive edge. Ken O'Flaherty, of NCR in San Diego, a long-time decision support developer and implementor, creator of new data mining solutions, and now a privacy expert has provided major contributions here. Ken has joined me in contributing his insightful views of managing customers and relationships through the use of data mining and knowledge discovery.

Data mining expectations need to be realistic, and they must be founded on a true understanding of what data mining is and what it can and cannot do. This chapter sets a foundation to relate real-world business problems where **data mining** can play a key role in relationship solutions.

There are other ways to define data mining and knowledge discovery. Here are some of the examples in recent literature:

- "Knowledge Discovery in Databases is the *non-trivial* process of identifying *valid*, novel, *potentially useful*, and *ultimately understandable patterns* in data" (Fayyad et al., "Advances in Knowledge Discovery and Data Mining," 1996).
- "Data Mining is the process of *analyzing detailed data,* to extract and present actionable, implicit, and novel information *to solve a business problem*" (NCR).
- "Data mining is the process of extracting valid, previously unknown, and ultimately comprehensible information *from large databases* and *using it to make crucial business decisions*" (IBM).
- "Data mining is the process of *selecting, exploring and modeling* large amounts of data to uncover previously unknown patterns *for business advantage*" (SAS Institute).

Many business managers and nontechnical people define data mining as one of the following. These are applications of the technology of data warehousing and/or data mining to solve business problems:

- **Customer Profitability**
- **Customer Retention**
- **Customer Segmentation**
- **Customer Propensity**
- **Channel Optimization**
- **Targeted Marketing**
- **Risk Management**
- **Fraud Prevention**
- **Market-Basket Analysis**
- **Demand Forecasting**
- **Price Optimization**

Business Context: The Mega-Issues

Why is this important to your organization? Today's businesses are continually challenged by a variety of factors that play a major role in determining their ongoing success. Among these, the four mega-issues are:

Increasing global or domestic competition. As trade barriers continue to be removed, and as new players emerge on the international scene, competition gets tougher. The new global economy favors foreign companies that benefit from lower wages or from specialized skills. It also offers opportunities for the best domestic companies to expand overseas.

Thus the world of banking is increasingly dominated by a small number of highly effective international banks, and retailing is witnessing a similar consolidation of large global enterprises. International deregulation of telecommunications industries, long the stronghold of national monopolies, is allowing service providers to cross borders and to form alliances or mergers.

Similar trends are at play domestically, with deregulation of telecommunications within various countries and with mergers in the banking field, resulting in lower overheads, reduced prices, and tougher competition.

Changing consumer patterns coupled with newly emerging technologies are giving rise to whole new markets or market opportunities, opportunities that are frequently seized by nimble new companies that can quickly spot new trends rather than by the established industry leaders. Thus mutual funds and other forms of retail securities investing have created new market segments that might logically have belonged to the established banks and insurance companies.

Similarly, retailing has seen the emergence of hypermarkets, toy supermarkets, microspecialty stores, airport shopping, and video rentals, and is now being challenged by home shopping via TV and the Internet. And cellular phones have created a major new market, with vigorous new players, in the telecommunications industry.

To respond to these challenges, established companies are engaging in major soul-searching and development of fundamental new strategies. There is an increasing focus on core competencies as the key sources of competitive advantage, resulting in abandoning peripheral activities, selling off major divisions, or splitting up into multiple corporations.

More effective distribution strategies are also being sought, typically leveraging newer technologies (e.g., ATMs, TV, and the Internet). Companies are looking for new relationships, such as cross-industry partnerships or transnational alliances. To survive, some companies are reinventing themselves, for example, by abandoning hardware and becoming software or service businesses.

While data mining cannot realistically be expected to be the genesis of such strategies, it can help companies compete more effectively and identify key business trends that become the impetus for new strategies. For example, data mining can be used to analyze the relative profitability of lines of business, products, or distribution channels. It can help grow revenue and market share by identifying new market or business opportunities or by focusing attention on the most valuable current initiatives.

As you will learn in Chapter 8 (which highlights companies using CRM and data mining), data mining can identify profiles of successful stores or branches and assist in site selection for new openings. It can analyze which products are most typically purchased with others, leading to new strategies for product promotions, store layouts, or new product developments.

Restructuring of Industries. As companies seek to reinvent themselves, so also are whole industries undergoing major reconstruction. Fueled by technology advances, the distinction between the telecommunications, personal software, and entertainment industries is becoming increasingly blurred, and the new world of "Infotainment" appears to be emerging.

Similarly, within major industries, the demarcations are disappearing: banks, building societies, and securities companies are competing and merging; and cable providers are new potential allies of long-distance carriers entering into the local telecommunications market.

In many guises, the traditional "middlemen" of earlier commerce, such as agents, wholesalers, and brokers, are finding themselves "disintermediated"—no longer needed as intermediaries, as technology such as data warehousing and electronic commerce combine the value chain and put customers in direct contact with suppliers.

The role of data mining in this environment is not yet well developed, but it is clear that the main technologies enabling these new ways of doing business, data warehousing and electronic commerce, are highly synergistic with data mining and will become increasingly dependent on it for their future success.

Data mining, as we will see, offers to fulfill the largely unmet promise of data warehousing by discovering knowledge in the growing mountains of data—knowledge about business activity and customer trends that can point to better ways of doing business. And the emerging field of electronic commerce will to a large extent depend on data mining technologies such as *intelligent agents* and *pattern detection* to match customers and suppliers and maintain customer satisfaction.

More-demanding and less-loyal customers. In this brave new world, customers are becoming increasingly discerning, more demanding, and less liable to remain customers unless they are happy with the relationship. They are demonstrating increasing independence, sophistication, and selectivity in their choice of vendors. Thus we see credit cards offering low introductory rates being snapped up at the expense of the established cards.

To compete effectively in this environment, companies are faced with the need to develop a deeper understanding of their **customers' values**—what attracts new customers, and, more importantly, what retains existing customers, because it typically costs five times more to get a new customer than to keep an existing one. It is in addressing business issues such as these that data mining is being used today most frequently and most successfully.

Data mining can classify customers according to their propensity to purchase a new product or service or to defect to a competitor; this can provide the basis for more effective marketing or retention programs, which in turn help reduce marketing costs and improve customer satisfaction.

Companies are also being forced to streamline their operations, with customer satisfaction being a paramount consideration. The focus is thus on reducing cost, offering customers what they want, and reducing "hassle." Data mining again can provide the insights into these difficult business issues, developing customer profiles according to factors that are satisfiers or dissatisfiers.

As businesses become increasingly knowledgeable about their customers, they realize that not all customers are alike. Some are profitable, others are not. Some like trendy products, others go for "value for money." Some travel a lot or frequent restaurants, while others stay at home. This leads to the concept of customer segmentation. Most customers will fit into a particular segment where they have much in common with others in the segment—"yuppies," for example, or "business travelers." Ideally, businesses would focus their attention on each individual customer (the concept of "segment of one"). But, for practical purposes, marketing can be successful by identifying key customer segments, classifying each customer into a particular segment, and developing products or campaigns targeted or customized by segment. Here again, data mining plays a vital role.

Time compression. It seems that the price of progress is that everything seems to be happening faster. The pace of change is accelerating, demanding faster decisions and responses. Consequently, businesses have to be more flexible and adaptable, ready to react faster to events or to move proactively to preempt their competitors. Innovation has much greater value in this environment, and the winning companies will be those that empower and reward their people (their main sustainable resource) to make their own decisions and to respond quickly to events.

This first demands reengineering of basic business processes and then requires better linkage throughout the value chain, so that information is available to make decisions, and systems are in place to automate the execution of decisions.

▶ The Role of Data Mining

The role of data mining is twofold:

1. **Convert data into information and knowledge, such that the right decisions can be made.**
2. **Provide the mechanisms to deploy knowledge into operational systems, such that the right actions occur.**

For example, in customer retention, models can be built that predict the profile of customers likely to switch to a competitor. These models can then be deployed in call center environments to provide guidance to operators who are in direct contact with customers, suggesting approaches that are likely to retain specific "at-risk" customers based on their particular profile, for example, to propose a new rate plan that reduces their costs based on their calling patterns.

Predictive models can be renewed regularly to reflect the changing nature of the customer base and the competitive environment.

This can significantly improve turnaround times in marketing, reduce inventories, and improve time to market for new products or promotions.

Relationship Technologies: Creative New Approaches

To respond to these mega-issues facing businesses today, IT offers three new approaches that separately offer major relief and together represent a major paradigm shift capable of revolutionizing the way business is transacted over the next decade. These are becoming known as *relationship technologies*.

▶ Electronic Commerce

The Internet has already radically altered the way many companies transact business. Corporate intranets are rapidly assuming the primary role of internal company communication, and extranets are extending the reach to customers and suppliers. Corporate and product information is already obtainable over the World Wide Web on a widespread basis. Software products are increasingly distributed over the Web along with their documentation. Products of all kinds are being sold and distributed through this medium by enterprises ranging from major corporations to individual home businesses. Fueled by the Internet, the Web, and electronic commerce, the "extended enterprise" is rapidly taking shape.

Many large companies have already established decision support or value-chain connections to suppliers or customers based on data warehouse technologies, which enable them to collect large volumes of historical data for analysis (primarily data about their customers).

In a data warehouse, data is input from a variety of operational, legacy, or external sources, cleaned and transformed to remove inconsistencies and duplications, and organized historically by subject. For example, all data pertaining to customers (e.g., personal data, geographic/demographic data, and account balances) is stored in a customer table.

By analyzing such data, large companies can better understand their customers and their needs, thereby to a large extent vicariously regaining through IT the customer "intimacy" once enjoyed by small family businesses. They can also gain insight into many other aspects of their business, such as operational efficiencies, product performance, or inventory movements, all based on historical fact rather than on surmise. Query and reporting tools, along with more recent *On-Line Analytical Processing* (OLAP) tools, have made such analysis increasingly easy and productive.

Operationalizing the Customer-Centric Data Warehouse

The more advanced data warehouse users have begun the process of operationalizing their data warehouse. This is also called *the Active Data Warehouse*. This entails linking the warehouse to users' operational systems, such that decisions made based on data in the warehouse are enacted automatically in users' operational systems. For example, analysis of inventory levels based on yesterday's sales activity can lead to reordering of inventory; this can be automated by programmatically generating a transaction from the data warehouse and transmitting it to the inventory management system.

Further levels of operationalizing the data warehouse can occur when customers and suppliers are linked into the data warehouse and given access to information they need to make business decisions. For example, suppliers of packaged goods can track the sales movements and inventory levels of their products at major retailers (e.g., Wal-Mart, Kmart) and can decide autonomously when to restock shelves; in effect, the suppliers are moving up the value chain by "renting" shelf space from the retailers. Electronic commerce is accelerating this trend.

Combining Data Warehousing and Data Mining

Properly executed, data warehouses can be extremely valuable tools for making intelligent business decisions. However, they frequently result in extremely large databases that grow like topsy and can easily outgrow the ability of the brightest analysts to fathom.

Data warehouses have also frequently been difficult to cost-justify. The payoffs are initially hypothetical and have to be subsequently realized by deriving value from the masses of data that have been accumulated. Without new insights from the data or tangible benefits from actions directly attributable to analysis of the data, frustration and disillusion with the technology (and its cost) may result. Data warehouse users thus often encounter the phenomenon of "Data rich, information poor" or "Drowning in data, but lacking in information."

The challenge then becomes one of turning *data* into *information* —for without information, *action* is either not possible or at best foolhardy.

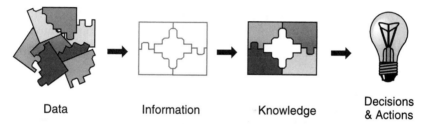

Data   Information   Knowledge   Decisions & Actions

Figure 4-1. Transforming data into knowledge for decisions.

Data mining can be thought of as the software and applications technology that turns data into information and thus promises to fulfill the promise of the data warehouse.

Data mining is really a means of knowledge discovery—discovering "knowledge," which can be viewed as a set of patterns that turns the data into information.

Until recently, data mining was the preserve of specialists—statisticians or machine learning experts who practiced their art using arcane, often home-grown tools. Usually faced with poorly organized data, much of their energy was spent on cleaning up data to get it into good-enough shape for their tools to be able to process. Now, with data warehousing, much of this work has already been performed during the construction of the warehouse.

Meanwhile, a new generation of data mining tools has emerged, aimed at the business user rather than at the expert. These tools mask the complexities of the algorithms beneath the covers and are easy enough to be used by sophisticated business analysts, people who know the business problems being addressed and understand the data involved in their solutions.

Communicating a Definition of Data Mining

Creating your own organization's definition can be an important communication throughout management and external relationships. Remember that you will be utilizing customer data; therefore, many parties will need to know what you mean by certain terms (like data mining). Definitions of data mining are abundant, covering a wide range of meanings and nuances, often slanted to support a particular vendor's marketing agenda. The following core definition is offered as a common denominator:

> Data mining is a process of extracting and presenting
> actionable, implicit, and novel information from data.

- **"Process"** implies that this is not just a technique or algorithm, but a series of interrelated steps.
- **"Extracting"** implies some effort (typically *analytical* effort) in finding information that may be hidden; but data mining can also be used to confirm known or suspected information.
- **"Presenting"** means outputting the discovered information in forms such as reports, models, or rules.
- **"Actionable"** means that the information is of the form that decisions and actions can be taken.
- **"Implicit"** implies that the information may be well hidden (or at least not well understood) but can be inferred or discovered using various data mining techniques.
- **"Novel"** means that the information will be new and useful (or even important).
- **"Information"** is distinct from **"data"** in that it embodies knowledge of a pattern or patterns that give meaning to the data. To maximize the chances for discovery, the data should be **detailed**, where no potential information has been already been lost through summarization.

The end goal of data mining is to uncover information that has value, typically significant business value. Thus, for business data mining, you should add to the definition: **"to solve a business problem."**

Suggested Definition of Data Mining

> *Data Mining* is a process of analyzing detailed data
> and extracting and presenting actionable, implicit, and
> novel information to solve a business problem.

The process steps of effective data mining are illustrated in Figure 4-2.

Therefore, an enterprise can build a step-by-step process for data mining, not only using data mining tools but also using the appropriate consulting services and mathematically experienced people to build specialized models. This is highly valuable to the enterprise or government organization.

Financial institutions and retail sales stores use data mining for target marketing customers. The IRS uses data mining to find taxpayers who do not match characteristics in tax compliance models. Railroads use data mining to construct trains and their piece parts of rolling stock. Airlines use data mining to plan schedules of specific aircraft and also their individual maintenance times. Health and social services organizations use data mining (or modeling) techniques to discover overpayments, fraud, duplicate claims, misaligned services, ineligible fund requestors, and requirements for service improvements.

The data mining process is iterative and can be duplicated throughout many aspects of generating and maintaining relationships with customers.

Clarifying Knowledge Discovery

The terms **knowledge discovery** and **knowledge discovery in databases** (**KDD**) are often used interchangeably with "data mining" or to describe a superset or subset of data mining. Some definitions talk of data mining as one step in the knowledge discovery process, the step where a model is built using a data mining algorithm. Other definitions talk of data mining as any form of discovery, with knowledge discovery applying only to a subset of techniques involving particular types of algorithms. In this chapter, no such distinctions are made, and the terms are assumed to be interchangeable.

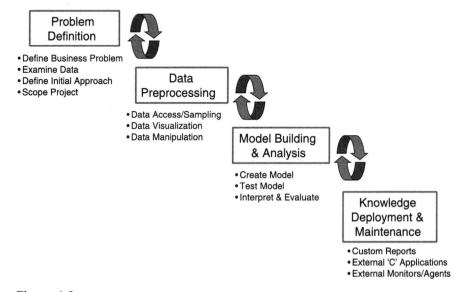

Figure 4-2. The step-by-step process of data mining.

Classes of Data Mining

The term "data mining" has been in use for a number of years and has frequently been applied to the use of more traditional types of knowledge discovery, such as query languages. To accommodate such usage, it is useful to divide data mining into two classes of knowledge discovery: "verification-driven" and "discovery-driven."

Verification-driven data mining involves the use of conventional techniques, such as SQL programming or SQL generation, via Query and OLAP tools, to verify hypotheses. Here, the analyst develops a hypothesis and uses conventional techniques to explore and hopefully confirm the hypothesis. The analyst must therefore know what to look for.

Discovery-driven data mining involves the use of intelligent software, such as machine learning, statistics, and data visualization to discover new hypotheses (versus confirming prior ones). Here, the software performs a significantly more active role in the discovery of new business knowledge. But the process is not fully automatic; it still involves the analyst intimately in the knowledge discovery process.

A popular misconception regarding data mining, to a large extent fueled by the press, is that it is performed magically by software that dredges through databases and automatically finds interesting information, coming back to the user, and saying "Did you know this?" The current state of the art is far from this.

There are some tools ("intelligent reporting tools"), driven mainly by expert-system technology, that can help automate information discovery, but they are still dependent on prior (expert) human input to provide guidance on what is "interesting."

More and more today, the terms *Data Mining* and *Knowledge Discovery* are commonly used to refer to *Discovery-Driven Data Mining*.

A Data Mining Taxonomy

Shown in Figure 4-3 is a simplified taxonomy of data mining, focusing on the most popular forms of data mining tools and techniques.

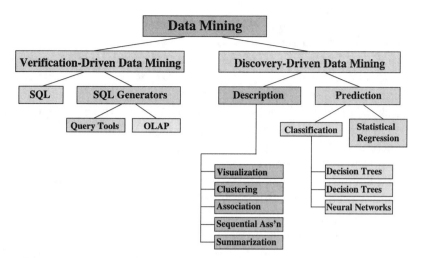

Figure 4-3. Data mining taxonomy.

Verification-driven data mining can be viewed as the use of SQL or SQL generators in verifying hypotheses. SQL generators can be broken into two main classes: Query tools and On-Line Analytical Processing (OLAP) tools. OLAP tools present the user with a multidimensional view of the data; some actually store the data in such a form ("MOLAP", or multidimensional database OLAP), whereas others ("ROLAP", or relational OLAP) work with data in relational form (in a "fact table") and generate SQL to access it. (MOLAP should be shown as a separate subclass of verification-driven data mining.)

It is often useful (but also sometimes confusing) to view discovery-driven data mining as consisting of two broad subclasses: description and prediction.

Prediction Prediction involves building a model that will predict the value of an outcome variable (e.g., "Yes, good credit risk" or "No, bad credit risk"), based on the values of other variables in the data set, such as: Age, Gender, Income, Debt, Number of Children, Homeownership (Yes/No), Checking Account (Yes/No), Savings Account (Yes/No). The model is built using "training"data with known outcomes, such as prior loans. The algorithm analyzes the values of all of the input values for each known case and identifies which fields are significant as predictors of the desired outcome.

Predictive models can be built using the more traditional **Statistical Regression** techniques (e.g., as embodied for some time in products such as SAS and SPSS) and with newer **Classification** techniques.

The most popular classification technique, **Decision Tree Induction,** consists of developing a decision tree of yes/no or multiple choice questions that classify the data set based on fields that most correlate with the known outcome variable (e.g., Good Risk/Bad Risk or Approve/Reject). For example, Figure 4-4 illustrates a simple decision tree for determining credit risk, where the tree might first split on Income as the most highly correlated field (e.g., one branch for Income > $50,000 and the other branch for Income < $50,000), and then each branch might split on another attribute (e.g., the first branch on Homeownership, the other branch on ownership of a Savings Account), and so on, until the data set has been classified (or until a predefined stopping point is reached).

The resultant decision tree can then be used to predict outcomes on new data, for example, to predict the likelihood that new credit applicants will be good credit risks. In our simple example in Figure 4-4, the decision tree could be deployed in an automated program that processes credit applications or in an interactive environment where bank officials are processing applications online.

Rule Induction consists of developing a set of rules that classify the data set. An example of a rule might be:

If Income > $60,000 and Homeowner Debt <10% of Income, then Good Risk = Approve,

or

If Income > $60,000 and Homeowner Debt = 0, then Good Risk = Approve,

otherwise

"Disapprove or reconsider using additional information."

Rules such as these can be automatically derived from decision trees or can be derived using different algorithms.

Both Decision Tree Induction and Rule Induction are examples of *Machine Learning.* They both have the advantage that they are understandable by humans.

Neural networks (Figure 4-5) offer a somewhat different approach to classification and prediction that produces a less understandable, but often more accurate model (sometimes referred to as a "black box" model).

Chapter **4** I Learning from Information: Data Mining

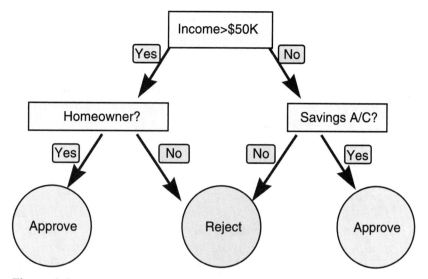

Figure 4-4. A simple decision tree.

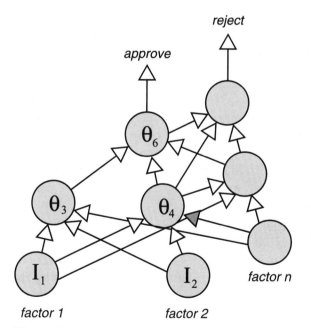

Figure 4-5. A simple neural network.

Neural Networks mimic the neurophysiology of the brain. They consist of collections of connected nodes with inputs and outputs organized into layers. Between the visible input and output layers of nodes are one or more layers of hidden nodes. The input variables are presented to the input layer and values are propagated from each node to every node in the next layer, continuing until a result is delivered from the output layer (e.g., Good Risk/Bad Risk or a score on the probability of default).

The values that pass through the network are modified at each node based on a simple mathematical transformation and on the node's weight. Weights are initially assigned randomly but are continually adjusted by the network based on the accuracy of the outputs for each case it processes. (This is an example of a "back-propagation" network.) Thus initial results are not meaningful, but the network learns through "training," using the training data, producing more and more accurate answers.

The resulting neural network model can then be deployed in a similar manner to a Decision Tree or Rule Induction model to predict outcomes on new data.

Description covers a class of algorithms and approaches that finds human-understandable patterns in data. Unlike prediction, description is not involved in predicting a particular outcome based on other values, but rather in characterizing data that has no known outcomes.

Data Visualization (Figure 4-6) is typically used throughout the data mining process and consists of a set of techniques that reduces large amounts of data down to more easily understood picture. It is useful for displaying intermediate or final results of an analysis and for suggesting new approaches to the analytic problem at hand. Examples include histograms, scatter plots, line graphs, and web diagrams (which show strengths of relationships among variables). These may be in two- or three-dimensional form.

The human faculty of vision is very highly developed; over 50% of the human brain is involved with vision. Visualizations of data can be highly intuitive to humans, often leading to insights that could never be discerned by examining the same data in tabular form. By exploiting the broader information bandwidth of graphics, complex patterns, relationships and exceptional values ("outliers") can frequently be identified.

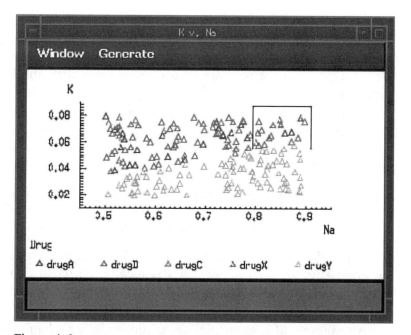

Figure 4-6. Data visualization of data mining techniques (also showing clusters and high potential sales opportunities).

Clustering (Figure 4-7) is a technique for grouping together subsets of records that have similar attributes or characteristics. Clusters can be mutually exclusive or overlapping. Clustering algorithms may use statistical approaches or may use a special form of neural network.

Clustering is useful for segmenting large populations (e.g., customer databases), thereby reducing the complexity of the business problem and permitting more targeted analysis. For example, having segmented a customer population, the analyst might then develop individual predictive models for each identified segment.

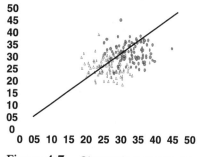

Figure 4-7. Clustering customers with regression analysis.

Association (or **Affinity**) is a technique that finds rules that correlate the presence of one set of items with another set of items, such as the joint presence of products in market baskets. Association algorithms can find all rules that correlate the presence of one set of items with another set of items.

Interest in association has escalated among retailers, as the use of scanners has enabled them to gather transaction-level detail that can be indicative of purchasing patterns. A specific association rule discovered for a supermarket might be:

> **When corn chips are purchased, 55% of the time cola is purchased, unless there is a promotion, in which case cola is purchased 75% of the time during the promotion.**

Sequential Association (or **Sequential Affinity**) finds associations that link events over time (i.e., identifies sequential patterns). To identify sequences, the transaction record must identify the transactor as well as the transaction detail.

An example of a sequential association rule for a bank might be: Customers who open a checking account and within three months open a savings account, will open a credit card account within six months 24% of the time.

So the time to execute marketing actions is essential for success. Many new opportunities exist as in Figure 4-8.

Summarization reduces large amounts of data down to easily understood, meaningful summaries. This typically involves the use of Knowledge-Based Systems (a.k.a. Rule-Based Systems), which apply rules or expert knowledge to data to find interesting information. This is sometimes referred to as "deductive" reasoning rather than "inductive" reasoning.

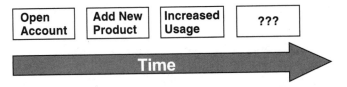

Figure 4-8. Sequential association or sequential affinity.

The value of summarization using Knowledge-Based Systems is dependent on the quality of the domain knowledge supplied by the expert(s). With high quality knowledge and business rules, a summarization tool can produce exceptional analytical results. An example "intelligent report" from such a tool reporting on one segment of the business might point out differences with other comparable segments and identify key contributing subsegments as well as probable causes of trends or anomalies.

Data Mining and Knowledge Discovery Technologies

When planning or implementing the various types of data mining and knowledge discovery technologies, it is important to note the experience and learning required by the human (user) versus the ability of the machine to provide the answers.

In Figure 4-9, you will find Gartner Group's view of the spectrum of data mining and knowledge discovery technologies. This can be very helpful in explaining the potentials or the requirements when selecting the type of technology for your needs.

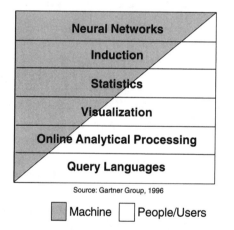

Source: Gartner Group, 1996

☐ Machine ☐ People/Users

Figure 4-9. Spectrum of data mining and knowledge discovery technologies.

Additional Techniques for Relationship Management Applications

The classes and taxonomy of data mining covered in this chapter are by no means exhaustive, and lesser used techniques such as Time-Series Forecasting, Case-Based Reasoning, Logistic Regression, and Genetic Algorithms can be helpful in meeting your needs.

The distinctions made earlier between predictive and descriptive techniques are in no way meant to imply that they should be separated.

In fact, data mining will usually involve using a mixture of both classes of techniques to solve a given business problem. Furthermore, the distinction is somewhat arbitrary, and in practice some techniques can be used for either purpose. For example, decision tree induction can be useful not just for prediction but also for describing the data to the analyst, especially when combined with visualization of the resulting decision tree.

Similarly, verification-driven data mining and discovery-driven data mining, while different in their technological origins, are more useful when used in combination than separately. Thus, OLAP techniques can be used to select and prepare data for analysis and can also be used to probe and verify insights derived from predictive or descriptive algorithms.

▶ The Data Mining Process

Data mining is highly iterative in nature, involving several key steps that are typically repeated many times before a satisfactory model is developed. A brief description of the process is provided in Figure 4-10.

At the highest level, data mining can be viewed as consisting of two phases: knowledge discovery and knowledge deployment. Deployment consists of taking the outputs from developed models and using them in one's business; outputs may consist of reports (e.g., discovered rules), models (e.g., in the form of code or tables), encoded actions that occur in operational systems (e.g., via monitors or agents), or data visualizations. Discovery consists of Data Preprocessing, Model Design, and Data Analysis.

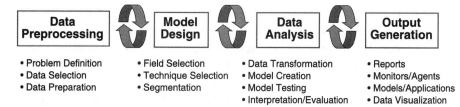

Figure 4-10. The data mining process.

At the front end of the process, in the **Data Preprocessing phase**, the specific business problem must be clearly defined; without this, the data mining exercise will likely lead nowhere. Based on domain knowledge of the business problem, this then leads to identifying, selecting, and preparing the data required to address the problem; in a well-structured data warehouse environment, these steps should be relatively straightforward but will still involve considerations of sampling and balancing the data.

The **Model Design phase** entails examining the data further and selecting from it those fields that appear the most relevant to the problem. It also entails selecting an appropriate data mining algorithm to apply to the data (e.g., neural network, rule induction). Then, segmentation at a minimum will usually entail breaking the data out into a training set and one or more test sets. Segmentation might also involve using clustering techniques to break the data out into separate subsets based on common characteristics and then analyzing each segment separately.

The **Data Analysis phase** typically involves a further preparatory activity (data transformation) to reorganize the data to best match the selected algorithm and the business problem, for example, to handle missing values in the data or to derive new fields that are better indicators for a predictive model, such as "Disposable Income" (Income less Outgoings). Then the selected data mining tool is applied to the data; this typically involves creating a model using the training set of data and then verifying the model with at least one separate set of test data. The model's accuracy and validity can then be evaluated.

It is very likely that the initial model will not meet the goals of the data mining exercise, and that many iterations will be necessary, especially among the Model Design and Data Analysis phases. This will involve trying out different data mining techniques or parameters on different subsets of the data before arriving at a successful outcome. **Data visualization** will be a key technique used throughout these iterations.

The entire data mining process is dependent on the domain knowledge of the business analyst in interpreting and evaluating interim results. Without this knowledge, the results may be of little value, or, worse still, they may be wrong. The algorithms involved in the process have minimal intelligence compared to the human expert, and the old maxim "garbage in, garbage out" applies to data mining just as well as to other applications.

▶ Using Data Mining and Modeling for Business Problems

Data mining is a broad technology that can potentially benefit any functional areas within a business where there is a major need or opportunity for improved performance and where data is available for analysis that can impact the performance improvement. The list of potential applications is therefore long. Examples of business applications that can most benefit from data mining include the following:

- Target Marketing
- Customer Retention
- Fraud Detection
- Market Basket Analysis
- Customer Segmentation
- Credit Scoring
- Credit Risk Assessment
- Portfolio Management
- Security Management
- Customer Profitability Analysis
- Resource Management
- Customer Service Automation
- Profitability Analysis
- Sales/Revenue/Demand Forecasting
- Cross-Selling/Up-Selling
- Campaign Management
- Insurance Claims Analysis
- Help Desk/Problem Resolution
- Capacity Management
- Distribution Channel Performance Analysis

- Store/Branch Performance Analysis
- Store/Branch Site Selection
- Inventory Control
- Process/Quality Control
- Equipment Failure Analysis
- Medical Treatment Analysis

Of these, the first four are perhaps the most popular, and possible scenarios for each of these are discussed in the remainder of this section.

Target Marketing A bank has a new or revamped product (e.g., a Gold Credit Card) that it wishes to market to its existing customer base. (For a telecommunications company, this might equally well be a new or revamped service, such as Cellular Call Forwarding or a multiphone dual-device specially allocated phone number).

The Marketing Department is tasked with developing a telephone and/or mail campaign to deploy the product. The Campaign Manager is given a goal of achieving a hit rate among contacted customers of 10% (previous campaigns have averaged only a 7% hit rate, with a range of 5–9%). This goal is based on the following simple cost/benefit analysis:

1. Anticipated average product life (length of time customer will keep the product) = 18 months
2. Anticipated average monthly product profit per customer = $8
3. Thus average revenue per hit = $144
4. Target hit rate = 10%
5. Thus average revenue per customer contacted ($144 x 10%) = $14.40
6. Planned cost per customer contact (to sell product) = $10
7. Thus average profit per customer contact = $4.40 (= margin of 4.40/14.40, or 30%)

Another way of looking at these sample numbers would be to say that, with a customer contact cost of $10, the campaign will lose money (i.e., cost more than it adds in future profit) if the hit rate falls below 7% ($144 x 7% = $10.08). Thus, unless there are special goals for the campaign (e.g., to increase market share even at the expense of profitability), the hit rate needs to be significantly above 7%.

Plenty of data is available from prior campaigns, and there are opportunities to test market the new product and review results prior to a major launch. The specific challenge is to learn from prior campaign experiences and some early test marketing to improve the hit rate to 10%, thereby achieving a 30% margin on this campaign.

Data mining could help this campaign in several ways, including the following:

1. Analyze data from similar recent campaigns to identify characteristics of those customers who responded favorably. Do this by developing a predictive model using training and test data reflecting a balanced sample of customers, some of whom have responded to one or more specific campaigns and others who have not. Then apply the model to the database of current customers to score them according to their predicted propensity to respond favorably to this campaign. Then select from the scored database those customers who are above a certain level of probability of responding favorably and target just this subset for the campaign.

2. Similarly, build a model based on a trial mailing for the new product. This would involve selecting a random sample of, say, 100,000 customers, sending out mail to them offering the new product, and then building a predictive model from the data resulting from the trial mailing. While more expensive, this is likely to result in a more accurate predictive model, since the data is current and relates directly to the actual product being marketed.

3. Identify customer segments based on a variety of personal and socioeconomic data, and build predictive models for each identified segment. This is likely to show that some segments will have a higher hit rate than others. Further analysis of each segment will also likely show varying profitability and varying customer retention rates, and tailored marketing campaigns can then be developed for each segment, each with its own set of more accurate assumptions regarding average product life and average monthly product profit per customer.

Customer Retention Essentially, customer retention is a similar business problem as target marketing is. Both involve building propensity models (i.e., predictive models indicating a customer propensity). In this case, the model identifies customers with a propensity to switch to a competitor (rather than to buy a product), using historical data with a mix

Chapter **4** I Learning from Information: Data Mining

of customers who have recently defected and others who have not. Campaigns would then be targeted at those customers who are most likely to defect. If customer profitability information were available, only customers above a certain profitability level would be targeted.

Customer retention also can benefit from customer segmentation to develop tailored campaigns for each segment with differing assumptions regarding cost of defection (lost profitability × estimated continuing longevity) and with separate predictive models developed for each segment.

Additional aspects of customer retention that are well suited to data mining include:

- Identifying key factors in retaining a customers
- Identifying key factors and activity patterns in winning back customers
- Determining characteristics of loyal customers

Fraud Detection Data mining can be applied to the problems of fraud analysis and detection in several ways. One example that is similar in approach to target marketing and customer retention involves developing a predictive model indicating customer propensity to fraud. In this application, data is analyzed relating to a sample of known previous fraudulent customers and nonfraudulent customers. A broad set of factors that might influence fraud is prepared (e.g., age, sex, in-state/out-of-state, rent/buy, amount of debt, 12-month balance trend), and a model is trained (using a neural network and/or rule induction) and tested using separate subsets of the data. The model could then be applied to the current customer database to score customers on their probability of fraud or could be applied against new applications for credit to predict likelihood of fraud.

A similar application could be developed by insurance companies to analyze the characteristics of fraudulent insurance claims. Using prior claims data that includes characteristics such as insurance type, vehicle type, age of policy, age of insured, and postal address of insured, a model might be induced that shows a high propensity for fraud among motorcycle vehicle owners below age 25 on policies that have been in force for less than 2 weeks.

A quite different approach to fraud detection involves *clustering*. Here, customers are grouped into segments by a clustering algorithm (a.k.a. a Kohonen network) based on similarities of multiple attributes. Then, those customers that do not fit well into any one cluster (the "outliers") are examined for possibilities of fraud; for example, irregular patterns of spending (or of cellular phone usage, insurance claims, or tax payments) are potentially good indicators of fraudulent activity. In this type of analysis, data visualization can be a very powerful technique to detect the outliers most worthy of further analysis, for example, a scatter plot or a Web diagram showing strengths of relationships among attributes (e.g., locations of purchases, types of item purchased, or amounts spent per day) can visually indicate significant anomalies.

Affinity Analysis   In the retail industry (but to a lesser extent in other industries), valuable insights can be gained by identifying product purchase affinities, that is, products purchased together in the same transactions ("market basket analysis"). Such affinity analysis could be used by a retailer to determine which products to stock up on if it is planning a sale on Home Electronics or by a catalog sales company to decide which attachments to include in a direct mailout. For many industries, this technique could also be used to identify customer profiling characteristics (e.g., to find association rules such as "10% of married customers in 50–59 age group have at least two cars"). In the communications industry, it could be used to identify combinations of products and services that drive network usage.

Data visualization techniques can provide an alternative or complementary approach to such analysis. In particular, Web diagrams can be used to visualize product or other affinities: Purchased items are each shown as a point on the graph, and the strength of the purchase relationship between any two items is indicated by the thickness of the line connecting them.

Retailers that have instituted customer loyalty cards, and therefore have customer data, can tie their market basket analysis back to customer characteristics by inducing the characteristics of shoppers with certain purchase habits. For example, having identified certain buying patterns or styles (e.g., joint purchases of wine, confectionery, and gourmet coffee might indicate a "chic" shopping style), customer records can be tagged with the style attribute, and a classification model can then be developed (e.g., using rule induction) that predicts the characteristics of each shopping style (e.g., "*chics* tend to be females aged 25–45 with high income"). Customer promotions (e.g., in monthly billing statements) can then be targeted at customers according to their predicted shopping style.

The complete process contains people, tools, activities, data transformed into information, extraction of specific resulting knowledge, and visualization through relationship technologies (see Figure 4-11).

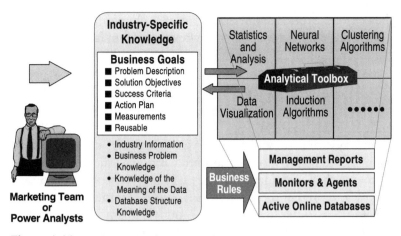

Figure 4-11. The elements and process of data mining. The end-to-end data warehouse and knowledge continuum.

The Future: Toward Continuous Insight

Each of the preceding examples shows the potential power of data mining. Not only does this technology help solve difficult business problems, but it does so in ways that are repeatable. In each case, models are developed that are subsequently deployed in some form to solve the business problem at hand. But since they are models, they can be reused on new data. As data in the warehouse is refreshed (i.e., with new rows of data), the models can be rerun on the new data, and new results can be obtained.

Furthermore, if the patterns in the data change significantly over time (e.g., if purchasing propensities evolve to new tastes), the models can be retrained using the new data and can give different results; thus, after analyzing the effectiveness of a Thanksgiving promotion, a retailer can retrain the model to analyze Christmas promotions. And more importantly, if new types of data are collected (i.e., with new columns of data), then the model can be revised to take the influence of these new attributes into account.

This phenomenon is sometimes called "generalized insight." This means that, unlike insights gained with query or analytical tools ("specialized insights"), data mining insights are reusable. They involve development of models, and these models have the special attribute that they can be applied again and again in a changing business environment. This represents a major step forward in information technology, toward the ultimate goal of "continuous insight," where the system will one day constantly monitor events and automatically adapt to a new environment.

As the next step toward this goal, companies should make data mining an integral and continuous part of their business processes. Having built a model, they can regularly calibrate its accuracy and revise it when necessary or on a scheduled basis. They can continue to build more sophisticated and more pinpointed models, such as around customer segments that they identify. They can map customers into segments and follow and predict their progress from one segment to another. They can develop "customer lifetime value" models to guide their marketing and to product development efforts, and they can feed results from one campaign into the development of models for the next campaign. Data mining then becomes a way of life and a means of staying ahead of the competition.

▶ Selection Criteria for Data Mining Technologies

The base of Evan Levy's (1999) thoughts on selection follow, and we've added some of our own experience for you to use.

Before purchasing a data mining tool, be certain it fits your organization's specific needs by asking prospective tool and consulting vendors some very specific questions. Keep in mind, there are no right or wrong answers per se. Here are some of the questions to ask:

1. Which algorithms are supported by the tool/service?
2. Describe and display results of the data mining techniques.
3. What "data formatting" does the tool/service require?
4. How does the tool/service acquire the data for its use?
5. How does the user or business analyst interact with the tool or service? Is it a graphical interface? Is it a command line? Are there precoded modules or objects?
6. What level of data or statistical analysis experience is necessary to utilize the tool/service effectively? What are the special educational and job experiences required?
7. Does your data mining tool/service support continuous or range value analysis? Can the system identify relative groupings for a continuous set of values, or is the user required to identify those values? For example, does the tool/service subdivide age ranges, or must the user define the ranges?

8. Does the tool/service really scale? (Can you add hundreds of megabytes of data and also dozens of tables or columns to the models/queries/visualizations?) Can it break problems into multiple concurrent steps? If so, how?

9. Is your data mining tool/service "business" or "function" focused? A "business-focused" data mining tool focuses on a specific function such as "churn." A "function-focused" tool is more aligned with the type of algorithm (such as clustering) and can usually apply to more than one business problem.

10. Is it a learning or static model tool/service? (A static model tool requires the user to identify the specific attributes and their relative weightings. A learning model tool analyzes all available data attributes and determines the appropriate weightings and values itself.)

11. What other organizations are using this tool/service for a similar business requirement? Will we have an exclusive on locally developed models using the tool? Is there some uniqueness to the solution for our organization?

12. Can you provide specific examples of results that achieved a major ROI through the use of the tool/service? How does that compare with the cost of the tool/service, people involved, computers, database, software, data collection and sourcing, and all maintenance charges? (Cost may be an insignificant amount, even in millions of dollars, if the ROI potential far exceeds the cost or if using these tools/services are required to stay in business and keep your best customers.)

Herb Edelstein of Two Crows Consulting, an expert in Data Mining, and author of "The Data Mining Technology Report" warns: "The most common error in data mining is relying too much on the tools to do the work for you." He continues with the two most important factors in data mining success, which I wholeheartedly agree with: "Getting the problem statement right. Then you've got to get the data right. Those two steps easily account for 80 percent—if not more—of the time and effort you spend on a data mining project."

Every user organization will have different scalability, process, formatting, and data sourcing requirements. Weight the responses received from vendors and select the tool/service that most closely matches your core requirements.

Management Considerations

Data Mining is a process that will provide valuable ROIs when utilizing a highly detailed customer-centric data warehouse to gain new insight to transactions and behaviors.

The multiplicity of data mining tools requires an organization to carefully select the types of models and processes.

The tools do not make up the data mining process or systems. The tools are only part of the total approach to integrating technology and process (e.g., consulting and applications) within the business framework for managing customers and marketing your offerings.

New knowledge will be gained through a continuous monitoring of the detailed transactions and their attributes in the marketplace environment. Selection of the right customer, for the right action, at the right time, can be accomplished through multiple processes within the data mining domain.

The Stages of Growth for CRM and Data Warehouse

The World Is Transforming from an Information Systems and Networking Era to One Based on Relationship Technologies with Customer-Centricity.

Leveraging CRM and Data Warehouse: Stages of Learning

Successfully using Relationship Technologies is a continually evolving learning process. The stages that make up the management maturity process are interdependent, interrelated, and the continuous learning becomes highly valuable to an organization over time. These periods of time can be shortened, as we will see, through an early understanding of the future maturation actions, experiences, and combination by learning of management. Knowing the future, based on historical experiences of the past, can truly accelerate the maturity process and position for greatly enhanced opportunities.

As your enterprise realizes new opportunity and potential, you'll gain much greater benefits from your info-structure with changes that are more than providing universal data access or a new and sophisticated management reporting system. Knowing the future drives enlightened people to seize the opportunity.

**Information and knowledge allow you to create new
wisdom of your customers and of your own organization.**

The "stages" theory has been introduced into many educational
courses, consultant white papers, and articles on change and management
planning. The foremost stages approach to discussing information
technologies and the management issues (in the adoption and maturing of
management) was published by Richard L. Nolan and Cyrus Gibson
(1974). In the initial visionary article in The Harvard Business review of
March-April 1974. Nolan and Gibson titled the article: "The Four Stages
of EDP Growth." The original four stages were: Initiation, Contagion,
Control, and Maturity. But this was only the beginning.

The "stages view of Information Systems" world discussed the
changes of perspective over time, including the shift from technology-
centricity into information (as an asset) and the management of
information with integrated applications. Exactly five years later,
Nolan published new knowledge gained and wisdom in the stages in
another hallmark article. He extended the "mature" stage into three new
stages, to total six stages, in (Nolan, 1979).

The stages approach has been utilized throughout the past 25 years by
my teams and our clients in thousands of strategic sessions and in executive
briefings or roundtables. We have utilized the stages approach for
positioning and evaluating the philosophies, strategies, learning,
experiences, management changes, and applications in the leading (and
not so leading) corporations of the world. Nolan, Norton (subsequently
part of KPMG), Curt Bynum Associates, The 4-2-1 Consulting Group,
Index Systems (subsequently part of Computer Sciences Corp.) and many
other consultants have found the stages approach very beneficial.

**Knowing where you are presently allows you to
position where you want to be.**

During my two decades with IBM, I found that the stages theory had
been a cornerstone of educating the executives and middle management of
our customers and prospects to ensure a clearer understanding of the
abilities and challenges of the IT organization. The stages also helped
identify the issues and appropriate priorities for the management team,
while also accepting that changes will occur regularly over time. Knowing
what changes are coming makes change easier.

"Facilitating change" and "maturing management"
accelerates opportunity, goals, and success.

The time horizons for the stages vary greatly based on such factors as willingness to accept change, management's commitment to the introduction of new technology, new uses of information, and the amount of management investment in both time and resources.

▶ The Six Stages of Growth

The Six Stages of Growth in the "Maturity" process include:

1. **Initiation**—Startup: Building and Learning
2. **Growth**—Application, Technology, and Data Spread
3. **Control**—Managerial Intervention/Positioning
4. **Integration**—Enterprise info-structure
5. **Distribution**—Cross-Function Sharing, Uses, and Marts
6. **Strategy/Maturity**—Shared Tactics, Planning, and Strategy

Using a time scale, as in Figure 5-1, facilitates proper position and perspective.

There are several methods of using this stage theory and the visualization approach to communicating the experiences, challenges, issues, concerns, and success criteria. Some enterprises have utilized it to understand their present and future positioning in technology, others in learning to use technology, in the formulation of their data bases, in the overall view of investments in technologies, or in understanding how they changed over time in the introduction and promulgation of technologies (such as in a data warehouse environment).

The identification of technological issues or measurements on the left/horizontal access becomes the first opportunity. (Nolan originally used financial applications as a key construct to view.) To understand the importance of the managerial issues, you need to "view" the long-term potential impact. Use this exercise as a beginning point of understanding the viewpoint of your businesses (IT) history and then extend the thinking to those who succeed by having a vision (whether forward vision or hindsight).

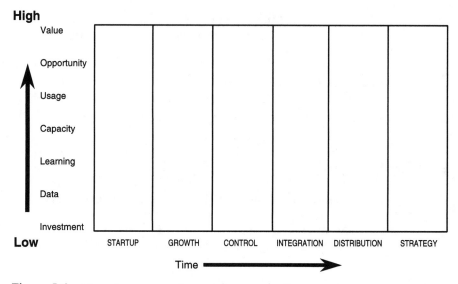

High

Value

Opportunity

Usage

Capacity

Learning

Data

Investment

Low

| STARTUP | GROWTH | CONTROL | INTEGRATION | DISTRIBUTION | STRATEGY |

Time ⟶

Figure 5-1. The six stages of growth or maturity.

As you read on, you will have an opportunity to overlay multiple thoughts, figures, diagrams, and strategic approaches to address the maturing of your management team. Use the stages process to think about how you will change your managing of customers, technology, databases, and the application portfolio, and seeking new knowledge and learning how to integrate all of these functions. You will find this view of your world to be of very high value.

In Figure 5-1 you should be seeking to plot your position (know where you are now). Plot where other business units are within the different stages, then understand and focus on the wisdom of what is coming in the next stage (or managerial phase) so that you can advise, direct, manage, or plan your positioning, changes, and maturity.

The vertical axis can be one or many items.

▶ Categorizing Analytical Approaches

As a foundation of understanding, consider that operational or transactional systems handle the "orders" and the financial processes within an enterprise. First, a key question for your management team:

What systems (by name or application) provide support for "xyz"?

1. Decision making
2. Planning (both tactical and strategic)
3. Resource allocations
4. Managing relationships
5. Predicting the future

List them carefully by name and purpose and add who uses them and how many people or systems either input to or output from them. (You may find that this list only has names of applications or systems and that later on you will want much more detail to truly understand your position in utilizing this type of information systems investments.)

The leading organizations I have come to know clearly delineate the types of systems (or philosophies) that provide the analytical and managerial information for *creating knowledge* about the best (or worst) processes, systems, people, financials, inventories, channels, or customers that might be involved with your organization. Good news travels fast; bad news should travel faster. Bill Gates, in his recent book, had this to say: "Moving bad news at the speed of light is important."

▶ The Types of Decision Support

There are several **managerial application types or uses** that are significant in a decision support environment (DSS). The types of DSS discussed here will provide insight to the (1) **characteristics of use** and (2) the **focus of questions** asked by people using a data warehouse **in differing stages** of the maturation process. Hence, DSS changes during the stages. Therefore, understanding "why" is very helpful in defining management thinking and productivity, and the stages will be helpful in positioning your technology, applications, data, and the integration or utilization of the information resources themselves.

The *managerial applications or types of DSS* are used to describe the scope of management thinking about applications and the types of questions asked of the decision support systems. The stages are a view of the maturity level or the experiences achieved through the use of each of the systems. So who uses the views and how they use each is critical.

Some enterprise executives do *not* have the experience with information or technologies to visualize the potential scope of the opportunity of cross-pollination of information and its far-reaching uses.

The main reason for this situation is that most managers (and even executives) are responsible during their careers for a single area of the business and/or utilize information systems to process transactions and report on the group's past actions. Few managers have experience in predicting the future using information technologies. It is result of maturity.

Limiting your management systems to "post-action" reporting inhibits the opportunity of exploiting your knowledge of the future.

Type One DSS/DW: Reporting   The first type of DSS is characterized by a large quantity of *predefined queries*. (Predefined queries are set up by the technologists after receiving requests from the business users or are predisposed managerial methods of communicating what needs to be known after a period or a process is completed. These types of reporting systems usually provide a complete set of charts/graphs/cubes about a specific area of the business, answering the most frequently asked questions, and trying to learn about your company and its market or customers. In Figure 5-2 is the distribution of use types and business value.

The underlying queries are known and the data is mostly summarized and presented quickly. It answers the strategic question, "What happened?" or what may be called "hindsight viewing." Some typical beginning data warehouse examples are:

- What are the total revenues, sales, expenses, volumes, or products produced?
- Where did most of the sales, revenues, deliveries, or services occur?
- What are the comparisons or differences to the past period(s)?
- What are our most/least productive resources (money, products, transportation, people)?

The initiation of new levels of information and reporting has its benefits. It provides easier access to previously inaccessible data, focuses on elements of information that are known by the management requestors, may have not been previously delivered or accessible, generates initial awareness of actions and problems, defines extensions to standard reporting systems, elevates the needs for more data and more data (transformed) into information, opens the eyes of several key managers on what they possibly "could" learn if they invested more in the info-structure. The journey has begun. But hindsight is the delivered result.

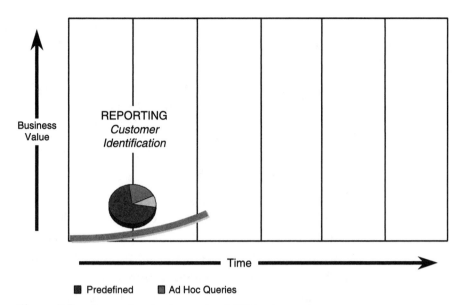

Figure 5-2. Reporting is the major DSS in the early stages.

There are particularly interesting characteristics that may inhibit future growth and maturity in the initial stage or early uses of DSS and DW. The first is overexpectation and the desire to see all of the data in one system, at one time, on all customers, and then realize that the initial implementation is only a fraction of the actual potential volume, quality, credibility, creative usage, and return on investment.

Additionally, the "view in the eyes of the beholder" is that the wonderful new graphical or creative display of information *is* the data warehouse itself or *is* the truthful exposition of a customer relationship. This is rarely the reality, and the management team must understand what is being achieved and what must be achieved over time.

The initiation or Startup stage focus is to build the framework, the infrastructure for getting initial results and reports, and allow for expansion of the information and the applications in future stages. Just learning what real transformation and data base normalization techniques is difficult enough for the IT and management teams.

Solving such business and data issues as "What is a customer?" "What is a product?" or "What is a channel to our customers?" can keep an experienced management team busy for months defining the business and data model. This can be shortened by adjudicating the characteristics among the various business divisions, applications, and data bases.

Figure 5-3 shows the distribution of the reporting type of DSS/DW usage. These include reporting, ad hoc queries, and possibly some analysis applications.

Effective management teams plan beyond the initial changes generated by the introduction of a new technology or process.

When using data warehousing for reporting in CRM, the focus is on defining the characteristics and habits of your customers. Some of the initial questions usually have been:

- Who are our customers? (age, income, gender, group)
- Where do they live? (geography, economics, styles, etc.)
- What have they bought in the past? (historical views)
- How have they bought it? (financial transactions information)
- Which are the most profitable? (known margins, etc.)
- How many times have we contacted each of them?
- When do we contact them? (cycle, calendar, event, etc.)
- What are the positive and negative responses to our contacts?
- What is the cost to support them via their chosen channel?
- Which groups of customers buy similar products?
- What is the average customer revenue? Our expenses?
- What is the annualized customer churn rate?
- What is the current response ("take") rate (to ads/contact)?
- What is the revenue by product, by customer, by channel?
- What is the acquisition cost by channel?
- Which customers pay, what kinds of bills, at what time?

Reporting applications provide some answers found in many business' data bases, but data warehousing provides new views and an ability to use combined cross-organizational detailed data to understand the past.

Stage One represents the core essentials—and the most immediate data needs—of the user's requirements. In some implementations, this is limited to summarized data. This is because the providers or requestors (the business management) have limited understanding of the real value of detailed data. Understanding its potential is yet to be discovered.

Stages 1-2 Questions:
What Happened?

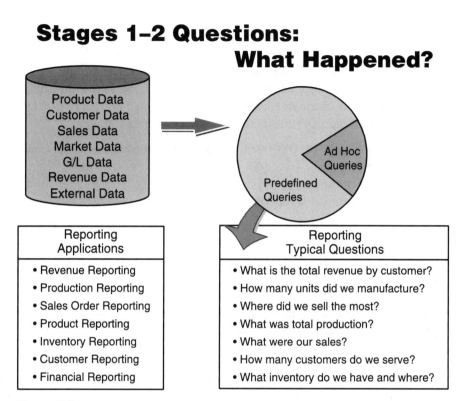

Figure 5-3. Reporting applications and questions in Stages 1-2: What Happened?

Some organizations, with only limited knowledge of the actual potential of data warehousing, limit their investments in the early stage to prove the initial value of the data warehousing or to deliver on the promise of better data.

Comment/Hint: It is very disconcerting to find companies that only predefine their queries into their corporate data warehouses *and* do not permit their business users to ask ad hoc queries of their historical customer data. Nevertheless, organizations control their data resources and limit the potential of creating new business opportunities and relationships. From experience, the controllers are usually one of two types: (1) The IT department wanting to maintain good security, quality, performance, or costs or (2) the business user department who wants to own the data, manage it, limit its use by others, secure it, or stop access or acquisition of the data. "Stupid is as stupid does?"

But creative and leading enterprises *do* have a strategy for getting information to users or making it available. But, because there is a lack of detailed experiences in the user community, the DSS/DW system focuses on the known and the internal business's happiness ratings.

Once the business users learn ways of interrogating the warehouse's detail data and access its multiple and complex combinations, the magnitude of the ROI changes to high growth and high profitability. This usually emerges (unfortunately) in subsequent stages.

Type Two DSS/DW: Analyzing   Once we have learned what happened in the initial use of a DSS/DW, we move onto the more complex ad hoc queries of the second type of DSS: Analyzing. This focuses on the question of "Why did it happen?"

This is an organizational process of understanding the factors that brought about the results "discovered" earlier.

This is an important transformation in understanding the value of the data warehouse or new Enterprise info-structure. As shown in Figure 5-4, the use of customer information now accelerates the ability to segment and analyze the customers and their actions. In addition, the types of questions become much more sophisticated, and the abilities of the information environment are increasingly becoming known throughout the organization. "You mean I can ask any question of that new DW system?" is a typical overheard comment. Some typical data warehouse ad hoc business queries that arise in this phase are:

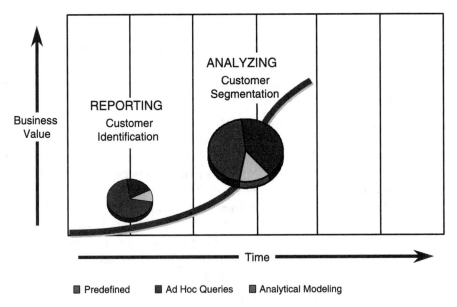

Figure 5-4. Analyzing customers creates segments.

- Why did our team not meet or exceed its forecast or goals?
- Why were volumes so low or later than expected deliveries?
- What caused the most positive results or highest margins?
- Where do we actually achieve our best ROI?
- Why are inventories or resources not moving well?

This type of DSS/DW encompasses data mining through models and detailed mathematical correlation, and has the ability to "drill down" into a data base for minute detail and come away with deductive conclusions based on the data. The business users discover trends and patterns not readily apparent from the straight reporting found earlier. So we also see that awareness and allowing people to ask questions drives a new desire to utilize the information infrastructure and begins changing the thinking of what the system(s) are there for.

Stages 3 and 4 CRM Analysis: Focus on Understanding Customers

- Why is average customer revenue down?
- Why is annualized customer churn so high?
- Why did the campaign not meet plan?
- Why are sales of a product below plan?
- Why did they buy it from you?
- Why has the cost of alliance channel declined?
- Why is the current response (take) rate lower than before?
- Why does revenue between specific products vary so much?
- Why is the acquisition cost increased for this channel?

The reporting applications now need to interact with one another to reveal a new reality. The types of applications now are using more sophisticated tools, but the hallmark of the change in this phase is the use of analyzing methods and analysis models to answer the questions surrounding "Why did it happen?" This move beyond reporting is significant because the detailed historical data is now being exploited to understand much more about past behaviors and other characteristics previously unknown to management.

This ability to understand the past is the key to understanding the future, which is the hallmark of Stage Three (see Figure 5-5).

Stages 3-4: Why Did It Happen?

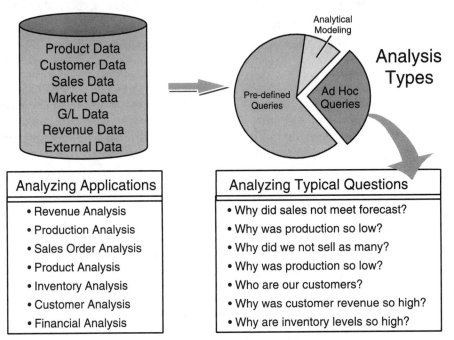

Figure 5-5. Analyzing applications and questions in Stages 3-4: Why did it happen?

Type Three DSS/DW: Predicting the Future Forming knowledgeable, high-percentage predictions is a specialized skill that truly separates the leading companies from the rest of the pack. Those who can anticipate trends and capitalize on them before they become common knowledge have an obvious edge in the marketplace.

In a comprehensive data warehouse having an "analytical modeling" capability, where the queries ask "What will happen?" provides immense abilities to achieve a prophetic facility (see Figure 5-6).

The more mature stages provide the pathway to highest profitability and high ROI. Some of the questions that Phase Three (with their corresponding predictive applications) can help answer are:

- What customers are at risk of leaving? (**customer retention application**)
- What products or services will the customer buy? (**market segmentation**)

- What is the best way to reach a customer? (**channel optimization**)
- How will a new product sell? (**demand forecasting**)

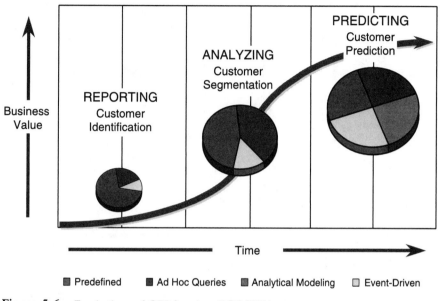

Figure 5-6. Evolution of CRM using DSS/DW.

These applications are now very sophisticated and utilize advanced techniques of decision support, parallel query functions, massive detailed historical data, cross-function information pertaining to customers, finite knowledge of behaviors, scoring of everything from credit to payment ability to behaviors to propensities to pure prediction to complex strategic decisions.

Once achieving a modicum of maturity in information management, data warehousing, extending the info-structure, distribution of resources, and massing of knowledge, the enterprise is more mature, networked, positioned, integrated, knowledge based, and highly flexible for change.

The enterprise is now positioned to ask questions that drive answers to "what will happen" in the future? This is the type of DSS or data warehouse that is characterized by the applications and questions in Figures 5-7 and 5-8.

Stages 5-6: What Will Happen?

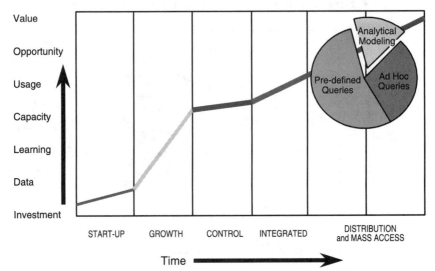

Figure 5-7. Stages 5–6: What will happen? Prediction capabilities.

Stages 5-6: What Will Happen?

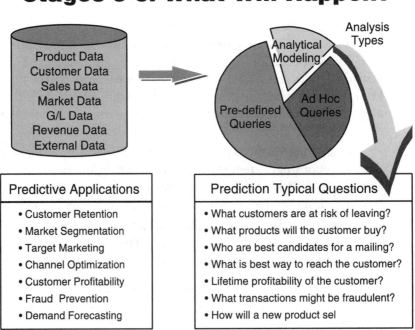

Figure 5-8. Predictive applications and prediction questions.

Type Three of DSS with CRM: "Thinking Like Your Customer":

- Which customers are more likely to leave?
- Which customers are more likely to buy?
- Are they likely to defect?
- What's the impact on profit when I change price?
- What's the best channel to reach a specific customer?
- What's the best product mix for each customer?
- What's the projected demand by area?
- What relationships exist between certain customers?
- Do segments share "like" buying/defecting behavior?
- Which segments have potential to grow/decline?
- What do the best customers want in the future?
- Are they likely to buy again?
- If so, what are they likely to buy?
- What is the impact of new products to each customer?

Types of DW/DSS—A Summary

Initiation or startup predefined queries (not glamorous) and new reporting are certainly the foundation. But the analytical and the predictive are the bellwethers of competitiveness. They soon become the indispensable elements in any company's ability to utilize and learn from information. Any organization, business or governmental, that seeks to gain a high return on investment desires to gain through a new learning environment: The Data Warehouse—an info-structure for the coming millennium.

A successful enterprise using CRM and the info-structure enables the triple view of knowing the past, analyzing the present and the potential, and predicting the future (with a high rate of accuracy, while also measuring and refining the processes and models).

The long-term view of the changing role of DSS/DW is shown in Figure 5-9. Notice that there are two stages underneath each of the major shifts in types of DSS/DW. We will discuss the management issues and maturation characteristics in the next section.

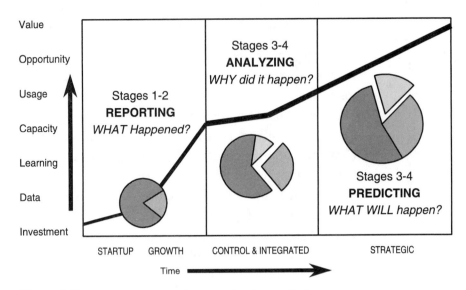

Figure 5-9. Migrations to a knowledge-based info-structure.

The focus of your information info-structure investment should be on the customers, not only on your products. The secondary focus might be on finances, resources, products/services, channels, distribution chains, inventories, franchisees, suppliers, transporters, servicers, partners, and others, but you will find fantastic returns from your data warehouse if you focus on your customers.

Using the "Types" of Data Warehouses for Growth Using the stages diagram to show CRM actions as individual stages, there becomes an overwhelming opportunity to foster not only the concepts of CRM, but attaining high profitability and high customer retention.

As you mature in the use of real data warehousing for management of your organization and for CRM, you will be able to traverse the wide plane of applications and achievements.

Figure 5-10 shows the applications and stages of growth, combined to provide a view for your organization to build sensible and communicative goals and an info-structure objective to support the CRM strategy.

     Chapter **5** I The Stages of Growth for CRM and Data Warehouse

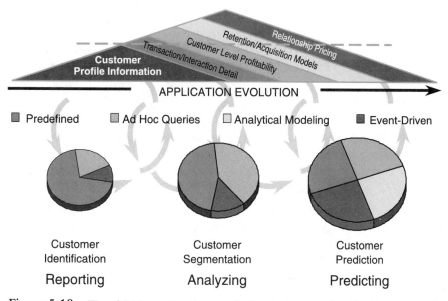

APPLICATION EVOLUTION

Customer Profile Information
Transaction/Interaction Detail
Customer Level Profitability
Retention/Acquisition Models
Relationship Pricing

■ Predefined   ■ Ad Hoc Queries   □ Analytical Modeling   ■ Event-Driven

Customer Identification
Reporting

Customer Segmentation
Analyzing

Customer Prediction
Predicting

Figure 5-10. The CRM application evolution integrated with the types of iterative decision support applications.

You *can* assume that you must go through both stages of learning and maturation as well as through the application evolution before you can achieve world-class status and competitive advantage. But this is always a subject for discussion and debate. There have been attempts to circumvent the stages and the applications, but please be aware that others have tried and experienced revisiting the growth-control-integrate stages and relearning to implement the approaches to CRM and customer management.

As shown in Figure 5-11, there are significant internal behavior and action changes that occur in customer-centric marketing and uses of data warehousing techniques.

The goal is for CRM to create profitable and loyal customers, then over time to foster customer trust and confidence to move them to the levels of customers referring new customers *and* customers using your organization as an advisor to their life-events and uses of their own resources. This is the ultimate loyalty and relationship. Any organization that continues this type of relationship has the opportunity to achieve lifetime value and lifetime returns at very low marketing and support expenditures.

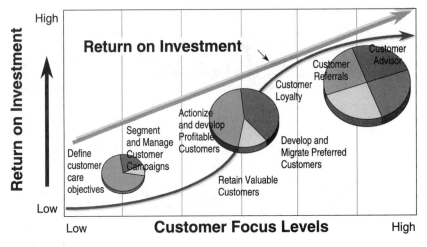

Figure 5-11. Customer focus levels and return on investment (source: Swift, 1998).

Managing the "Stages of Growth" in Customer-Centric Enterprise Info-Structure Environment

In the earliest stages of decision support or data warehousing, there is a propensity to build a rather small database for reporting or queries to meet a specific business requirement. The focus in these systems is usually on a single subject for (generally) a single problem or single business unit or department (see Figure 5-12).

These databases are usually copied or extracted from the major transactional business files or databases of the organization. Sometimes these are extracted or copied regularly from the mainframe or main server of the organization to provide more effective management reporting. At this stage, little is known of the real potential of the use of the data warehouse or info-structure; therefore, the solutions are funded by IT (in error) or within the individual department requiring the new database.

This type of activity can be very productive in the short term and educational for all parties involved. But it limits any high potential of cross-organizational sharing of information until the "maturation" activity really begins. So this is known as the *startup* or *initiation* stage or phase, and most management decide to replicate this environment or even to build new departmental data bases or data warehouses. This is also pleasant, since the IT technologists remove the pressure for more information from the various groups involved and also only have to provide the data.

Marketing data bases, built in many cases to foster new campaigns or to generate new management reporting, are usually within the first two or three of these decision support or campaign management solutions. They are usually limited in scope, limited in data, and require supporters to reinvest or enlarge the data or its usage within the organization. Because this is an early stage, most managers are not believers, and therefore long-term perspectives and organizational strategies are not the driving force. Most organizations using decision support have already implemented some form of this situation. Management that are believers at this stage are usually the proponents of more use and more data bases.

As duplicates of the data base contents have to be in different distributed solutions, there is also a redundancy of the data and multiple personnel seeing differing views of similar data, because they are only interested in the details of their area of the business.

Once the second data base or departmental data warehouse is built, another set of characteristics in the environment begins.

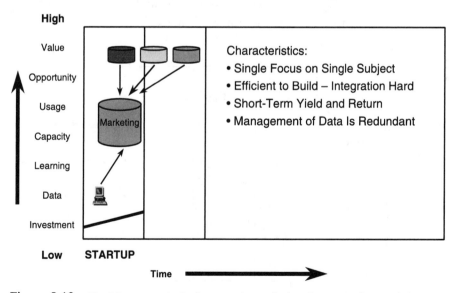

Figure 5-12. Problems and challenges in early implementations of data warehousing.

As more than one solution has been created (see Figure 5-13), there arises a set of managerial and strategy issues that have confounded IT for three decades. And these managers, having little knowledge of their predecessors to live by, are repeating history already experienced in the central mainframe environment. If your organization is relatively new to managing computing and managing data bases, you can learn from a historical view of the problems and challenges faced by others.

The **major issues created by multiple data bases** or multidepartmental distributed data warehouses are:

- **Single business focus on single subject**
- **Efficient to build—No integration of data or uses**
- **Short-term yield and return**
- **Management and storage of data redundant**
- **Applications usually are stove piped**
- **Transformation not standard, multiple methods**
- **Summary and reporting is fast, little detail to access**
- **Use of data mart is in each group or business unit only**
- **Management is not understanding scope of opportunities**
- **Business user or executive expectation high or unknown**
- **ROI not measured or no goals have been established**
- **Customer data is not yet utilized**

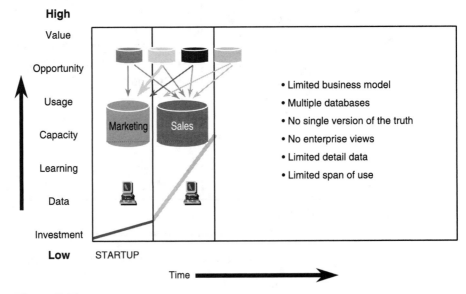

Figure 5-13. Incorrect growth strategies for data warehousing.

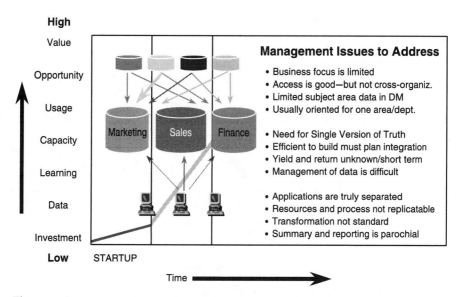

Management Issues to Address

- Business focus is limited
- Access is good—but not cross-organiz.
- Limited subject area data in DM
- Usually oriented for one area/dept.

- Need for Single Version of Truth
- Efficient to build must plan integration
- Yield and return unknown/short term
- Management of data is difficult

- Applications are truly separated
- Resources and process not replicable
- Transformation not standard
- Summary and reporting is parochial

Figure 5-14. Management issues to address for strategic plans for DW.

To resolve many of the problems and organizational issues, management must concentrate on the key business requirements. The issues require some insight, not of just the technology but also of the usefulness and meaningfulness of a shared information environment that provides for and enables a *"Single Version of the Truth."*

Many organizations fail to achieve their objectives because they do not have this "Single Version of the Truth" and spend enormous amounts of time and resources to understand and manage their finances, supply, people, skills, customers, channels, margins, taxes, and opportunities.

In addition, there must be enabling of access to and use of information from all departments and applications that touch customers. Without this info-structure environment, built on "subject areas" (e.g., customer), there will be inaccuracies and conflicts on communications and actions.

Figure 5-15 shows the correct switch of focus to the "centralized approach" and provides direction for resolving the problems and management challenges created in the earlier stages.

The requirements at this juncture of management maturity require control and integration to resolve the issues and problems. This is an extremely important aspect of maturing. In many instances, the leader or manager (and sometimes) the top technology executive is replaced.

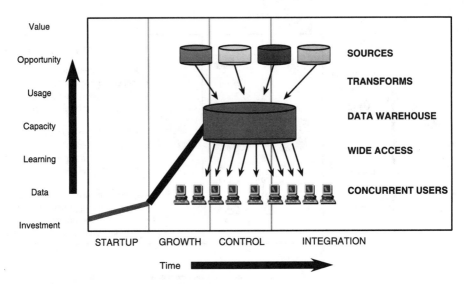

Figure 5-15. Resolving problems and management challenges.

The characteristics of **successful maturation** at this stage of require complete change of focus to create:

- **Single Version of the Truth (on each subject)**
- **Corporate memory and history of transactions**
- **Integrated subject areas of data and tables**
- **Historical detailed data**
- **Multiple complex queries**
- **Summarization anytime**
- **Online/real-time analysis**
- **Integrated Info-structure to support infrastructure**
- **Centralized knowledge management**

One example of bringing together multiple data bases in a decision support environment occurred at Sears, Roebuck and Co. This retailer had multiple mainframes, departments, tools, and answers for their management team. Figure 5-16 shows a philosophical change that occurred when Sears decided to bring together data into their *Strategic Performance Reporting System* (SPuRS). This system supports management from the top to the store level of the company and provides over 2,500 standard reporting solutions and has over 3,000 potential users on any day. You can also read more details on Sears in Chapter 14 or find success stories at www.ncr.com/subscribe.

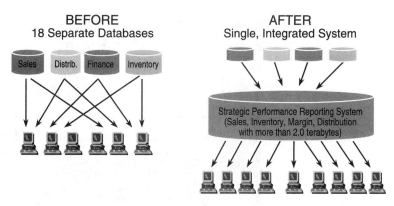

BEFORE
18 Separate Databases

AFTER
Single, Integrated System

Sales Distrib. Finance Inventory

Strategic Performance Reporting System
(Sales, Inventory, Margin, Distribution
with more than 2.0 terabytes)

"It won't matter if someone is the company president or a replenisher. *They'll be looking at the business the same way.*"

Figure 5-16. Consolidation of decision support systems at Sears.

The Info-Structure or Framework

The flow of information for a mature organization starts with understanding the full info-structure environment of the data warehouse and all of the associated decision support and relationship technologies.

In Figure 5-17 is a framework that allows your organization to utilize its past, present, and future investments in technology, data, people, training, some user software tools, and the support infrastructure. Notice that the flows begins at the top and can move through the levels to meet all organization's requirements for access and use of data (or now: transformed data into information).

Operational and source data is accessed, obtained, copied, or extracted from internal and external data files and data bases. Many organizations have built "home-grown" programs to move or transform the source operational data to decision support files or Data Warehouses.

Data transformation is a process that utilizes both business rules and commonly accepted field transforms to convert or transform the data into common characteristics. This usually involves some masterful programming and business knowledge plus a very clear understanding of the data sources and the meaning of the data. This is the most difficult of the processes for building a data warehouse. If you do not have these skills, acquire them or utilize a consultant.

An Infrastructure for Shared
Enterprise Information Management

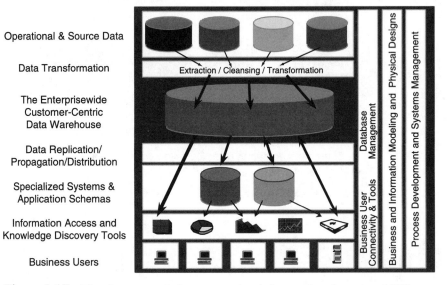

Operational & Source Data

Data Transformation

The Enterprisewide
Customer-Centric
Data Warehouse

Data Replication/
Propagation/Distribution

Specialized Systems &
Application Schemas

Information Access and
Knowledge Discovery Tools

Business Users

Figure 5-17. The framework for enterprise information (source: NCR Corporation).

The **customer-centric enterprisewide data warehouse** (EDW) can begin very small or grow from one of the previously implemented departmental DWs. The EDW needs to be customer-centric if your organization truly requires understanding the customers and all of your touch points and interactions with your customers. The EDW needs to be available to all departments and managers that will handle touches or communications with your customers. It also needs to maintain a historical view (meaning long-term detailed transactions and interactions) in the central (DW) repository accessible by all decision-making tools.

Two excellent examples of EDWs are 3M of St. Paul, MN and Anthem Blue Cross and Blue Shield of Indianapolis. Each of these organizations has matured its strategy, planning, implementations, merging, usage, and value of its data warehouses to greatly enhance the ability to serve customers and constituents (providers or suppliers). Each has also gone through the difficult task of merging data warehouses, decision support databases, and user-initiated files into one centralized EDW. See Chapter 14 for more organizations that are experiencing high returns from such info-structure investments and reinvestments (of the returns/savings).

Data replication or propagation provides for the distribution or movement of elements of data (rows and/or columns) to noncentral technologies. This allows for building of local departmental, or dependent data warehouses that can still have the "Single Version of the Truth" maintained in the entire organization. This is important when you seek information on customers, make decisions about your various business units and their customers/products/finances, and therefore build strategies or messages for increasing business.

The major reasons for distributing or replicating data are for performance or ownership reasons. Some organizations may need to give up control and share information that they create or have responsibility to maintain.

By propagating or distributing data, you can also provide for localization of information for **specialized applications or visualizations.**

Information access and knowledge discovery tools are those selected software solutions that business users utilize to access and manipulate the data required for providing answers to their business questions. See Chapter 4 for additional uses and applications that fit into these categories. Information access tools can be as simple as query languages, spreadsheet accesses, decision support query tools, executive information systems, specialized applications tailored to your own business, or external tools that allow access to your data (i.e., for your customers, suppliers, or distribution channels). Common tools are now used through the Internet and other networks for accessing and manipulating data within a data warehouse info-structure.

Business users are defined as anyone with appropriate access authority who has a need to access and/or use the core info-structure to perform their responsibilities. Business users include multiple levels of people with varying knowledge and experience with the technologies. Some have been classified as: Power Analysts, Statisticians, Modelers, Managers, Executives, Customer Service Personnel, Customers, Suppliers, Channels, Partners, Investors, Transporters, Servicers, and even the Internet connections to other types of users.

DW Successes from Long-Term Detailed Historical Enterprise Data

Whirlpool Corporation, Benton Harbor, Michigan has imple-mented various manufacturing, quality, customer service, and distri-bution decision support systems through a data warehouse environment. In Figures 5-18 and 5-19 you can view the value chain approach and the framework of a data warehouse overlayed with the organization's major external applications.

A study on "The Benefits of DW at Whirlpool" conducted Drs. Hugh Watson, Dale Goodhue, and Barbara Haley, all with the University of Georgia in 1997 was published in the "Annals of Cases on Information Technology Applications and Management in Organizations" Magazine Volume 1 in 1999. Whirlpool discussed their implementation successes and framework for creating their initial info-structure using a Scalable Data Warehouse (SDW) Framework shown in Figure 5-19. Whirlpool is a major supplier to Sears and you can see where the Sears application fits into their decision support structure.

Whirlpool uses its "gold mine" of customer service data for marketing, sales, and product design

15 Million Customers
20 Million Appliances
Up to 30 Years of History

One of a dozen DW Applications Creating New Value from Historical and Detail Data

Higher quality and profits come through close cooperation of the supply chain and customers.

Manufacturer | Manufacturer's Warehouse | Retailer's Distribution Center | Retailer | Consumer

Outbound Logistics | Delivery | Store Delivery

Figure 5-18. Whirlpool Corporation: Managing quality for customers.

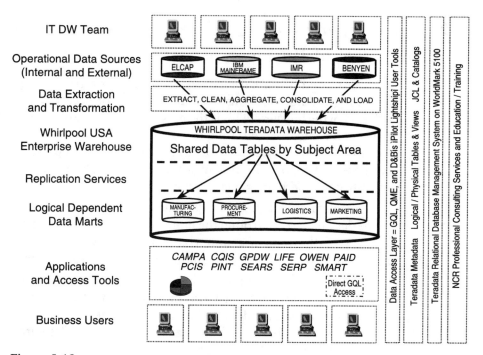

Figure 5-19. SDW Framework at Whirlpool (circa 1997).

The study showed that Whirlpool utilizes product maintenance and replacement part data to understand the longevity of products and the opportunities for selling new products to their customers. It also has the potential of using the customer service data to ensure that products do not fail for the customer in the future. This will provide opportunity for predictive maintenance and higher customer satisfaction.

Sears and Whirlpool are just two of the hundreds of organizations that have successfully utilized this SDW Framework for planning and implementing a high-ROI data warehousing solution. Each has also used the tenants and functions shown in the methodology chapter.

Any Question—At Anytime—of Any Data—from Any Level of Business

The centralized historical memory repository of a truly integrated infostructure (or data warehouse) should provide for access and query from any level of the business. This is the most highly profitable strategy because it allows for thinking, initiating new questions and ideas, and questioning potential actions before each goes to market. This concept is a hallmark of excellent and mature IT organizations who seek to provide significant flexibility for the management team.

The data models for your database should reflect your business and not be designed to get around the limitations of the technology. The access and use of the data are important, and you will need to foster an environment of unplanned or unknown characteristics of growth.

Your systems and your database contents will grow exponentially as more questions are answered and more users become familiar with the opportunity of really understanding your customers. In Figure 5-20, there is a business question requiring data from multiple tables within the data warehouse database. Note that this is a simple version of a data model to show that complex questions can be answered without preparing the data. This is done through strategy called *normalizing* (the data). Now, think about changing the question. How much restructuring of the data organization would have to be done if your database managers were required to access other tables or other data?

The strategy and organization shown here can save you hundreds of hours of query time and workdays per year.

If your IT or database managers must reorganize the data, extract special subsets just for one query, or write specialized applications to handle a new query, your design and infrastructure is probably built around the limitations of your technology investments (probably a popular but limited, database on a transaction processing server or mainframe).

Recommended major areas for resolving these situations:

1. Parallel processing for decision support and analytics
2. Parallel database on parallel hardware technology
3. Concurrent users with multiples of concurrent queries
4. Direct connection to other hardware for fast data loading
5. Design of the database and the tables: normalization versus denormalization

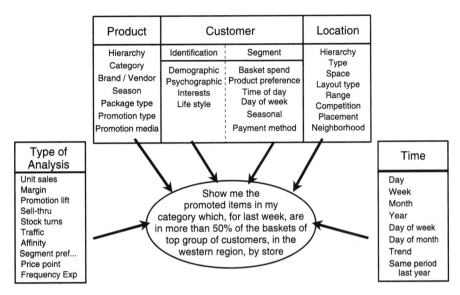

Figure 5-20. Modeling for customer-centric "anytime" queries. Your Info-Structure should allow you to ask *any* question at any time.

You don't know what questions your business will ask in the future, so you must plan for any question, from any data, at any time.

Mature Data Warehousing and CRM Decision Support

As organizations learn, experience, and mature in their use of decision support and data warehousing, there are significant changes to their scope of use and ultimate ROIs. After consolidation and centralization of the core information and transactional histories of customers or another major area of the business, there is a high growth rate of leveraging information into knowledge for decisions.

The advanced stages of DW include characteristics that are shown in Figure 5-21, which highlights the use of the info-structure for strategic purposes and integrated value-chain processes. Flexibility and knowledge become the hallmarks of many organizations leading their industries. These are the key characteristics for long-term growth and strength of organizations. Utilizing a centralized and distributed architecture, along with integration of information sources from throughout the internal and external business systems, joining process flows and interchanging decisional information and allocating the right resources at exactly the right time provides for advanced business management.

The characteristics of mature or advanced data warehousing include:

- **Enterprise focus with integrated information**
- **Numerous sources and growing subject areas**
- **Transformation (a process that is duplicated)**
- **Single business model with multiple uses**
- **Quick collection and insertion of data**
- **Wide transaction collection and usage**
- **Customer-centric and/or mission critical**
- **Single version of the truth**
- **Anywhere, anytime, any type of questions**
- **Wide access and managed security**
- **Applications that cross departmental boundaries**
- **Tools are utilized to expand the "views"**
- **Dependent data marts or dependent DWs**
- **Management decisions by using DW**
- **Expectations continually extended/exceeded**
- **Known ROI and reinvestment is strategy**

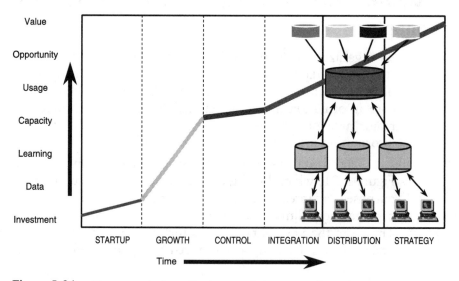

Figure 5-21. Characteristics of advanced data warehousing.

CRM and the Stages of Growth for Customer-Centricity

The value of the information infrastructure is to begin through multiple stages of developing and using customer data and new knowledge. As you proceed through the stages, you will find that your perspective, strategy, database usage, applications, and benefits will increase exponentially.

In Figure 5-22, there are four levels of applications in a customer-centric organization compounded over time. Notice the changes occurring in the thinking and use of the data over time and the opportunities to master competitive advantage.

Now we must formulate strategies to create and maintain effective communications with our prospects and customers. For success, many enterprises need to think about the major functional types of contacts or campaigns to achieve this objective. As you amass more data and transform it into significant information, there are significant differences in your approaches to customer interactions.

In Figure 5-23 you will find an insightful approach to the sequencing of real applications and campaigns as you move through the stages of implementation and managerial change.

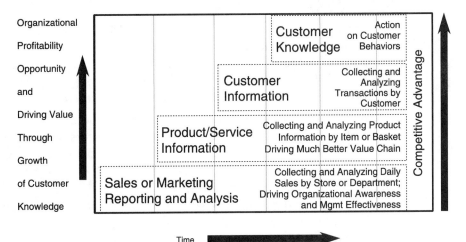

Figure 5-22. Four Levels of CRM Information uses for High Growth, Customer Profitability, and Competitive Advantage.

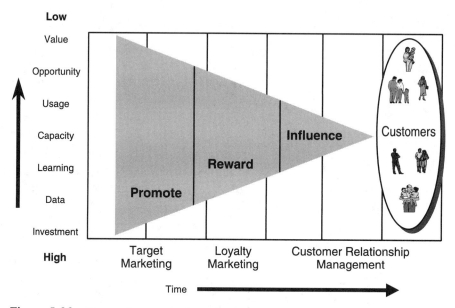

Figure 5-23. Types (stages) of marketing to mature relationships.

Extending the Info-Structure

Now we have completed the maturation of the three major types of decision support systems for use by management. In organizations that have matured in the philosophy and creation of the info-structure defined here (and the framework and stages shown in the previous figures), you will find a fourth type of foundation: **interactive knowledge**.

Interactive Knowledge systems enable your customers and your organization to have an active environment that fosters the integration of your processes into those of your channels or your customers. In Chapter 11, you will find a detailed description of active (DW) info-structures for competitive advantage. This is not a trend, it is reality, and it drives extremely high ROI for those organizations that have the experience and maturity to foster such an environment.

The Internet has driven many organizations to create collection systems from their transactions and interactions with customers. But it will be the analytical and decision-process driven applications that will truly make the difference in the future.

So, we have moved from the beginning stages of creating a database for data warehousing purposes and providing SQL Reporting in the earliest of stages. Then the provision and inclusion for Ad Hoc Queries allows your people to ask any question at any time from the data warehouse.

When organizations learn from the systems and the information, they then build enablers and infrastructures for Predictive Modeling. The combining of all of these applications and systems for real-time management of customers is in the Interactive Knowledge era. The distribution and use of these DW applications is shown in Figure 5-24.

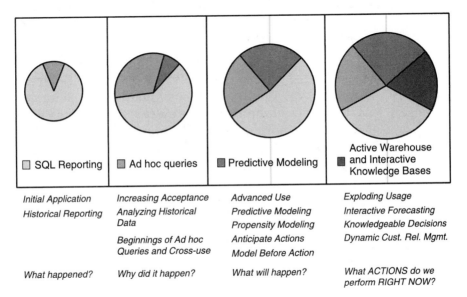

☐ SQL Reporting	☐ Ad hoc queries	☐ Predictive Modeling	☐ Active Warehouse and Interactive Knowledge Bases
Initial Application Historical Reporting	Increasing Acceptance Analyzing Historical Data	Advanced Use Predictive Modeling Propensity Modeling	Exploding Usage Interactive Forecasting Knowledgeable Decisions Dynamic Cust. Rel. Mgmt.
	Beginnings of Ad hoc Queries and Cross-use	Anticipate Actions Model Before Action	
What happened?	Why did it happen?	What will happen?	What ACTIONS do we perform RIGHT NOW?

Figure 5-24. Accelerating the stages of DW/DSS.

Management Considerations

- There is a maturation process that most enterprises need to address early in the CRM or data warehousing process.
- The highest rewards (or ROI) come through widespread use of information resources and allowing for unlimited thinking and questioning (also see Chapter 12).
- The CRM applications do change over time through the stages.
- Most managers don't foresee change coming as they mature.
- Extending the experience of preceding stages, actions, processes, applications, and information movement drives a much better facilitation of the opportunity for competitive advantage.
- Enterprises do not learn in the early stages to position for the future and create a strong info-structure for flexibility.
- Scalability is a problem of most enterprises because the foundations of information infrastructures, particularly for decision support, constrain the growth.
- Management needs to be informed and an active participant in the evolution to maturity.

Data Warehouse Methodology

▶ The Proof Is in the Experience

Hundreds of consultants over the past fifteen years have refined a consulting methodology and practice to the point where it now covers the full spectrum of data warehouse tasks. The methodology and processes shown in this chapter have been utilized around the world. It gives you insight to actual experiences and shows how you can perform the planning, design, building, implementation and support of data warehouse. These consultants have used their skills in industry-specific implementations, in areas such as retail, financial services, communications, transportation, government, insurance, and electronic commerce.

The Scalable Data Warehouse Methodology shown in Figure 6-1 consists of three major phases:

1. Planning
2. Design and Implementation
3. Usage, Support and Enhancement.

Each phase provides a series of processes clearly defined.

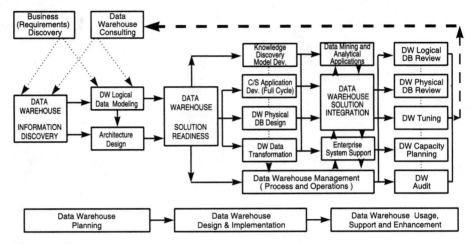

Figure 6-1. A Scalable Data Warehouse (source: NCR Corporation).

The Planning Phase

The *Planning Phase* identifies *business problems*, and models and develops the architecture for initial DW solution plans. It accomplishes this by providing five services. The *Business Discovery process* determines practical, information-based solutions to issues that the organization is facing. The *emphasis is on the business issues, not technology*. The result of Business Discovery is to gain consensus on and prioritize key business issues, identify quantifiable benefits to getting the issues resolved, and provide an analysis showing the "bottom line" impact.

The *Information Discovery process* helps enterprises refine the solution requirements by validating critical business needs and information requirements. Next, data modeling is used to show the customer how data can be turned into useful information and used to address the critical issues. The external (or internal) consultants should provide a data model supporting the business needs, which forms the foundation for the technical data warehouse solution.

You may need to run a workshop or a walk-through to help identify the type of data warehouse best suited for your organizational plans and requirements, which can be comprised of dynamic presentations and interactive interviews. Educating decision-makers, the user community, and technical or operations personnel about the advantages and disadvantages of the different data warehouse architectures, database engines, access methods, management methods and data sourcing methods is necessary.

Logical Data Model Design process produces a logical data model for particular solutions, including the confirmation of requirements, creation of a project plan, and the generation of the logical data model showing relationships and attributes. The logical data model is not specific to any platform or database and is separate from any physical dependencies. Instead, it represents a metadata layer, which, in the simplest terms, describes data about data.

The *Data Warehouse Architecture Design process* designs the specific architecture for the customer-defined environment and it specifies the data warehouse location (centralized, virtual, distributed), network requirements, types of users' access, and so on.

The Design and Implementation Phase

The *Design and Implementation Phase develops full-scale design and implementation plans* for the construction of the data warehouse. Solution Readiness, for example, is a collection of six assessments combined into a single engagement, the overall intent of which is to provide a comprehensive evaluation of the environment and to assess the organization's readiness to implement a data warehouse.

Technology Assessment ensures that no technical issues could prevent the implementation of a desired solution. The process includes interviews with business and technology representatives from all groups that could impact the data warehouse, and also evaluates your readiness for a client/server solution. It assesses the hardware, network and software environment, and analyzes the requirements for remote data access, data sharing, and backup/restart/recovery. The result of this service is the identification and prioritization of issues that could impede solution implementation, and a follow-up plan to eliminate issues. At the end of the process, you should have assurance, with concurrence from your technical staff, that no technical issues could prevent implementing the identified solution.

Data and Function Assessments evaluates the existing data structures and their characteristics to ensure that data warehouse sourcing requirements are met and that the data models supporting the solution truly address the business requirements. The function assessment identifies the technology and business processes that will be supported by a data warehouse, and confirms that the system under consideration will meet business needs.

Change Readiness Assessment defines how people using the data warehouse are affected by it and how they might react to the changes caused by implementing a data warehouse. It should explore barriers to success caused by cultural issues and identifies potential education to address the problems. It focuses on the impact of the proposed solution on the technical and user communities and their disposition to accept the changes.

Education and Support Assessments will organize and plan education for project participants and end-users to support the integration of a data warehouse into their environment. The support assessment identifies the requirements for ongoing support of a data warehouse solution.

Knowledge Discovery Model Development begins when conventional database access methods, such as Structured Query Language (SQL) or Online Analytical Processing (OLAP) are not enough to solve certain business problems. The service defines the specific business problems not served by these methods, then documents the data, resources, constraints and assumptions, and prepares the data set for the model. Knowledge Discovery utilizes predictive data modeling to make more informed decisions about these problems. An example of an answer derived directly from data is a list of customers located in New York City who hold certificates of deposit with a bank. An example of the results of a predictive modeling or Knowledge Discovery effort might include the long-term revenue potential associated with each of those customers.

Data Mining and Analytical Application selects the Data Mining tools or analytical application that best fits the business problem defined by the Knowledge Discovery service. This process should also perform tool-specific transformations, run the chosen application against prepared data sets, validate the results, and present them to end users.

Client/Server Application process includes both client/server design and development. The client/server design provides for specific applications and the query interface required, and includes an iterative definition and prototyping of the desired applications. The process requires the consultant to work closely with the user community to define the type of access required (ad hoc or planned), possible access methods, tools for development and access, report look-and-feel, and testing processes. The result of the design process is a working prototype of the applications, a specification of the technical requirements of the design, specific deliverables, and development tools to support implementation, as well as complete plans for the required applications.

The *application development process* implements the query interface for a data warehouse solution. It uses the prototypes, specifications, recommended tool sets and other outputs of the design service to develop and validate the applications that give users the data and information they need to perform their business functions. The development service provides the tools and the programmed applications that access, transform and represent to users the data that supports their analysis and decision-making. These applications and tools provide collection, analysis and presentation of information with graphical user interfaces, allowing for both pre-defined and ad hoc analysis of data. Training and documentation are included with the delivery of the application and access tools.

Data Warehouse Physical Database Design process provides the customer with the physical database design and implementation optimized for a data warehouse. It is built using the project plan, logical data model, and data warehouse architecture design plan. The primary activities in this service are as follows: translating the logical data model to a physical database design, database construction, design optimization, and functional testing of the constructed database. The Physical Database Design process should also provide design guidelines appropriate for the environment and for the specific database platform used in the project.

Data Transformation process designs and develops the utilities and programming that allow the data warehouse database to be loaded and maintained. This service locates, extracts, conditions, scrubs and loads data onto the data warehouse. Also included is the operational planning that allows the reloading or incremental loading of the data warehouse periodically.

Data Warehouse Management process implements the data, network, systems, and operations management procedures needed to successfully manage a data warehouse. Included are data maintenance routines to update, load, backup, archive, administer, and restore/recover data, ensuring consistency and compatibility with existing procedures. The service also identifies workgroup databases and provides the procedures required for the DW updates. It implements procedures for application version control, hardware and software maintenance, error reporting, and other management tasks. Operations management looks at the operational procedures that affect the solution environment and recommends changes to meet the customer's needs. Design areas include: archive procedures, change control procedures for hardware and software upgrades, application version control, report logging, and preventative maintenance.

▶ Usage, Support and Enhancement Phase

The **Usage, Support and Enhancement Phase** focuses on data warehouse maintenance and expansion planning (data warehouses often grow rapidly in volume and usage). Changes can affect performance and sometimes the integrity of the data warehouse; therefore, expansion should be carefully planned. There are six services and programs in this phase.

1. **Enterprise System Support** provides three tiers of integrated system support for all solution components, such as the database, tools, applications, basic software, and hardware. Account management and hardware support are featured with different levels of service delivery for each tier. Customized application support is also offered as an additional chargeable feature.

2., 3. **Data Warehouse Logical Data Model Review** and **Physical Design Review** process adds skills to your organization to allow use of your own staff for some of the design and implementation. Your external consultants review the requirements of the users along with their model construction, and offers analysis and suggestions for improvement. Reviews examine and validate the current logical model design for correct technique and the ability to meet all requirements.

4. **Data Warehouse Tuning** would typically be engaged when performance problems are encountered. Consultants should conduct a detailed analysis to pinpoint the source(s) of the problem. The analysis looks at the network, applications, users, database structure, systems utilization, and other areas, and once complete, recommendations are presented to resolve performance issues.

5. **Capacity Planning** helps enterprises plan for the initial definitions of capacity and sizing, and then for the expansion of their data warehouse. Expansion includes the addition of applications, users, data, remote applications, and operations. Any of the aforementioned additions could affect the performance of the data warehouse. Proactive planning for changes will allow the user community to continue to work with limited or no disruption.

6. **Data Warehouse Audit** (or *ROI Discovery/Audit*) helps ascertain the business value of an existing data warehouse by validating its current state against its business "best practices." This service recommends changes that will ultimately maximize the value of the data warehouse to the business. The areas of assessment include: flexibility and extensibility of the database design, metadata richness, consistency, and consumer access, as well as the use of third-party extraction and conditioning tools, use of summary tables, and so on. Consultants also audit operational aspects of the DW for improvement opportunities.

This (NCR) Scalable Data Warehouse Methodology, unique in the industry, has multiple entry points. Most methodologies, developed for project management or information processing applications development, have one starting point and a specific finishing point. What makes this methodology unique is its ability to segment the sections and provide services for various organizational experience levels. Many companies have already performed steps within the total methodology. Multiple entry points allow them to 'pick-up' from where they are, flow through the final points and then repetitively return. This provides for greater flexibility. Somewhat mature organizations are able to utilize the methodology's proven techniques to increase their positive results from a data warehouse. Figure 6-2 displays entry points 1 through 5.

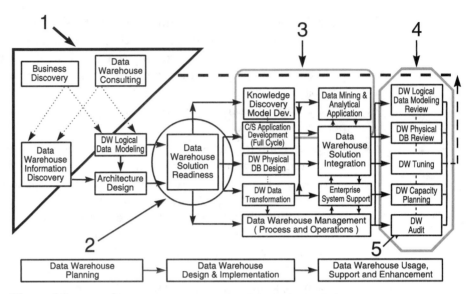

Figure 6-2. Multiple Entry Points into a SDW Methodology.

Organizations, which have little or no experience with data warehouse planning and development activities, will require going through the normal process groups from upper left (#1) to lower right (#5). You should start with the Business Discovery process block in the upper left and end with the grouping of review activities on the far right. Not all of the processes will be required to implement the first stage or even subsequent stages. (Many organizations skip certain processes, which they learn about later, after cycling through the methodology in different pathways.) This methodology allows using only those activities required to be successful in the implementation of the current stage (or data warehousing project goals).

Organizations with prior experience in data warehousing, decision support, or data mining may also use this methodology. The entry point is determined by an analysis of the present DW, DSS, or Data Mining implementation(s).

When an extensive data warehouse has already been implemented, you may begin with the *"DW Audit"* process (entry #5). This reviews the presently-implemented processes, and also reviews the results of actions taken prior to beginning any new data warehousing activity. It is also important to determine the extent to which the previous implementations have met and are meeting the business objectives for the data warehouse environment. The follow-up activities would flow back through the *Data*

Warehouse Consulting and *Data Warehouse Business Discovery* processes to ensure additional contributions and successes for the enterprise or department using the data warehouse.

Organizations that already have data warehouse project plans may need to begin at point #2, to ensure that proceeding with their plans have been through a complete *"DW Readiness Assessment."* Many unsuccessful data warehouses have skipped this process and failed. Through this process and the hundred plus questions, your IT team probably will need to acquire additional outside experience to ensure that all of the key specific items are completed prior to building or enhancing a data warehouse. This step is essential in ensuring success. The process then continues through the normal methodology flow.

Organizations seeking to implement a data mining or knowledge discovery environment can begin with entry point #3. In most cases, these organizations should have very detailed data, stored in a data warehouse environment or database, which allows these two process groups to succeed without the need to build or rebuild an entire information environment.

Organizations that have already implemented a database, striving for a data warehouse or data mart environment, may require a complete review of their designs and models. This may be due to performance problems, including the inability to extend the data models or to easily grow the data within the desired environment.

Physical and Logical Database Design Reviews are an entry point for the methodology. These are usually performed in the normal process of building a data warehouse. Organizations that do not have experience in designing and building a complex, open-systems, query anytime-anywhere-any-data environment, will require a review of their physical and logical database designs as they continue to grow the data warehouse environment.

One of the most neglected or forgotten data warehouse processes is to perform *Capacity Planning*. Your team will find this a major challenge without experienced knowledge. You must pre-determine the growth path, performance considerations, and capacities required to maintain high-performance response times for simple, detailed, and complex queries. Entry point #4 includes a key process for capacity planning.

How to Achieve a High Degree of Scalability

The goal of a scalable system is four-dimensional: to allow the maximum number of users the ability to input and/or extract data while running complex queries against complex data models with minimal support.

The first of the four dimensions of scalability is the ability to input and extract data with consistent response times. The second dimension is the number of users or queries that run simultaneously. The third is environmental complexity, represented by the complexity of the data model and the queries run against the model. The fourth is the degree of support needed to maintain scalability.

You will need to achieve a high degree of scalability through a combination of software automation and hardware parallelism. Through intelligent use of algorithms, and sophisticated Database Optimizer Technologies, make sure your IT architects understand the use a hybrid of the two basic kinds of Optimizers: rules-based and cost-based. With rules-based, a DBA knows the rules and sets up queries to take advantage of those rules. Using cost-based, an Optimizer tries to find the least costly way to handle an SQL query. You can use both in one system and in one architecture if you desire.

Another factor contributing to the optimization of queries is the intelligence in the way data is loaded and placed in the warehouse. Through the use of Automated Data Placement, based on a "hash algorithm" (a division algorithm), data is divided in a way that permits scalability and accuracy. A repeatable randomizing routine places data in a random, balanced way that doesn't make assumptions based on time.

Management Considerations

- The most important contribution of this DW Methodology is the iterative nature of the process. The small company, or newly-formed data warehouse team, can grow their data warehouse using this methodology and consultants' expertise.
- You should expect either outside consultants to transfer their data warehousing knowledge and experience, or have an outsourced DW environment. Consultants should view the DW relationship as a partnership, for example, the more it contributes to your

business success, the more the data warehouse is used and, in turn creates the additional need for data warehouse applications, technology, and services. Everyone wins !!!

- Wal*Mart Stores started with 30 Gigabytes (in Spring of 1990) in their initial data warehouse and implemented true scalability to create the largest commercial data warehouse environment in the world with 101 Terabytes of storage (Summer, 1999) on multiple NCR WorldMark and Teradata RDBMS data warehouses.

- The methodology highlighted in this chapter is founded on the premise that to be successful the sharing of information, experience, and expertise is essential for long-term joint relationships. Therefore many of the companies that have utilized this methodology have started out with relatively small data warehouses (now called: Data Marts). They have since grown these investments into very large data warehouses with industry-leading uses and applications. Time, experience, and reinvestment show real success.

Building the CRM Data Warehouse and Info-Structure

The greatest value from data warehousing occurs when the data warehouse is used in the redesign of business processes and in the support for strategic business objectives. This is the most difficult value to achieve, however, because of the required amount of top management support, commitment, and involvement, and the amount of organizational change involved.

As a result, many organizations are not realizing this kind of value.

Hugh Watson and Barbara J. Haley,
"Managerial Considerations with Data Warehousing,"
Communications of the ACM 41, (1998) and
"Implementing Successful Data Warehouses,"
Journal of Data Warehousing, 1998).

▶ Defining Your Timeframes and Objectives

Organizations desiring to succeed in CRM will require an info-structure of customer-centric information as well as a framework to dynamically integrate future technologies within the CRM process.

Because many companies building a data warehouse are entering *terra incognita*, they should ensure a careful preparation of the venture (Sean Kelly, 1997). Usually, they have experience with initiatives for building information systems or with implementing "island"-like solutions for some corporate departments. But an "enterprise-wide" approach has either failed when first attempted or has resulted in another isolated solution.

For years, people have been asking us: "How can I build a Data Warehouse within a reasonable period of time and budget?" We believe that you can begin with a reasonable objective (knowing the questions that have high payback and high priority) and complete the initial phases and implementation with three to six months. In his article "100 Days to Data Warehousing Success," Marcel Bhend discusses his experiences in such a project and the success criteria. I've included additional ideas and materials from research of over 500 meetings and strategy sessions with data warehousing and decision support implementations on five continents.

This chapter discusses the sensible way to approach the creation of a data warehouse environment and is followed by the methodology that you can utilize to succeed. You will also learn about the data warehouse project elements. Each step of the preparation and implementation phase is discussed in detail, with emphasis on the tasks necessary to analyze, design and implement the data warehouse system. In addition, the requisite resources for a successful data warehouse project are described.

▶ Defining a DW Framework and Building a Data Warehouse

The *NCR Data Warehouse Framework,* shown in Figure 7-1, provides the blueprint and foundation for building a truly scalable data warehouse (SDW). The framework includes a series of steps (or levels) to transform existing operational data into informational data, thereby rendering a company's data more organized, consistent and valuable to its business in many ways. Informational data can be the source of strategic perspectives about how a business ought to be run to achieve maximum advantage in its market. In order to achieve *informational data* (that which is used for analytics, not for operational transaction activity and updates), it is necessary to perform data transformation on raw transactional or operational data.

The goal of a data warehouse is to co-exist with operational systems, extracting significant operational data from those systems for use in a centralized, relational database. Significant **operational data** is defined according to the customer's line of business; generally, though, it is mission-critical information generated by the business from such day-to-day operations as sales, orders, request for payments, shipping, or activities that start or complete a cycle (such as manufacturing, delivery, production, or customer contacts or requests).

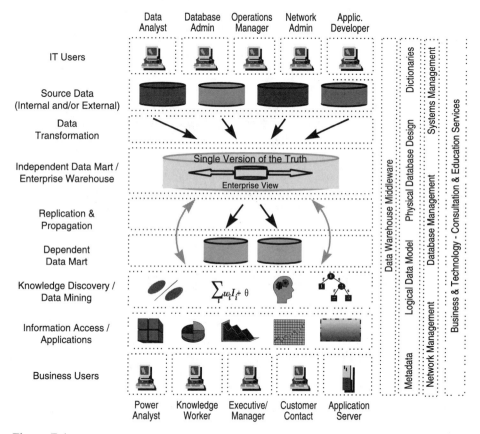

Figure 7-1. The NCR Scalable Data Warehouse Framework. Copyright, NCR Corporation 1996.

Managing Operational Data into the Warehouse

The DW Framework actually provides a solution to a number of common Information Systems problems. Inconsistent data formats make it difficult (and sometimes impossible) to use increasingly common Decision Support Systems (DSS) to analyze raw operational data for changes in customer behavior, market trends and changes, or product/market cause-and-effect relationships. DSS technology requires consistent information that cuts across functional departments. A company without the ability to use DSS tools effectively to understand cross- functional aspects of the business, can be at a distinct disadvantage against its competitors.

Operational data applications are frequently the result of customization based on individual user or departmental requirements. *Customized applications* were designed in isolation, without taking into account how other applications use and store the same data. The way operational data has been stored and organized depends on how it has been used; for instance, on whether it undergoes high or low volume transactions. The style for updating data may differ; that is, on a field-by-field or block basis. Often, there is data that has accumulated over years without being maintained. All of these circumstances can make it difficult to apply operational data to DSS technologies that were built to add value to a business.

Transforming Data into Information

One of the greatest challenges in creating a usable SDW Framework is in the process of transforming operational data into the informational data needed to facilitate analysis and decision-making for creating business value. Despite the challenge, however the process is crucial. It creates a consistent format, which paves the way for the kind of advanced decision-making rendered possible by technologies such as DSS and Data Mining.

Data transformation is the logical transformation and physical movement of data from operational systems into informational systems. Depending on existing conditions, data transformation activities can include accessing, reconciling, extracting, conditioning, condensing, filtering, scrubbing, merging and loading. The exponential value of a warehouse is realized when companies use it to ask cross-functional, complex questions of detailed data without limitations of data storage organization or database structure.

Architectural Strategies—Centralized Versus Distributed

The key business decision, at the outset, is in the architectural approach to data warehousing. Whether to build a small or single focused data warehouse, sometimes called *Data Marts*, is a critical decision.

There are two classifications of data marts: Independent and Dependent Data Marts. *Independent Data Marts* are unconnected and non-integrated. Very few of these independent data marts grow up into real data warehouses, unless they are designed, from the beginning, for expansion of both the business model and the data model.

A *dependent data mart* is a logical and/or physical subset of data from the enterprise warehouse that is selected and organized for a particular set of usage requirements. Performance and cost are often the key reasons dependent data marts are implemented.

The dependent data mart provides an enterprise view, as it resides closer to power users in specific financial and marketing departments. Marts can be organized by user group (physically located in users' departments), or by subject area (organized logically in a separate partition within the data warehouse). Data replication and propagation synchronizes data between the enterprise data warehouse and dependent data marts.

Independent Data Marts Versus Enterprise Data Warehouse

The goal of the data warehouse approach is to provide a centerpiece of collected and transformed information in a single data store of clean, accurate detail and summary data for the enterprise. This foundation alleviates much of the problems associated with "stovepipe" or non-integrated operational or decision support systems. Independent data marts do not provide a "single version of the truth," therefore continuing the frustrating and limited-ROI reporting environment of the past. Users of the Data Warehouse should be successful in eliminating inaccurate reporting, incorrect detailed data, and ineffective management information.

To enter into the process of building a scalable data warehouse, it is recommended that you start with a small or manageable *enterprise data warehouse,* which is focused on one or two particular subject areas. Within this context, we also recommend that a dependent data mart be a part of the planning and architecture of an enterprise strategy. Although we have seen many data marts, it has become clear that multiple, unconnected, non-integrated, and un-modeled data marts are not acceptable for high return on investment and successful growth of the data warehouse.

As a smaller version of the data warehouse, the dependent data mart instantly provides *power users* with the most current information possible. Users don't have to wait for a *database administrator (DBA)* to allocate space or provide authorization to access data, or to build queries. They can use the dependent data mart independently, meaning they can react more quickly to market changes. Sometimes these data marts are physically located within the data warehouse database. The business user believes that they have a special data warehouse (e.g., data mart) prepared for them, when it is actually part of an integrated environment within the enterprise data warehouse. These are known as **Logical Data Marts**. This approach saves enormous amounts of time and money.

The exponential value of an enterprise warehouse (multiple functional areas sharing the same data) is realized when you can begin to ask cross-functional complex questions about your business. It is only then that you can analyze your products or services in relation to time, geography, distribution channel, customer, and resources to maximize profitability and the lifetime value of your customers.

Data Replication and Propagation

Data Replication and Propagation synchronizes data between the enterprise warehouse and the dependent data marts. Independent data marts do not really utilize replication and propagation, but merely use copy utilities (in most cases) to move data from the originating source (operational) files and databases.

Middleware Requirements

A scalable data warehouse does not stand alone. Instead, it must fit into an existing systems environment, which may include a diverse collection of legacy and client/server applications, logical data sources, external data sources, and so on. For maximum effectiveness, all systems components must work together as a single "virtual" system, accessible to end users through a consistent graphical user interface (GUI) or a Web-based application.

The glue that dynamically connects all the disparate components comprising an integrated system is called *middleware,* which can connect the databases in the operational environments to the data warehouse. It can also connect the business users to the data warehouse database(s) for access to and use of Information Access and analytical tools.

The *Data Access Layer* of middleware refers to the industry standard interfaces or APIs, such as ODS and ODBC, which allow access to both data managers and legacy operational data sources. Middleware is the essential connector for a successful and complete data warehouse solution.

Data Modeling and Design of the Data Warehouse

The *Data Modeling and Design Layer* of the DW framework represents the creation of a logical data model to support the business information needs, and the physical design of the database to support the logical model. This layer also includes the data dictionary (for consistent data definitions), and the *metadata* for establishing an efficient directory and usage of the data. *Metadata* is the detailed properties and characteristics of the information within your database and/or systems. This is one of the most crucial aspects for creating a sustainable data warehouse solution. Metadata contains the internal pointers and specific information for the applications and operating systems to know the location of the data, the level of code, the owner, the security level, the latest update (time/application/file/person), and the characteristics which allow for access and use. In the future, the metadata will become a most important part of the process flow and connection to information resources in information technology systems.

▶ Building a Data Warehouse in 100 Days

What are the key factors to consider when embarking on a data warehouse project, and what resources are needed and where are some of the traps to be avoided? Once the decision to build a data warehouse has been taken, operational questions like these become important. The following description of a data warehouse project is based on the assumption that the long-term vision for the data warehouse is to evolve into a corporate-wide information platform (Inmon, 1998). Experience shows that starting with a small data warehouse and laying the foundation for future growth can be achieved within a reasonable timeframe, that is, within 100 days. In order to stay within the given limit, the complexity of the first data warehouse implementation should be restricted to no more than one or two departments with similar interests and similar data sources. Of course, this is also true for all subsequent development cycles.

A large part of the project's future success depends upon the preparational activities undertaken before the project actually starts. Preparing and implementing a data warehouse project cannot be completely separated (Swift, 1998). The project will succeed (as described below) only if all those in charge have done their homework. When do specific tasks have to be completed, and how long before the project is launched? The answers depend largely on the circumstances surrounding the project. An important date is when management decides to build a data warehouse. From this "milestone," preparation work can be started, with the following topics usually requiring two to three months duration (see Figure 7-2).

- **Identify beneficiaries**

  Which user groups or departments can profit most from a data warehouse? Whose work would be simplified by a data warehouse; that is, who is already working with databases, or employs statistical methodology?

- **Secure financing**

  The departments who need the data warehouse most are not necessarily the ones with the biggest budgets. Hence, financing must be ensured before the project is launched.

- **Define goals**

  Any strategic decision for a data warehouse must be based on quantifiable target figures. These figures, for example, the expected benefits, must be clearly visible if this project is to compete successfully with other projects considered in the boardroom.

- **Assess current situation**

  How satisfied are users with the available information? Are there any operational problems that should be solved before launching a data warehouse project?

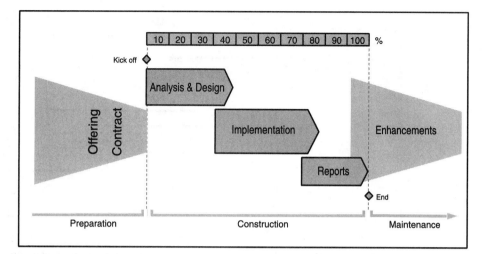

Figure 7-2. Data warehouse project cycle with an extented preparation phase for the initial project.

- **Analyze business issues**

  A data warehouse enables people in a company to resolve business issues that eluded them before, and to find answers to questions that have always been unanswerable. Therefore, an initial overall analysis should identify the business fields with the greatest benefit potential.

- **Identify possible data sources**

  Frequently, a company will have a most interesting business query, and either the data needed for answering it are not available or too difficult to access. To guard against this, all potential sources of data must be reviewed to see if the pool of usable data is big enough.

- **Set up technological "info-structure"**

  The technological info-structure such as workstations, network integration, and so on should be provided and in place as early as possible, so that the project will not suffer unnecessary delays.

Project Outline

Figure 7-3 illustrates an outline of the project that starts with the kick-off meeting, and is divided into three phases:

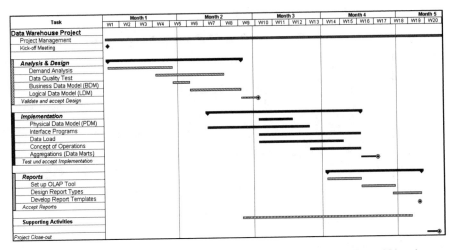

Figure 7-3. Outline of all substantial tasks connected to a Data Warehouse project.

- Analysis & Design
- Implementation
- Reports, queries, and/or analytical tool uses

A detailed description of all steps to be taken follows below.

Project Team Resources

Illustrated in Table 7-1 are the positions needed in the project team. The abbreviations are used in the project plans of each phase.

Table 7-1. Team Roles and Responsibilities

Position	Job Description
Project Manager	Project managers are responsible for the entire project, and need to have a thorough understanding of data warehouse concepts. They direct all assignments in close cooperation with their data warehouse architect. If they handle the project in this manner, they need not to be physically present for more than 2 to 3 days per week.

Table 7-1. continued

Position	Job Description
Business Consultants	Business Consultants are industry experts. They define project goals and benefits from the department's point of view. Additionally, they identify and analyze the business fields to be included, and they model the appropriate business processes. Their activities focus on analyzing business transactions; once the project is implemented, they also keep their eye on the results.
Data Warehouse Architect	Data warehouse architects are responsible for the overall technological concept; that is, the transfer of departmental requirements into a technological solution. This includes modeling the data, designing and implementing the data warehouse architecture, and managing all interfaces. Their task requires their permanent on-site presence.
Data Modeler	Data modelers are primarily engaged in creating various data models. These data models include a normalized data model for the data warehouse and specific data models for the data marts. For this job, a person needs a profound knowledge of customer structures and business processes. Successful data modeling requires close coordination with the user representatives. The completed models should be reviewed by experts external to the project (Whitten, 1999).
Database Designer	Database designers are responsible for transforming and integrating data into the data warehouse as well as for configuring and administering the database. Other activities include optimizing the performance and developing a task scheduler. Because of the heavy workload during implementation, some activities are executed simultaneously, and the individual assignments will determine whether knowledge of SQL and/or operating systems is required.
Application Programmer	Application programmers are primarily engaged in transferring the users' requirements into reports, using OLAP tools. For this, they analyze the requirements from the corporate departments and develop application-specific data models, the latter in cooperation with a data modeler. Application developers should be included when data sources are analyzed, so that they have a better understanding of the data contents.

Table 7-1. continued

Position	Job Description
Systems Engineer	Assignments that concern the system directly are bundled under the heading "System engineer." These include installing hardware and software, setting up user profiles and implementing security concepts. Each of these activities is usually handled by a specialist.
Training Educator	In the context of a data warehouse project, the term "training" consists of educating IT staff in data warehouse-related matters, such as databases and SQL, or introducing users to handling the OLAP tool and the applications (reports) developed with its help.
Systems Administrator/Customer	System administrators who administer our customers' systems know their operative systems, from which the data for the data warehouse will be extracted, and make the necessary data available.

With each step, only the lead position is listed, although other positions may be involved. The data warehouse architect is involved in each step and/or assignment.

Understanding Data Organization Differences

There has been much discussion and debate on the methods of organizing data for query, decisions support, analysis, data mining, knowledge discovery, and complex prediction applications. Before we begin the phases of the project, it might be valuable for you to more clearly understand the differences and the issues related to data organization in an informational (not operational) database system.

Modeling Methodology—Let's discuss Third Normal Form (used by Teradata and other mature databases) versus Star Schema (utilized mostly by application-oriented or small data warehouse DBMSs).

Structured Query Language (SQL) runs against any kind of data model, but the two most common model-building methodologies are star schema and third normal form. While some database companies are just now beginning to add third normal form versions to their star schema-based products, NCR Teradata has been fine-tuning third normal form products since 1983.

Third normal form is a flexible data modeling methodology that does not make assumptions about the basic functions of a business. Deployed as an accurate yet adaptable model of the business, third normal form shows how and why patterns (as well as anomalies) in a business are occurring. Having knowledge of these patterns is particularly valuable when the business leverages that knowledge through data mining activities.

Experienced Relational DataBase Management Systems architects know that data models based on "star schema" data models limit business intelligence which requires any question, at any time, queries and ad hoc modeling. This can be illustrated when a company misses an opportunity by organizing its sales information based on the assumptions inherent in star schema. If the company looks at sales data only by how sales have done in the past week, the assumption is that there is no variation in days or hours of the day, and that customers' behavior is even and predictable throughout the week.

For instance, during the Christmas season, retailers know which store has sold what merchandise and when. If they discover in time that they have overstocked inventory of product X in one geographic area, but under-stocked it in another region, they could move product X to the needed location where it is selling well. But if retailers only look at sales data by the week, then Christmas day will come and go by the time they discover where merchandise needs to be in order to sell the most. If retailers gain knowledge of this a day or two in advance, then they can act quickly to move the leftover merchandise from low-selling regions to the high-selling areas in time to realize profits from this information.

The *star schema* approach makes certain assumptions about data, presuming to know relationships between data in advance. One of the ways in which assumptions are made is through a process called denormalizing, which reduces the complexity of information so that a DBMS can handle it better. Denormalizing two or more pieces of data by combining them into one may make the DBMS job easier, but it decreases the quality of the information. In the process of denormalizing, assumptions about relationships are set in stone to relate in ways when they often don't relate at all. When internal business or external market circumstances change, the process the model takes must be completely be redone.

A typical example of denormalizing is in the health insurance industry when a claim is filed for a doctor's visit. The doctor may have taken ten separate actions during the visit and reported each one separately. Yet in denomalizing the data, by combining health actions in a claim, the perimeters do not reflect the real circumstances.

Utilizing third normal form for both the logical and physical aspects of a computer model minimizes the need to denormalize data. It avoids the data integrity compromises that can lead to business problems. However, you will need to develop a strategy and process for working with existing star schema data by allowing the requisite joins resulting from a star schema model to be viewed within a third normal form model. This process will accept star schema data without letting the data compromise the faster, more accurate third normal form model. Still, we encourage enterprises to build enterprise data with third normal form models that require minimal denormalization of data.

▶ Phase 1: Analysis & Design

Almost half the time allotted for the project will be spent on analyzing business requirements and designing the technological solution necessary for meeting them. The reason is that the results that will be achieved using a data warehouse cannot be predicted to the last percentile, and therefore enough time should be spent on careful preparation (Bhend, 1999). In order to promote a mutual understanding, the results of each step should be discussed with the customer who should formally accept these results.

Demand Analysis

The demand for a data warehouse will usually arise because a department, or business unit, has problems that cannot be solved by more traditional approaches. Often, the data necessary to solve the problems have already existed, but were not available or accessible. Therefore, one of the first orders of business is to find out if this data can be provided in the data warehouse, so that there will be no illusions as to how useful the data warehouse is going to be.

Analyze Business Needs

Each data warehouse project will begin with the analysis of business transactions. By interviewing members of several corporate departments, who are potential users of the data warehouse, the project team will determine the kind of business questions that a data warehouse is supposed to answer. The main thrust of activities will be to evaluate and prioritize the questions to be answered, considering the available data. Limitations regarding the availability or quality of data will usually result in putting business transactions with a high priority on a back burner, until the appropriate data become available.

Evaluate Data Sources

First, the potential data sources already identified are characterized by describing, both technologically and by content, the data elements to be extracted, and by describing the amount of data to be expected. If interfaces to other systems are already in place, it will check if they can be exploited for the Data Warehouse. The team will also pay attention to the availability of this data, and to the possibility of transferring them to the Data Warehouse.

Data Quality Test

Frequently, the data quality of operational systems is overestimated. Therefore, even a careful analysis of the source systems should be bolstered by samples from existing data.

Create Test Data

Customers provide data from their source systems for various quality tests (see Figure 7-4).

Analyze Test Data

Samples are taken from the data, and evaluated according to various criteria. Of course, the content-related quality of this data cannot be verified. For this, the team will have to rely on statements from expert users of these operative systems.

Task	Days	Position	Month 1					Month 2				
			W1	W2	W3	W4	W5	W6	W7	W8	W9	W1
Analysis & Design	*40*											
Demand Analysis	**20**											
Analyze Business Needs	10	BC										
Evaluate Data Sources	15	MO										
Data Quality Test	**20**											
Create Test Data	10	(adm)										
Analyze Test Data	10	DB										
Business Data Model (BDM)	**5**											
Design BDM	5	MO										
Accept BDM												
Logical Data Model (LDM)	**15**											
LDM Design	15	MO										
Accept LDM												
Validate Results	5	DWA										
Accept Design												

Figure 7-4. Data models are generated by comparing business needs to data sources.

Business Data Model (BDM)

Starting with the submitted business issues and the demand for information defined by them, a business data model will be created as outlined in Figure 7-5. This data model comprises business objects and the relationships between them.

Tablename	Columnname	Analysis	Value	Occurs	% of Rows
Transaction	Effective_Date	CHAR	19980821	30956	100,00 %

Tablename	Columnname	Analysis	Value	Occurs	% of Rows
Transaction	Key_Level_1	CHAR	ALL	30953	99,99 %
		CHAR	V01	3	0,01 %

Tablename	Columnname	Analysis	Value	Occurs	% of Rows
Transaction	Key_Level_2	CHAR	DPC	12466	40,27 %
		CHAR	DTX	9080	29,33 %
		CHAR	FEA	7199	23,26 %
		CHAR	DIS	2050	6,62 %
		CHAR	DPD	98	0,32 %
		CHAR	AD	58	0,19 %
		CHAR	CB	3	0,01 %
		CHAR	DCR	2	0,01 %

Tablename	Columnname	Analysis	Value	Occurs	% of Rows
Customer	Account_Conversion_Date	CHAR	19930917	33695	55,09 %
	Active_Merchant_Indi	CHAR	N	31149	50,93 %
	Advice_Correspondence_Indi	CHAR	1	53846	88,04 %
	Affinity_ID	CHAR	_SPACE_	61061	99,83 %
	Agent_Control_Accnt_Nr	CHAR	_SPACE_	61164	100,00 %
	Agent_Relationship_Indi	CHAR	N	61164	100,00 %
	Allow_Dscnt_Credit_Indi	CHAR	Y	60945	99,64 %
	Alt_Accnt_Company_ID	CHAR	00000	61164	100,00 %
	Alt_Accnt_Nr	CHAR	000000000000000000000000	37904	61,97 %
	Alt_Accnt_Title	CHAR	_SPACE_	61164	100,00 %
	Alt_Accnt_TR_Nr	CHAR	0000000000	37900	61,96 %
	Apply_Minimum_to_Dscnt_Indi	CHAR	N	47816	78,18 %

Figure 7-5. Analyzing the contents of data by defining threshold values.

- Typical business objects: customers, orders, products.
- Relationships correspond to business rules, such as: A customer can have received one or more orders. One order cannot relate to more than one customer.

Logical Data Model (LDM)

The logical data model in a normalized form is derived from the BDM (Moss, 1998). Attributes are added to the business objects (entities) and their relationships are represented by keys. Figures 7-6 and 7-7 illustrate an LDM expanded by history tables for selected attributes, such as *Customer* and *Contract*. The entity *Distr_Channel* refers back to itself, and thus indicates a multilayered distribution hierarchy.

The LDM is not bound to any platform, or database, and is created independently from physical restrictions.

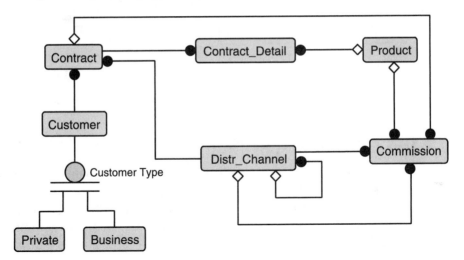

Figure 7-6. Example for a business data model regarding a sales division.

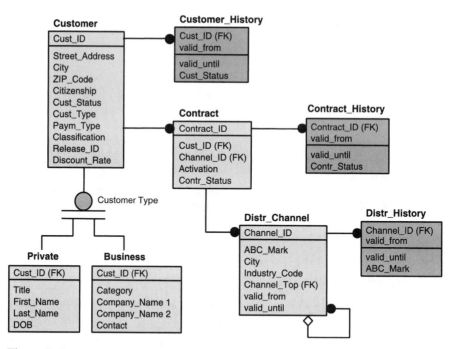

Figure 7-7. Example of a logical data model with historical tracking in some fields.

Validation of Results

The design must be reviewed before its implementation begins. The question must be asked: Does it really generate the benefits originally associated with it? If not, then this is the time when a company can still cancel the project without losing much, as the resources committed to the project to date—financial and otherwise—have not been large.

A review should focus on the following issues:

- **Function**

    This evaluation examines the processes that a data warehouse's implementation is to support. It also asks if the system, as proposed, fulfills the users' needs, and if the benefits it offers are clearly recognizable. This part of the review verifies that the system to be implemented will meet the company's requirements.

- **Technology**

  The technological review looks for system- or data-related obstacles that may hamper the implementation or even make it impossible. It also includes the question of whether the internal IT resources of the company are adequate for running the data warehouse, so that it will fulfill its potential. If there are not enough qualified employees, it may be better to postpone the project.

- **Acceptance**

  This part of the evaluation will determine what impact a data warehouse will have on the users' working habits, and how they will react to changes in their environment. The company should plan information campaigns and workshops early-on in the project to increase the employees' acceptance of the data warehouse.

▶ Phase 2: Implementation

Figure 7-8 shows the timeline in the implementation phase, when the actual data warehouse system is built. If the team has the necessary resources, several steps can be taken simultaneously. Some steps require more resources than others. For instance, programming the interfaces and transferring the data are very resource-intensive. Developing a sequence control does not require quite as many resources, but does need its fair share, as extensive testing is necessary. By contrast, building data marts may only be required if the performance is not sufficient.

Physical Data Model (PDM)

The physical data model implements the logical data model in an actual database system and is optimized toward its features. Ideally, the structure of the LDM can be transferred to the physical database design without major changes (see Figure 7-9).

Task	Days	Position	Month 3						Month 4			
			W8	W9	W10	W11	W12	W13	W14	W15	W16	W1
Implementation	*45*											
Physical Data Model (PDM)	**10**											
Design PDM	10	DB										
Accept PDM												
Interface Programs	**25**											
Extract Data from Source Systems	20	(adm)										
Transform Data into Data Warehouse	20	DB										
Data Load	**30**											
Provide Historical Data	10	(adm)										
Initial Load	5	DB										
Provide Actual Data	5	(adm)										
Periodical Data Transfer	15	DB										
Concept of Operations	**25**											
Schedule Control	25	DB										
Backup & Recovery	5	SE										
User Access	5	SE										
Aggregations (Data Marts)	**15**											
Design Data Marts	10	MO										
Implement Data Marts	5	DB										
System and Integration Test	5	DWA										
Accept Implementation												

Figure 7-8. During the implementation phase, interface programming and data loading will require the most work.

Interface Programs

The initial steps toward creating interfaces can be taken even before the design has received final approval, because the time needed is sometimes very difficult to calculate. For the data warehouse it would of course be desirable if only the required data—in the correct format—would be delivered. But because this takes extra computing time from the operative systems, this approach is frequently unrealistic.

Extracting Data from Source Systems

The conclusions drawn from analyzing business processes and operative data sources provide a starting point for defining rules regarding the extraction of data from source systems. This allows the creation of interface programs in accordance with the specifications of the physical data model. The expenditure for the programming will increase linearly with the number of interfaces needed.

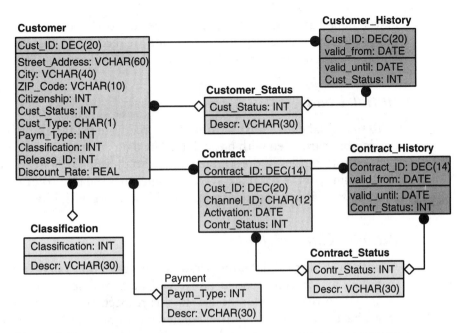

Figure 7-9. Example of a physical data model with historical tables.

Transforming Data into Data Warehouse

As a part of the data warehouse system, interface programs are created that will be appropriate for transforming the data into the relational data model. Depending on the number and diversity of the data sources, additional features must be provided that may be used for combining and comparing data.

Data Loading

As with programming the interfaces, loading the data can also be subject to delays, the primary reasons being that the data quality is bad, or that the delivery of the data from the source systems is unstable.

Provide Historical Data

For initially filling the data warehouse, historical data are usually provided, so that it will be possible to work immediately with values related to the past. If old backup tapes are used as a source, the problem arises that newer data have often changed with regard to formats and contents. However, unpleasant surprises of this kind are recognizable early on, at the latest when test data are provided for a data evaluation.

Initial Load

With the initial data transfer from the source systems, the empty tables of the database are filled with basic data. The data entered must be provided as fixed-format files in the source systems so they can be loaded using the load routines of the database system. Sometimes the best solution may be to write special loading programs for this one-off initial load.

Provide Current Data

As with the historical data, the person in charge of the system must ensure that the data, usually loaded daily, will be available on time for their transfer into the data warehouse. In this respect, the special limitations regarding the size of the (nightly) batch window must be kept in mind. The same thoughts apply for the loading of weekly or monthly bulk data.

Periodic Data Transfer

During a periodic data transfer, data will be loaded from the source systems into the data warehouse in regular time intervals, according to the procedures determined by the schedule control. Current data will be transferred daily; aggregated data may also be transferred on a monthly basis.

Concept of Operations

The concept of operations describes the technological aspects of the data warehouse system, including:

- listing all data models and programs
- data flow diagrams and interface definitions
- acquisition and maintenance of metadata
- a description of the loading procedures
- instructions for backing up and restoring the system
- the concept for administering user access

Schedule Control

The schedule control regulates all steps taken during the nightly batch data processing. Various checks prevent the data warehouse from loading inconsistent data. Appropriate procedures must be implemented to enable the system to reload data manually if errors occur.

Backup & Recovery

The data in the data warehouse must be backed up regularly; one way is to back up any newly loaded data daily, and to back up the whole data stock on weekends.

Although the data warehouse is not initially a mission critical system, a procedure for restoring its operations must be prepared to be ready in the event of disaster. Therefore, consideration should be given to creating a 'hot site,' which is a duplicate of the original site plus offsite storage capabilities for total backup and recovery capabilities for data.

User Access

Protecting the data from illegal access is a very important point, and failing to protect the data can have legal repercussions. Therefore, the corporate departments and IT must develop a viable concept for ensuring that the data are protected. To have a regulated administration of access will grow ever more important as more and more data are added to the data warehouse.

Aggregations (into Data Marts)

On the level of reports and analyses, people always work with aggregated data. The expected performance determines whether these aggregated data, e.g., monthly sales figures, are also to be stored in the database. Data marts are the appropriate place to store aggregated data together with desired analytic parameters, such as geography or time (Inmon, Imhoff and Sousa, 1998).

Design Data Marts

Data models for data marts are usually implemented as star schemas (see Figure 7-10). While normalized data models represent the relationships between a company's business objects globally, **star-schema data models** are oriented toward the specific needs of a user group. Star schemas include both key figures (facts), mostly in aggregated form, and analytic parameters, so-called dimensions.

Star Schemas have become popular with consultants who wish to provide relatively small amounts of data in a warehouse, and to make reporting the key factor in their analysis activities. Leading data warehouses use star schemas for the user-site database technology, not for the master or major data warehouse schemas. De-normalized data schemas are much more valuable in their ability to allow for users to ask previously unknown questions (or queries) of the data, since they are not pre-designed or pre-prepared for performance considerations (as usually required by most data marts). Data Marts can be normalized (star schema) or de-normalized, depending upon the long term usage plans and the requirements for the usefulness of the database.

Implement Data Marts

Data marts may be implemented either logically or physically.

- **Logical implementation:** As views over the tables of the normalized data model.
- **Physical implementation:** As additional tables in the database, or in the form of an OLAP cube.

If the performance is unsatisfactory when working with views, parts of the views can be realized as physical tables.

System and Integration Test

The implementation phase concludes with a comprehensive test of all features. At this stage, two problems tend to come up much more frequently than others. One is incorrect or inconsistent data, and the other is insufficient query performance.

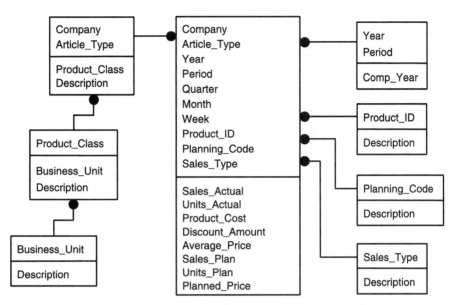

Figure 7-10. Star schema with multilayered dimension tables on the left.

▶ Phase 3: Reports, Queries, and Analytical Uses

Figure 7-11 illustrates the lists of report types and durations required for development. Do not forget meetings and documents for final acceptance of the reports, graphs, charts, and screens. It is usual that in addition to the expected benefits, the participants in a data warehouse project also determine a certain number of reports to be created. Based upon the flexibility of OLAP tools, they tend not to be rigid reports, but rather report types for application in certain situations, such as:

- analysis of customer behavior down to a single customer (Peppers and Rogers, 1998)
- summaries of monthly sales numbers

Task	Days	Position	Month 4				Month 5		
			W14	W15	W16	W17	W18	W19	W
Reports	30								
Set up OLAP Tool	10	AP							
Design Report Types	10	AP							
Develop Report Templates	10	AP							
Accept Reports									

Figure 7-11. The initial report templates for users are derived from various report types.

Based upon this flexibility, the users can employ changeable report templates that will facilitate their introduction to the data warehouse. Figure 7-11 illustrates the span of these activities.

Set Up OLAP Tool

As the logical data model is transformed into a physical database design, so the OLAP tool represents data in accordance with the data models used. Most OLAP tools allow access to normalized and denormalized data (models).

Designing Report Types

The report design activity is primarily aimed at transforming user requirements into concrete analyses. Therefore, it is important that similar requirements are bundled, and represented by one report type. Thus, it is easier for other user groups to reuse reports by adapting them to their field.

For instance, a time series analysis with a graphical representation of one department's sales figures (as shown in Figure 7-12) can be adapted by other departments with only small modifications.

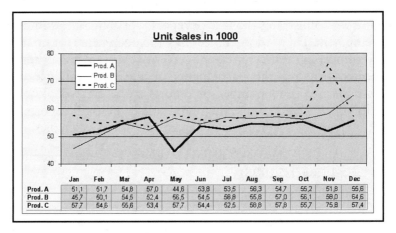

Figure 7-12. Example of the report type "Time Series Analysis".

Developing Report Templates

Report templates are very helpful for introducing new user groups to the data warehouse: the users can start their first queries quickly, and the templates are easily adaptable to individual needs.

Supporting Activities

Installation: Hardware and Software and Networking Extensions

Installing a data warehouse includes not only setting up the hardware, but also connecting the data warehouse to the operative systems for loading the data. Figure 7-13 shows the time of these activities.

Training (IT and Users)

An intensive training will be offered for both system administrators and end users. Experience has shown, however, that the expenditure for training can be cut dramatically if a person works with the project team on getting the data warehouse up and running. Training is an essential ingredient for success of your project. Investments in training are sometimes overlooked and this is a big mistake. Investments in culture transitions, system and application usage, and concepts of queries will drive higher return-on-investment to the business.

Conclusion—100 Days to Success !!!

Building a data warehouse in 100 days is feasible. There have been successful data warehouse projects at real customers' sites that followed this timetable, and produced a fully functional data warehouse as described above. Therefore, this chapter can help you to begin your focus on the elements and frameworks for a practical guide for your own project.

Task	Days	Position	Month 3					Month 4				
			W9	W10	W11	W12	W13	W14	W15	W16	W17	W18
Supporting Activities	50 t											
Installation: HW, SW	10 t	SE										
Training (IT and Users)	20 t	EDUC										

Figure 7-13. In addition to meetings with the customer, installation and training are the most important supporting tasks.

Author's Notes:

Much of this chapter was originally written by Marcel Bhend and edited later by Ronald Swift (ron.swift@ncr.com), with major contributions from the NCR Professional Services Consulting Organization, plus data from many other practitioners who have assisted in the collection of experiencial advices in the case studies in this book, as well contributions from numerous industry experts throughout the world.

Thanks also to The Data Warehouse Institute and Digital Consulting Incorporated (DCI) for support in our efforts. The core of experience written about here is from the experience of hundreds of consultants at NCR Professional Services who contributed to the successful DWs over the past fifteen years.

Critical Success Factors for CRM and DW

When formulating objectives for an enterprise or even a project, there should always be a set of specific criteria for success. Until the latter part of the twentieth century, the phrasing of these objectives, or goals, into a concise set of measurements and known (or communicated) achievement-oriented statements did not become prevalent. The term now commonly used is *Critical Success Factors (CSF)*.

In this chapter, you will read about numerous suggestions on "success criteria" and "questions" to ask your providers/vendors/partners that should enable you to increase your success rate of implementations and also your contribution to your enterprise. These viewpoints are included to assist you in accelerating your contribution while also providing leadership strategies. They range from strategic, to project, to vendor selection, to business user support, all for your review.

During my time with IBM in the 1970s and 1980s, we promulgated the use of "CSF" terminology. In 1961, U.S. President John F. Kennedy gave a speech about the expectations of new goals for NASA. His hallmark management statement, subsequently used in many academic and business circles as *the* simplest—but yet most profound—statement of success criteria, was: *"We will put a man on the moon, by the end of this decade (1960's), and bring him back safely."* His statement to the people at NASA, the American public, and to the world clearly stated the objective, the timeframe of the project/activities, and the criteria for successful completion. (The only major item missing was the investment or cost of the resources to achieve the objective within the timeframe.) All of the thousands of contractors and government employees then knew the goal (or CSF) and, even after Kennedy's tragic death, the dream and goal lived on. As the years moved on, each success generated additional project milestones, CSFs, and incremental re-investment.

The formal use of the term *CSF* was originated by Dr. John F. Rockart and his team at MIT's Sloan School of Business in the late 1970s. Rockart's premise was an interviewing procedure to determine those factors that were critical to the business and were of such importance that the organization could not succeed without them. His use of the criteria clearly set them above all other objectives, strategies, or goals.

In Rockart's article in the April 1979 edition of the Harvard Business Review, he enumerated his initial findings from reviews with leading executives of major firms throughout the USA. Rockart found a number of strategic issues and one startling fact:

Most executives do not appreciate the value achieved from the investments made in information technology.

Executives receive little feedback or formal reporting on the usage, value, and transformations achieved by IT organizations and their stakeholders. Mainly because there are no CSFs for IT.

This reminds me of the famous line from the movie "Cool Hand Luke," starring Paul Newman: "What we have here is a failure to communicate." And that is the key issue and challenge to all business and technology managers throughout the world.

Many of the Directors of Data Processing, VPs of Information Systems, and the newly-crowned CIOs required a clearer vision of their opportunity for success.

One such VP of IT was John Eggerding at St. Louis Union Trust Company, which subsequently merged into Centerre Trust, then Boatmen's Bank (now merged into Nation's Bank). John was a favorite because he had three characteristics which tested our philosophies, theories, and practices:

1. Senior management needed to more clearly understand the true value of IT.

2. Their IT team was managed through a specific budget and had specific projects and deadlines, but required additional vision of what could be achieved for the entire enterprise.
3. The receptivity of ideas and allowance for continuing change.
4. All these made the communications and the business relationship profitable for both sides. John and his management team utilized the CSFs listed below as did many others throughout the world.

The CSF for Success:

Create and Communicate Value and Contribution

Before we begin itemizing several sets of CSFs for your management team to strategize upon, let's spend a few moments defining the base for this chapter's significant knowledge and examples.

There can be several levels of CSF that organizations have successfully forged. Some CSF pertain to the highest of strategic issues and priorities, and some relate to, or are driven by, the lower levels of the organization into departments and even work groups. Whichever is the case for you and your CRM team, you can use this philosophy and process. We hope you learn from the research cited, questions and hints provided, and practical experiences itemized in this book.

▶ Strategic "IT and Business" Enterprise CSFs

Let's begin with a high-level, strategic set of CSFs to focus on key elements of your business and your customers at the same time. These seven CSFs were initially presented to provoke thought and conversation to build a more purified set of CSFs, but they can stand as-is for your organization. They include:

1. Planning and setting the direction
2. Service and communication management
3. Relationship technology strategies
4. Personnel development and enterprise management
5. Information and asset protection
6. Process and application strategies
7. Contribution

Planning and Setting the Direction

Determining your strategy and defining your mission, goals, and expectations of management, employees, stockholders, partners/channels, and customers is essential. This has been excellently stated as "vision" by some of the recen great business leaders. Driving the CSFs into allocation of resources and definition of how the organization will support the CSFs through their own goals is a process that must be accomplished. Finally, there must be executive commitment to these plans and allocations of resources. The achievements will be reported and analyzed in the final CSF: Contribution.

Service and Communication Management

Providing quality services and support for both your customers and your internal organizations can make or break any organization. Most negative experiences that I have witnessed have a breakdown of support for processes that are essential for servicing either or both internal or external constituents. Establishing exciting and acceptable external marketing communications and integration of your communications facilities are key, whether they are telephone, Internet, email, e-commerce, or personal contact devices.

Technology Relationship Strategies

Every organization, large or small, should have an effective strategy to maintain forward movement and also determine actions required to ensure the organization is successful. Integrating the communication and delivery systems, through an info-structure described in this book, provides advanced and flexible linkages to all parties involved in your success.

The integration of technologies to achieve your objectives determines your ability to change your processes quickly to meet market needs, and to be responsive to your internal and external customers.

Positioning for the unknown, through information and communications technologies, can mean the difference between a follower and a leader in most industries or governments today.

Including on-going training or educational learning on how to better utilize the technologies is also a very important part of this strategy. This can be accomplished through electronic or physical learning technologies to educate and inspire the recipient. Most formal classroom or structure learning sessions are boring, and can create a wall-of-refusal on the part of employees, associates, partners, and channels.

Customers appreciate creative learning techniques when doing business with you and also to make use of your electronic tools to benefit themselves or their organizations. Integrating your technology into that of your customer drives a stronger business linkage, and it is therefore more difficult to sever later on in the business relationship. This will become a key part of CRM for your team.

Personnel Development and Enterprise Management

Improving organizational effectiveness, through personnel productivity and inter-departmental cooperation with communication drives the enterprise to handle customer requests, develop new products and services, and forge new relationships.

People make the difference. They always have and always will, even in an electronic (non-personal) environment. People communicate to each other their knowledge and experiences *and* their perception of value.

Repeat business, in a relationship which drives Life-Time Value, is built upon the trust of people (who make up the organization). Although some businesses will come and go, especially in the commodity worlds of pricing and fast delivery, it is service and people that make the difference and which will provide the highest contribution to the growth of any enterprise. This can be at the highest or lowest levels of any organization, and the investments you make in your people will show in the long run.

Setting objectives for personnel productivity should not only be centered on transaction volume, but on development of the business and/or increasing the value of the relationship to both sides of the business equation. Too often businesses seek the "order" instead of growing the business, over the longer term, through meaningful relationship management.

To achieve your goal, concentrate on the work environment, user's tools to achieve people's goals, information to manage processes, and education/training to develop people's knowledge and skills. This must be a key investment strategy for long-term growth and strength for an organization to have great success. (Note: in all too many cases, when a company is having profit problems, it tends to reduce this area of its present budgets and future investments. This is a major mistake and has been proven so.)

Information and Asset Protection (Including Privacy Issues)

Protecting and securing your corporate assets is mandatory (and in some countries there are penalties for not assuring protection). Information is a key asset of any enterprise. Customer information may be the most valuable asset of some organizations.

Developing and setting enterprise rules, guidelines, standards, and policies are surely required. The effective enterprise communicates the actions required, responsibilities of management and employees, and assigns individual responsibilities to such tasks.

Establishing accountability and reporting processes will provide a clearer understanding as well as a reduction in risk for your enterprise. All too often these tasks are assigned to low-level people, with little specific knowledge of the value of these tasks, and also little or no reporting on the completion or enhancement to this process.

In the electronic world of today, customer privacy issues are extremely important. See Chapters 10 and 11 for this issue.

Resource Investments and Application Strategies

Managing customers through information technologies requires a strategy for an extensive portfolio of investments in resources and applications of information technologies. Defining a short-term vs. long-term portfolio of technology investments, tied to specific processes and applications, usable by both internal and external parties, is essential for initiation and growth of the business relationship.

Implementing decision support, analytical processes, and systems (i.e., data warehouse, data mining, knowledge discovery, knowledge management systems) enables enterprise management to continuously learn by doing. Merging and reconciling data into information in a centralized repository enables sharing or distribution of the new "Single Version of the Truth" environment with the info-structure. This environment also generates numerous undefined questions, or queries, which drive more questions to the system and its information.

The transformation from data into information is the core of the data warehouse infrastructure. But the usefulness of the information *and* the transformation of the information into knowledge (and then actionizing it) are much more productive, and therefore profitable.

Determining the resource investments requires information from the past, prediction of potentials in the future, and a set of CSFs which drive toward making the right decisions. Decisions on allocations of resources started in the *Planning CSF* and continue here.

Contribution

The ultimate CSF is **contribution** to the enterprise, business unit, project, team, or task.

The most effective management teams reward their people appropriately when communicating specific contributions.

This ensures an understanding of multiple factors in their quest for success. These include everything from financial factors, to personnel factors, to customer sales or growth factors, to channel management measurements, to margin factors, to profitability factors, to stock price factors, and even customer satisfaction factors.

Contribution measurements should be based on more than past performance for a period, more than just present performance (although that is important), *and* use projections of opportunities (and/or customer propensities through customer histories) which culminate in intelligent allocations of resources (financial and physical).

If positioning is half the game in an electronic world, then building the info-structure and making it available to all appropriate parties for their interactions and transactions, drive the highest of opportunities (even before the portals or connection are opened).

When an organization, a team, or an individual person contributes to the enterprise, there should be public recognition of the achievements *and* the explanation of why it is so important to everyone. This drives other people to contribute more and more.

▶ Information Infra-Structure CSFs

Over the years, leading organizations have succeeded in accelerating their abilities to communicate and manage their customers effectively through information technology by enumerating "learned valuable lessons." As you invest in an increasingly important "info-structure" for decision-making and customer relationships, you should include:

1. Identifying and prioritizing issues carefully
2. Managing expectations through small successes
3. Creating appropriate cost justification measures
4. Delivering substantive depth of information
5. Defining requirements for decision information
6. Creating a single, complete view of the customer
7. Forging a business and IT "team"

The best CSF trick seems to be to build an "iterative process" for learning and action.

Customer-Centricity Information and Application Systems

The information systems discussed in this book are related to managing customers and channels to increase profitability, service, marketing, business velocity, and long-term growth.

The integrated CRM flow and process includes:

1. knowledge discovery
2. market planning
3. customer interaction
4. analysis and refinement

To develop an ongoing strategic and tactical process, you will need to consider multiple processes to create a total iterative flow of learning and action. By sequencing the functions and the analytics into the process, you then integrate an ongoing process.

In Figure 8-1, you will find an example of the flow of the integrated CRM and DW process for success.

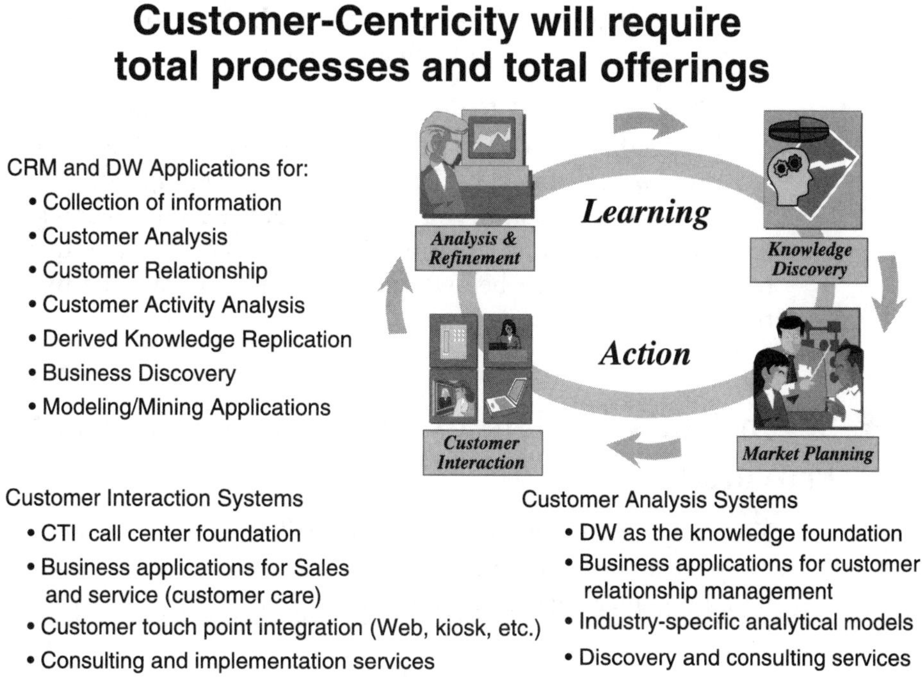
Customer-Centricity will require
total processes and total offerings
CRM and DW Applications for:
• Collection of information
• Customer Analysis
• Customer Relationship
• Customer Activity Analysis
• Derived Knowledge Replication
• Business Discovery
• Modeling/Mining Applications
Analysis & Refinement
Learning
Knowledge Discovery
Action
Customer Interaction
Market Planning
Customer Interaction Systems
• CTI call center foundation
• Business applications for Sales and service (customer care)
• Customer touch point integration (Web, kiosk, etc.)
• Consulting and implementation services
Customer Analysis Systems
• DW as the knowledge foundation
• Business applications for customer relationship management
• Industry-specific analytical models
• Discovery and consulting services

Figure 8.1. The CRM Iterative Learning Process

Guidelines for Success—Knowing Your Providers

This section is intended as a guideline to help you decipher significant questions and delineators for your success. The ideas and questions here are drawn from experience with consultants, vendors, and developers of successful information infrastructures for decision-making and management of customers. It also includes suggestions and "words of wisdom" from hundreds of conference sessions and numerous industry publications.

When discussing a provider's previous experiences in the field that you require their product or services, ***references*** can be misleading, either intentionally or otherwise. By asking the proper questions, you can better understand what is really going on. By understanding the reference sites, you can better understand the suitability, viability, and potential success of a particular solution for your environment.

Why references? Vendors and customers make a lot of claims. It would be difficult to cite an example where claims and reality are so widely separated without going back to the days of traveling snake oil salespeople. By visiting reference sites, you can understand exactly what is going on and translate that to your situation. Simply stated, effective questioning of references (as shown below) allows you to separate the hype from the truth.

Seven Rules for Discussions with CRM Solution Providers

Keep the following rules in mind when talking with a provider's references. They are all just common sense, but it's very easy to lose sight of possible miscommunications if you are not careful.

Rule Number 1: Never Take a Vendor's Claims at Face Value.

Many "facts" are significantly distorted by the time they get to you. For example, consider the simple statement, "MegaCorp has a data warehouse exactly like you want." Some quick questions: What does MegaCorp mean by "data warehouse"? Is it the same thing your vendor representative means? Is it the same thing you mean? How much actual data is on it? What type of user access is allowed? By directly asking MegaCorp, you can understand what they are doing and make an informed decision.

Rule Number 2: Never Assume a Vendor Reference Is Valid.

The biggest mistake you could make is to assume any reference a vendor provides must be a good one—after all, who would give you a bad reference? Many vendors provide references and pray you do not check them out. Who would give you a bad reference? A vendor who couldn't come up with a good one.

If a vendor throws a customer name out during a sales call, make a note of it. Don't be shy—call the company on your own. If the vendor says the system is for risk management, ask the switchboard to speak to anyone in risk management—then ask who is in charge. Always start with the users when using this approach. They are generally very happy to talk about what their information systems (IS) organization has accomplished or failed to deliver.

Rule Number 3: Always Talk with the Reference's IS Staff.

The IS organization supports this environment. They are aware of the issues confronting them. Talk with them to get a sense of what they are facing on a daily basis.

Rule Number 4: Never Take IS Claims at Face Value.

Yes, the IS organization is important, but there are problems with relying too heavily on them. First, the IS folks you talk with will most likely be the same ones who made the original vendor decision. If they just spent $20 million on a disaster, do you really think they are going to tell you?

The most common IS response when a system does not work as anticipated is to simply redefine the problem. If the system cannot handle the ad hoc processing requirements, simply redefine it as pre-defined access only. IS can get away with this for one simple reason: They do not live with the system, they only babysit. This leads to rule number 5.

Rule Number 5: Always Talk with the Users of the System.

Users determine the real value of the system, because they are the only ones who have to live with the system; they are the ones trying to solve business issues; they are the drivers of a data warehouse. You must understand if the system does what they expected, and you must understand how their expectations match yours.

Make sure you involve your users in this conversation. This accomplishes a couple of things. First, it gets user involvement at an early stage. If a data warehouse project is going to be successful, you will need their involvement. Second, the users understand the business impact of what their counterparts are saying. If a reference user says, "It's fine, but I can't run these queries," does that matter? It may be the single most crucial issue to your users.

Rule Number 6: Always Talk Without the Vendor Present.

If a vendor has chosen a site as a reference, it is likely they have a good relationship with at least part of that organization. If there are problems, it is less likely you will hear an honest appraisal if the vendor is in the same room. If the vendor's product works, then this should not be an issue for them.

Rule Number 7: Always Talk with the Users Without the IS Organization Present.

In many organizations there is a strained relationship between the users and the IS organization. These tensions make it unlikely that you will get an open, honest opinion if they are in the same room. Divide and understand.

▶ Business Questions and Issues

Before you can effectively use a reference, you must have a good idea of what you are trying to accomplish with your data warehouse. Unlike traditional systems, these definitions might be somewhat fuzzy.

For example, consider one of the most common requirements of a decision support, marketing analysis, or data warehouse environment: Be able to answer any reasonable business question with no worse than overnight turnaround. How do you translate this into a tangible deliverable? The point here is you might not know exactly where you are going, but some quick introspection can save you a lot of trouble down the road. Below are some simple questions to ask yourself before checking references.

Internal Question 1: How Is Your Risk Tolerance?

This question has many facets. There is **tangible business value** to building a info-structure or implementing "relationship technologies." This implies there is risk in not being successful, or in only being partially successful.

What is the **business impact** of a delayed implementation? If the product you choose is difficult to set up and tune, delays are likely. If you are relying on a product that has not yet been released, you cannot be sure it will work in production. What is the impact if the new release does not work? What is the impact if the release is delayed six months? A year? Two years?

What is the impact if the product you choose simply will not work? Can you really afford to start again? Can you afford to re-define the problem to match what you've built?

How is the vendor support? You cannot build and support this environment on your own. If you must train the vendor every step of the way, what is the risk of failure?

Can you afford to be the first site? There can be strategic advantages to being first, but there is always significant pain and/or risk as well.

Internal Question 2: Is Your System Mission Critical?

Don't answer this one too quickly. If it's not mission critical today, how quickly will it become critical? Hopefully, you are implementing relationship technologies because there is a business reason to do so, and business issues are mission critical. While many info-structures do not start off as mission critical environments, they very quickly become so important that you have difficulty scheduling preventative maintenance. If your answer to this question is "No," then you need to ask yourself another question: "Why are we building this?"

Internal Question 3: What Is Your Processing Environment?

Do you require iterative processing? It would be difficult to overstate the implications of this response. Iterative processing means an unpredictable environment, and an unpredictable environment means more complex support. For example, in a traditional systems environment, database administrators (DBAs) tune all queries. In the iterative environment, this is simply not feasible. Your database marketing people will need to take over much of the work you used to rely on DBAs to do. The real value is in the ability to ask unpredictable questions and get a quick response. If the users are asking for the moon, it's probably because they need to get to Saturn to be competitive but do not think Saturn can be reached. They've already lowered their expectations based on past experience—be careful not to lower them any further.

Internal Question 4: How Much Data Do You Have?

This is a tricky question. Don't worry about how much data is on your archive tapes; it's compressed, it's blocked, and it's not all useful data. When you have completed a logical model, how much data is out there to support it? Now, multiply by ten. Why ten? This is a fairly average increase in data volume over the first two to five years of data warehouse or relationship technologies.

When you check the references, be very careful on this point. Vendors like to tell you how much disk space their systems support. More often than not, this indicates the shortcomings of the database managers, not the amazing data volumes they can access. It is not unusual to find systems in excess of 1 terabyte of disk to support less than 100 Gigabytes of real data. Before you know if the solutions can support your data volumes, you must know what your data volumes are.

Consider this question in conjunction with your level of risk tolerance. The largest reference out there for a product got there through much pain. Can you afford to be larger? Can you afford to be as big? Can you even afford to be within 80% of it?

Internal Question 5: How Many *Concurrent Users* Will There Be?

While this is not as easy to predict as it is in a traditional systems environment, reasonable estimates must be attempted. A system that runs well with one user might turn out to be the world's most expensive personal computer.

In analytical systems it is very common for there to be dozens or even hundreds of users all asking questions (queries) at the same time (when many of these interactions are not pre-defined or pre-coded). The most effective analytical systems provide for any question, at any time, to any data (correlations, as an example), to any user for any potential business opportunities.

In customer relationship systems, such as on the Internet and e-commerce, there is a requirement for more users to access more data in order to be able to make more decisions in an instantaneous timeframe. Be prepared to discuss vast magnitudes of scalability and performance requirements if your system is being opened to your customers and outside users (prospects or channels).

Information Technology Questions

The first thing to determine when speaking with the IS organization is that you are indeed talking with the right people. If they cannot answer simple questions like these, they are probably not the people you need to see. As you ask these questions, it is likely that they will generate additional leads to follow. Be alert. If something does not seem to add up, ask them why.

The questions are divided into three subject areas: System Size, System Utilization, and System Administration.

IS people can give you a great deal of solid background information, but, remember, it is highly unlikely that they know the answer to the two most important questions: "How does the system meet the business requirements?" and "How much of a contribution to the business has the system provided?"

IT Question 1: How Big Is the System?

Look here for the number of processors, the amount of memory, the amount of disk storage (also known as total disk space), and the number of processing nodes (there may be dozens or hundreds in a parallel processing system). Please note that the answer to this question by itself is of extremely limited value. Once you understand how big the system is, you must also understand what type of environment it's supporting. This will give you a good indication of how large a system you can expect to need.

Let's follow a real-life example of system size. The vendor has told you about a 1.4 TeraByte site for a data warehouse. The reference's answer to question 1 is ONE Terabyte. OK, so what's 400 Gigabytes between friends? No big deal, we only need to bring up 500 Gigabytes of data, or half the reference size.

Be specific in understanding size, real data, used data, historical data, index data, standard reporting data, multi-dimensional data in a cube/file/database, and also differentiate the data that is in summaries or summary tables (which are accessed easily, but provide little or minimum value).

IT Question 2: How Much Detail User Data Is on the System?

You have to ask this directly, but it is unlikely the answer you get will be correct. Few people take into account the impact of free space and block factors, although they can consume considerable unused space on the system. Many people include mirrored data or indexes as part of the user data. The need to mirror, the number of indexes, the impact of data blocks, and the amount of free space required will depend greatly by product. Ask this question, then dig deeper with the following questions. (In the example above: there's about 700 Gigabytes of user data.)

IT Question 3: How Much Index Space Is on the System?

The amount of index space is going to depend entirely on the database managers. Most references will include index space when they first answer question 2.

Our example: there's 400 Gigabytes of indexes. (Don't laugh, this number is actually low for many sites.) That leaves us with 300 Gigabytes of data.

IT Question 4: How Much Summary Data Is on the System?

The strange thing about summaries is the number of them it takes to be useful. If you summarize on one set of criteria for one question, you will probably need to summarize on another set for the next question. Systems that rely on summaries quickly contain more summary data than detail data.

Our example: let's be generous and only assume 100 Gigabytes of summaries. Now we're at 200 Gigabytes of data.

IT Question 5: Do Some Applications Go Against Specific Sets of Tables?

They might not call it summary data, but if they have designed certain tables for specific applications, they are probably not accessing part of the detail data base. Some vendors claim 3 TeraByte data warehouses, when closer inspection reveals 3,000 unrelated data bases of about 1 Gigabytes each.

Our example: let's say we find a very conservative 20 Gigabytes. We're now left with 180 Gigabytes of data.

IT Question 6: How Much Workspace Is on the System?

Workspace takes on many flavors. There is workspace required for temporary database work areas and workspace required for sort activities. For some systems, there is also workspace required for staging data from the source systems. This is particularly true if the source system is a mainframe.

Our example: let's say they tell us 300 Gigabytes. This is the difference between our original 1 TeraByte system size and the original claim of 700 Gigabytes of detailed user data. Now their original number makes sense. We're still at 180 Gigabytes of data.

IT Question 7: Are the Data Mirrored for Recovery?

On most systems, a disaster recovery plan involving system reloads is not feasible. Be particularly careful of true fault-tolerant environments, where everything, including work spaces, is mirrored.

Our example: yes. Now we're at 90 Gigabytes of data—less than 20% of what the business needs, and we still don't know about free space. So much for the 1.4 Terabytes reference site. This example shows the nonsense and games that you will experience if you do not do your homework and plan for the questions you really need to get answered.

Now that we've figured out how big the system really is, let's look at how it's being used. The big question in this section is if they are using it in a manner similar to your needs.

IT Question 8: Who Are the Users?

Which departments are using the system? For example, if the answer is customer service, there is a good chance the system is really a call center application. Make sure the user departments are the same ones you plan to support. Make sure they are the people you are meeting with later.

IT Question 9: Do These Users Have Direct Access to the DW Corporate Historical Detailed Data?

Now you know how much data is on the system and who uses it. There is still a good chance that the database managers cannot support access to the detail. Look for clues like PC download files or departmental summaries for the users. Or, in some cases, preloaded (nightly) summaries and details by division or locations. This is because of major performance limitations of the central enterprise system or the inability (or lack of knowledge in the IT organization) to manage both normalized and/or de-normalized information databases.

Many organizations familiar with transactional databases for customer accounting and product or financial invoicing do not really know how to build an analytical decision support, managerial planning, or customer interactive environment. Not having direct access to detailed DW data is a major limitation. Your architecture or plan uses business applications, and managerial applications should provide access to the master repository of historical detailed data.

IT Question 10: How Many Users Utilize this System?

How many users were on it initially? How many are on it today? Data warehouses increase every year in data volume, number of users, and number of daily queries. The percentage of iterative queries also increases as the users become more familiar with the system. Indications to the contrary are generally signs that the system is not providing what the users need from a data warehouse.

One company I heard present at a conference told of their great data warehouse system. It was an IBM MVS Mainframe environment, and at first they were concerned that the resources required by the additional TSO (time-sharing) address spaces would cripple their system. To their surprise, the number of users had dropped by nearly 80% in the first two weeks. IS took this as a sign that their users had "become smart about how to use the system."

A call to their primary business user confirmed what some had suspected: they gave up because it did not work. And it took the users less than two weeks to reach this conclusion.

IT Question 11: How Many *Concurrent Users* Are Supported?

How many different people can concurrently use the database system for basic or complex queries and be logged on at the same time? How many different queries are running concurrently? How many of the queries are likely to be doing iterative processing, how many are repetitive, and how many fail to complete their total problem solution?

Many products allow you to tune the amount of parallelism on a query by query basis. While this has benefits in a very low concurrency environment, it can create problems in an environment with a high degree of change or growth. You may have to tune down the level of parallelism as the number of users increases, and sometimes limited computing environments must often turn parallelism off completely to support as few as a dozen users.

IT Question 12: What Types of Access Are Supported?

Is there any iterative processing allowed at all? Be careful of distinctions here. Some environments call things like multi-dimensional analysis ad-hoc processing. Ad-hoc processing means you can ask anything.

Some systems allow you to change parameters, e.g., date ranges or customer numbers. This is still repetitive processing—the questions you can ask are all pre-determined. These are not ad-hoc queries, this is changing the pre-defined fields or columns of data or characteristics, and does not allow for true, timely creativity in asking questions. People learn by inquiring, trying, doing, then measuring in ways they never thought of before.

The most valuable uses of decision support, DW, or analytical systems allow for complex, parallel, detailed data, historical, correlation (or complex modeling) queries that define whole new opportunities. Wal-Mart stores makes major decisions every moment of every day on what to do with their inventories, supply chain elements, prices, and future allocations of resources.

IT Question 13: Was this Designed to Replace Another System?

Sometimes systems are put in to replace older technology that is either out of date, not meeting user requirements, or simply does not fit into IT's overall architectural vision. If this is the case, what did the old system do? Is it still supported? If it's still there, it's unlikely the new system really meets its objectives.

What will the new system do and provide (in info-structure) that enables the employees and management to think, learn, and do?

Although analytical or relationship technologies decision support systems are different from traditional computer systems, they do share some common characteristics.

IT Question 14: What Are the Data Sources?

The data sources should be consistent with the user community and overall goal of the system. If, for instance, a financial DW has the Human Resources system as its primary input, there is probably a problem somewhere. The required financial systems probably have too much detail for the database managers of the data warehouse to handle. This answer is not appropriate. We are handling customers and must know about financial transactions, rebates, payments, refunds, costs, resource allocations, margins, and so on. We may be in the process of negotiating a major new contract for new prices, new services, or new channels. Quality detailed data is essential.

IT Question 15: What Is the "Batch" Window?

Knowing the time limitations and asking questions about loading are very important to your future success. You must get data into the warehouse, and, unless you have *a lot* of money, you must delete old data off the system. How often is this done, and how long does it take? What is the standard in *your* industry? What do *your* customers, channels, or partners expect of *you*?

IT Question 16: How Do You Get Data In?

What is the physical process for loading data? Are utilities available? How much work is required to set it up? How much work is required every month to make sure it works? What is the physical process to move data from the operational environment to the warehouse? Does data have to be staged? Careful—data staging generally indicates a serious problem in the ability of the traditional database to handle effective management techniques.

Mainframe databases also want you to copy the data, or stage it, because they cannot handle loading the data directly and distributing it evenly into the DW database for effective performance. Using people to define data spaces, changing space allocations due to data volumes, and defining segments of the database all require time.

People are required to do all of these detailed tasks. If people are the roadblock to loading data, they will also be a part of the problem in providing access, distributing, tuning, and managing the database itself.

IT Question 17: How Do You Get Data Out?

Most people do not think about this issue until it's too late: If you add 20 Gigabytes of data tonight, you will probably need to delete 20 Gigabytes of data tonight. How are you going to remove the oldest time series data within a realistic batch window? Are utilities available? How do these utilities maintain data integrity?

IT Question 18: Can I See the Data Model?

The logical model should match the physical model. Any deviation indicates a potentially serious performance issue with the database management system. Ask them to explain each variation. Every deviation restricts the users' ability to conduct iterative processing, limits the business value, and adds a support nightmare as the environment evolves. (In order to gain access to some of the industry's leading models, you may need to sign a non-disclosure agreement.)

IT Question 19: Do The DBAs Tune All or Most Queries?

If you need iterative processing, you cannot have database administrators controlling the access or volume of queries in your decision support, analytical, or customer relationship applications. If the DBA controls the access *or* the queries (or even has to build each of them for your business management team), you will have major limitations in your business opportunities.

The system that you invest in for CRM and DW must have the ability to handle future predictive models and applications, and allow for your customers to access their data for decision support or analytical applications. If the most important queries and the volumes of customer data must be managed by humans, you will suffer from having relationship technology that is not of much value to your management team. It may give you the impression that you are leading the world or your competitors, when actually you are not leading. It takes money to have enough people to perform systems administration tasks and also manage the data and the queries.

No one has this much money, and no one has this much time. Many IS directors are unaware of the limitations of their database systems due to the requirements of volumes of DBA activities. Therefore, these managers are also unaware of how they are holding up the progress of their company.

IT Question 20: How Many DBAs and Systems Administrators Does It Take to Really Support the System?

What is the biggest cost in most warehouse environments? Hardware? Software? How about system support? It is a simple equation. Multiply the loaded cost per year for Systems Administrators and Data Base Administrators by the number of people by the number of years you think this system will be in production. It's probably more than the hardware, software, environmental requirements, and maintenance combined.

IT Question 21: If the System Size Doubled Tomorrow, How Many DBAs and SAs Do You Think It Would Take to Support It?

What if the number of users doubled? What if the daily query load doubled? What if the number of concurrent queries doubled? What if the data volume doubled? Are you in an industry that has potential for your enterprise to merge or be a channel with another enterprise? (Most IT people say no, then suddenly it happens to them.) Assume sudden, unexpected growth. Can you still support the business? The Decision Processes? The access to historical detailed data? The volumes of business users? Ad Hoc Queries? Would DBAs easily handle the explosion?

Remember Bank of America and Nations Bank? Think about Chrysler and Daimler. MCI and WorldCom. Union Pacific and Southern Pacific. Toronto Dominion and Waterhouse Securities. AOL and Netscape and Time-Warner and CNN. Wal-Mart and Asda. Pfizer and Warner-Lambert. Or Southwestern Bell Corporation (SBC) and Pacific Telsis, add Ameritech, then add SNET; and many smaller enterprises that join forces.

IT Question 22: What Is the Disaster Recovery Plan?

If the system is truly useful, it is *mission critical*. If it is mission critical, it should have a disaster recovery plan. How long will it take to recover the system in case of a minor component failure? How long will it take to recover the system in case of a critical failure?

IT Question 23: Are You Where You Need to Be Today?

The answer should be "never" if you do it right. The warehouse evolves as the business evolves. Still, if the things they have described above are "ready to go into production" at some future point, be it next year, next week, or tomorrow, it is a useless reference. There was a particular reference who told a customer of mine all about their 600 Gigabytes warehouse. After half an hour, they talked about their upcoming 40 Gigabyte test. They were asked if they had concerns that decreasing data volumes from 600 to 40 Gigabytes would cause problems. The answer was "Well, we actually have 6 Gigabytes loaded today, but, if it works with 6, why wouldn't it work with 600?"

IT Question 24: How Much Time Do You Spend Training the Vendor?

There are few vendors out there who understand what it means to build production, mission critical systems. An amazing number of support people have never heard of MVS, let alone GCOS or TPF. If you are not careful, you will be training them every step of the way. As we move forward, there are even more people who know little or nothing about managing databases and network accesses on the Internet.

IT Question 25: How Long After The Hardware Arrived Did You Deliver Your First Application?

Were there unexpected delays? Does it seem an unreasonably long time? Are there ways they could speed it up without sacrificing quality? What is the value of bringing up a new customer relationship decision-support application a month earlier?

IT Question 26: If You Started Over Today, What Would You Do Differently?

This is a good way to tie up dangling questions from the conversation.

Business Users' Questions

There are far fewer questions for the users, but they are as critical as the IS questions. If the system does not meet the business needs, then it does not matter what answers IS provides.

User Question 1: What Did You Expect the System to Do?

Inherent in this question is the anticipation that what you expect is close to what they expected. Also learn here about expectations.

User Question 2: Does the System Do What You Expected It to Do?

How important is this? How important would it be to you? What is missing? Can you infer other limitations from this?

User Question 3: Are You Where You Need to Be Today?

You must understand whether the users and IT agree on their answers in this area. If not, you could be uncovering a problem area.

User Question 4: What Else Do You Need?

What is it that they need and don't have? Learn from this answer.

User Question 5: How Much Time Has Passed Between When the Contract Was Signed and When You Could Actually Use It?

This is indicative of problems with the implementation or software. Problems could result from a selection of an unacceptable (but well-liked or advertised) database management system, the vendor's lack of experience building a similar analytical solution, or other factors. Understand what has happened. Remember: Relationship technologies and customer relationship management solutions and software are relatively new.

User Question 6: If You Started Over Today, What Would You Do Differently?

See if the Information Systems and Business user perspectives match.

▶ Red Flags

If you are building a list of CSFs, which should include questions for various groups to discover the answers, then you will surely need some Red Flags.

If these things happen when you go researching a reference, they should set off red lights and sirens in your head.

Red Flag Number 1: No References Are Available.

Many claims fall apart because references simply do not exist. If the product can do what the vendor claims, there should be at least one site in the world doing it. After all, the world's a big place, and you aren't the first to build this solution. If you are, then know the risk and participate in the rewards.

Red Flag Number 2: The Vendor Reference Doesn't Check Out.

If a vendor has provided a reference that was way off base from what you expected, it's probably not a mistake. They were most likely counting on your not following through. If the vendor provides references which do not check out, a second chance would be unwise. Clearly, someone doesn't know their business.

Red Flag Number 3: The Vendor Must Be Present at the Meeting.

The only reason for the vendor to be present at the meeting is to guide the conversation away from uncomfortable topics. If the system works as advertised, they should not be afraid of a few warts. Also, if the vendor has to "explain" situations or products, the reference customer you are visiting doesn't know what they have, or how it works, or how they gain advantage from it.

Red Flag Number 4: The Users Cannot Make the Meeting.

If the users are happy with the system, they will be happy to talk about what they've accomplished. Lack of user presence is probably lack of user satisfaction. Many times a vendor or IT will set up a meeting and then the user does not participate, due to unforeseen or higher priority reasons. If the user is aware of your business need to know about the use or value of the system, they usually should be prepared to discuss it. (Hint: the vendor selected the account and the users should be happy and knowledgeable.)

Red Flag Number 5: The Only Reference Is Halfway Around the World.

References that are thousands of miles away present a convenient logistical problem for the vendor. It is difficult, if not impossible, to meet in person. It is difficult to talk over the telephone because of timezone differences. The difficulty imposed by not being able to draw images of what you mean makes telephone references more challenging. Language differences might make it difficult to convey complex concepts you need to explore.

Given all of this, it is still possible that the best reference for you is in another country. A simple way to do a first-level qualification: Tell your vendor that you need to see the reference in person, but, if the reference doesn't check out, you expect them to pay for all expenses your company incurs. If they balk, the reference is probably worthless. If they agree, make sure you follow through—the reference still needs to be checked.

If this is unacceptable to the vendor, then arrange for a teleconference connection using full-motion video and ask them to prepare a presentation of their system, project, and results. The vendor can attend this session, if they agree to remain silent; you must be in control of the communication and conversation—so that you can learn the most and get all of the required answers for an effective evaluation.

▶ Management Considerations

- Some conference speakers, mostly consultants looking for you to hire them, tell disaster stories of implementations and how to avoid them. They focus on "how to fail." It is much more important to *know* how to succeed. You should do business with people who succeed and speak about success.

- This chapter was specifically designed to provide you with the keys to success and how to succeed—at multiple levels of your enterprise. Use it as a base for your research.

- There are key questions and reasons for business managers, technical evaluators, information systems managers, application users, and systems administrators to become familiar with to ask their outside providers and partners. Be careful, read the insightfulness in this chapter, provided by hundreds of experiences ...think... and use common sense. Sometimes in the heat of urgency, people forget the basics of questioning and the possibly untrue answers.

- Everyone wants your business. Everyone wants to believe that their solution is the best. If you desire to be a pioneer, do so, but understand the risks and the inherent costs. Ask questions that determine where others had problems or issues to resolve. (Remember, you will have to resolve some of these issues.)
- Few implementers will tell you about their failures. Remember that once a commitment is made to a solution, few people will tell you of their "bad" choices. Honesty is worth more than your spending millions to find out. Find truths.
- Be careful, there are a lot of unsupported claims being made. By checking and questioning business and technology references closely, you can help ensure you're a success.

Data Privacy: Ensuring Confidence

▶ The Need for Data Privacy

Many of us receive phone calls from telemarketing firms citing information which was provided by their contracting firms through the Internet, financial applications, credit bureaus, mailing lists, surveys, and the like. We are stunned by certain facts that these firms may know about us. Therefore, during the creation and administration of databases there *needs* to be a clear set of policies, procedures, and guidelines for the collection, usage, dissemination, and administration of customer information and of our choices about the data.

Privacy is the subject of mounting public concern worldwide. While it has been a background issue for database administration, especially in relation to database marketing applications, privacy has recently sprung to the forefront as a major focus of government, media, and consumer attention. This is largely due to the Internet, and more specifically "Web commerce." But the issue of privacy pervades all forms of commerce, not just in the online environment.

An example of increased collection of personal data is in retailing, whereby retailers have recently introduced "membership" or "loyalty" cards. The card provides the consumer with reduced prices for certain products, but each time the consumer uses the card, information about the consumer's buying habits is collected. This personal data is in some cases then stored and processed by retailers in databases or data warehouses for their own business purposes, without the knowledge or approval of the customer. The same personal information can, with today's technology and online environment, also be collected from purchases with smart cards, telephone cards, and debit or credit cards.

"Privacy," in relation to CRM, means individual control and protection over the use of personal information. "Personal information" is any information of a personal nature about an individual (e.g., age, gender, income). When personal information is stored in databases, mailing lists, or data warehouses, it is incumbent upon the owners (i.e., "data controllers") to protect customer data from abuses.

As more and more data is collected, the rights of individuals regarding the use of data pertaining to them are becoming increasingly codified in legislative declarations and statutes. These started with the OECD Guidelines of 1980, and continued when the European Union's Data Protection Directives went into effect in October 1988. The USA has relied on several sectoral laws, tort law, and self-regulation, as articulated in the Clinton Administration's 1997 "Framework for Global Electronic Commerce," as well as in the June 1998 formation of the Online Privacy Alliance, a private industry initiative of which NCR is a founding member. More recently, the White House has begun to shift toward a stricter enforcement policy, initially supporting legislation in the areas of medical-records privacy, identity theft, and children's privacy online.

You will need to define an approach to support the handling of privacy, first by formalizing a consolidated set of general privacy requirements, then by examining their impact on information system's info-structures, data warehousing, data mining, and database marketing. We will help you interpret the requirements into measures that must be taken to bring data warehousing applications into compliance, using a set of comprehensive privacy protection solutions.

You need to identify the opportunity to leverage the privacy issue as a means of expanding and enhancing the customer relationship. We will show you how privacy can be addressed within the context of Customer Relationship Management solutions. We will also outline a methodology for building privacy mechanisms into your info-structure and data warehouse environment in order to provide "Privacy Views." This will assist you in achieving 1) compliance, and 2) the concept of applying the emerging P3P standard (from the World-Wide Web Consortium) to support privacy in data warehousing.

Let's review the events and major initiatives that are driving privacy to the forefront of management teams worldwide.

Alert: Recent Alarms in the U.S.

CVS/Giant Food

Three recent news stories illustrate the rising concern over privacy and the use of data. In February 1998, it was reported that the CVS pharmacy and Giant Food supermarket chains were selling medical information (gleaned from filling prescriptions) to a marketing company (Elensys), who used the information as an aid in marketing other drugs for the same conditions. Front page *Washington Post* coverage and a public uproar caused Giant Food and CVS to retreat and cease sending such information to Elensys, as well as offer customers the right to remove their names from the database.

American Express

In May 1998, American Express issued a press release on a new agreement with KnowledgeBase Marketing, a database marketing firm. *USA Today* gave it front page coverage, reporting that American Express would be selling detailed purchase profiles based on customers' credit card activity to small businesses for marketing purposes. The "Today" show's Katie Couric, for one, was outraged, asking how she could stop American Express from doing this to her. Two months later, American Express terminated the database marketing agreement.

Sabre

In July 1998, top officers of the Sabre Group, operator of the Sabre reservation system, gave an interview to *PC Week* in which they spoke about a planned project intended to provide the airline and other industries with a treasure trove of passenger information—"a potential gold mine." By knowing who is flying where, when and for how much money, they explained, Sabre could gather valuable data to sell to airlines and other businesses, such as travel agencies, hotels and real estate firms. Sabre could find, for example, who is flying to a specific city in the next three weeks. Sabre CEO Michael Durham was quoted as saying, "Think about how much companies would pay for [the names of] people who have reservations to go to specific places at specific dates and times." Within days, Sabre Group was forced to issue a clarification, noting that, "We do not sell passenger names or other private information to third parties without the consent of the passenger, and have no intention of doing so in the future."

Lessons

A common theme among these recent stories is the major discrepancy between consumer expectations regarding the use of their personal data, and the actual or planned uses of the data collector. In all three cases, a failure to be sensitive to consumers' privacy expectations resulted in:

1. damaging public attention for the firms
2. damaging public attention for data warehousing (as an instrument for privacy invasion)
3. dampening corporate enthusiasm for a data warehousing project

▶ Guidelines—The OECD Principles

The *Guidelines Governing the Protection of Privacy*, adopted in 1980 by the Organization for Economic Cooperation and Development (OECD), is the seminal work that laid the foundation principles of personal data protection.

The voluntary guidelines encouraged member nations to adopt laws and practices that recognize rights which individual citizens can rightfully expect will be accorded them by data gatherers. These rights, or principles, can basically be described as follows:

- **Purpose Specification.** Consumers should, at the time of collection of personal data, be provided with an easily understood notice of the data collector's intent with regard to the collection and processing of the personal data.
- **Collection Limitation.** The collection of personal data should be limited to that which is needed for valid business purposes, and any personal data should be obtained only by lawful and fair means.

- **Data Quality.** Personal data should be relevant to the purposes for which they are to be used, and should be accurate, complete, and kept up-to-date.
- **Use Limitation.** Personal data should not be disclosed, sold, made available or otherwise used for purposes other than those specified during the time of collection, except with the consent of the consumer (via an opt-out or an opt-in[1]), or by the authority of law.
- **Openness.** Consumers should be able to receive information about developments, practices, and policies with respect to personal data. Means should be available to establish the existence and nature of personal data, and the main purposes of their use, as well as the identity and the usual residence of the data controller.
- **Access.** Opportunity should be provided to consumers to have their personal data communicated to them in a readable form, and to challenge data relating to them and if the challenge is successful, to have the data erased, rectified, completed, or amended.
- **Data Security.** Personal data should be protected by reasonable security safeguards against such risks as loss or unauthorized access, destruction, use, modification, or disclosure.
- **Accountability.** A data controller should be accountable for complying with measures which give effect to the principles above.

Generally, this means that, before collecting or making use of personal information, companies should notify their customers about the data they are collecting, and why. They should also provide their customers the ability to opt out of collection and uses of their data, unless it is required by law or needed to complete a contract with the individual or to protect the rights of the individual. Some uses of data that consumers generally would want to opt-out of are the use of personal data for purposes such as direct marketing, and disclosing or selling personal data to third parties. This in turn means that data controllers should implement mechanisms that control the collection, the uses that they make of the data, access to the data, and other similar processing. (Note: This requirement is non-negotiable in certain countries, e.g., Hong Kong.)

---

[1]*"Opt in" and "Opt out" are terms commonly used to describe consumer control over the use of their data. If consumers opt in to a use (e.g., for direct marketing), they are expressing agreement to that use. If consumers opt out of a use, they are denying permission for that use.*

Indirectly, all these principles raise the further issue of anonymity:

- **Anonymity**—Maintaining personal data in an anonymous form. **HINT:** Most consumers and local data protection legislation do not object to collection of information about individuals if it is done anonymously for statistical purposes, in such a fashion that the data cannot later be used to target the consumer, or otherwise invade the consumer's privacy (unless consented to).

Web Commerce and Privacy

Within recent years, Internet marketing and advertising have mushroomed and become increasingly invasive, attempting to divert the consumer's attention to Web sites that wish to sell something. And, as businesses attempt to cash in on the emerging world of electronic commerce (seeing the Web as the ultimate channel for achieving "one-to-one" marketing), a multitude of sites have sprung up that seek personal information from their visitors. Internet businesses seek personal background data, areas of personal interest, credit card information, and other forms of individual identification. This has the dual annoyance of seeming to invade privacy, and doing so repetitively for each commercial site visited. "Cookies" emerged as a technique for minimizing such annoyance by "remembering" your prior visits to a site, but these in turn create the impression of being spied upon.

Recent surveys in the USA have shown that public concern over privacy is now the number one factor holding back the much anticipated explosive growth of Web commerce. This concern relates not only to issues of revealing financial information and security of business transacted over the Web, but also to the broader issue of giving up personal information, as well as identity, without knowing what "creative" uses might be made of such data.

This type of collection and use of personal data can prevent many consumers from signing up to membership award programs. It can also discourage use of emerging technology, such as cash cards, and foster continuation of more conservative payment methods such as cash and checks.

Beginning Resolutions—U.S. Self-Regulation Policy

In response to the mounting concern over Internet privacy, the US government adopted a policy of "self-regulation." In July 1997, the Administration issued "A Framework for Global Electronic Commerce," which among other things called on the private sector to develop self-regulatory mechanisms to protect privacy online, from both a process and a technological point of view.

The Framework reiterated the fundamental OECD principles, stating that, under these principles, *"consumers are entitled to redress if they are harmed by improper use or disclosure of personal information or if decisions are based on inaccurate, outdated, incomplete, or irrelevant information,"* but is vague on how such redress mechanisms would be implemented: "The Administration considers data protection critically important. We believe that private efforts of industry, working in cooperation with consumer groups, are preferable to government regulation, but if effective privacy protection cannot be provided in this way, we will re-evaluate this policy."

In May 1999, President Clinton announced his new Financial Privacy and Consumer Protection Initiative, which stated the intention to act on protecting the privacy of medical records, but also pushed for stricter control over financial information: "Clearly, we have to do more to protect every American's financial privacy. The Vice President led our efforts to identify areas where privacy is at risk, and financial areas came up over and over and over again as a matter of great concern. The technological revolution now makes it easier than ever for people to mine your private, financial data for their profit. While some of your private financial information is protected under existing federal law, your bank or broker or insurance company could still share with affiliated firms information on what you buy with checks and credit cards—or sell this information to the highest bidder. This law, to put it mildly, is outdated and should be changed—to give you the right to control your financial information, to let you decide whether you want to share private information with anyone else."

Study of Web Sites by the U.S. Federal Trade Commission

During the first few months of 1998, the Federal Trade Commission conducted an analysis of the effectiveness of current privacy self-regulation on the World Wide Web. Its findings, published in a June 1998 report, conclude that *"industry's efforts to encourage voluntary adoption of the most basic fair information practices have fallen short of what is needed to protect consumers.*" In a survey of over 1,400 Web sites, the FTC found that, while 85% of U.S. commercial sites collect personal information, only 14% provide any notice of what they do with the information, and only 2% publish a comprehensive privacy policy.

This study prompted some privacy advocates to push harder for legislation in the U.S., arguing that self-regulation will never work. However, a recent major step by U.S. industry—the formation of the **Online Privacy Alliance**—represents the first real concerted effort at self-regulation, and has succeeded to some extent in spurring U.S. companies into action on the issue of privacy, at least with regard to online privacy.

A follow-up study of Web site privacy practices conducted by Georgetown University in early 1999, under the sponsorship of the FTC, and published in May 1999, showed that about two-thirds of the 7,500 most-visited commercial Web sites now post some form of privacy notice. But only 12% have addressed all of the elements of "basic fair information practices," according to FTC chairman Robert Pitofsky. Thus, while significant progress has been made, "preliminary assessment of these results suggests that more work is ahead," according to Vice President Al Gore in 1999.

▶ Online Privacy Alliance

In June 1998, nearly 50 major U.S. companies and trade associations announced the formation of the Online Privacy Alliance, dedicated to protecting the privacy of individuals in cyberspace. Although originally intended to address privacy more broadly, the Alliance decided to initially limit its attention to the Internet. In a letter to President Clinton, the Alliance members pledged to "work hard to ensure that our member companies take steps to adopt and implement" their self-regulatory privacy plan.

The Alliance's approach is two-fold:

1. **Adoption of a unified set of key elements** of privacy protection that its member companies commit to implement.
2. A plan of action to promote broader adoption by the online community of privacy policies that include **consumer recourse mechanisms** for resolving consumer complaints and answering privacy inquiries. The plan includes encouraging customers,

suppliers, and other companies to participate in programs to protect privacy.

Thus, we strongly encourage you to engage in privacy protection and practices.

More recent moves by the Online Privacy Alliance are in support of **third-party enforcement** entities (specifically TRUSTe and BBB Online). These entities provide **privacy seal** programs to assure consumers that organizations bearing the seal adhere to their stated privacy principles and practices, and that these are consistent with the principles and practices of the Alliance. Seals will be accompanied by periodic verification and monitoring, either via self-assessment systems or independent compliance reviews, together with dispute resolution mechanisms for consumers to seek recourse if they have privacy complaints.

▶ The Emerging "P3P Standard"

The primary technology mechanism that has emerged in the USA to support privacy self-regulation is the Platform for Privacy Preferences (P3P) standard, under development by the World-Wide Web Consortium (W3C). A first draft of the P3P standard was issued on May 19, 1998; various drafts of updated and enhanced standards are coming forth regularly. The standard already has widespread support, particularly in the U.S., and both Microsoft and Netscape have expressed an intent to implement support for it in future versions of their browsers.

The goal of P3P is to provide a standard means of implementing privacy controls in electronic commerce. The approach is to define a standard mechanism whereby users supply personal information to Web sites along with privacy rules regarding its usage.

P3P consists of three major elements:

1. A **personal profile** detailing both **personal information** (e.g., identification, contact information, demographic/lifestyle data, transaction data, clickstream[2] data, personal preference data), and **privacy rules** regarding usage of the data (e.g., opt in/out for receiving marketing solicitations, or for disclosure to third parties). The profile would be set up for each user and typically

---

[2]*A clickstream is a detailed record of mouse-clicks for a given Web user, indicating which Web pages have been visited by the user.*

stored on his/her hard disk (optionally encrypted for security). It would be administered by the user's Web browser, and could be updated at any time by the user.

2. A **profile of Web site privacy practices**, developed by each Web site, describing the personal information requested by the site, and its usage practices.

3. A **protocol** for negotiation between the user's agent (a browser extension) and the Web site, to reach automated agreement concerning what personal information will be provided, and how it will be used. On the user's attempt to enter a Web site, the user agent acquires the Web site's profile request, and compares it with the user's profile. If they match (or if an agreement can be negotiated automatically), the user agent provides the requested personal information, and the user enters the Web site transparently. If a match is not achieved, the user is notified, and may attempt manual negotiation, or consent to the site's privacy practices, or withdraw from further interaction with the site. The personal information and associated privacy rules can thus be dynamically negotiated, either by the user agent or by the actual user, for each Web site visited, or even for each visit to a site.

P3P Standards—Applicability to Data Warehousing

While P3P is clearly designed for electronic commerce, it is a major advance in the field of privacy technology, and incorporates features that can equally well be applied to the world of data warehousing. In particular, the P3P definitions for a personal profile, down to the level of specific data fields, provide an extensible framework for the collection, storage and usage of personal information in customer-centric databases (i.e., data warehouses).

Given the anticipated standardization of user profiling, covering both personal data as well as privacy controls, that will rapidly come about in commerce in the electronic environment, it makes sense to adopt (and adapt) these standards into your data warehousing. We believe that those companies with data warehouses that are **the first to adopt this approach to privacy will gain significant competitive advantage, primarily through improved relationships** with their customers. They will also be taking a step to avoiding potential litigation, or civil or criminal sanctions for non-compliance with local legislation when performing data mining or customer data distribution.

(Note: Although, as currently defined, P3P in itself is not sufficient to ensure compliance with legislation in certain European countries, as well as Hong Kong and New Zealand, it does provide a convenient mechanism for the data controller to comply with some of the requirements in national data protection legislation.)

▶ European Legislation

While the U.S. focus on privacy is largely recent and has centered around self-regulation in electronic commerce, Europe has for some time taken a broader view of the problem and developed a more comprehensive, legislation-oriented approach to its solution.

Most European countries have had significant **privacy laws** in place since the early 1980s, largely based on the principles laid down in the OECD Guidelines of 1980 and the subsequent "Convention for the Protection of Individuals with Regard to Automatic Processing of Personal Data" of 1981. With the emergence of the European Union, the need has arisen for a consistent set of privacy laws across member countries, particularly since, in a common market environment, personal data needs to be exchanged increasingly among member countries.

In October 1995, the Council of the European Union adopted a new blueprint for privacy: **Directive 95/46/EC** on "the Protection of Individuals with Regard to the Processing of Personal Data and on the Free Movement of Such Data." This directive **applies to all forms of data and information processing**, not just electronic commerce. It is applicable within electronic environments and non-electronic environments, and will affect all companies operating in Europe or using information about European citizens.

As a second step, the Council of the European Union adopted a supplementary Directive 97/66/EC concerning "The Processing of Personal Data and the Protection of Privacy in the Telecommunications Sector." Both directives require member countries to enact legislation by October 24, 1998, supporting an extensive set of privacy principles (see section 4).

The legislation in Europe provides certain rights to individuals about whom individually identifiable information is collected (personal data), including the rights to:

- **Notice.** With reasonable intervals and without excessive delay or expense to be informed as to what personal data is being collected about them, and where the data originated if it was not collected from the individual himself (e.g., in monthly billing statement or in member card monthly report as well as upon request).
- **Receive an explanation of the knowledge of logic behind the automatic processing** which produces automated decisions which affect the individual (e.g., based upon a data warehouse analysis using statistical or data mining algorithms, a decision to reject or approve an application for a loan or credit).
- **Correction/Deletion/Blocking.** The ability to erase, block, or rectify inaccurate or incomplete data or data which does not comply with the rules set out in legislation.
- **Right to object** to the processing (opt-out) on compelling grounds; when the objection is justified the controller may no longer process the information. In the case of certain "special categories" of personal data (e.g., race, religion), the objection is assumed to be the default, and an explicit opt-in is required in order to process the information.

The directive also imposes certain obligations upon the data controllers, including the obligations to:

- Only collect data for specified, explicit, and legitimate purposes and only process information according to those purposes.
- Only collect personal data for which, for instance, explicit consent has been given or when it is required by law or to fulfill, or enter into, a contract between the collector and individual about whom data is collected.
- Ensure the data collected is accurate, and kept up-to-date.
- At the point of collection, provide the individuals about whom personal data is collected with information containing, among other things, the name of collector, the purpose of collection and other processing, recipients of the data, and how to access information and have it deleted.
- Ensure data security, preventing unauthorized access and disclosure.

HINT: Encryption is one example of a method of ensuring that data is not disclosed without authorization to third parties during transmission or storage.

- Notify supervisory authorities in each country before carrying out processing of personal data relating to citizens of the country.

A further directive (EU Directive 97/66/EC) applies specifically to telecommunications providers established in the European Union. This directive gives users/subscribers additional rights to:

- Opt out of itemized bills
- Opt out of certain calling line identification procedures
- Opt in or opt out of being listed in directories (fully, or specifically their address and/or reference to gender)
- Opt in or opt out of directory information being used for direct marketing or purposes other than identification.

It also requires communications providers to:

- **Inform subscribers of potential risks** of data security breaches, and possible remedies/costs
- **Erase (or make anonymous) traffic and billing data on subscribers** after expiration of payment dispute periods, unless subscribers have opted in to their data being used for marketing purposes.

The Impact on Companies Operating in Europe

The European Union's Directive on Personal Data Protection affects any company (U.S. or European) that operates in the European market, if it collects or uses any personal data relating to EU citizens. Companies that do not uphold the strict legal requirements set forth in national legislation may be subject to civil and criminal sanctions, as well as face large lawsuits from individuals who feel their privacy has been damaged through a breach of law. Companies processing data about EU citizens should thus implement privacy practices that conform not only to general norms but also to the further safeguards adopted in the EU Directive.

Furthermore, under certain circumstances, the free flow of data from EU to non-EU countries may be impacted if the destination country is considered to have inadequate privacy controls. This is due to a further requirement of the EU Directive:

Transfer of personal data to third countries—May take place only if the country ensures an adequate level of protection, with assessment based on:

- Nature of data
- Purpose and duration of processing
- Country of origin and destination
- Rules of law of third country
- Professional rules and security mechanisms complied with in third country

As an example, the Swedish Data Protection Board prohibited a foreign airline from transferring personal data about its passengers for processing and storage in the U.S. This could potentially also become the case for large corporations who may wish to enter personal data about their global customers into a data warehouse located in a country outside the EU which does not uphold an adequate level of protection of personal data.

In light of the U.S. policy of self-regulation in privacy, the burden is on individual companies, rather than the U.S. government, to institute privacy controls. It is thus advisable for U.S. companies that process EU personal data to put in place privacy practices which conform with the EU Directive (as well as to conform to the guidelines of the Online Privacy Alliance).

U.S. "Safe Harbor" Principles

In order to address the requirements regarding the transfer of personal data to the U.S., the U.S. Commerce Department has proposed a set of "Safe Harbor" principles to serve as guidance for U.S. organizations seeking to comply with the "adequacy" aspect of the EU Directive. Organizations within the safe harbor would have a presumption of adequacy, and data transfers from the EC to them would be allowed to continue. Organizations could come into the safe harbor by self-certifying that they adhere to these privacy principles.

The EU has agreed to avoid disrupting the flow of data to the U.S. as long as the U.S. is engaged in good faith negotiations with the EC regarding the terms of the safe harbor principles.

The seven safe harbor principles cover: **Notice, Choice, Onward Transfer** (Choice regarding Third-Party Disclosure), **Security, Data Integrity, Access,** and **Enforcement** (Accountability). The two main areas of difference between these principles and the EU Directive are in Access and Enforcement. In Access, the safe harbor wording is weaker, stating that "individuals must have *reasonable* access to personal information about them that an organization holds, and be able to correct or amend the information *where it is inaccurate.*" In Enforcement, the safe harbor is vaguely worded, especially in the area of sanctions, and has no concept of a government enforcement mechanism.

Agreement between the U.S. and the EU over the "Safe Harbor" principles would be a major step forward for U.S. companies with European operations, and would provide a template for them to adhere to. However, the principles are most likely well beyond current privacy practices of most U.S. companies, and will exact a significant compliance burden on them. To ease this, there is expected to be an agreed transition period for implementation of the principles.

▶ The Approach to Privacy in Data Warehousing

Threat and Opportunity

From the viewpoint of data warehousing, privacy can be considered both a threat and an opportunity. Perceived abuses of privacy (such as the Giant Foods/CVS or American Express cases) not only damage goodwill that companies have built with their customers, but could also put data warehousing and data mining in a bad light. Increasing public outrage at such perceived abuses could hinder the adoption of these technologies. However, the root problem lies in the inappropriate use of the technology, rather than in the technology itself.

In places such as Europe, Hong Kong, New Zealand, and Canada, inappropriate use of consumer data could lead to judicial sanctions if companies do not comply with local data protection legislation. Elsewhere, the penalty may not be legal, but may be just as damaging in terms of poor public relations. On the other hand, companies that adopt effective privacy policies will reap the rewards of improved consumer trust and a better public image than their competitors, as well as providing confidence that they are in conformance with legal requirements.

Moreover, a well implemented privacy program will offer companies opportunities to collect more accurate and detailed data on consumers (with their cooperation and consent), and get closer to the goal of one-to-one marketing.

To support privacy, the NCR Privacy Center in San Diego has developed a comprehensive program comprising specific privacy services, framework, architectures, privacy views, and associated understanding of how to use software products. You need to have a legal review when using a privacy blueprint. The blueprint also shows how to turn the privacy threat into an opportunity for enabling you to gain a competitive edge by treating privacy as a part of a larger strategy of enhanced customer relationship management.

General Privacy Requirements

Individual countries, states, or areas of business (e.g., telecommunications, banking) may have specific privacy laws that vary in their details. The telecommunications sector, for example, is subject to the additional EU Directive (Directive 97/66/EC) in Europe, and to FCC regulations regarding the use of Customer Proprietary Network Information (CPNI) in the US. The financial services industry in the US and most other countries fall under various relevant legislative and regulatory restrictions, especially as concerns disclosure of credit and other sensitive personal data. You should identify any such additional privacy requirements. **But it is important to get your own legal counsel to ensure compliance with all legal requirements of the jurisdiction in which you operate.**

Global Privacy Requirements

(Note also that the requirements discussed here relate only to the handling of customer [consumer] data. Other privacy requirements exist beyond these, for example in the handling of employee records.)

A comprehensive set of privacy requirements is recommended for the following classes of organizations:

1. All companies processing personal data relating to citizens
2. Companies processing any personal data that operate in countries that have adopted similar privacy laws to those of Europe (e.g., New Zealand, Hong Kong, Czech Republic, and Canada)
3. Companies processing personal data that wish to enhance their data warehousing solutions and competitive advantage without negative government, media, and/or consumer responses

The following requirements are based on a consolidation of the privacy provisions of the OECD Guidelines, the "key elements" of the Online Privacy Alliance, and the Articles of the EU Directive, and thus represent a "high bar" for how companies worldwide should handle their customers' personal data:

Notice—Your customers should be given notice of:

1. The existence and nature of personal data collected or used
2. The policy for collection
3. The intended purposes for any type of processing, such as collection, use and/or disclosure
4. The identity of the "data controller" and other recipients of the data
5. The "logic involved in any automatic processing"
   HINT: Where a customer-accessible Web site is maintained, notice should be given in a Privacy Policy statement. Additionally, notice would typically be provided via mail communication, e.g., in a special mailing or in conjunction with a regular billing, and could be combined with requests for opt-in (or opt-out). Data mining implications of "logic involved in automatic processing" are discussed in the section below.

Collection and Use Limits—Organizations should consider limiting the collection and use of personal data to what is appropriate and needed:

1. Limit collection and use to explicit, specified and legitimate purposes.
2. Data must be "adequate, relevant and not excessive" in relation to original purposes.
3. Data must be kept in identifiable form for no longer than necessary for original purposes.
   HINT: The spirit of this principle is somewhat at odds with data warehousing, where data is collected for later analysis, sometimes unforeseen. However, even in cases of "ad hoc" queries, the general categories of purposes are typically known. In order to conform with this principle, you will need to carefully think through and spell out to your customers the categories of existing and planned uses of personal data (e.g., "market research", "product design", or "analysis of effectiveness of marketing programs"). And where a major new category of use is identified for collected data, this should be communicated to your customers prior to implementation and allow for the opt-out when a consumer or a customer of yours does not want to be part of the processing purpose.

HINT: Data warehouses clearly keep detailed data for long periods of time. Where personal data is involved, it can be kept in identifiable form for purposes that have been specified earlier to customers (and where they do not opt out); otherwise, it should be erased, or made anonymous (e.g., by forming new tables stripped of identification columns, or by applying as an example: "Teradata Privacy Views" that remove visibility of identification columns). Thus, if your customer opts out of their data being used for direct marketing, it can in most jurisdictions still be retained and used to develop predictive models or for other analysis purposes, as long as the data is made anonymous to the analytic applications and users, and as long as the customer is not later targeted for direct marketing purposes. This is just an interpretation of European requirements; however, as local privacy laws are put into practice, it is possible that some local courts might rule otherwise.

Choice/Consent—Your customers should be given the choice to opt out of the processing of personal data (such as collection and uses of personal data and disclosure of personal data to third parties).

1. Customers should specifically be able to opt out of the use of personal data for direct marketing, and to opt out of disclosure of their personal data to third parties.

2. Customer consent via explicit opt-in is desirable (versus defaulted opt-in; i.e., assuming opt-in unless the customer explicitly specifies opt-out), and in some jurisdictions required for certain types of "special categories" of data. These are: data revealing racial or ethnic origin, political opinions, religious or philosophical beliefs, trade-union membership, and the processing of data concerning health or sex-life.
   HINT: Consistent with the spirit of this EU requirement, customers should also be able to opt out of the use of other sensitive data, such as income, home value, family details, personal interests.
   HINT: The most comprehensive approach to this requirement would be to seek explicit opt-in for all uses of all categories of personal data. Such an approach would build the greatest level of customer trust and loyalty, but has implementation issues since direct communication with customers typically achieves low response levels. To achieve a high response level may require creative approaches toward customer communication, possibly

involving the use of incentives. An alternative approach of assuming opt-in (except for "special categories"), but clearly and conspicuously providing the "opt-out" choice (e.g., via a prepaid return mail-in), is currently interpreted to be compliant with the EU requirements (although this may vary by country, and may need to be clarified by test cases).

3. Customers may also opt out of automated decisions with legal or other "significant" effects (e.g., automated evaluation of work performance, creditworthiness, reliability or conduct).
HINT: The implications to data mining of opting out of automated decisions are discussed later in this section.

Data Quality/Access/Accuracy/Correction—Organizations should ensure that personal data they process is accurate and up-to-date.

1. Data should be adequate and relevant and not excessive in relation to the purpose for which it was collected.
2. You should provide your customers the ability to review and correct inaccurate or incomplete personal data.
HINT: A direct interface allowing your customers to review their personal data is preferable, but may present implementation issues, including security and system performance. Correction of personal data is additionally complex, and will involve execution of specific new privacy-related business processes to verify the validity of requested changes, before updating the data warehouse.
3. Customers should have the right to "erasure or blocking" of personal data which has not been collected in accordance with the rules of local legislation.
HINT: While some organizations may wish to take a safe approach of complying with requests to erase personal data, database technologies such as Teradata Privacy Views with associated security levels can effectively accomplish "blocking" of access and other processing of the data.

Data Security——Secure personal data against loss, and against unauthorized access, destruction, alteration, use or disclosure.
HINT: Your customer-centric database should be designed to provide such data protection and security. Measures to prevent data loss or destruction are standard requirements in data warehouse environments. Unauthorized access, destruction, alteration, use or disclosure can be

prevented through good logical and physical database design, including the use of Privacy Views with appropriate usage privileges.

Accountability/Enforcement/Recourse—Establish systems for individuals to seek resolution or redress of possible violations of stated privacy principles and practices.

1. Support enforcement of existing legal and regulatory remedies
2. Requirement to notify privacy authorities in each country of intent to collect personal data relating to their subjects.
   HINT: You should set up a supervisory authority responsible for monitoring compliance to privacy laws. Where personal data relating to citizens is involved, you must notify the privacy authority of each country involved regarding the existing or planned processing of such data.

Notification should include:

1. Name and address of the data controller
2. Purpose(s) of processing
3. Description of categories of data subject (consumer) and data relating to them
4. Recipients, or categories of recipients to whom data may be disclosed
5. Proposed transfers to third countries (i.e., non-EU countries)
6. General description allowing preliminary assessment of data security measures.

It is anticipated that agreement between the United States and the EU regarding a "safe harbor" will result in U.S.-based companies being exempted from these requirements, in return for agreeing to adhere to the "Safe Harbor" principles—including the conditions of an agreed U.S. Enforcement mechanism.

1. Judicial remedies, liabilities (including compensation) and sanctions for breaches of privacy rights (country-specific).
2. Enforcement via national codes of conduct, national supervisory authorities, and, where the data in question relates to an EU citizen, the European courts.

   HINT: The "key elements" of the Online Privacy Alliance should be treated as the de facto U.S. national code of conduct for

U.S.-only businesses. U.S. businesses that process personal data relating to EU citizens should conform to the eventual "Safe Harbor" principles.

Privacy Impact on Data Warehousing, Data Mining and Database Marketing

The "key elements" of the Online Privacy Alliance include the element of consumer choice—to opt out of personal data collection and use, and to opt out of disclosure to third parties. In essence, this boils down to two kinds of opt-out:

1. Opt out of identifiable personal data being used to target an individual for direct marketing
2. Opt out of disclosure of identifiable personal data to third parties (typically also for marketing).

In some cases, a third opt-out may be appropriate relating to disclosure of identifiable personal data to affiliate organizations.

The EU Directive establishes the following additional privacy requirements:

1. The right not to be party to an automated decision with legal or other "significant" effects (e.g., creditworthiness) to the individual, unless there are suitable measures to safeguard the individual's legitimate interests.
2. Notice of the "logic involved in any automatic processing."
3. Explicit opt-in for "special categories" of data.
4. Right to "rectification, erasure or blocking" of certain data.

The implications of these requirements on data mining, data warehousing, and in particular database marketing, are significant, but also manageable.

Opt-Out of Direct Marketing

The purpose of direct marketing is to contact "prospects" who are likely to be interested in a product or service. This is in contrast to "mass marketing," which may involve untargeted "junk mail" or other forms of contact. Thus, if a customer opts out of direct marketing, it is likely that he or she would not have responded positively to being contacted, and moreover would have become a less happy customer.

The "direct marketing" opt-out should therefore be considered beneficial in terms of improving customer satisfaction and decreasing marketing costs. This benefit can be expanded by implementing more fine-grained marketing opt-outs based on individual customer preferences (e.g., by product type, or means of contact), thereby eliminating marketing of low-interest products, and likely marketing higher-interest products more successfully, with customer consent and satisfaction.

A "direct marketing" opt-out does not eliminate the use of personal data relating to opted-out customers for purposes of devising successful marketing campaigns—as long as the data is used in an anonymized form. Thus, analytic programs, ad hoc queries, and Query® or OLAP tools can be used to perform statistical or other forms of predictive analysis of personal characteristics, and to identify types of customers that are likely to be good prospects.

Additional Hints:

- This can be achieved by separating the columns of data of personal characteristics from the columns that provide any form of identification; separation can be achieved physically, by setting up separate tables, or logically by using an "Anonymization" view that filters out the identification columns of data.
- Thus data mining techniques such as regression, decision tree induction, rule induction, and neural networks can be used to automatically detect such patterns, and (usually with human involvement) to develop predictive models ("propensity models") that can be applied to a customer database to select targets. But here is where the opt-out applies: customers who have opted out of direct marketing must be excluded from the selection.
- This can easily be achieved with a DW Relational Database by forming a conditional query (e.g., via a "Direct Marketing" view) that checks the relevant "opt-out" flag and excludes rows where the flag is on. (Note that this exclusion of opt-outs at the selection stage applies whether data mining techniques or any other methods are used to determine propensity.)
- In data mining terms, this means that personal data attributes can be used (anonymously) in the *knowledge discovery* phase, but not

in the *knowledge deployment* phase, where action is taken based on the discovered knowledge.

- A common additional refinement in data mining involves "*scoring.*" This is the process of applying a predictive model against a potential target set, and appending to each record a score indicating a propensity (e.g., the likelihood to respond positively to a direct marketing offer). Although scoring could be viewed as an early form of knowledge deployment, it occurs prior to taking action (e.g., forming a target list of customers with a score above a certain level), and therefore is considered legitimate. The consequence, however (if the score is recorded as a value in the customer record), is that the consumer is considered to have the right to see any scores relating to him/her, as part of the consumer access right.

Disclosure to Third Parties

Disclosure of identifiable personal information to third parties can be controlled by similar mechanisms.

For example, disclosure can be prevented by requiring applications that read personal data to gain access via an ***Anonymizing View***, or via a view which checks a disclosure "opt-out" flag and excludes rows with the flag on, or via a combination of these approaches that selectively anonymizes those rows that have opted out of disclosure.

Opt-Out of Automated Decisions with Significant Effects (Example: Customer Creditworthiness)

The term "automated decisions" is assumed to mean computer-generated, based on some set of rules or some algorithm—e.g., in an application that incorporates a predictive model for creditworthiness (an example of knowledge deployment). Allowing a customer such a choice may appear unusual (e.g., for a bank extending credit). The EU Directive does include provisions that this choice can be overridden if the data controller has a "legitimate purpose" for such processing of personal data, or by a contract agreed to by the data subject; thus a bank can require an individual to sign a contract agreeing to automated decisions, before extending credit.

The EU Directive may be interpreted as allowing automated decisions to occur during a process, provided that a human is involved in the process—e.g., to review the decision, either before notification to the consumer, or following notification, but prior to taking action.

HINT: An "automated decision" opt-out can be implemented in a similar fashion to the prior two examples—e.g., the application goes through a view that checks an "automated decision" opt-out flag, and does not execute the decision for each row where the flag is on. In this case, it may also be necessary to create an additional result table of opted-out rows, for further processing (e.g., to refer to a human for a decision).

Notice of "Logic Involved in Automatic Processing"

Related to automated decision opt-out is the requirement to provide every data subject the right to *"knowledge of the logic involved in any automatic processing of data concerning him at least in the case of automated decisions."* This is assumed to mean an explanation of the logic used in an application in making a decision—e.g., the rules contained in a predictive model, such as: "If estimated disposable income is greater than x, and if homeowner, and if no known bad loans, and if checking account in good standing for more than 12 months, then good credit risk."

In order to meet such a requirement, the logic used in automated decisions should be understandable by a human—e.g., the rules produced by a decision tree induction algorithm. Decisions based on neural networks may not meet this requirement, unless the key influential attributes used by the neural network are made available by the program (note that the SPSS Clementine and SAS Enterprise Miner products do provide such information, via a sensitivity analysis of the generated neural network).

"Special Categories" of Data

It is always a good practice to consider prohibiting the processing of certain "special categories" of data such as: personal data revealing racial or ethnic origin, political opinions, religious or philosophical beliefs, trade-union membership, and the processing of data concerning health or sex-life, unless the data subject has explicitly opted in.

The most obvious way of complying with this requirement is to not collect any personal data in these special categories (as well as any other personal data that might be considered sensitive, such as income, home value, family details, personal interests). However, there may be good reasons for collecting such data, in which case the explicit opt-in of the customer should be obtained before its collection or use. A valid example might be a telecommunications company's use of ethnic origin as an indicator of customers who are more likely to be interested in certain special-rate overseas calling plans.

HINT: The processing of such data may pose difficulties, in cases of large percentages of opt-outs. This would be the case if the columns of data for "special categories" were made null in the database for opted-out customers. An alternative would be to keep such data in the database, but to use views to restrict access to such data to those users or applications that have a valid reason to see it. Another alternative would be to use a similar approach to that discussed above for "direct marketing" opt-out: to keep the data (if it is provided), and to make it anonymous through a view; also to incorporate an opt-out flag for "special categories" (or a separate flag for each category), and to respect such opt-outs in any deployment application (e.g., omit opted-out customers from any overseas call-plan communication that is based on ethnic origin).

"Erasure or Blocking" of Certain Data

In real life, data is rarely erased; it probably exists somewhere—perhaps on an archive tape. So the right to actual erasure may be somewhat unrealistic.

However, the erasure option may be a requirement in your country. Some organizations may be able to undertake actual erasure of certain data to comply with this requirement. However, it is generally more feasible to support the other two alternatives: rectification and blocking.

HINT: Rectification can be achieved by providing a direct interface to customers to handle review and correction of personal data; this should take care of the "incomplete or inaccurate" issue. Blocking can be accomplished through RDBMS Privacy Views, in the manner discussed for opt-outs: views that block access to subsets of the data, or views that provide anonymity during processing of personal data, coupled with views that respect "opt-out" flags in any application that takes action on the data, such as marketing or disclosure.

Opportunity for Enhanced Customer Relationship Management

The prior section has shown how some of the various privacy requirements impacting direct marketing and data mining can be achieved. The basic approach is to keep personal data in the database, but to protect it through views by restricting access, by providing anonymity and by respecting opt-outs. This same approach can be expanded to develop a richer relationship with each customer. This will be important in the long run for your company.

The need to communicate with customers on the subject of privacy opens up the opportunity to also seek more detailed personal background and personal preference information from them, along with their wishes regarding the use and protection of such information. Thus companies could find out more details of the current demographics, lifestyle, life-cycle positioning, and financial profile of their customers. Banks could additionally seek out the financial product/service interests of their customers (including use of competitor offerings). Retailers could gain detailed profiles of the specific interests and preferences of their customers, by product category and by brand. And telecommunications companies could investigate the near-term communications needs of their customers and research the product or service factors that they value most in a long-term relationship.

In a direct marketing context, such information will result in a richer, more individual profile of each customer, together with a more fine-grained set of marketing opt-outs based on individual customer preferences (e.g., by product category, and/or by means of contact).

Furthermore, the methodology for identifying customer preference information, including the data elements making up the profile, and the associated customer privacy rules (opt-outs), can be based on the P3P profile discussed earlier. The P3P standard is expected to achieve widespread implementation in the world of Web-commerce.

The framework of the P3P profile is designed to be extensible, and can thus be extended to include customer-specific information deemed important to enhance the future customer relationship.

This represents a major opportunity to advance direct marketing and other aspects of customer relationship management towards the goal of marketing to a "segment-of-one."

Building Privacy into the Data Warehouse

The prior section has provided an analysis of global privacy requirements and their anticipated impact on data warehousing, data mining and database marketing. It has also explored some opportunities for enhanced customer relationship management that a comprehensive privacy solution where the same basic approach can be expanded upon to develop a richer relationship with each individual customer.

We now need to propose a framework for meeting these requirements and building privacy controls. The main elements of this framework are:

1. Enhancing the Logical Data Model.
2. Using "Privacy Views" to Support Restricted Access, Opt-Outs and Anonymity.
3. Providing an Interactive Customer Service Interface for Personal Data Administration.
4. Providing Reports to verify Privacy Adherence within the Data Warehouse Operation.

Enhancing the Logical Data Model

In order to address privacy, it is first necessary to examine the logical data model that has been developed for the enterprise, and identify all data entities related to "customer" that:

1. Reveal identity (e.g., account number, name, address, phone number).
2. Provide personal information (e.g., age, gender status, number of children, estimated income, shoe size, purchase habits).
3. Provide sensitive personal information (see special categories of data discussed earlier in this chapter).

The customer profile (i.e., the current set of data entities related to "customer") should then be reviewed, in order to identify possible additional data entities that would be worthwhile adding, in order to gain better insight into individual customer preferences. This review should in turn lead to brainstorming of possible further data entities that would be of value to the particular business situation. For example, a retailer specializing in fashion merchandise might decide to collect customer-specific details and preferences within key merchandise categories (e.g., shoe size and favorite shoe type/brand).

Opt-out tables or columns should then be added to the logical data model, to support individual customer opt-out of certain uses of personal data. At a minimum, four opt-outs should exist for: "direct marketing," "third-party disclosure," automated decisions," and "use of sensitive data"; a fifth opt-out for "affiliate disclosure" would be appropriate for companies with affiliate organizations.

HINT: "Direct marketing" and "disclosure" could be further broken out into separate opt-outs based on the type of customer contact. Opt-outs could be set up to apply across all of the customer's data, or to be selectable separately for each data category or even for each data item. Your Privacy Modeling should include a Logical Data Model for consumer privacy. You will need to base it on a clear definition for a "customer," and ensure additional "consent tables" for recording customer privacy preferences. The data model will typically require adaptation to existing data models, and it is recommended that you utilize a normalized approach to your database for easy expansion and queries that will become more complex over time. You should plan to utilize a consulting firm that has specific experience and professional service consultants who specialize in privacy services. This will save you time, money, complexity, and growth pain in the coming years.

Using Privacy Views to Support Restricted Access, Opt-Outs and Anonymity

Having established an enhanced logical data model with identification of personal data fields, sensitive data fields, and identity-revealing fields, and with an opt-out structure of appropriate detail, a review should be conducted of all data warehouse applications, including those involving interactive users engaged in ad hoc queries or other forms of analysis.

Database Views should be set up for the various classes of users of the data. At a minimum, views should be built for the following purposes:

1. Restricting access to personal data ("Standard" View)—for routine users and applications.
2. Allowing full access to personal data ("Personal Data" View)—for special privileged applications or users, such as privacy administrators. (Other classes of users might have restricted access views that show a particular subset of personal data.)
3. Making personal data anonymous ("Anonymization" View)—for analytic purposes.
4. Excluding rows, i.e., whole records, ("Opt-out" Views), where customers have opted out of the use of their data for a given purpose (e.g., direct marketing, disclosure, or automated decisions)—a row is excluded if the applicable opt-out indicator is on for the customer in question. Such opt-out views should also take into account any "Special Categories" opt-outs that customers may have expressed. Where opt-outs have been set up at a more fine-grained level, (e.g., by data category or data item), then the Opt-out View (e.g., for disclosure) would return row subsets containing the data items that are opted in, with nulls in the other fields. This could be used to handle situations where consumers have opted out of the use of "Special Categories" data items, but have opted in to the use of other personal data.
5. Selectively anonymizing personal data ("Selective Anonymization" View)—for disclosure of personal data—a row is anonymized if the appropriate "Disclosure Opt-out" indicator is on for that row.

Organizations with long-term understanding and experience with customer databases define the data warehouse applications into classes.

You should use application classes to apply the Five Types of Views as follows:

1. Analytic applications: "Anonymization" View.
2. Action-taking applications (e.g., direct marketing): "Direct Marketing Opt-out" View/Views (incorporating, where applicable, "Automated Processing Opt-outs" and/or "Special Categories" Opt-outs).

3. Disclosure applications: "Selective Anonymization" View (incorporating, where applicable, "Special Categories" Opt-outs). Alternatively "Anonymization" View or "Disclosure Opt-out" View—see Chapter 11 on use of Views in a privacy solution.
4. Special administrative applications/users—"Personal Data" View
5. All other applications—"Standard" View.

See Chapter 10 for implementation information for "Using Privacy Views to Implement Privacy in a CRM Environment."

Providing an Interactive Customer Service Interface for Personal Data Administration

Having set up the database according to the extended schema, incorporating additional personal data fields and additional opt-out indicators, a means is now required for populating these additional columns with customer-specific data. Certain columns can be set by default—e.g., by setting opt-outs on, assuming that explicit opt-in will be sought before using the data for the related purpose.

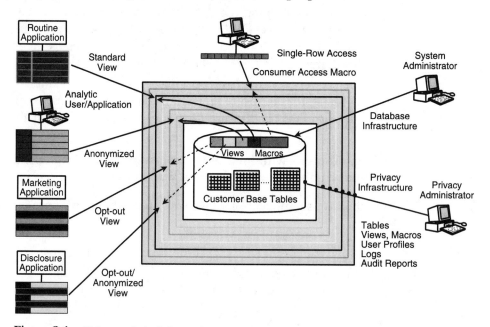

Figure 9.1. Privacy Administration and Views.

Customer profile information can be obtained directly from customers via a Web site, or through a call center interface, or through a mail/phone campaign. Such a campaign could be centered around privacy (and timed to coincide with increased public attention on privacy), and would also provide a statement of one's privacy practices.

An interactive customer interface (via Web site and/or call center) is needed for the additional purposes of providing customers access to their personal information, and allowing review, updating, and correction. Such an interface is important for generating customer goodwill, but does raise security and performance issues. Before any data is updated in the customer database, an intermediate form of review may be necessary, possibly involving person-to-person communication to validate requested changes. Validated customer input will typically be accumulated in a separate table, and entered into the customer database later.

HINT: Your organization will require a "Consumer Access Interface" product that will provide a set of software components and interfaces on which customers can build a consumer access application, allowing establishment, review, updating, and correction of personal information and associated privacy rules.

Providing Reports to Verify Privacy Compliance

A further aspect of privacy impacting the management of your customer data is the need to verify compliance. Verification may be conducted by an independent group (e.g., TRUSTe, BBB Online, or CPA WebTrust), by a government agency, or via self-verification. Reports should be made available showing details of the logical data model, the database schema, the various Privacy Views and related privileges, and the full set of applications and related users that have access to the warehouse through the views.

HINT: To ensure compliance your organization should institute a "Privacy Administrator" function and manager. This function would be responsible to create and review a variety of reports on the privacy infrastructure and on privacy-related activities. The reports may be based on information held in the Database Data Dictionary and on access activity logged in the Database Access Log, as well as in an additional Privacy Log maintained by a software utility. The administrator should also be able to set up or modify privacy rules and graphically view the Logical Data Model and the associated Table/View/Macro structure, along with the definitions of users and their privileges. These are very important functions for manageability.

▶ Management Considerations

- The issue of privacy—the protection of personal information—has reached a turning point worldwide. Government restrictions, laws, guidelines, and increasing media and consumer advocacy are driving the need for privacy action. Already, public attention is being drawn to privacy horror stories that relate directly to abuses of data analysis and database marketing. It is therefore incumbent on the leaders of customer-centric organizations to initiate effective privacy controls in databases, data warehouses, and on Internet applications.

- The benefits can accrue to your organization very quickly. Early compliance with the governmental directives will bring accolades in certain markets while also enhancing public perception. But it is not just a question of compliance. By becoming early implementers of privacy, your organization can gain substantial goodwill among your present customers. You also have the opportunity to gain new customers, and develop a relationship of confidence and trust that will lead to lasting customer relationships (e.g., Life-Time Value of customers). By expanding your strategy and vision of privacy into one of serving the needs of their customers better, you have the opportunity to build a new generation of customer relationship management applications that will bring them significantly closer to the ultimate goal of "one-to-one" marketing.

- As you offer your customers privacy-compliance solutions and privacy-enhanced CRM solutions, the value of your info-structure increases. More sophisticated applications will be deployed, database size and value will grow, and more users (and eventually your customers) will be totally online and connected throughout your intelligence and customer communications systems. The result will be more business, and privacy will become a major opportunity for long-term growth and strength of customer-centric organizations. As Ken O'Flaherty says from his real-world development and interaction with companies that have developed new strategies and architectures:

"Privacy Is Good for Business."

Implementing Privacy and Customer Views

▶ **Applying the Privacy Policies to a Data Warehouse for CRM**

Why the Platform for Privacy Preferences (P3P)?

The emerging P3P standard (Platform for Privacy Preferences) is to provide a standard means of implementing privacy controls in electronic commerce. A first draft was issued on May 19, 1998. There are updates which you should access and study in relation to your situation and needs.

The purpose of P3P is to provide a standard mechanism whereby Web-users supply personal information to Web sites and specify privacy rules to be followed by Web sites they visit. Briefly, P3P consists of three major elements:

1. A **personal profile** detailing both **personal information** and **privacy rules** regarding usage of the information.
2. A **profile of Web site privacy practices**, developed by each Web site, describing its rules of usage regarding personal information.

3. A **protocol** for negotiation between the user's agent (a browser extension) and the Web-site's agent, to reach automated agreement concerning what personal information will be provided, and how it will be used.

While P3P is clearly designed for electronic commerce, it is a major advance in the field of privacy technology, and incorporates features that can be equally well applied to the world of data warehousing. In particular, the P3P definitions for a personal profile, down to the level of specific data fields, provide an extensible framework for the collection, storage, and usage of personal information in customer-centric databases.

Application of Privacy Policies to a Data Warehouse

Companies with a data warehouse typically collect personal information about their customers from multiple sources, e.g., from application forms or questionnaires, from customer interactions, from transactions, or from third-party suppliers of demographic/psychographic data. They typically use this information for marketing purposes—e.g., to cross-sell a new product or service more effectively, to intervene prior to a perceived potential switch to a competitor, or to develop new products, services, or promotions. Often companies use data mining to analyze prior behavior patterns in samples of historical data (e.g., transaction details, market baskets, call-detail records, tied back to personal characteristics) to come up with predictive models (e.g., rules such as: if female, unmarried, under 28, city-dweller, with income over $50K, then propensity to buy is high). Sometimes these models are of a form (e.g., neural network) that is not understandable by a human, but is accurate in capturing generalized patterns hidden in the data.

Each company in the world with a major database of customers, or a customer-centric data warehouse, has the opportunity to be the first company to apply the P3P standard.

The framework of the P3P profile is designed to be extensible, and can thus be extended to include customer-specific information deemed important to enhance the future customer relationship. This represents a major opportunity to advance direct marketing and other aspects of customer relationship management towards the goal of "segment-of-one."

The basic idea is to take the P3P profile, and:

1. **Incorporate the personal data fields and privacy preferences specified under P3P into the logical data model of the data warehouse.** This means extending the personal information collected about each customer by taking advantage of the additional information supplied in the P3P profile (e.g., personal interests/preferences).

   HINT: You need to acquire the profile information either via their Web site, or through a mail/phone campaign to their customers requesting them to fill out a personal profile. Such a campaign would be centered on privacy (and timed to coincide with increased public attention on privacy). It would also state your privacy practices.

2. **Respect the privacy preferences expressed by each customer in their P3P profile.** This means that your company would most likely have to modify any privacy practices (e.g., in marketing solicitations, to exclude those customers who have opted out of direct marketing). It may also involve changes to some existing applications. However, such changes can be minimized by use of the special **"Views"** features of your DW/DSS RDBMS.

You can gain a competitive advantage by developing privacy extensions to your corporate **logical data model** and implementing the revised logical data model into your existing data warehouse (including the use of Views to both minimize application changes and to implement restrictions on access to personal data fields). You might also develop sample applications that implement privacy controls (e.g., to input P3P profiles and from them create additional tables and/or columns in the database; also to handle ad hoc user requests to view/update/protect personal data fields).

Further, you should consider **extending the P3P profile to collect additional personal information** from your customers, such as more fine-grained preference information. For example, information about preferences in books, magazines, music, and videos could be used (with customer consent) to identify items that might appeal to your customers, based on the preferences of other similar customers. This could include consideration of customer ratings of purchased products.

Customers who may want to opt out of receiving broad marketing solicitations might well agree to being notified on items of special interest. For example, a customer who is interested in hiking and nature might opt out of receiving marketing information in general, but with exceptions for promotions on outdoors equipment, or for books on nature. Other customers might agree to being notified about many broad classes of items, but may have some aversions (e.g., to sports). Customers might also agree to receive certain types of promotions, such as for semi-annual sales, or for new product introductions, or for categories, such as fashion merchandise or securities investment opportunities. A few customers will undoubtedly opt in to everything—but this may not be the ideal situation.

Better long-term customer relationships are more likely to develop based on serving the interests of each customer, rather than aiming everything at them.

In summary, the basic concept is to apply P3P to Data Warehouses, thereby **applying an advance in the field of electronic commerce to the field of commerce in general**. The advance is in terms of both improved privacy of personal information, as well as improved marketing and improved overall customer relationships, through using more detailed personal information.

If your organization is **resistant to changes,** particularly changes **that restrict freedom in marketing,** you may find it easier to hire a Privacy Center consultant to review your practices and polices. Also, to counter such resistance, we should underline the benefits of **improved targeting** (they only market to people who are more likely to buy) and **improved customer goodwill** regarding privacy. We should also point out that they would soon be affected by P3P anyway. Companies who have Web sites will have to implement P3P profiles on them. When they do, their customers will be unhappy if their preferences are respected in electronic commerce, but not in other forms of commerce. See the next section regarding this situation.

Can Companies with a Data Warehouse Ignore the Privacy Issue?

Although privacy is a general issue that pervades all aspects of information technology, it is currently in the spotlight of electronic commerce. This is largely because it is here that consumers are confronted with requests to supply personal information (often repeatedly), with little or no disclosure regarding what is done with the information. From a wider perspective, it is typically in **operational systems**, such as electronic commerce, ATM usage, POS systems, and call centers where privacy issues initially occur and must be handled.

But privacy is a broader issue, and pervades all forms of data processing. And the realms of data warehousing and data mining are particularly susceptible to public concerns regarding what is done with their data. We believe that you must face the privacy issue squarely, and implement appropriate privacy controls within your marketing, database, and data warehouse environments.

1. **European Union Directive 95/46/EC on Privacy**

   An initial consideration for many of organizations is the EU Directive on Privacy. Started on October 24, 1998, this affects any company operating in Europe, or receiving data imported from Europe (from their own or other operations). The directive applies to all forms of data processing, not just electronic commerce. Broadly speaking, the easiest way for data warehouses to comply with key aspects of the directive will be to provide anonymity to any personal data stored in the warehouse. This can be accomplished through the use of database Views, a standard SQL feature in Teradata. It will normally involve changes to the logical data model and physical database design, with possibly minor application changes. Professional services are available to assist you in effecting such changes. An auditing service should be used to provide an independent assessment of such voluntary compliance with the EU Directive.

2. **Customer Goodwill**

   A further consideration for all of companies is the preservation of the goodwill of their customers. The issue of privacy continues to grow as a public concern. Numerous newspaper articles and TV pieces have focused U.S. attention on the issue over the last year, fueled by stories of business disregarding the privacy of consumers or benefiting from the sale of personal information (see section 2.1 of the main document). All EU countries are implementing, or have already implemented, legislation on consumer privacy rights in conformance with the EU directive. And the U.S. government is stepping up to the issue by promoting its policy of "self-regulation" and by focusing public attention on U.S. activities in this area.

With increasing public awareness around the privacy issue, consumers will expect and increasingly insist that companies operating data warehouses will respect their wishes in regard to handling their personal information. In fact, it is often "data warehouses" and "data mining" that are singled out as the most pernicious form of snooping into personal information. Increasingly, the data warehouse is the infrastructure supporting the business intelligence activities that generate the direct mail and telemarketing solicitations that annoy so many consumers.

3. **Adoption of P3P in Electronic Commerce**

The P3P standard will be rapidly adopted in electronic commerce over the next two years. Following solidification of the standard in late 1999, new versions of the Netscape and Microsoft Web browsers can be expected that will implement all or part(s) of the P3P standard. Consumers will then begin to grow accustomed to defining their own personal profiles, and deciding how their personal information should be used in electronic commerce. They will also expect their privacy preferences to be respected in all forms of commerce, not just when they are dealing with Web merchants.

You will have to formulate privacy practices and publish them on your Web sites. Your customers will expect you to abide by these practices in your Web commerce. As you grow your electronic commerce activities, you will negotiate privacy agreements with an increasing percentage of your customers. These customers will naturally expect your privacy agreement to apply in all dealings with the enterprise, not just in Web commerce.

Thus the rapid spread of P3P in electronic commerce will spill over into all forms of commerce, and will force companies operating data warehouses to respect their privacy agreements with customers in all applications of the data warehouse.

▶ Opportunities for Managing Your Customers

Rather than waiting until they are forced to confront the multiple privacy forces that will impact their business, our data warehouse customers have the opportunity to take preemptive action in adopting new privacy practices that will benefit both themselves and their customers.

Specifically, by incorporating the framework of the emerging P3P standard into their data warehousing as well as their operational and electronic commerce systems, and by devising appropriate extensions tailored to their business goals, most organizations have an opportunity to "kill two birds with one stone": that is, increase the effectiveness of their business through improved customer relationships, while also meeting the privacy expectations of their customers.

▶ P3P Adoption Scenario: Retail Data Warehouse

New/Enhanced Loyalty Card or Credit Card Program

Retailers can initiate or enhance existing loyalty card or credit card programs within the framework of the P3P standard, and thereby gain access to a significant amount of personal information about their customers (while also respecting their privacy wishes). The enhanced personal information can be used in three broad ways:

1. In an aggregated, anonymous manner, to improve business operations (e.g., better selection of merchandise per store, based on aggregated demographic/psychographic profiles of each store population).
2. In a non-anonymous manner, to target customers who match behavior profiles (e.g., customers who match the profile of buyers of high-fashion merchandise). Note: Targeted customers would have opted in to receiving such promotions.
3. In an anonymous manner, to develop improved profiles of customer behavior (e.g., propensity-to-buy profiles for various categories of merchandise). Such profiles could be used to improve business operations (e.g., identify new types of products that could be stocked at specific stores), or to target opted-in customers who match the developed profiles.

Enhanced Personal Data

The following types of personal data could be collected from customers within the framework of the P3P profile:

1. P3P Required (Base) Data Elements
   - Birthdate, gender, employer, job title, time zone
   - Identification, contact information (including zip code)
2. Additional Optional Data Elements
   The retailer could ask for additional personal data such as:
   - Household income, disposable income, household size, home ownership, lot size, swimming pool ownership
   - Personal interests, favorite items (e.g., books, CDs, videos), style preferences (e.g., fashion, furniture, home furnishings)
3. Transaction and Behavioral Data Elements
   - Additional transaction detail and behavioral detail (e.g., clickstream, other contact occurrences) could also be used to gain a better understanding of customer buying habits and interests
4. Specific Privacy Opt-Ins

The retailer could request specific opt-in/opt-out selections for each data element for each customer. For example, a customer might opt in to receiving information about each of their personal interests or favorite items, or information about store events such as semi-annual sales, or targeted sales (e.g., high-fashion shoe sales). A customer might also agree to opting-in to transactional or behavioral targeting, if presented positively and with the future option to opt out if not satisfied.

Potential Marketing Initiatives

The following marketing initiatives might be implemented by the retailer towards opted-in customers:

1. Customize content of monthly billing or other mail communication, based on individual or household interests, buying habits, or favorite items.

2. Initiate specialized promotions or sales events around interest groups (based on declared interests, and/or interests observed via analysis of transaction and behavior detail). Examples: fall fashion, high-fashion shoes, country music, colonial furniture, nouveau beaujolais.

3. Develop an ancillary customized catalog business (via mail and/or Web commerce), with catalog content highly-personalized based on analysis of preference data, buying habits, and (for Web commerce) individual click streams.

4. Initiate a Frequent-Shopper Discount program for valued customers, e.g., offering a 10% discount or an occasional highly discounted special offer to customers exhibiting certain buying patterns.

5. Cross-sell product lines based on analysis of preference-based customer segments, e.g., promote rock-music videos, magazines, books, and concert tickets to buyers of rock-music CDs, and identify affinities in fashion preferences or other merchandise for the same segment.

▶ Using Privacy Views to Implement Privacy in a CRM Environment

This section will review the concepts and specific implementation uses for customer views within the data warehouse environment and for CRM. The section will discuss:

- Reasons for Using Views
- Concepts of Views
- Standard Views
- Privileged Applications
- Anonymous Views
- Opt Out Views
- Disclosure Applications
- Selective Anonymization Views
- Fine-grained Opt-in/Opt-out Actions
- Verification of Privacy Procedures

Reasons for Using Views

There are various methods of using Privacy Views to implement controls on access to personal information. Views become very valuable when your requirements are:

1. To allow consumers to "opt out" of or to consent to their personal data being used for certain purposes, e.g., for marketing purposes, or from being disclosed to third parties.
2. On request, to provide consumers access to personal information collected about them, and the ability to correct, erase, or block certain data.
3. To provide methods of verifying usage of personal data.

Views are part of the SQL standard and therefore also present in most relational DBMS's. **Views exist primarily to provide:**

1. Data Independence—where each application or user may have its own logical view of what data exists in the database, and where all such views are mapped to a single logical data model for the enterprise ("single version of the truth"), which in turn is mapped to the actual physical database design. This allows for both independence and flexibility.
2. Security—where different security levels and associated access rights can be established based on what elements of data are visible via each view.

The implementation of Views is particularly strong. **Competitive advantage is gained** through the following aspects of using views with your database:

1. You must be able to store and manage large volumes of detailed data, so that the logical data model can be in (or close to) "pure" third normal form (3NF), and multiple different views can easily be constructed into the logical data model.
2. Your database
3. Your customer's database
4. Your channel partner's database

5. Views tend to generate wide SQL expressions, which exploit the parallelism of a RDBMS (such as Teradata) in order to provide the ability to optimize complex SQL statements to achieve parallelism.

6. The high-performance implementation of views makes the use of views a practicality for implementing privacy, whereas competitive systems may typically avoid using views, for performance reasons.

7. You will need security features that include the option to log all accesses to a table (or a view), and to log the SQL expression that was used to perform the access. This means that all accesses to views or to base tables are auditable.
HINT: A privacy view generates SQL for selecting the appropriate columns and rows into the result table. Many of the standard, more popular relational databases do not generate optimized views. This prevents the systems from quickly obtaining the data and presenting it to the users. Some systems, such as NCR's Teradata RDBMS, provide privacy views automatically, and they are also optimized mathematically by the query and the database working together. If you do not have this function available, you will find that your database systems require much human set-up and administration. Some RDBMs companies say they have "views" but these may be very elementary "views" of customer data or sales data based on pre-coded queries, SQL, predefined specific definitions, or data models that only allow access to the data in a particular method. This can be very cumbersome, time-consuming, and costly for your information technology data management people.

The Concept of "Views"

1. **"Standard" Views** are Used to Exclude Personal Data from Routine DSS Applications
DBAs set up Views into customer tables (any tables containing personal information about their customers), so that, for routine users, all columns of personal information are hidden. Thus, all routine DSS applications and tools are precluded from viewing personal information. All end-users of these applications and tools are also precluded.

To minimize disruption, views should be set up using the same names that are used for base tables in any existing applications that access private data, and corresponding base table names would be changed to some other value. Thus, whenever an existing application attempts to access private data (now via a view), the private data can be screened out by the view, depending on user privileges. Using this approach, existing applications would not need to be modified. Instead, the logical data model and database schema would be modified, and additional naming conventions would be introduced.

2. **Privileged Applications Have Access to a "Personal Data" View**

   A special class of privileged applications ("Class A") would be able to access columns containing personal information, via a "Personal Data" View. These privileged applications would include administrative and maintenance applications (e.g., for inserting new customers, deleting ex-customers, handling change of address). They would also handle privacy functions, such as informing customers about personal information collected about them, changing/updating personal information, and applying "Opt-in/Opt-out" controls.

3. **"Anonymization" Views are Used for Analytic Applications**

   Certain applications may perform analysis on personal data, in order to gain insight into customer behavior (e.g., to identify trends or patterns). Such applications may be driven by business end-users (knowledge workers or "power analysts") performing "ad hoc" queries, typically using either custom-built software, standard Query or OLAP Tools, where the end-user spots the patterns. They may also involve the use of data mining tools, where statistical or machine learning algorithms, in conjunction with the analyst, discover patterns and from them, build predictive models.

   To derive the greatest value, analytic applications must have access to all available forms of personal information. In order to enable this, while at the same time respecting personal privacy requirements, special "Anonymization" Views are used. These views are designed to provide access to personal data fields, but to screen out all fields containing information that can identify the owner of the data (e.g., name, address, phone number, social security number, account numbers). Serendipitously, identity fields such as these are generally useless for data mining, and in fact would typically cause "noise" (confusion) in the model building process.

4. "Opt Out" Views are Used for Action-taking Programs, such as Marketing Applications

A further class of privileged applications would be any application that uses the personal information to take some form of action, such as marketing applications (e.g., to create mail or phone solicitations). These marketing applications would be subject to the "Opt-in/Opt-out" controls set for each customer, and would access customer information through a special view, which removes all records where the indicator is set to "Opt-out." For example, any customer who has not opted into receiving marketing solicitations would be omitted from any hit-list created by the marketing application.

"Opt-out" indicators would be new columns added to customer tables, or would compose a new table joined to existing customer tables. The value of these columns for each customer row would initially be set to "Opt-in" (or "Opt-out" if required by law), and could be modified via a new customer application that handles customer requests regarding privacy controls.

Multiple "Opt-out" indicators would typically be set up for each customer record. At a minimum, four opt-outs should exist for "direct marketing," "third party disclosure," automated decisions, and "use of sensitive data;" a fifth opt-out for "affiliate disclosure" would be appropriate for companies with affiliate organizations. However, it would be advantageous to design a scheme of more fine-grained opt-outs, based on more detailed customer preferences. For example, "direct marketing" and "disclosure" could be broken out into separate opt-outs for contact by telephone, direct mail, fax, and electronic mail. And, where it makes sense, each class of opt-out could be applied separately to each category of personal data (e.g., demographic data or preference data), or even down to each specific item of personal data (e.g., age, gender; hiking interest, shoe brand preference).

HINT: A "Special Categories" opt-out could be handled by associating an opt-out indicator with all "Special Categories" of data. For example: race or ethnicity, political opinions, religious or philosophical beliefs, trade-union membership, health or sexual orientation, and/or use of any disclosure application would be subject to a view that nulls out these columns for any opted-out row. This would make it relatively impossible for an unauthorized viewer to see pertinent data.

5. **Disclosure Applications Would be Subject to "Selective Anonymization" Views (or to "Opt-out" or "Anonymization" Views)**

   Special RDBMs services and applications or queries that disclose personal data to third parties or to affiliates (e.g., for marketing or analytic purposes) could be subject to a "Selective Anonymization" View. If the customer has opted out of third party or affiliate use of his/her data, this view will eliminate any identifying fields from their row (record) of data. Otherwise, where the customer has opted in to disclosure, the personal data is output along with identifying data columns.

   Alternatively, disclosure applications might be subject to an "Opt-out" View that eliminates all rows with the "disclosure opt-out" indicator on (thereby creating a result comprising the full rows of those customers that have consented to disclosure), or to an "Anonymization" View, that anonymizes all rows. The "Opt-out" View would be used in cases when the recipient needs to be able to identify any of the individuals, whereas the "Anonymization" View would be used when the recipient is using the data for analysis purposes.

6. **More Fine-grained Opt-in/Opt-out**

   In each of the three previous cases, a more fine-grained approach to opting in or out can be implemented. Specific opt-ins or opt-outs could be agreed upon with each customer for a variety of permissions and protections. For example, disclosure to third parties or affiliates could be based on specific data fields: a customer might agree to their address and interest profile being provided, but not their financial information and their telephone number.

   Opt-in/opt-out could also be further extended to gain a more detailed profile of each customer and their interests. For example, each class of opt-out identified in Section 4 could be applied separately to each category of personal data (e.g., demographic data, preference data), or down to each specific item of personal data (e.g., age, gender, hiking interest, shoe brand preference). In this manner, customers could opt out of certain actions relating to certain interest areas, but could opt in to others (e.g., to receive direct marketing by mail for running shoes, or to receive mail or phone notification of sales events for fashion merchandise). This approach is explained further in Appendix A.

7. **Verification of Privacy Procedures** Privacy audits may be required on a periodic basis, or to investigate complaints. Verification of privacy procedures can be performed via a self-audit by the organization's privacy administrator, or in cooperation with an independent auditing service (e.g., BBB Online, TRUSTe, Price Waterhouse, TRW, DMA, or CPA WebTrust), or with a government privacy officer. This would typically be achieved as follows:

a. Examine the logical data model and view structure to confirm the existence of:

- **"Standard" Views** for normal users (restricting access to personal information)
- **"Anonymization" Views** for analytic applications (and possibly disclosure applications)
- **"Opt-out" Views** for action-taking applications (and possibly disclosure applications)
- **"Selective Anonymization"** Views for disclosure applications

b. Examine the applications and users that exist for the system, and the access rights that have been granted to them:

- **Privileged applications**/users only have access rights to the "Personal Data" View.
- **Analytic applications**/users only have access rights to "Anonymizing" Views.
- **Action-taking applications**/users only have access rights to "Opt-out" Views.
- **Disclosure applications** only have access to "Selective Anonymization" or "Anonymization" or "Opt-out" Views.
- **Other applications** use the "Standard" View.

c. Examine the RDBMS Security and Access Logs to review access activity.

Author's Note:

The NCR Privacy Center in San Diego provided much of the information in this chapter. Specific thanks go to the core materials originated and compiled by Ken O'Flaherty under the leadership of Bob Henderson and Peter Reid and their worldwide privacy team. The research and governmental guidelines included herein are derived from white papers. We hope that this chapter provides significant understanding on how to manage this touchy issue and also how to facilitate it within a small or large organization.

11

The @ctive Data Warehouse

"As the world of electronic commerce and CRM increases velocity... strategic leadership forges the potential of operational and analytical systems as being one entity for everyone to access and use to service their customers."

Dr. Stephen Brobst
"Strategies for Managing Customer Information"
Presentation at Partners Conference, Orlando, 1999.

▶ A New Breed of Decision Support

The development of **@ctive data warehouse** implementations change the landscape of advanced decision support in competitive business environments. This will also become true in the governmental applications, and the immediacy in decision-making required in the new millennium.

The implications of actionable decision support capabilities are four-fold in nature:

- A company or government uses a shareable real-time decision support environment instead of an *operational data store* (or ODS) with both short (daily, hourly, or nano-second) update combined with long-term (many years of) transactions and interactions with customers, suppliers, channels, and multiple internal business units.

- The @ctive warehouse **enables all levels of management to make instant decisions and drives knowledgeable measurements** plus vast process changes to the operational (day-to-day and, in the future, minute-to-minute) activities. This also involves changing the methods of allocating resources and marketplace changes to price, quantity, logistics, deliveries, and meeting customer requirements.
- The environment **enables long-term investment analysis** and customer relationship analysis with short-term resource allocations and responsibility changes.
- The ability to **engage in marketplace velocity**, increasing speed of change to product, price, markets, channels, and relationships.

The evolutionary steps from first generation decision support or initial data warehouse implementations to cross-organizational active data warehouse deployment, described in Chapter 5, provided a means for incrementally delivering business value in the path toward advanced decision support and significantly profitable info-structure capabilities.

In this chapter you will learn about the advanced approaches and also read specific case study examples in the diverse areas of transportation customer relationship management, medical services customer management, and inventory management. Each illustrates the "active" or concurrent velocity approach to CRM.

▶ Knowing Differences—Old World Versus Active Info-Structures

The scope and impact of "info-structure" (or data warehouse) implementations are rapidly expanding and transforming to address today's new set of business requirements. These requirements have evolved to demand a decision support/capability that is not simply oriented toward corporate staff or summary reporting activities in the central headquarters offices, but on an actionable, day-to-day (or minute-to-minute) basis.

Decisions such as when to replenish Barbie dolls at a particular retail outlet may not be strategic at the level of customer segmentation or long-term pricing strategies, but when executed properly, they certainly make a big difference to the bottom line. Those capabilities are referred to as "tactical" decision support. Tactical decisions are the drivers for day-to-day management of the business. Businesses today want more than just strategic insight from their knowledge-based info-structure implementations—they want better execution in running the business through more effective use of information for the everyday decisions that get made thousands of times per *day*.

The bottom line impact of a well-placed info-structure for tactical decision support capability often rivals that of strategic decision support. In the end, the business wants and needs both.

▶ First Generation Implementations—The Refreshment Cycle

The first stages of decision support capability provided in the evolution of the data warehouse marketplace focused primarily upon batch-oriented decision support capability. These implementations focus on delivery of cleansed and integrated data to the "information starved" marketing, finance, actuarial, and other corporate decision-making groups. Information from across the organizational silos created by operational systems (usually along product boundaries) is made available for query purposes to knowledge workers. Value to the organization is huge: for the first time, a customer-centric view of the business or, perhaps, integrated sales and inventory data is available to decision-makers.

The Enterprise Scalable Data Warehouse environment consists of multiple levels of data and its movement into the true historical memory detailed database. See Figure 11-1, which shows the various sources and repositories throughout the multilayer environment. At the bottom are sample applications and processes that become active in the management systems to marketplace.

This diagram uses the Data Warehouse Framework shown in the early stages of DW and the top-to-bottom flow of information resources. This flow continues overtime, but the uses of the information change over time, which is the maturity process highlighted in Chapter 5, and the economic value increases with velocity and usefulness.

Using the Data Warehouse as Your "INFOrmation-InfraSTRUCTURE"

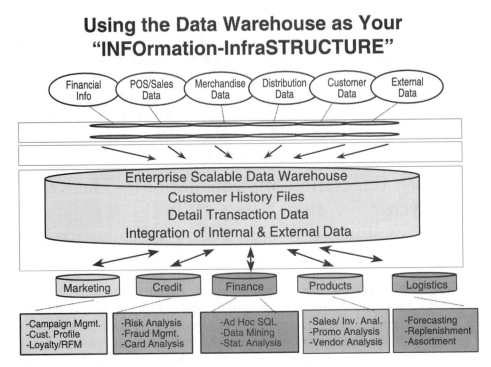

Figure 11-1. The DW as "Enterprise Info-InfraStructure."

The refresh cycle for a first-generation Data Warehouse implementation is typically monthly or weekly. Queries are often launched in a batch-oriented environment with somewhat long turnaround times. A typical implementation allows ad hoc queries during the day and batch scoring algorithms for customer segmentation, profitability calculations, predictive response models, and so on, using the overnight window of available time.

Advanced organizations may even take the results from the overnight (batch scoring) jobs and feed them back into the operational systems to assist in customer care (e.g., providing customer product affinity scores to customer service representatives to assist in cross-selling and up-selling).

> **Extensive support for multi-user query workloads, or even complex queries, is a rarity in the early stages of a cross-organizational knowledge-based environment.**

During the early stages, roll-out of decision support capability is limited to a small number of *"power users"* and analytically oriented decision-makers, so supporting widespread deployment is not yet an issue. To the extent that a large number of users exist, they are usually limited to pre-built summary tables (sometimes called "data marts" or "multi-dimensional databases" or "cubes") for satisfying queries in a highly parameterized reporting environment. This is efficient, but may not be effective in the long run and may not allow for thoughtful maturation.

Despite the limitations of early designs, substantial value is delivered by bringing detailed data and a total organizational view of customer relationships together for the first time. Of course, a successful data warehouse implementation always begets demands for even further enhancement to the value proposition for the business. It is in this light that many of the pre-turn-of-the-century decision support implementations were limiting in the strategic sense. Many have begun moving toward the "active" data warehouse, bringing vast new thought of information uses and capability into the mainstream of the business.

▶ Current Generation Data Warehouse Implementations

The key to maximizing the value derived from a customer-centric info-structure is to make the decision-making actionable and relevant to the business.

First generation data warehouse implementations are often consigned to one of two extremes: either purely strategic endeavors, such as studying long-term trends in the business or for an individual department to perform customer segmentation activities. The value of these activities, while certainly critical, is difficult to quantify; that is, unless the organization provides effective managerial sponsorship, measurement, analysis, and growth plans.

"Measurable value comes when the results of strategic analysis get translated into actionable decisions."

Mark Hurd, Senior VP—NCR Corporation
Address to Barcelona I/T Conference, April 1999

Many such decisions are possible with initial implementations: pricing, market positioning, business strategy development, and so on. Getting to the next level of value, however, requires wider deployment of decision support in the business. Rather than relegating customer-centric information to the narrow domain of a think tank exercise, organizations are leveraging them into a more proactive role in the management and execution of the enterprise.

One of the most effective approaches used is **"event-based triggering."** The technology uses quantitative decision-making techniques to analyze business events with the goal of proactively generating triggers for initiating operational activities.

Customer retention is a particularly good application of event-based triggering. By detecting events that may lead to customer attrition, proactive steps can be taken to retain the most valuable customers to the enterprise.

Example: Transportation/Airline Customer Sensitivity

A recent experience of a friend of ours by a major airline provides an excellent example of the technique. After a long day at a client site, he made his way to the airport for a flight to a conference at which he was scheduled to speak early the next morning. At the airport, he found out that his flight—the last one that night—was delayed indefinitely due to a mechanical problem. He had encountered a similar delay (with the same airline) only a few weeks earlier. (It is also important to note that he flies over 100,000 miles per year on this airline.)

It was well past midnight by the time he arrived to his destination.

Upon dragging himself out of bed at 6 A.M. for the keynote speech, loyalty to the airline was definitely not at its peak. Allegiance to an airline goes only so far when on-time performance or service is not up to par.

The interesting part of the story occurred when he arrived home that very next Friday night. A letter of apology from the airline was waiting for him in the mailbox, complete with some statistics about on-time performance (demonstrating that his two recent bad experiences were an unfortunate statistical anomaly) AND two first class upgrade certificates along with a free round-trip flight voucher. With an apology and certificates in his hand, the inconvenience of a couple of late night flights didn't seem quite so bad to him anymore.

Learn by Having Very Detailed CRM Data About Customers

This particular airline is relatively sophisticated in its use of data warehousing. Clearly, after the second major flight delay in as many weeks they identified him as an **"at-risk customer"** based on a scoring initiated by the delayed flight event. Interestingly, the airline didn't react to the first delayed flight that month. Even more interesting is that not all passengers on the plane received compensation for the inconvenience. The airline sent nothing at all to his companion traveler, who flies much less frequently than our friend, and who had not experienced the previous delay.

> **Selective inclusion in a retention program is an important aspect of its effectiveness and long-term value.**

The combination of his risk of attrition and high value to the airline triggered inclusion in an aggressive retention program designed to re-build confidence in on-time performance and re-enforce loyalty through flight rewards.

The customer retention program described above can be translated into a variety of other industries and scenarios. Providers of wireless services often use **dropped call events** to trigger customer retention activities. **Missed or late deliveries** may be the events to look for in the package shipping business. A botched wire or transfer is a likely candidate in the financial services arena.

> **Sophisticated event-based triggering uses combinations of different events to optimize a customer retention program.**

The key is to have integrated detailed data (and events) from across *all* customer relationships and touch points within the enterprise. This should include all of the transactions and all of the *customer-touch* interactions.

Event-based triggering is certainly not confined to customer retention programs.

Example: Health Care CRM Before the Doctor's Services

In health care data warehouse implementations, for example, event-based triggering is used in proactive intervention programs when high-risk patients are identified and steered into case management programs. By scoring patients as early as possible when acquiring pre-admission certification for illnesses, health care costs and quality can often be managed more effectively by case managing the individual back to health rather than relying on traditional health care processes.

Identification of candidates for case management using quantitative scoring techniques with significant breadth and depth of patient data enables earlier and more effective allocation of case management resources. Using these quantitative decision-making techniques allows the traditional physician referral process for case management to be augmented to benefit the health of individual patients, as well as the overall management of health care costs. Areas of particular success include case management for high risk pregnancies, chronic diabetics, chronic asthmatics, congestive heart failure patients, and other illnesses where close monitoring by skilled nursing professionals can significantly impact the health of an individual.

Scoring will usually be initiated based on an event such as a pre-admission certification request or on-line nursing call, and will use both patient characteristics (age, gender, heredity, etc.) and past medical patient history to make individual decisions regarding placement into a case management scenario.

Medical claims data may also be used to initiate scoring, but lags in acquisition of this data often make its use outside of chronic illnesses less beneficial than data that can be acquired earlier in the medical process.

Examples in Banking, Insurance, and Other Industries

In the banking industry, events such as a large deposit into a checking account may trigger communications to a customer regarding alternative investment vehicles (with higher yields). The specifics of the communication should be based on the customer's individual needs.

Assessment of these needs should be based on an understanding of the investment portfolio, risk tolerance, cyclical monetary movements, and other aspects of the individual, and should be scored considering the multiple account relationships within the bank.

An impending payment date on a life insurance policy may be used to trigger customer communications to minimize the probability of lapse. Life events also play a large role in triggering action within the business. For example, a "right-selling" approach in the insurance industry would certainly involve working with a customer to re-evaluate the appropriate coverage upon major life changes such as marriage, birth of a child, or purchase of a new home. Depending on the customer relationship, life events may be reported directly by the customer, or acquired from external service bureaus.

Notice that all of these examples are utilizing a proactive role in triggering action within the business, based on event detection and scoring. First generation implementations often provide the ability to perform list selection and extracts for purposes of direct mail and telemarketing campaigns. However, these list pulls are largely initiated by human intervention or pre-defined scheduling criteria that are largely independent of individual customer events.

Mature IT groups are much more focused on proactive management of customer events, rather than just reacting to them.

Part of making a decision actionable and relevant is to ensure that it is timely. Monthly refresh cycles are not nearly frequent enough for proactive management of events. Nightly (incremental) refresh is typically a minimum requirement for proactive event-based triggering. For example, win back campaigns in the long distance calling marketplace degrade almost exponentially in effectiveness for each day lost after a competitive disconnect.

As you move through the maturity stages, your organization will require more frequent updates and workload characteristics that are much more sophisticated. The need to score many different subsets of customers, based on event classifications (using different quantitative models appropriate to each scenario), leads to more sophisticated use of database optimizer capabilities in query execution. The beginnings of true multi-user query capabilities also emerge as a requirement for supporting a more diverse workload.

▶ The @ctive Data Warehouse Strategy

The "active" data warehouse implementations will need to support real-time analytics to assist in managing the customer relationship at any and all touch points. The focus on CRM in a competitive business environment will drive toward leverage of the capability in directing customer interactions for one-to-one relationship building. The @ctive data warehousing concept comes to maturity as analytical decision support capabilities are integrated directly with customer interactions.

Consider, for example, interacting with a customer service representative (CSR) in pursuit of a retail catalog purchase.

Pre-defined responses for cross-selling and up-selling are often scripted for interacting with customers based on product of inquiry. This is not what it means to deliver one-to-one customer service (see Peppers and Rogers: "One-to-One Marketing Handbook," 1998).

The key is to understand the individual needs of each customer and service these needs rather than produce the same response for everyone asking about a particular product.

While cross-selling and up-selling based on product inquiry can certainly be effective, this technique falls short of one-to-one relationship building because it does not seek to understand the customer as an individual.

Next generation customer service interactions will need to use scoring techniques based on product of inquiry AND customer specific purchase patterns and demographics to suggest the best offer for each individual customer.

Moreover, customer-specific marketing techniques will allow special offers and pricing to individual customers based on the loyalty and profitability of each customer.

Notice that real-time scoring is essential because pre-defined scoring (even if it is based on customer-specific attributes) ignores the most influential attributes of all—those that describe the content of the customer interaction at this very moment.

Providing on-line scoring to help representatives interact with customers is only the beginning of real-time customer relationship management utilizing a data warehouse. The trend toward integrating the data warehouse with customer interactions will be adopted even more aggressively and evolve toward more sophisticated use of information as corporations explore ways of developing a customer relationship management strategy in the face of e-commerce as a way of conducting business.

So, the "active" data warehouse encompasses numerous data collection customer touch-points and internal applications systems, as well as the abilities to drive new forms of knowledge bases to create new applications and environments. In Figure 11-2 you can view the integrated entities of your total info-structure of the active environment and process.

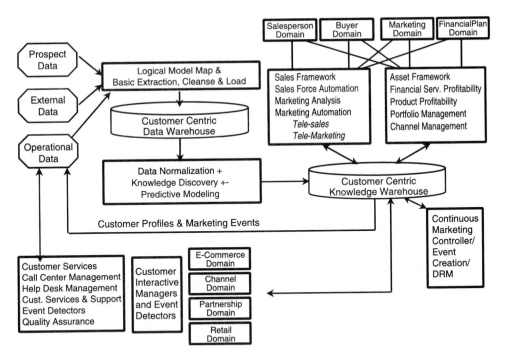

Figure 11-2. An @ctive Data Warehouse Info-Structure.

Web-Based Business Opportunities

Conducting business over the Web will augment traditional channels of relationship building. Bank tellers, travel agents, retail salespersons, brokers, and so on are quickly being out-moded by self-service models using the Internet for a large number of business-to-business and business-to-consumer enterprises.

Reaction to this trend from an operational perspective has been very positive. Reduced costs in customer service resulting from the self-service model are very attractive. However, marketing organizations in astute corporations are grappling with the impact of losing direct contact with the customer.

Brand image and quality of a relationship are largely based on the "experience" of doing business with an enterprise.

Because human customer service representatives are becoming disintermediated in the world of e-commerce, the intelligence necessary for superior customer care must be built into the Web interactions. The intimacy of experience previously provided by human interaction now needs to be delivered using advanced CRM techniques in an automated fashion. This means that individual customer profiles and on-line scoring capability need to become accessible from within the transactional model for implementing best-of-breed e-commerce solutions.

Specific applications of data warehousing capability that we have seen in the context of e-commerce solutions include cross-selling, up-selling, yield management with customer-specific pricing, fraud detection, and so on, will become the norm.

Each of these applications requires heavy duty analytics and yet must be delivered in the transaction-oriented world of e-commerce.

The goal is to provide an interaction which is uniquely customized to each individual based on specific needs that can be gleaned at the time of the e-commerce event, combined with as much demographic, purchase, inquiry, and other information as can be leveraged to refine the interaction.

▶ Paving the Future for Knowledge Commerce

Next generation "customer relationship management systems" and "knowledge-based data warehouse" implementations will push the envelope of technology in a big way. Response time requirements for on-line scoring of individual customer events will be nearly instantaneous. This requirement combines the large database size and query complexity of a traditional decision support environment with the response time requirements of a traditional transaction processing system.

Moreover, data acquisition needs to become much more real-time than in current or previous implementations. This is much more than a two-phase commit on a database. Continuous "trickle feed" and advanced replication mechanisms are now required.

The bar of successful integration and viability will also be raised for Reliability, Availability, Serviceability, Privacy, Electronic-Commerce, and Recoverability (**RASPER**). These are the characteristics of newer generation info-structures.

Active data warehousing is all about integrating advanced decision support with day-to-day decision-making. Success in this endeavor inevitably escalates the RASPER requirements for the data warehouse because enabling tactical decision-making becomes mission critical. Moreover, in the world of e-commerce there is no downtime—the channel for delivering products and services is open twenty-four hours a day, every day of the year.

Another requirement that first and current generation data warehouse implementations are not prepared for is the orders of magnitude increase in concurrent query workload. No longer are we talking about dozens or even hundreds of simultaneously executing queries—concurrency will reach into the thousands when customer service representatives and Web sites begin accessing the data warehouse for sophisticated scoring capabilities. Middleware software, such as TUXEDO and TOP-END from BEA Systems, will become a critical component of active data warehouse architectures. The ability to assist in managing service levels for performance and availability in the face of thousands of concurrently launched queries will be a key role of the middleware layer in these implementations.

> **"The hallmark of a competitive management team is to position itself for the unknown _and_ to enable the organization for the immediacy of knowledge-based decision-making."**
>
> Robert Fair
> **"The Value of Knowledge-Based Decision-Making in Competitive Industries,"**
> **Presentation at Communications Industry—Leaders Roundtable, 1999.**

▶ Coming of Age in the New Age of E-Commerce

The marketplace is coming of age as we progress from "passive" decision support systems to "active" customer-centric data warehouse implementations. Convergence of requirements from traditional decision support and transactional systems presents challenges previously not dealt with in high-end database implementations.

Technology is in the position of playing catch-up to these requirements. Phased implementation strategies will be the best way to ensure successful deployment within the constraints of today's technology.

The key is to design today with an eye toward tomorrow.

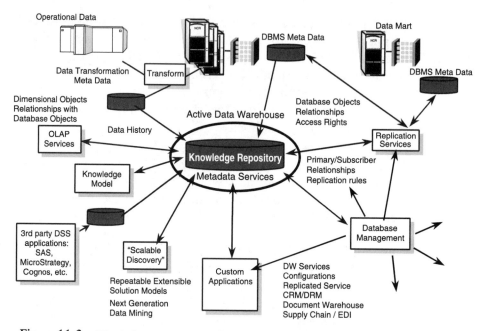

Figure 11-3. The info-structure using the "@ctive Data Warehouse" and the "Corporate Knowledge Repository.

Finally, there is quite an impressive group of organizations in the U.S. and worldwide that is moving to the truly tactical (active) and strategic info-structure environment. Some of them are highlighted in Chapter 8 and as "excellence examples" in various chapters throughout this book. The architectural view of these new environments can be summarized in Figure 11-3.

▶ E-commerce and E-business

Each day companies collect large amounts of customer online data through many of the numerous systems, as well as the Internet interactions. Some companies use an application to parse and filter the data they find important to their business processes. Other companies may have an application that takes that data and generates reports on customer activity. The real question is how do you combine online customer information with information obtained from kiosks, ATM's, delivery channels, sales channels, the call center, the customer service department, or third parties?

To make educated decisions about your customer, many companies have developed a "single repository" for customer knowledge that absorbs information from all of these disparate sources and also provides interaction internally and externally through the Internet for e-business and e-commerce. The development of active data warehousing provides the capability of continually "feeding" the knowledge base giving a 360-degree view of the customers.

Click-Stream Analysis Opportunities

Click-stream analysis programs deliver standard reports based on online data and actions of the prospect or customer. Companies perform sophisticated profiling and learn the effectiveness of trial promotions and propensities of customers to look, inquire, purchase, or reject offers. Some of the most valuable information gained from click-stream analysis is the rejections. This type of knowledge may point to the type of offer, the price, the timing, or possibly a better understanding of the individual needs of the prospect.

Collecting positive as well as negative interactions and transactions provides a wealth of knowledge, especially over long periods of time. People have two common behaviors in life. The first is repetitive behavior and the second is seeking to find new knowledge. When each of these behaviors occurs, it becomes a signal of psychological behaviors that a company can foster. Knowing that repetitive behavior is happening, provides opportunity to use historical transactions to generate repetitive (accepted) offers or similarities in new products or services. Knowledge gathering, or knowledge seeking, can provide opportunities for presenting new (and sometimes related) offerings.

The high profitability use of DW and CRM happens when events are "discovered" as they occur. Then an "active" process, application, human, or relationship technology is initiated to communicate with the individual. Having continuous, timely, detailed, and correlated data, in an active data warehouse environment, enables many new opportunities.

@ctive Data Warehousing for E-business on the Internet

@ctive data warehousing and supporting applications with decision making is an essential requirement for successful e-commerce and e-business on the Internet.

Over the past century the old economy has evolved from mass marketing to segment marketing, and is now moving towards one-to-one marketing. The new e-business economy is following in the same footsteps but at an accelerated pace. To target customers individually, you will need the info-structures described in this book and the use of new relationship technologies.

For example, when using data warehouse tools for a new promotion of your product or service, you can identify a trial group by geography, demographics, and propensity to buy, based upon prior purchase history and behaviors.

Then, you can test-market different banner ads to optimize the effectiveness of your promotion. This optimization allows you to do this one-to-one marketing in a single or multi-channel scenario improving customer profitability and loyalty.

Advertising analysis programs typically deliver standard reports based on campaign impressions and click-throughs. By contrast, data warehouse mining and online analytical processing tools (OLAP) allow you to obtain sophisticated, ad hoc analysis of ad campaign data with customer segmentation data.

For example, an advertiser is looking at a standard report that noted the number of impressions, click-throughs, and conversions to a sale, by banner, ad and publisher. Seeing that one specific publisher had higher conversions, the advertiser can drill down to look at segmentation, contextual data, and time-of-day to learn how to be more effective on other Web sites. In addition, advertisers can take this information and test it against other publisher data. Using these tools, the advertiser can design or fine-tune a campaign to maximize its effectiveness and ultimately help to build higher margin marketing services.

Advertising campaigns are becoming more sophisticated. In particular, to reach their target audience, advertisers use multiple channels, banners, television, wireless devices, and e-mail. How does one manage the use of these channels to deliver an effective campaign message in the most optimum way? For example, what if a consumer clicks on a banner ad but doesn't purchase from the advertiser's site? You could use this event to trigger the delivery of an e-mail with a special message to encourage them to complete the purchase. You will need the capability to manage marketing campaigns and promotions across multiple contact channels.

Privacy and The Internet

In Chapters 9 and 10 you will find significant information regarding the requirements and planning for a privacy policy. You will want to implement a privacy strategy and policy for the protection of your customers, your company, and potential audits of activities or uses of the data that you acquire and maintain in your knowledge repository. (see Chapters 9 and 10). This subject and its future uses in your organization can be an excellent way of maintaining of winning customer confidence in your organization (especially on the Internet). Assuring customers of your commitment to their privacy is not only good business; it is an effective method of communicating one of your CRM principles.

▶ Excellence in Business Transformation: Delta Air Lines Takes Off Using Advanced @ctive Data Warehousing for CRM

Delta Air Lines carries more than 100 million passengers annually on more than 2,600 daily flights. The airline began by dusting crops in 1924 and, for the past three-quarters of a century, has built a strong route structure and many partnerships throughout the world. Delta believes that superior customer service is behind its most recent successes and will be its defining, competitive focus for years to come.

Millions of dollars in increased revenues and decreased costs, and a better understanding of its customers and operations, are a few of the initial benefits Delta Air Lines has realized through its investments in data warehousing and CRM.

Delta Air Lines' Challenge

In a fiercely competitive, mature industry, Delta strives to find ways to get closer to the customer to differentiate itself in the marketplace and reduce costs.

For many years Delta had created numerous decision support and customer information systems throughout the many divisional areas of the company. Delta found that information was difficult to correlate across the organization, especially for marketing and resource decision-making, due to over 25 different "data marts" used in multiple organizations, each data mart for their own purposes.

"In the past, we wasted a lot of energy trying to get numbers from different analytical systems to correlate with each other," explains Brent Lautenschlegar, Director of Data Warehouse Services at Delta Technology (the wholly owned information technology subsidiary for Delta Air Lines).

"With the existing systems, we would gather the information we had available and make an educated decision," says Keith Drewski, Manager of Data Services for Delta Marketing.

Without a **"single version of the truth,"** Delta's existing data mart strategy made accurate decision making difficult. To take advantage of the operational and customer data it collected, Delta knew that users needed easy access to enterprise business information.

Delta Air Lines' Solution

Delta had the data it needed within its systems, but with it fragmented across various functional areas, users weren't able to obtain an enterprise view of the business or the customers. The airline quickly set out to develop an enterprise-wide data warehousing strategy to provide users easy access to a central view of near real-time enterprise business information.

Wayne Hyde, Vice-President of e-Delta Systems at Delta Technology, had previous experience with data warehousing and felt confident in its ability to solve these and many other challenges. Delta needed total scalability, easy business user access, easy data collection and loading on a faster basis than before, and very fast turnaround to its hundreds of requests and queries generated by a changing, competitive business environment.

Delta consolidated the dozens of data marts into one centralized data warehouse to gain a single version of accurate information across the organization. Delta's business user community routinely asks challenging questions against this very detailed data using statistical analysis and analytical tools.

This approach allows Delta to rapidly optimize cross-organizational business opportunities that would lead to improved levels of service to their customers and improved profitability to its shareholders.

At the beginning of the 21st century, Delta estimated that it was supporting 1,300 data warehousing users across its major business areas, estimating that number to grow to 2,300 within the following year.

Marketing was the initial DW subject area, with technical operations, cargo, and many others following.

"We're constantly uncovering new subject areas and new pieces of information that people want to bring into the warehouse so they can have quicker and easier access to it," Lautenschlegar explains.

Delta developed a strategy to complete all project phases within a 60-day period. Typically, the first phase of work involves populating the warehouse with transaction or detailed level information and training users. In subsequent phases, summaries and predefined reports, and analysis are developed and placed on top of the detailed information in the data warehouse. "This approach has been valuable in terms of quickly putting information in front of users and enabling them to provide feedback to the IT organization to shape subsequent phases of projects. It also gives IT people a sense of accomplishment by getting things done in a faster period of time," summarized Lautenschlegar.

Delta Air Lines' Benefits

By providing users with fast and easier access to very detailed information, Delta has increased the confidence in the quality and the speed in which new questions and decisions can be achieved.

"In addition to having a single source of high integrity and reliable data, you must also provide tools that allow large numbers of users to have fast, easy access to their data. Having one without the other really doesn't make much sense," added Hyde.

In the first 18 months of the *enterprise-wide @ctive data warehouse*, Delta estimated the *ROI was seven to eight times its investment*. Delta's executive team and its more than 1,300 data warehouse users are making fact-based business decisions that positively impact customers and operations on a daily basis.

Using NCR's Teradata @ctive Data Warehouse brought together data from more than 25 major operational systems into one enterprise system. Previously, a typical information request submitted to the technology department would take, on average, three to eight weeks to get a response. Now, with company-wide self-service through the Web, Delta's business and management users get most answers within minutes.

One example is how Delta measures customer value. Traditionally, the airline industry rewards passengers for the number of miles they fly. Delta changed that practice by matching revenue to frequent flyers and found a low correlation between passengers flying the most miles and those generating the most revenue. Armed with that information, Delta focused greater attention on its highest value flyers, not merely those customers who fly the most miles.

"We must treat our passengers as individuals. The data warehouse provides some of the tools we need to understand who those individuals are and how we can best take care of them," says Keith Drewski, marketing manager of Delta Air Lines.

Delta also uses the data warehouse to improve its understanding of sales and distribution channels—how passengers buy tickets (i.e., through travel agencies, over the phone or via the Internet). By understanding that mix and how changes in areas such as advertising, ticketing practices, and incentives can influence how passengers purchase tickets, Delta can improve the efficiency and effectiveness of its marketing and operations. Previously, Delta used a sampling of ticket sales to gather this information. With the data warehouse, Delta now can use a 100-percent sample to get a much more accurate assessment of its sales channels to determine the best way to sell to customers.

Delta is using the data warehouse as an integral component of developing Delta's CRM strategy, which will tie in to all customer touch points of the "travel ribbon" (i.e., making a reservation, going to the airport and checking bags, boarding a flight, being in-flight and the post-airport experience). The goal will be to integrate real-time analytical decision-support capabilities directly with customer interactions.

Hyde explains, "Our CRM program really looks at targeting our customers much more closely than they've ever been targeted before, where a passenger can be a 'market of one.' It all goes back to knowing the value of an individual customer and recognizing that value."

Delta's expectations for its data warehousing solution were high, requiring fast analysis for a large number of users while housing vast amounts of data. Using a combined CRM and @ctive data warehousing strategy, Delta Air Lines' employees around the world are empowered to make better decisions based on sound knowledge day in and day out.

"We are moving more and more of our business and larger numbers of users to a reliance on this data for day-to-day decision making, which makes it even more important to have a reliable platform...to provide consistent performance as use increases," Hyde continues.

As customer information, e-commerce, e-business, e-sales, e-travel, CRM, and relationship technologies become more tightly intertwined, Delta sees the active data warehouse becoming more central to all it does. At Delta Air Lines, employees are empowered throughout the business with the information necessary to make better decisions each and every day, using CRM, data warehousing, and relationship technologies to achieve new goals, strategic objectives, higher profitability, and increased share value.

▶ Management Considerations

- For the business managers reading this book, drive your information technology investments to create an analytical environment which encompasses data from all of the systems that touch your customers. Then utilize this new info-structure to foster both analytical and predictive applications. The business management team that sponsors these enabling information technologies can then implement the future.

- For the technical people reading this book, begin your next generation data warehouse by introducing advanced indexing techniques for your detailed customer data. Also, create an environment of mixed workload support for both operational and informational (analytical) applications available to your usiness management users. These approaches are particularly important in light of the impending tidal wave of e-commerce capability that will be required in your new customer care solutions.

You can achieve a successful and profitable future when you have the info-structure to support it.

Chapter

12

The Economic Value of CRM

▶ One-to-One Marketing

While the "one-to-one" marketing mantra is familiar to most people, it is all-too-often misunderstood as simply "database marketing." According to one-to-one guru Martha Rogers, "The difference is about customization—about generating feedback from customers so that marketers can learn more about their preferences, so future offers of products, packaging, delivery, communications, or even invoicing can be tailored to these preferences." To substantiate the concept of CRM, let's look at four one-to-one customer experiences in Figure 12-1.

We should remember that the One-to-One Marketing concept (published by Peppers and Rogers in many books and articles since 1997) has embodied the four key elements of:

1. Identify
2. Differentiate
3. Interact
4. Customize

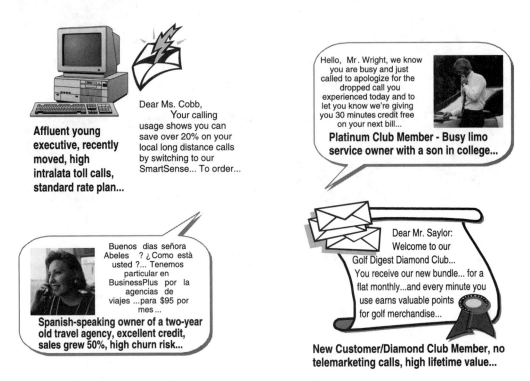

Figure 12-1. Customer One-to-One Marketing Communications.

The one-to-one approach is included in the foundations of the tactical and strategic processes and frameworks to support relationship marketing. Please make sure that you fully research and clarify your enterprise's understanding and objectives in these areas. In addition, an investment in a truly supportive information-infrastructure, driving to the "single version of the truth" will be required for successful growth and strength of your CRM process.

With the advent of data warehousing and data warehouse-enabled CRM *technologies and applications* (e.g., data mining, campaign management), companies are making huge investments. The average 1997 DW-based project required $1.9 million to implement. Sparked by expectations of improving "customer relationship management," sales of data warehoused-enabled CRM products and services are growing at an annual clip of 21% (Source: International Data Corporation, 1999).

Since the concept of CRM is unique in IT management, defining a successful project is especially important compared to traditional operational systems such as billing, financial statements, inventory control, and order entry processing. For example, there are many schools of thought concerning investment justification in CRM. Below we will review some of the more effective ideas on this subject.

While operational systems address relatively structured business problem(s), Data Warehousing with CRM is an "enterprise enabling technology." Hence, investment justification can be argued on the basis of strategic reasons, such as becoming a learning organization or "knowledge colony." Considering the unique nature of CRM technologies, we will use the following definition(s) of success as:

- **Build core competencies** to more effectively and efficiently acquire, retain, serve, and grow customers. According to Don Peppers and Martha Rogers,[1] "one-to-one marketing is made possible by three important capabilities that information technology now provides: customer tracking, interactive dialogue, and mass customization. Taken together, these new capabilities not only make marketing possible, but competitively essential." The biggest problem in justifying information technology is not the cost of the technology itself, but the lack of a reliable way to calculate return on investment (ROI).

Peppers and Rogers argue that the strategies they have been proposing are especially difficult to justify because the strategies themselves are new and different, and the benefits are primarily on the revenue side. You should possibly evaluate investments in such strategies/ capabilities (technologies, processes, and people) based on the *strategic* advantage over competition, evaluating anticipated ROI on the overall, long-term value of your customer base.

However, such strategic benefits are intangible and often difficult to measure (yet theoretically drive increased fundamental shareholder value). Adopting Michael Porter's "Value Chain" creates a conceptual framework for understanding the strategic value of core CRM competencies. The illustration in Figure 12-2 shows that CRM capabilities can impact other value-added activities, thereby further enhancing customer experience and gaining competitive advantage.

---

[1]*"Enterprise One to One," Copyright 1997 by Don Peppers and Martha Rogers, Ph.D*

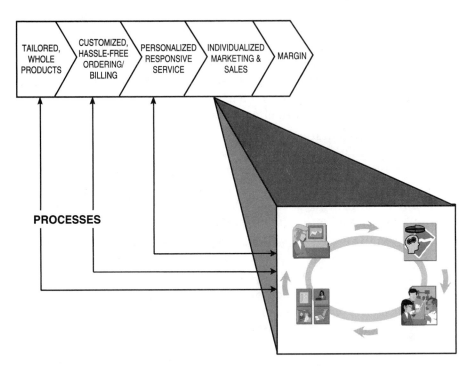

Figure 12-2. The Value Chain Model and the CRM Process Model.

Some of the benefits that CRM achieves include:

1. **faster, more informed decision-making**
2. **improved accuracy**
3. **improved customer service**
4. **faster product-to-market realization**
5. **migration from a product focus to a customer focus**

Thus, investments in such technologies are considered enterprise-enabling. Under this justification approach, the **focus is on speed,** no longer whether or not we should invest. How quickly can you build such capabilities compared to your competitors?

- **Solve the defined business problem** (albeit a clear definition may not exist in some CRM projects) and deliver the anticipated benefits in the form of incremental revenue, cost reduction, or both. Using this more traditional justification approach, Patricia Seybold Group[2] suggests there are two aspects to the economics of customer management.

One involves acquiring customers more efficiently (customer acquisition), and the other involves holding onto them for longer periods of time (customer retention). Figure 12-3 uses an adaptation of the Malcom Baldridge Quality Scoring Framework to see the emphasis on traditional business results.

Victor Sassone, Director of Customer Learning at Hogan Quality Consultants of Dallas, Texas, states: *"Companies with a penchant for excellent customer service and life-time customer relationships know that CRM-type activities are essential to their success."* Sassone is a leading consultant and educator of Southwestern area small- and medium-sized businesses desiring to learn and practice Baldridge Quality, and CRM techniques. Sassone goes on to say: "We see many firms achieving revenue and profitability increases far beyond their initial expectations."

But many companies still do not believe in the value of CRM.

While CRM strategies are somewhat new, quantifiable business impact models can be developed using more traditional methods of ROI analysis for many applications of CRM technologies.

Business Impact Models (BIMs) are designed to gain insight into the investment requirements and the investment returns in CRM. BIMs focus on tangible benefits such as:

- Increase in return on marketing campaign expense (target marketing)
- Increased average customer profitability
- Reduced customer defection (customer retention)

---

[2] *Wayne Eckerson, "How to Architect a Customer Relationship Management Solution," 1996.*

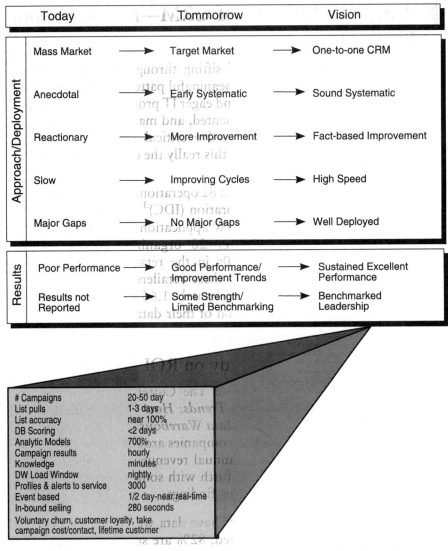

Today		Tommorrow		Vision

Approach/Deployment

Today		Tommorrow		Vision
Mass Market	→	Target Market	→	One-to-one CRM
Anecdotal	→	Early Systematic	→	Sound Systematic
Reactionary	→	More Improvement	→	Fact-based Improvement
Slow	→	Improving Cycles	→	High Speed
Major Gaps	→	No Major Gaps	→	Well Deployed

Results

Poor Performance	→	Good Performance/ Improvement Trends	→	Sustained Excellent Performance
Results not Reported	→	Some Strength/ Limited Benchmarking	→	Benchmarked Leadership

# Campaigns	20-50 day
List pulls	1-3 days
List accuracy	near 100%
DB Scoring	<2 days
Analytic Models	700%
Campaign results	hourly
Knowledge	minutes
DW Load Window	nightly
Profiles & alerts to service	3000
Event based	1/2 day-near real-time
In-bound selling	280 seconds
Voluntary churn, customer loyalty, take campaign cost/contact, lifetime customer	

* Source: Adapted from Macolm Baldridge Quality Assessment

Figure 12-3. Malcom Baldridge Quality Scoring Framework.

Thus, success is defined as achieving the anticipated tangible business benefits of deploying such technologies. This is a much more significant method of maintaining management commitment to CRM and increasing their understanding of the continuing investments in information technology for decision-making, modeling, forecasting and predicting, as well as long-term storage of very detailed customer historical data.

Anticipated Results of CRM—Key Assumptions and Verifications

The science (and art) of sifting through immense collections of very detailed data to identify meaningful patterns and relationships is enticing to innovative marketers and eager IT professionals. As we shall see, when properly planned, implemented, and managed, CRM provides powerful information required to solve critical business problems and gain a competitive advantage. Is this really the case or is it hype? Let's review it now.

A well-known study of 62 operational data warehouses conducted by International Data Corporation (IDC)[3] indicated an average three-year ROI of 401 percent and DW application payback of 2.3 years. The NCR Corporation studied over 20 organizations that invested in data warehousing in the 1990s in the retail industry. The results of the NCR study showed that these retailers achieved between 300% and 1000% increase in approximately 1.66 years from the implementation date of the first application of their data warehouses.

Cutter Consortium Study on ROI in DW

In mid-1999, Curt Hall of The Cutter Consortium published *"Data Warehousing Issues and Trends: How Organizations Worldwide Are Adopting and Applying Data Warehousing Technology"* which is based on detailed surveys of 94 companies around the world. Forty-two (42) of the companies reported annual revenues about the $500 million (U.S.) mark. Hall's study came forth with some interesting results, and I have added my comments to his findings:

- 65% of respondents have data warehouse or data mart type applications deployed, 82% are still deploying;
- The goal of "providing better business intelligence" was the perceived primary benefit among 39%; "consolidating of information sources" and "improved data access" were other major benefits achieved;
- 73% of larger companies and 55% of smaller companies have dedicated data warehousing groups, making DW a mainstream activity;

[3] *"The Foundation of Wisdom: A Study of the Financial Impact of Data Warehousing,"* Copyright, IDC, 1996 (Toronto, Canada).

- Only 17% of 11 companies have commissioned ROI studies of their applications. Those that have, however, report an average 180% ROI, with larger companies reporting approximately 230% and smaller companies reporting approximately 118%;
- Only 21% report that at least 50% of their data warehouse applications are yet deployed. Therefore, many companies have not fully implemented their customer centric solutions and have not studied their ROI because they are unsure of their payback and profitability;
- A surprisingly high number of companies—77%—have **adopted an application development methodology** of some kind, and 40% of them are homegrown. This may attribute some of the **failures** to inexperience and trying to build this new DW and CRM environment without a proven methodology (see Chapter 6);
- Interestingly, 79% have built their own programs for extraction, transformation, and loading of their data from the multiple sources into their data warehouse;
- 49% had predicted that by the end of 1999, they will deploy Web-enabled or Web-based OLAP tolls for end-users, and 49% will deploy Web Reporting or Query Tools.

Although most companies do not have a formal mechanism for establishing goals and determining ROI, we suggest that you review Chapter 6 and the formal SDW Methodology. The first steps include understanding the business issues, setting goals and priorities for the DW and CRM, and establishing responsibilities and joint agreements on the measurements and achievements to be accomplished. This is also one of the critical success factors in Chapter 9.

President Franklin Delano Roosevelt is credited with an interesting statement, encouraging all of us to have the proper perspective: "Certainly I learn from my mistakes, I can repeat any of them." His point, (and mine), is that we should not make continuous mistakes in implementing technology. *And* that we should set goals and know how to evaluate them before we embark on the journey, especially the second time.

Risk of Failure?

Some consultants and magazine writers have been stating high failure rates in data warehousing. They know of losing situations (some as high as 50%–75%).

But it seems that these people are seeking to alarm the uneducated into buying their services or instructional courses. The truth is that you can succeed with a proven methodology, based on business needs that are documented and identified, and the management team working together to achieve a common goal. The team must include both the business management and your information technology management working as a team. See Chapters 6–8 on how you can define, perform, and succeed.

How to Get Your Economics Around CRM

Considering both the novel concept of, and the potential benefit in enabled CRM customer-focused strategies, as well as the unique, unstructured nature of such business problems, to understand the key success factors is potentially very useful for the successful planning, implementation, and management of CRM technologies.

You will need to adopt a set of processes to facilitate analysis of the issues concerning successful CRM applications. There are four chief factors necessary to achieve a successful CRM effort.

1. **Strategic Impact:** A core CRM capability (competency) or a core CRM capability and measurable business problem. Both the capability and business problems must be linked to operating and management processes, corporate strategy and demand-side value chain.

    Generally, use of CRM is aimed at solving less-structured problems, in comparison to traditional operational systems, making problem definition very difficult. Some of the biggest pitfalls of CRM projects are insufficiently defined business requirements,[4] suggesting lack of understanding of the IT impact (strategic and tactical) on CRM. In many of the failed CRM attempts, companies have focused on the "sizzle," diluting resources on "interesting" but useless insights—i.e., that senior citizens don't buy rap music—or have overlooked those that can help solve a real business problem, such as the loss of highly profitable customers to competitors. Hence, CRM is most cost-effective when used to solve a particular problem.[5]

---

[4]*Pieter R. Mimno, "Cost-Justifying a Data Warehouse,"* Patricia Seybold Group Research Report Series *(July 1997).*
[5]*"Debunking Data Mining Myths".*

Fleet Bank, which invested $38 million in a top-notch database marketing infrastructure, has reported an ROI of more than 70%. A major problem at Fleet is that nearly 40% of their customers and products are unprofitable, but current systems limited their knowledge of who these customers were and why.

By using CRM to micro-market the different products to distinct customer segments rather than offering all customers the same products at the same prices, Fleet has reduced the interest rate paid to customers by one-tenth of one percent without changing the total amount of deposits, saving $40 million a year.[6]

In many CRM projects, early ROI is one of three key success factors[7]. The above examples validate the transforming nature (changing the basis of competition) of CRM technologies, and thus, the importance in understanding the strategic and tactical impact (and implications in the successful planning, implementation, and management) of CRM technologies. The strategic advantage comes from being better at managing the information that these (CRM) systems create.[8]

2. **Technology Integration:** Includes the integrated planning, implementation and management of the full spectrum of CRM technologies, and the many CRM business opportunities based on the integration across these and other technologies (e.g., billing, customer care).

Another key factor to CRM failure and, conversely, success, resides in the integrated planning and management. This is particularly relevant to CRM for two major reasons:

- CRM is based on a decision-support architecture and requires feeders from a vast array of internal operational and, more recently, external data sources.
- CRM is enterprise-enabling, cutting across management function and operating activities to solve a particular problem such as how to reduce high value churn. Figure 12-4 is a CRM information flow, which illustrates the previous assumptions concerning integration.

[6]From Wayne Eckerson, "How to Architect a Customer Relationship Management Solution," Patricia Seybold Group (October 1997).
[7]Mitch Kramer, "The Pulse: WorldCom's Large-Scale, Realtime, Data Warehousing," Patricia Seybold Group Case Study (August 1998).
[8]Rob Mattison, "Data Warehousing and DataMining for Telecommunications" (1997).

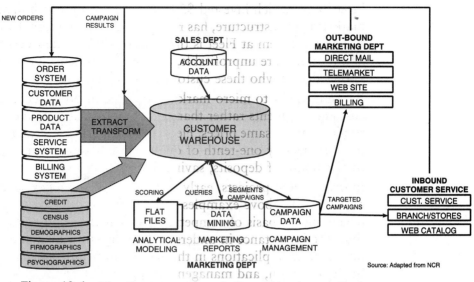

Figure 12-4. The Customer-Centric Data Warehouse Environment.

Once a problem has been defined, such as profiling high value/ high risk customers of long distance services, the process of CRM may involve mining through data collected from various sources systems. Data is analyzed for meaningful patterns about a customer's behaviors to derive valuable profiles that can be used in a target market campaign to retain those customers. This campaign may involve deployment though a customer care system and the results (both in terms of the campaign and order provisioning) feed back into the Data Warehouse or "knowledge repository."

Integration is particularly relevant in CRM for communications but also are: Poor quality integration of CRM strategies, policies, architecture and technology standards, and integration with existing technological platforms can lead to inconsistent results.

3. **Technology Assimilation:** The structure / processes / skills / metrics to successfully drive the process of implementing CRM technologies.

CRM technologies enable radically different ways of doing business from traditional mass-market approaches.

CRM and Relationship Technologies are used for data mining, business rules, and the Internet to dramatically improve customer loyalty, achieve operational goals, and gain a sustainable competitive advantage.

Hence, by not having the organizational capabilities (structure/processes/skills/metrics) integrated to the added intelligence from CRM technologies to either confirm or change past decision criteria, companies will not gain the strategic and economic benefits associated with CRM.

As an example, an insurance company's IT department has analyzed information that shows a valid relationship between the customers who purchased insurance polices and employment length. Unless the new information is imbedded in business processes and made useful to the decision-maker, the information is useless. Even with the new information integrated to business processes, without the necessary skills to use the information to produce a business action (e.g., target market campaign), the mined information adds no value to the company. Hence, in order to realize the full impact of this new approach to target marketing, users must be reasonably data-literate, particularly in strategies where more decision-making authority is moved to the marketing/product manager level, and involved early in the planning/implementation.

Finally, such new CRM strategies require structures and metrics to be aligned in order to operationalize the use of the newly "mined" information. Marketing processes and techniques need to evolve to take advantage of flexible CRM infrastructure. To realize the impact, companies will need to beef up the skill level and experience in the marketing organization, involving rewriting job descriptions, adjusted salaries, and other managerial issues.[9]

4. **Strategic Partnership:** Relationship of executive, IT, and operational (user) management, and support/capability in understanding the managerial and technology issues that transcend organizational boundaries in successfully implementing and managing CRM technologies.

---

[9]*Wayne Eckerson, "How to Architect a Customer Relationship Management Solution," Patricia Seybold Group Research (October 1997).*

A partnership of constituencies[10] is critical to the successful planning, implementation, and management of CRM technologies. This is particularly relevant in CRM for two major reasons:

  a. CRM strategies are aimed at building a sustainable competitive advantage through radically new, technology-enabled approaches. Thus, it requires very close integration between CRM technology management and business strategy;

  b. CRM technologies are "different" compared to traditional operational, or process automation technologies and applications. Data warehousing, unlike its operational brethren, is an approach that involves no specific discipline, no science, and no clear rules or guidelines.[11]

Hence, efforts to exploit competitive advantage are inherently risky and require close partnership with the business.

"Technology issues today (concerning investments in Internet technologies, data warehouse, data mining, and call centers) ironically don't involve technology," says Allan Woods[12], CIO at Mellon Bank. "The issues really involve business, and the attempt to show a very tangible, measurable relationship between technology and successful business strategy. A lot of processes are being developed and implemented to ensure that companies have a shared vision for technology (for CRM), and that they can prove that technology is a strategic enabler."

Another great example is at Federal Express, which earns up to 400% ROI for marketing programs. FEDEX states that to achieve such dramatic results, major investments are required in understanding the customer/problem, organization change, and technology infrastructure (Patricia Seybold Group case study, October 1997).

Consequently, judiciously managing the above key factors in the planning, implementation, and management of CRM technologies can minimize the risk associated with exploiting such technologies and have proven to dramatically transform customer marketing, delivering solid business value and competitive advantage.

[10] Applegate/McFarlan/McKenney, Corporate Information Systems Management: Text and Cases (1996).

[11] Rob Mattison, Data Warehousing and Data Mining for Telecommunications (1997).

[12] Beth Davis, 'Shared Vision' Makes IT Pay Off, Information Week, September 14, 1997.

The Payback from Detailed Information...and the Cost of Not Having It

As most of the world's financial institutions start moving away from aggregated and summarized business information to atomic (very detailed) levels of information made available through Massively Parallel Processing and data warehousing, new opportunities for performance improvements become available to these institutions. Each of these "informatted" institutions will have the opportunity to become the ultimate information competitor, bringing customer intimacy, operational excellence and product superiority to new levels. If not, they will face the alternative of doing business in a hyper-competitive world, without the ability or means to compete or defend.

High Returns

The early investors in detailed information or decision support technology have found ROIs atypically have high returns relative to returns from other technology investments. Some of these financial institutions were achieving a tremendous competitive advantage; thus began the wave of information-based competitors. The firms recouped their investments between one and four years later. Most were in two to three year time frames.

The thinking of the informated leaders was not how many years it would take to reach break-even from their informating investment, but how they would fundamentally transform their competitive approach to the same markets. The very beginning of this type of transformation was yielding exponential ROIs up to 50 times the normal ROI.

One financial institution stated that a ten-month payback on a $3 million investment for target marketing was "somewhere between 10 times and 50 times the normal ROI."

When comparing these returns to the single digit returns realized from the introduction of new products, building a new branch, or installing an ATM, the return on investment clearly placed the informating investment in a different category.

Payback Performance

The payback examples in this study are predominantly performance improvements, which were readily quantifiable with traditional approaches. In many cases, these quantified areas represent only a fraction of the payback on the information investment.

The following areas are considered the main activities upon which financial institutions focused their efforts to achieve payback from data warehouse with very detailed historical customer information:

- Sales and marketing
- Profitability
- Debt management
- Distribution
- Risk

Sales and marketing appeared to have the fastest and greatest payback, followed closely by the remaining areas. These activities, along with other areas, proved significant in terms of ROI.

Nimble Response

The speed at which financial institutions are able to react to change and respond to the market is an important factor contributing to the ROIs achieved by these financial institutions. Several of the institutions conveyed stories of being able to identify a market, enter it, and take market share—all before the competitors understood what had happened.

A good example of this is based upon an institution that decided to target a very competitive market. In the months between the time the decision was made and the time the program was ready to execute, market conditions had changed. The mailing campaign was launched into a market with conditions alien to the institution's original purpose. Because the market presented an opportunity to the organization for only a specific period of time, the opportunity was lost.

In an informatted environment, speed can be the difference between opportunity seized and opportunity lost.

Now, utilizing their data warehouse information, the institution can respond rapidly. It can very quickly compile a list of all the people who have invested in their products in certain periods, with certain types of economic activity. They can also have a breakdown of customer characteristics so they can go after other people in the database with similar characteristics. Their information engine gives them the ability to almost instantaneously react to changes in market conditions.

They are also able to predict future behavior, depending on market conditions. In other words, the institution has built a high degree of prediction into their operations, by capturing marketing conditions and people's behavior, and then correlating this information to actions under certain conditions.

Guarding Against Competition

In another scenario, the primary competitor of this institution has attacked a highly profitable product group. After the competitor attacked, this institution attempted to quickly assess the impact on their business (if they responded to the competitor's attack with the same offer).

The competitor was able to come into their market, quickly take profitable market share, and retreat without as much as a single response. By the time the institution had figured out the bottom-line impact, the battle was over.

After informatting, the dynamics between the two competitors change dramatically. When a competitor attacks, the institution can "knowledgeably" react in a short time. Reaction time can equal market share.

Many enterprises can react quickly, but do so without a true understanding of the specific consequences. These actions are possible because the financial institution had effectively applied predictive behavioral models to its atomic information (to predict future behavior of customer segments from past behavior). This type of capability is difficult to compete against, because most other institutions cannot currently compete at this level.

Accurate Direct Marketing

Many organizations using data warehouse information for direct marketing reported significant payback. One commercial enterprise noted that although they initially justified their entire project in direct marketing benefits, as management began to learn how to use the information to determine market direction and strategy development, the **business benefits eclipsed** the strong direct marketing benefits they were obtaining.

Many enterprises found significant cost reductions from many areas within multiple organizations within the enterprise. The three biggest areas were:

- insight into distribution channel closure and relocation
- the ability to operate with fewer employees in central office positions, as well as fewer distribution channel employees
- reduction in marketing campaign costs through more accurate segmentation

Many executives also predicted that costs savings would increase significantly as brick-and-mortar and physical currency continued to disappear.

Better Portfolio Management

Many organizations have found significant payback from a more sophisticated portfolio management approach using detailed information. After they implemented their data warehouse, they discovered behavior occurring after the initial transaction, which significantly changed the complexion of their spread on a particular loan. An example financial institution which was studied, using the more detailed information, quickly restructured and re-priced loans to account for customer behaviors post closing.

Service Versus Profits

Another area in which many organizations have utilized historical detailed information was to discover what services were used and were of most value to customers. These programs were initiated because of the high cost of providing services. Specifically, one group had many costly customer account services which provided little value to customers. They didn't have sufficient detail to determine how many customers used or valued specific services. Then the management team utilized the data warehouse to track customers' usage of account services and eliminated the poorly used ones **... at a savings of over $1 million per service.**

Many customer-centric organizations have found sizable payback from a more detailed understanding of their fee income. It was not that they had discovered some overwhelming revelation about fees, but they simply now had the details to understand the dynamics of their fee income. After an analysis using new levels of detail, they changed the structure and amount of some fee types, and increased their income significantly. Many of these institutions found that just by changing small dynamics of fee generation and management of customer relationships—**increases in fee income up to 20% could be gained.**

Measuring Success

Many enterprises have found that drastically reduced cycle times for obtaining current market information allowed them to make rapid movements, adjusting for hot or cold market conditions. Most did have information prior but couldn't quickly measure the success and failure of these new product launches in a timely and organized way. One stated that their bigger benefit was to **discover where the business was coming from** (existing customers, a competitor's customer, which competitor?). This gave them tremendous advantage when deciding how to redirect their campaigns and find the competitor's real weaknesses.

Identify Profitable Customers

Profitability was perhaps the most surprising area for some organizations. Many were astonished to find just how small the percentage of truly profitable customers was, relative to the total number of customers.

Most institutions agree that only a small fraction of their current customers are actually profitable. Several stated that the number is under five percent. It had been difficult for most of these management teams to come to terms with this realization. With data warehouse information, they can determine which customers to target for heavy retention programs and which customers to direct toward more profitable interactions with their organizations.

Smarter Marketing

Another institution which invested very heavily in aggressive marketing campaigns prior to informatting spent tremendous campaign dollars for mass marketing. Vast amounts of mail were sent to unqualified groups of customers. People were inundated with paper despite the fact there was little, if any, possibility of their ever buying any of the institution's products and services. By using the power of the data warehouse to correlate customers to products, the quantity of mailings decreased significantly, while the response rate increased.

Driving Propensity Models for New Profits

Other institutions were using their information to drive the use of their most profitable products. Consider how you could use transactional information to compare and construct "behavior scoring" to develop propensity buying models. Using the detailed information and scoring it resulted in **cross-sell ratios being boosted by 3X.**

Several data warehouse management teams, in using the detailed information, were able to increase their profitable business by **proactively modeling default propensity.** One utilized performance scores to increase the number of personal loan applications they could approve without increasing bad debt.

Channel Analysis

Many mature enterprises have learned to use detailed customer information to understand, adjust and proactively manage planned changes in their distribution network. As part of the planning process, they proactively modeled behaviors to ensure that the customers remained their customers during distribution channel transitions. Certain types of modeling questions to ask are:

- Do they have to go to competition?
- Do they use an alternative location of ours?
- Which customers stay?
- Which customers walk?

The answers to these questions are then used to develop sophisticated treatment strategies for many different scenarios. This team also used the information to put in place non-brick-and-mortar distribution systems to supplement the removal of traditional locations.

Keep the Satisfied Customers

What many mature organizations have found with atomic information is that they could be more intelligent and aggressive. They were able to turn away less business to competitors because they could more finely and predictably respond to customers' needs. The result is a significant improvement in decision time, higher margins, less risk, and more satisfied customers.

Increasing Productivity

One of the most compelling but least talked about areas is the ability of informatted institutions to supplant workers with an informatted environment. It has long been thought that the age of automation was over: "We did that in the 60's and 70's."

We could probably have redeployed 40% of the work force in the marketing environment.

Banks have found that the employee time and resources required to find, extract, understand, and apply information for business in their current mainframe environment is many times greater than that in an informatted bank. Informatting is giving enterprises another opportunity to do significant downsizing.

Retaining (and Gaining) Customers

Retention was a major concern for many high volume or competitive industries. This concern becomes even more acute in the information age. An informatted enterprise's ability to "poach" customers generally exceeded an un-informatted enterprise's ability to protect itself.

Applying detailed data analysis extended customer turn from 7 to 10 years.

The real issue is not the identification of an un-informatted enterprise's customers in common, but rather its most profitable customers. Clearly, top customers are increasingly available to competitors.

Rapid Application Development

Speed of development was a significant benefit accelerating the time to market. Many successful organizations that were studied related stories of market opportunities which were not even attempted, because the applications required to address the opportunities would have taken far too long to develop. The opportunities would cease to exist by the time they had reached the market.

One institution benchmarked equivalent projects for the new application development environment with their previous environment, based on mainframe architecture. The benchmarks for the application were **8 FTE (full-time equivalent) years versus 90 FTE years** to perform the analysis and development of new queries to achieve customer knowledge.

Competitive Speed

Many of the institutions commented that the ability to quickly understand and react to changing market conditions was one of the key benefits of their new environment. Three of the characteristic problem areas addressed in the new information environment were slowness at:

- spotting changing patterns of risk
- spotting changing patterns in market share
- implementing changes even when needs are spotted

One way to look at your business is to view it as simply a series of questions and answers about the business. The criteria then would be: At what speed and cost do the people (or management) ask and answer those questions? The costs of asking and answering business questions in a mainframe environment are exponentially higher than with a specialized informatting data warehouse and decision support system.

The number of questions answered by the IT system for the same dollars dramatically increases in the data warehouse environment.

Another payback area is the hours required to answer a question in a mainframe environment in comparison to those necessary in their current informatted environment. In the mainframe environment, the experience had been that a typical query requires exponentially longer to run than with a customer-centric specialized DSS information system.

In many cases, companies in your industry are already using some form of new detailed information to improve market segmentation. Others are specifically applying it to discover profitable market niches that currently weren't addressed by the competition. If you perform a detailed segmentation analysis using transaction information and competitive information, you will find that a niche may not be addressed by your competition.

Those who do not master the art of detailed information will be mastered by those who do.

Investment Payback Results

If the litmus test for success is measured by conventional ROI from their current "information" technology initiative, most organizations with data warehouses have far exceeded this definition of success.

▶ Advancing Toward Strategic Economics of CRM

After initiating the formal CRM process, and developing and integrating the info-structure to support the new value-chain environment—the acceleration of ROI is at a higher velocity in each subsequent year. An updated view of the CRM process and opportunity changes over time, therefore, creating a strategic view of CRM and the processes surrounding CRM. Illustrated in Figure 12-5 is a strategic matrix of functions performed and activities achieved.

As you progress through the maturation phases, refer back to Chapter 5 on "Stages of Growth." Your management and executive teams have the opportunity of gaining insight to the three strategic activity groups, which are Analyzing, Knowing, and Relating to your customers and the marketplace. (Notice how this directly relates to the initial and subsequent CRM processes/cycles in Chapter 2 and beyond). These three functions are both distinct and integrated processes, views, and actions within the CRM processes.

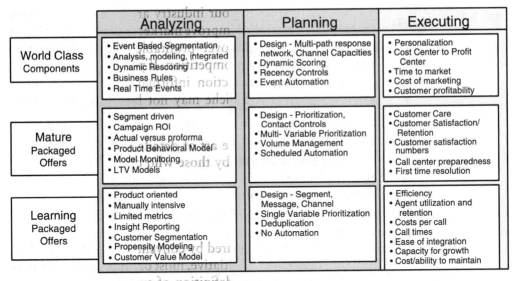

	Analyzing	Planning	Executing
World Class Components	• Event Based Segmentation • Analysis, modeling, integrated • Dynamic Rescoring • Business Rules • Real Time Events	• Design - Multi-path response network, Channel Capacities • Dynamic Scoring • Recency Controls • Event Automation	• Personalization • Cost Center to Profit Center • Time to market • Cost of marketing • Customer profitability
Mature Packaged Offers	• Segment driven • Campaign ROI • Actual versus proforma • Product Behavioral Model • Model Monitoring • LTV Models	• Design - Prioritization, Contact Controls • Multi- Variable Prioritization • Volume Management • Scheduled Automation	• Customer Care • Customer Satisfaction/ Retention • Customer satisfaction numbers • Call center preparedness • First time resolution
Learning Packaged Offers	• Product oriented • Manually intensive • Limited metrics • Insight Reporting • Customer Segmentation • Propensity Modeling • Customer Value Model	• Design - Segment, Message, Channel • Single Variable Prioritization • Deduplication • No Automation	• Efficiency • Agent utilization and retention • Costs per call • Call times • Ease of integration • Capacity for growth • Cost/ability to maintain

Figure 12-5. Strategic Matrix of the CRM Functions.

The strategic matrix of the three CRM processes (i.e., functions) encompasses previous investments and experiences (i.e., learning and maturity) to achieve new goals and focuses on major paradigm shift opportunities within the enterprise and out in the marketplace. The functions can then be mapped to various levels of sophistication in the types of relationship technology investments that are utilized. This becomes an excellent opportunity for assessment of the enterprise position within the three levels (vertical axis) of maturity in CRM.

The three levels of maturing include CRM implementations of:

1. **Early entry or Learning** (through packaged offer from software providers)

2. **Mature** (through packaged offer and tailoring through customer experiences and requirements)

3. **World-class** (integrating the best components, designs, inventions, and previous investments in software and relationship technology resources)

▶ Management Considerations

- CRM can create significant return-on-investment (ROI) when managed through a customer-centric data warehouse environment.
- Institutions in many industries, including banking, insurance, communications, manufacturing, airlines, retail stores, and government, have achieved high magnitudes of success and ROI.
- The value of CRM increases with the amount of relationship technologies available and the use of highly-detailed historical transaction and behavioral data on your customers.
- The processes and frameworks described in early chapters will guide you to faster and more complete success while also reducing risk of failure.
- Organizations that fail to succeed with data warehousing or CRM have not utilized a proven methodology, and also do not have strategic objectives to manage profitability (and measure it) to ensure motivation and the culture to succeed.

The Strategic View of Data Warehousing and CRM

When your strategy is deep and far reaching, then what you gain by your calculations is much, so you can win before you even fight. When your strategic thinking is shallow and near-sighted, then what you gain by your calculations is little, so you lose before you do battle.

Much strategy prevails over little strategy, so those with no strategy can only be defeated. So it is said that victorious warriors win first and then go to war, while defeated warriors go to war first and then seek to win.

The Art of War,
—Sun Tzu

During the mid-1990s, a group of our associates fostered strategic thinking in the use and application of Information Technology. One of the great thinkers and documenters of such principles and thought was Bernie Boar, formerly of AT&T and NCR. Bernie and our professional consulting services group around the world generated numerous white papers and reports encompassed in the ideas expressed in this chapter.

You will also wish to read more on this subject in: *The Art of Strategic Planning for Information Technology,* Bernard H. Boar, John-Wiley & Sons, 1994, and in *Practical Steps to Aligning Information Technology with Business Strategies,* Bernard H. Boar, John-Wiley & Sons, 1995.

As mentioned earlier, data warehousing is one of the four trends that are dominating IT industry attention and investments as shown in Table 13-1.

Table 13-1. Four key subjects dominate IT landscape.

Subject	Technology	Strategic Logic
IT processing architecture	Client/server	Maneuverability
Electronic commerce	The Internet	Reach
Developer productivity	Object-oriented	Leverage
Knowledge and learning	Data warehousing	Customer relationships and/or resource management

Numerous companies in multiple industries are achieving tremendous benefits from data warehousing. The typical reasons given are faster and better decision making, push down employee empowerment, leveraging of operational data, scenario analysis, customer intimacy, analysis of anything and everything, and process control.

These are certainly good reasons but are they adequate motivations to maximize the return on data warehousing? What is the underlying deep and compelling logic of data warehousing? How are we to understand data warehousing strategically so that we may fully optimize the investment?

To understand data warehousing strategically, we must first understand strategy and strategic thinking. Once we understand those concepts, the strategic logic of data warehousing becomes clear and the path to an optimum implementation emerges.

Data warehousing is best appreciated as a realization of the strategic idea of a *rising tide strategy*, which will be described later in this chapter. The maximum return from data warehousing occurs when it is conceptualized, implemented, managed, and evolved within that context.

▶ Sustainable Competitive Advantage (SCA)

From an academic perspective, the purpose of strategic planning is to provide direction, concentration of effort (focus), constancy of purpose (perseverance) and flexibility (adaptability) as a business relentlessly strives to improve its position in all strategic areas.

Strategy is mathematics and is equal to direction plus focus plus perseverance plus adaptability.

At a very pragmatic level, strategy can be understood as finding a way short (the shorter the better) of *brute force* to accomplish one's ends. Strategy should be comprehended as the movement from a current position to a more desirable future position—but with economies of time, effort, cost, or resource utilization. There is neither elegance nor insight in brute force, but there must be both in strategy.

The Eternal Struggle of Business

The one with more advantage wins, the one with less advantage loses. The purpose of strategy is the building, compounding, and sustaining of advantage. Consequently, business strategy must focus on:

- Building new advantages, which increase customer satisfaction and *create distance* from competitors.
- Maintaining existing advantages, which *increase customer satisfaction* and create distance from competitors.
- Compressing or *eliminating the advantages* of competitors.

> The lone purpose of business strategy is the nurturing of advantage. Advantage can be realized through infinite combinations of strategic moves.

While there are many ways to build advantage, all advantages can be classified into five generic categories:

- *Cost:* Results in being able to provide products/services more inexpensively.
- *Value-added:* Creates a product or service that offers some highly desirable feature or functionality.
- *Focus:* More tightly meets the explicit needs of a particular customer.
- *Speed:* Permits you to service customer needs more quickly than others.
- *Maneuverability:* Permits you to adapt to changing requirements more quickly than others. Being maneuverable permits you to constantly refresh the other types of advantage. It is the only advantage that your competitors can't take from you.

So you win by being less expensive, more unique, more focused, faster, or more adaptable than your competitors in serving your customers. Minimally, your advantages must satisfy your customers and, at best, delight or excite them.

> "The one with many strategic factors on his side wins...
> The one with few strategic factors on his side loses. In this
> way, I can tell who will win and who will lose."
>
> —Sun Tzu

> An action is of no strategic interest if it does
> not lead to the development of an advantage.

The struggle always has been, and remains, the perpetual struggle for competitive advantage.

The culmination of advantage is the building of a set of *sustainable competitive advantages* (SCA) for the business. An SCA is a resource, capability, asset, process, and so on, with specific attributes that provide the enterprise with a distinct attraction to its customers and a unique advantage over its competitors.

Table 13-2.

SCA Attribute	Definition
Customer perception	Customer perceives a consistent difference in one or more key buying factors
SCA linkage	Difference in customer perception is directly attributable to the SCA
Durability	Both the customers' perception and the SCA linkage are durable over an extended time period
Transparency	Mechanics/details of the SCA are difficult to understand by competitors
Accessibility	Competitor has unequal access to the required resources to mimic the SCA
Replication	Competitor would have extreme difficulty reproducing the SCA
Coordination	SCA requires difficult and subtle coordination of multiple resources

Without a well-designed set of sustainable competitive advantages, a business engages in a frantic life and death struggle for marketplace survival; after all, there is no compelling reason for consumers to choose that company's products or services.

The basic problem, of course, is to determine from where advantages emanate. How do we discover which will be elegant and insightful so that we may win without using mindless brute force? The answer is that we postulate, analyze, and select strategic actions through *strategic thinking*.

▶ Strategic Thinking

Figure 13-1 below illustrates *three dimensions to thinking:*

- *Time:* We think across time in the past, the present, and the future.
- *Substance:* We think between the concrete and the abstract.
- *Cardinality:* We may think about one or more issues concurrently.

Most of the time, most of us engage in point thinking where we think about only one issue in concrete terms in the present.[1]

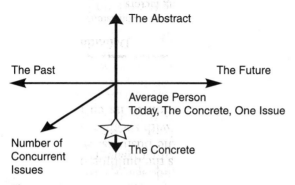

Figure 13-1. Mundane Thinking.

Figure 13-2 illustrates *strategic thinking.* A strategist uses the same dimensions as the mundane thinker, but thinks dynamically within the thought bubble defined by those three dimensions. A strategist concurrently thinks about many issues in multiple dimensions, at many levels of abstraction and detail over time (past, present, and future). Strategic thinking is a creative and dynamic synthesis—the exact opposite of point thinking.

---

[1]*The Art of Strategic Planning for Information Technology,* Bernard H. Boar, John-Wiley & Sons, 1994.

Bernie Boar has continually challenged thinking issues. He has stated that most of the time, "most of us engage in *mundane thinking* to solve our daily problems. All we need to do, to meet our needs, is to think about one issue, in the present, and in the concrete, one at a time. Anything more sophisticated would be overkill. This thinking pattern is also referred to as *point thinking* because all our problem-solving efforts converge on one point."

When looking at a problem, a strategist thinks about it in terms of certain established strategic ideas or themes. While new perspectives can always be developed, time and experience have demonstrated the power of looking at problems through certain enduring and tested strategic lenses.

Your management team will succeed greatly if you converge on one grand strategic idea—the building, sustaining, and extending of advantage. Your vision and strategy should begin with:

- Choosing a problem (or set of problems).
- Sampling strategic ideas (singularly and simultaneously).
- Thinking about solving the problem(s) by applying the strategic ideas within Figure 13-2.
- Fostering intuitive, holistic, dynamic, and abstract thinking.

Since the combinations of strategic ideas are inexhaustible, strategic thinking is a very powerful way to develop insight about problems and solve them in novel, unanticipated, and creative ways. Advantage is born and nourished from this kind of thinking.

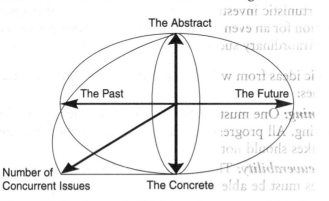

Figure 13-2. Strategic Thinking. Strategists think dynamically within the bubble of the three strategic dimensions.[2]

---

[2]*Ibid.*

Data Warehousing and Strategic Thinking

To understand data warehousing strategically, we should now appreciate that it is the consequence of strategic thinking, which means that it is the result of some combination of strategic ideas. In this case, we must reverse-engineer strategic thinking. We know the result of the strategic thinking process and data warehousing, but what are the strategic ideas from which it emanated?

Data warehousing, along with CRM, is an unusually rich strategic action. A strong case can be made that it is the product of numerous strategic ideas. What are the key ideas that it realizes?

In Miyamoto Musashi's classical book on strategy, *The Five Rings*, he teaches that all weapons have a distinctive spirit. It is the challenge of a warrior to understand that spirit, master it, and become in harmony with it. In that way, there is perfect integration between the warrior and his weapon.

When you think about data warehousing's distinctive spirit, think about *time*. More than any other strategic theme, believe that data warehousing permits one to compete across time:

- *Past:* One must *learn* from the past, so that the best lessons can be learned and deployed, and mistakes not repeated.
- *Present:* One must be able to quickly analyze current events, so that one can *maneuver* in real-time to adapt to them.
- *Future:* One must have *prescience* about the future, so that opportunistic investments and actions can be taken today to position for an even better tomorrow. *Foreknowledge* is the source of extraordinary success.

The strategic ideas from which data warehousing emanates are the time-oriented ones:

- *Learning:* One must continually learn and adapt based upon that learning. All progress includes making mistakes, but the same mistakes should not be made twice.
- *Maneuverability:* This skill requires finding the best way to go. Forces must be able to maneuver to exploit gaps.

- *Prescience:* The leadership must have deep and far-reaching foresight. Leaders must see and know what others do not. The height of prescience is to see the formless and act on it.
- *Foreknowledge:* All matters require competitive intelligence. Nothing is more important than understanding the plans of your opponents and the needs of your customers.

These four strategic ideas are not just any set of strategic ideas; they are uniquely important because they overlay the time dimension of strategic thinking (Figures 13-2 and 13-3, lateral axis).

Time is one of the three fundamental dimensions of strategic thought, and data warehousing enables one to think in that dimension. By giving employees robust access to information about customers, markets, suppliers, and financial results, they are enabled to strategically *learn* from the past, *adapt* in the present, and *position* for the future. To the non-strategist, data warehousing, marketing or CRM is about spending (wasting?) money. To the strategist, data warehousing is about winning the endless battle against time, fostering better relationships with customers, and using knowledge to know how to maintain and extend relationships with customers, suppliers, partners, channels, and even competitors—all of the ships you will encounter on your sea.

▶ A Rising-Tide Strategy

There is a special name given to certain strategic actions—*a rising tide*. As the tide comes in, it raises all the ships in the harbor. The tide does not discriminate; it raises the dingy, the canoe, the yacht, the warship, and the ocean liner. All of them, by no action of their own, enjoy the effect of the rising tide.

A rising tide symbolizes the strategic notion of *leverage*. Leverage is what gives strategy muscle, and means that you do one thing but derive multiple benefits from it. Mathematically, the value of leverage equals individual payoff multiplied by instances of payoff.

CRM with Data Warehousing supports a rising-tide strategy.

By the single action of making information readily available to employees, we can bring benefits to all employees as they go about their daily work. Hundreds of times every day, employees solve problems, make decisions, control processes, develop insights, share information, relate to others, and attempt to influence others.

All of these actions can be made more efficient and effective if better information is made available in a timely manner at the point of need.

Rising-tide strategies are cherished strategies because of the *multiplier effect.* While data warehousing permits you to compete in time, what is remarkable is that it can permit *all of your employees* to compete across time. The single act of making information available creates distinct strategic leverage for the business. You have the ability to further increase your leverage by increasing the amount of data available and the number of employees to whom it is made accessible. Data warehousing is an awesomely powerful rising-tide strategy—a strategy that is most effective when the tide is kept as high as possible and raises as many ships as possible.

Strategic Paradox

In conducting our daily lives, purposeful opposition to our routine efforts does not exist. No one has the goal to deliberately and continually thwart our actions. We use what is called *linear logic* to solve our problems. **Linear logic** consists of using common sense, deductive/inductive reasoning, and concern for economies of time, cost, and effort to problem solve. One is commonly criticized for taking a circuitous route when a more direct one is available. Daily life applauds the logical, the economic, and the application of common sense.

Business strategy, to the contrary, is executed against a background of hyper-conflict and intelligent counter-measures. Able and motivated competitors purposefully and energetically attempt to foil your ambition. Because of this excessive state of conflict, many strategic actions demonstrate a surprising paradoxical logic.

There are two types of strategic paradox:

- *Coming together of opposites:* A linear logic action or state evolves into a reversal of itself ("A" becomes "not A") or "you can have too much of a good thing." An example of this is that an advantage, unrefreshed, becomes a disadvantage. This paradox occurs because conflict causes an inevitable reversal due to the complacency of the winner and the hunger of the loser. While the current winners gloat in their success, this same success lulls them into a false sense of permanent security, while it paradoxically stimulates the current losers to tax their ingenuity to overcome it.

- *Reversal of opposites:* To accomplish your objectives, do the reverse of what linear logic would dictate. So, "If you wish peace, prepare for war," to accomplish "A," do the set of actions to accomplish "not A," or your primary competitor should be yourself. This occurs because the nature of conflict reverses normal linear logic. While taking a long, dangerous, and circuitous route is bad logic under daily circumstances, in a state of conflict (i.e., war), this bad logic is good logic exactly because it is bad logic (it is less likely to be defended). The logic of conflict is often in total opposition to the logic of daily life.

Conflict causes strategic paradox to occur, bad logic becomes good logic exactly because it is bad logic, and the able strategist must learn to think and act paradoxically. Figure 13-3 updates the illustration of strategic thinking to extend the thought bubble to a fourth dimension of linear logic and paradoxical thinking. Paradoxically, strategists often have to recommend, to an unbelieving and astonished audience, that they should take actions that are directly contrary to routine business sense.

An example of reversal of opposites thinking is illustrated by the *Kano Methodology*, an analytical method used to stimulate strategic thinking. As illustrated in Figure 13-4, the logic of Kano suggests that candidate strategic actions be divided into three types:

- *Threshold actions:* For every dollar invested in this type of action, customer satisfaction increases but gradually reaches a point where less than a dollar of satisfaction is achieved for each dollar of investment. It therefore doesn't make sense to invest beyond the break-even point.

- *Performance actions:* For every dollar invested in this type of action, there is a constant positive increase in customer satisfaction in excess of your investment. It pays to continue to invest in these actions.

- *Excitement actions:* For every additional dollar invested in this type of action, there is an exponential increase in customer satisfaction. These are prized actions and are the best actions to invest in.

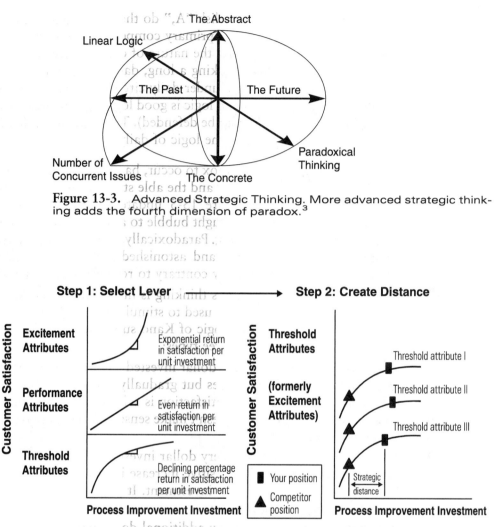

Figure 13-3. Advanced Strategic Thinking. More advanced strategic thinking adds the fourth dimension of paradox.[3]

Figure 13-4. The Kao Methodology uses the notion of paradox by converting excitement attributes to threshold attributes.[4]

[3]*Practical Steps to Aligning Information Technology with Business Strategies,* Bernard H. Boar, John-Wiley & Sons, 1995.
[4]*The Art of Strategic Planning for Information Technology,* Bernard H. Boar, John-Wiley & Sons, 1994.

While this is solid linear thinking, the true brilliance of the methodology occurs next through paradoxical thinking. What is suggested is that after one has developed the excitement capability, it be presented to the customer as a threshold attribute, i.e., paradoxically, the truly exceptional is most exceptional when it is the ordinary. This positions your capability as minimum ante to play the game. A customer may be willing to forgo the exceptional, but will minimally expect and demand the ordinary.

Since you can do it and your competitors can't, you create strategic distance between yourself and your competitors. While they struggle to do the exceptional as the norm, you raise the tempo of the game and work on converting another excitement attribute to a threshold attribute *ad infinitum*. So the great insight of the Kano Methodology is not the linear thinking of excitement attributes, where most people would have stopped, but the recognition that maximum value and market disruption occurs when excitement capabilities are presented, paradoxically, as the ordinary (reversal of opposites).

▶ Data Warehousing and the Strategic Paradox

Data warehousing also needs to be understood in terms of reversal of opposites. As we move from the industrial society to the knowledge society, knowledge becomes the premier weapon of advantage. Business-to-business conflict migrates from competing on industrial age economies of scale to information technology (IT) fighting. Therefore, key strategic information technologies, such as client/server computing and data warehousing, become subject to strategic paradox in their implementations.

The strategic paradox of data warehousing is that strategists concerned about cost do not seek to use just enough means, but an excess of means to accomplish their end. Data warehousing achieves, paradoxically, its greatest value for the business when it is used in high volume to discover new things that were never known or thought about before.

It is typical to observe customer teams engage in extensive and exhaustive cost justifications exercises (NPV, ROI, cost/benefit justification, payback period, and so on) to convince cost-conscious decision makers to approve data warehousing expenditures for a predetermined fixed set of uses. Their actions are linear logic, understandable but inappropriate because of reversal of opposites. When the weaponry shifts to IT fighting, data warehousing becomes subject to strategic paradox and must be managed as such to achieve optimum results.

Consider a military commander who needs to engage his enemy. If he uses linear logic and deploys *just enough* resources, he will win but it will be an expensive (Pyrrhic) victory. If he applies a force far in excess of his opponent, he will achieve his ends with minor casualities.

All the downstream costs of battle will be avoided (damaged weapons, confusion, wounded/killed soldiers, and so on). At the point of conflict, the efficient commander does not seek to use *just enough*, but applies far in excess. He does not use accounting logic that holds in non-conflict situations but applies paradoxical logic, which rules at the point of battle.

In the information age, data warehousing is a key strategic weapon.

As we have discussed, not only does it let you compete across time, it is also a rising-tide strategy that can elevate the strategic acumen of all employees. The attempt to cost-justify such powerful weaponry in terms of net present value misses the point. As an example, when one invests in a national highway infrastructure, one does not cost-justify or attempt to anticipate each event of commerce that will transverse the highway. Rather, one has the strategic vision to understand that the strategic action is putting in place the enabling infrastructure, and then you permit the marketplace to take care of the rest.

The same is true with data warehousing. Once the infrastructure is in place, you have raised the tide for all employees. Your initial justifications are constrained by the limits of your imagination. How the data warehouse will ultimately be beneficial will emerge as your employees use it to respond to the dynamics of the marketplace and it is exploited by their creativity. As they respond by using the *excessive* data warehouse, they will experience the same phenomena as the military commander. Though they will be spending in excess at the point of conflict, it will ultimately prove to be much cheaper because all the downstream business processes will be more efficient and effective. So while cost-consciousness is always in vogue and a specific set of business needs to be addressed is welcomed, the absence of *a priori* adequate tactical savings should not dissuade you from the deep and far-reaching strategic merits of an encompassing data warehousing initiative.

Unquestionably, it is easier to accept this paradox with regard to the military commander than data warehousing, due to the differences between cause and effect in the two situations. In the military situation, the cause and effect are tightly coupled in time and space. One can immediately see the results of the excess and correlate the success to that excess. In the data warehousing situation, the cause and effect are often dispersed across wide gaps of time and space. The use of excess data warehousing will have the desired effect, but it will occur perhaps months later, at a remote branch office.

The strategist must take solace in that he or she is engaged in deep and far-reaching strategy, not tactical, short-term decisions. Things that are readily cost-justifiable are things that are obvious and known to all. Strategic thinking is involved in seeing victory before it exists. How can anyone cost-justify the formless? While cost-conscious accounting methods are appropriate for sustaining wealth, strategic vision has always been the required ingredient to create it.

▶ Data Warehousing and Maneuverability

Businesses must always be prepared to respond creatively to marketplace dynamics. The normal marketplace state is constant change and upheaval. It is, therefore, obvious that those companies that can navigate with greater alacrity, speed, and dexterity have a distinct advantage. In fact, with speed, dexterity, and alacrity as your allies, you can further exaggerate your advantage by deliberately promoting marketplace mayhem to the benefit of your customers and the detriment of your competitors.

Companies take two basic roles in engaging the marketplace:

- *Attrition Fighter*: Marketplace supremacy is achieved by taking a strong but fixed position and "slugging it out" for marketplace dominance. Through confrontational marketplace battles and by concentrating superior assets against inferior foes, you win by exhausting the opponent's will and ability to compete. The optimum situation is to win in a few decisive battles and, by virtue of your proven superior power, deter prospective competitors from stepping into your marketplace and challenging you. An attrition fighter, like a classical heavy-weight boxer, wins by brute superiority of assets, and the ability to deliver a crushing and decisive knockout blow.

- *Maneuver Fighter*: Marketplace superiority is achieved by staying in a state of perpetual motion. A maneuver fighter continually looks for opportunistic gaps in the marketplace and swiftly moves assets to maximize the opportunity. The maneuver fighter attempts to continually disrupt the marketplace by changing the rules of competition. It is through the actions of movement that advantage is gained. Advantage is best understood as a succession of overlapping temporary advantages, rather than a set of sustainable competitive advantages.

The maneuver fighter expects that the maneuver process will cause friction and disruption in the ability of opponents to respond. At best, this will eventually lead to a collapse in the opponent's business systems. A maneuver fighter uses speed, flexibility, opportunism, and dexterity to chip away at the edges of the marketplace until the entire marketplace has been taken. In doing so, unlike the attrition fighter, a deliberate attempt is made to avoid expensive, time-consuming, and exhausting confrontations with competitors. You win by artfulness and indirection—not by brute force. The great heavy-weight fighter, Mohammed Ali, summed up the defining style of the maneuver fighter when he said, "Float like a butterfly, sting like a bee."

There is now a global and fundamental marketplace transition occurring from national wars of attrition to global wars of maneuver, and successful companies must adapt to this shift.

Sun Tzu described the eternal character of maneuver warfare when he said:

> **"Go forth where they do not expect it;
> attack where they are unprepared."**

As advantageous as this is, it is not easy to do. It demands intelligence. A maneuver fighter must continually zig and zag. The problem is to decide where and when to zig and zag. Done well, the maneuver fighter will delight customers and drive competitors crazy. Done poorly, the maneuver fighter will inadvertently zig or zag directly into the attrition fighter and be crushed.

Data Warehousing and CRM Are Prerequisites to a Maneuver Strategy

An infrastructure of knowledge must be available to engage in maneuver fighting. With a solid infrastructure of accessible information that can be manipulated as demanded by swirling times and circumstances, the maneuver fighter can make calculated judgments as to where and when to move. Without such knowledge, a maneuver fighter will make one guess too many and be cornered by the behemoth attrition competitor.

The way to understand CRM and data warehousing implementations strategically is to understand it as the necessary foundation for changing your business from being a slow and ponderous attrition fighter to an agile and quick maneuver fighter.

Attrition fighters stand still. If you're going to stand still, of what value is knowledge to you? To the contrary, a maneuver fighter, as shown in Figure 13-5, is a business in constant motion. Maneuver fighters win through intelligence, not brute force. In this way, by virtue of knowledge-enabled maneuvering, you act sooner rather than later, you learn rather than repeat, you anticipate rather than react, you know rather than guess, you change rather than atrophy, you exceed rather than satisfy, and ultimately, through the accumulation of *rathers*, you win rather than lose.

How Strategic Executives Think of CRM and DW

- Strategy is about building advantage. The business need to build, compound, and sustain advantage which is the most fundamental and dominant business need and is insatiable.
- Advantage is **built through deep and far-reaching strategic-thinking.**
- Strategic ideas that support data warehousing as a strategic initiative are learning, maneuverability, prediction, and foreknowledge. CRM and data warehousing meet the **fundamental business needs to compete** in a superior manner across the strategic dimension of time.
- **Data warehousing is a rare instance of a rising tide strategy**, which occurs when an action yields tremendous leverage. Data warehousing raises the ability of all employees to serve their customers and out-think their competitors.
- **Data warehousing achieves optimal results when one understands strategic paradox.** When used as a weapon of conflict in the information age, data warehousing, paradoxically, achieves the greatest economies when it is applied in excess. One always wants the tide to be at high tide.
- Data warehousing is a **mandatory prerequisite** to engage in a maneuver market style, which will be the dominant form of marketplace warfare as we begin the next millennium. To continually and abruptly change business direction requires both judgment and knowledge. Hard-won experience provides the former, and data warehousing provides the latter.

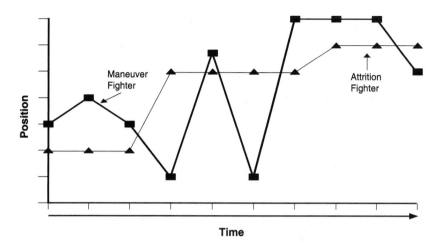

Figure 13-5. A maneuver fighter moves, stands, and moves while an attrition fighter stands, moves, and stands.

> **Companies enter markets to win profits, not to engage in expensive and endless pitched battles with competitors.**

Data warehousing is of strategic value because it enables us to achieve the former while deftly avoiding the latter.

This is the strategic emphasis which we should understand, implement, and Accelerate Customer Relationship Management through Information Technology.

 # Management Considerations

- **Strategic paradox** is an important dimension in the spirit of data warehousing. Understand its value and use it for developing management to think about the potentials within your business.
- Intelligence is both the sense of being smart and having knowledge about your competitors and customers.
- Ultimately, experience will prove that those who use data warehousing in excess will **achieve greater benefits** then those who attempt to rigorously cost-justify and constrain its deployment.
- You do not want a rising tide, you want a **permanent high tide** of information with which you can win the competitive battles by knowing more about the past, understanding the present, and positioning and predicting the future.

- **Use data warehousing to position yourself** so that you will surely win. **Positioning is everything** when it comes to an ever-changing marketplace and competitors that are vying for your customers.
- **Win through intelligence,** not brute force. Create an information infrastructure that enables people to think and act, then analyze, measure, and learn, and ultimately strategize and put new plans in actionable successes.
- Cost-justification is supposed to be a **tool of strategy,** not the reverse. Strategic paradox alters the rules; understand and justify data warehousing strategically.
- Those who enter the journey of data warehousing do not know where they will ultimately be in the information world, or the analytical world, or the CRM world, until they **experience the unknown.**
- The faster an organization shares its information **info-structure** within itself across business units, and subsequently with its partners, the larger the positive impact and achievements of goals.

> **"Measurable value comes**
> **when the results of the strategic analysis**
> **get translated into actionable decisions."**

Mark Hurd, Senior Vice President
NCR Corporation Addressing a Management Conference
Barcelona, 1999

How Companies Succeed Using CRM, Data Warehousing, and Relationship Technologies

> *"Organizations derive different kinds of value from data warehousing. Some value is ubiquitous; nearly every user of a data warehouse can show that he or she has better and improved information, and better support for decision making."*
>
> Barbara Haley Wixom, Dale Goodhue, and Hugh Watson
> "The Benefits of Data Warehousing at Whirlpool Corporation"
> Annals of Cases on IT Applications and Management

There are hundreds of excellent experiences of many companies—small businesses and large multinational corporations—around the world as a result of implementing an integrated "info-structure" utilizing a scalable *data warehouse as the base for business intelligence.* As was discussed in Chapter 5, it is important to understand that many data warehouses have advanced into more mature stages of management's utilization and far beyond reporting and query functionality.

Companies that have implemented a customer-centric information infra-structure have excelled in their industries.

The leaders are not always the first adopters of integrated information infra-structures (or data warehousing) in their industry, but you can be assured of ever-increasing insight into the process developed, the knowledge gained and utilized, and the results that have been achieved. Not all results are monetary.

Results achieved may include change of organizational behaviors, change in customer behaviors, change in channel operations and achievements, or ability to drive value through fast market entry with a new product or service. When companies enable marketplace velocity, there is supreme positioning of competitiveness and profitability.

Speed is more than just using technology to drive operations faster. Speed can be alarmingly potent in an industry that requires competitiveness through changes in prices of products or services, or a requirement for the management team to believe in and use business intelligence information—and therefore act upon it—regularly and with confidence, using a closed-loop decision support environment.

The following successful examples span multiple industries, including financial services, manufacturing, retailing, telecommunications, government, air travel, and tourism. This chapter will review the successes of:

The Financial Services Industry

- Bank of America—Data Warehousing for All
- Barclays Bank (UK)—The Challenge: Profit Management Initiatives
- Royal Bank (Canada)—Targeted Marketing Successes
- Union Bank (Norway)—Increases Productivity and Profitability

The Manufacturing and Distribution Industries

- Western Digital—Takes Quality to the Next Level
- Hallmark Cards—Evolving Excellence—see Chapter Three

The Retailing Industry

- Migros—Optimizing Sales Campaigns and Inventory Levels
- *"The Warehouse"* (New Zealand)—Specialized Retailing Down-under
- SEARS—Reinventing Itself for Success

The Airline Travel and Tourism Industries

- Continental Airlines (U.S.A.)—Managing Diverse Operations
- QANTAS (Australia)—Seeing the Future Through Information
- Travel Unie (Netherlands)—Keeping Its Customers Coming Back
- Kinki Nippon Tourist (Japan)—Driving Towards "One-to-One"
- "One World"—British Airways, American Airlines, and Qantas

Ground Transportation Industry

- Burlington Northern Sante Fe Railway (U.S.A.)

The Telecommunications Industry

- Pele-Phone Communications (Israel)

The Health Insurance Industry

- DCB Demo-Centrum (Czech)—Creating a New Future for a People
- Anthem Blue Cross/Blue Shield (U.S.A.)—Managing Health Care

The Entertainment Industry

- Harrah's Entertainment—Reinvention Abounds

The Financial Services Industry

Bank of America—Data Warehousing for All

Bank of America, originally based in San Francisco (now part of Nation's Bank headquartered in Charlotte, North Carolina), has several of the largest data warehousing and massive parallel processing systems in the world. For Bank of America, the advantages of data warehousing include employee empowerment, stronger predictive modeling and, over time, the bank has seen a close correlation in capacity to positive revenue and stock value performance. The bank has many times presented the value of the data warehouse and decision-support technologies and how it uses DW to understand its customers, employees, and banking partners better and more profitably.

With nearly 2,000 consumer banking branches in the western United States, Bank of America processes approximately 1.6 million transactions, each day handles more than 2.6 million transactions through its 7,000 proprietary ATMs, and in the back office processes 20 million checks. Needless to say, the bank manages a lot of valuable information about its customers, which is why B of A was an early adopter of data warehouse technology in banking in 1986.

The evolution of the bank's data warehouse began with its credit card division. When first installed, the warehouse was approximately 15 gigabytes with 10 parallel processors. Only three people accessed information and the average cost per query was about $2,500. At that time, reports were developed on a monthly basis. However, the benefits were readily seen and gradually new departments, such as mortgage and consumer loans, signed on. These new users also began requesting more information, more frequently.

In 1996, Bank of America's California-based data warehouse had grown to service 16 separate departments within the bank and had begun producing more than 3,000 reports on a daily basis. Needless to say, the size of the warehouse had grown, from 15 to 2,300 gigabytes and to 161 parallel processors. By late 1997, over 1,500 employees accessed Bank of America's warehouse and the cost per query has dropped dramatically, from $2,500 to $18. Demonstrating the cost benefit to Bank of America, the warehouse cost has stayed relatively flat as bank expenses increased.

The true value of the warehouse was to be found in the diverse business uses that have developed over the years. Today, the warehouse is used for product development pricing and risk analysis, as well as sales tracking, branch forecasting, and usage.

Bank of America's marketing department uses the warehouse to accurately segment customers for more accurate and profitable campaigns because of the detailed understanding the warehouse brings to bank employees. On the management side, the warehouse is used to audit departments and create complex financial models.

The more complex data mining functions have been underway since 1988, when the bank began customer analysis and portfolio management. Using predictive modeling, the bank has been able to effectively analyze, measure, and target profitable customers. On a particular direct mail effort, according to Charles Griffith (formerly a top manager in the bank's MIS department and now a consultant), the data warehouse at B of A in California had reduced the overall population of customers to be mailed by 40%, while increasing the response rate by 97% and the commitment rate by 21%. This one application generated in excess of $45 million for the bank. And there have been dozens of other applications built over the recent years, many of which are highly competitive (and withheld from publicity), and have provided even more return on investment.

Griffith has presented the bank's story at numerous conventions during the 1990's and stated that the bank's management quickly became dependent on the tools and interpretative results provided by the data warehouse. By capturing the vast amount of data that passed through the bank's systems each day, Bank of America is able to leverage that asset to the benefit of its customers and the bank itself.

In the fall of 1999, at The NCR Partners Conference in Orlando, Bank of America presented a major update on its data warehouse, showing new applications developed in the areas of product sales and profitability, regulatory reporting, risk management, extended bank marketing programs, balance sheet management, and customer product-usage with cross-selling opportunities. The business focus of the data warehouse is now "targeted programs" to meet customer needs, product and channel fit programs, household profitability, customer individual profitability, retention programs, loyalty programs, and use of data modeling for propensity to buy, wallet-share expansion, and risk of attrition.

The bank also builds detailed information to better understand its channels with decision support applications for channel expenses, profitability of each channel, usage patterns and trends, and customer migration planning and marketing activities.

Bank of America's leadership in the use of customer-centric knowledge –based data warehousing has progressed over the past decade from inconsistent and unintentional random marketing experiences, to predictable consistent intentional experiences, then onward to branded consistent intentional differential and highly valuable experiences. Along with this maturation experience the journey is toward loyal customers who differentiate and understand the value of Bank of America to them and their individual needs.

At Bank of America, CRM is defined as "a process that leverages customer transaction data, marketing models and life event triggers, to efficiently and continuously cultivate customer relationships, manage a customer contact strategy, and create a sustainable competitive advantage." This is then translated into **marketing goals**, which are to:

1. Create relevance with customers
2. Optimize marketing expenditures
3. Support the development and execution of strategies
4. Create a dialogue with customers to achieve the goals

Bank of America plans to have 80% of customer transactions triggered by predefined rules and use real-time methods to optimize all of the customer transactions. This spawns a new corporate vision of "every interaction contributes to customer knowledge AND customer knowledge contributes to every interaction."

Barclays Bank

The Challenge: Profit Management Initiatives

Although the financial services industry has had access to more customer data than most industries due to the high transaction nature of financial services, it didn't embrace CRM until recently due to phenomenal industry change—new competitors, such as supermarket chains; branch closings, which reduced access to customers; high demands from customers for more convenient channels, such as ATMs, telephone banking, PC on-line transactions, and the reporting of investment and banking services.

At the same time, banks wanted closer relationships with high-value customers and/or households—those customers who require the whole range of financial services and advice. In return, these customers would receive benefits in the form of discounts, rewards, benefits, advice and exceptional customer service.

By implication, low-value, one-product customers will be managed using the economies of scale that may or may not be afforded by automated or semi-automated channels, such as automated voice response or touch-tone interactions with the financial institution. And, unprofitable customers will be gently discouraged and even eased in the direction of financial services organizations that have turned price-busting into an art, but who do not stress service as part of their offering.

Knowing the customer, and knowing the profitability of individual customers, is highly lucrative in this industry. Many banks, through the effective use of their data warehouses, have discovered that over 50% of their customers are non-profitable customers and that less than 30% provide more than 100% of their profitability.

Although this was suspected by financial institution management for decades, leveraging data warehousing, they now are not only discovering the "single version of the truth," but also have detailed information to identify and know why their high-value and low-value customers do and don't perform business with their institution.

The rapid adoption of new technologies by banks is essential both in terms of managing profits, and improving and leveraging customer relationships. One international financial services group that has successfully faced this challenge is Barclays Bank.

Barclays is a leading financial services company operating in more than 70 countries around the world. It provides retail and corporate banking services to a wide range of international customers, as well as investment banking and asset management expertise to a global client base.

In the United Kingdom, Barclays serves more than 10 million personal customers and has a total of 9.3 million credit cards in circulation—making it the largest card issuer in Europe. Barclays serves around 500,000 small business customers—a significant proportion of the small business market—nearly one in three middle market businesses, and some 400 of the United Kingdom's largest companies.

In 1992, Barclays experienced its first financial loss in 300 years of operation, largely due to credit losses stemming from a significant economic downturn in the United Kingdom, where most of the group's borrowers were located. The Barclays management team needed to find a way to solve the situation. Barclays needed to be able to predict more precisely the default risk on every loan, and make its portfolio of assets more diverse to minimize the impact of economic swings. The Barclays' Teradata Information Warehouse enabled the bank to get the right balance between risk and reward. This is vital for any bank and a key component of Barclays' drive to market the right products, to the right people, at the right time.

At the core, Barclays needed more information about its customers: It wanted to develop a closer understanding of the probability of being paid back by its loan customers by analyzing past trends and predicting future behavior. The management team decided that Barclays did not have enough detailed understanding of the influences on the profitability of its loan business, and it was this that made them unable to manage profits successfully.

Geoff Horn, IT director of Barclays' Information Warehouse realized that new technologies were going to be needed to address these ambitious targets with a customer management solution that met their ongoing business needs. Barclays decided upon using combined scalable data warehousing, with data-driven business modules, and outside consultant services to enhance the team and foster success.

Barclays' management team—including the Finance and Planning Directors—endorsed the data warehouse program. In October 1992, Barclays committed to a feasibility study, which took place over the next two months. By April 1993, Barclays' team had worked closely together to achieve their common goal. The data warehouse—known as the *Barclays Information Warehouse*—was up and running.

Barclays had to make a major decision about centralizing its decision support database, while also architecting a strategy which brought data from its traditional mainframes into the data warehouse, as well as drove business users and management to utilize the new infra-structure. In the beginning, business analysts in the group's Central Policy Units were allowed to access the data warehouse directly across a private network. The management team's ultimate goal is to make the data warehouse available to all of Barclays' business units as and when they need it.

In October 1993, Barclays reviewed the data warehouse project and decided that although it started as an initiative to manage risk, the group would get more benefit out of its capabilities if it were opened up to more business units across the organization. By 1996, the data warehouse had been expanded significantly and was made available to all business units that demonstrated a need for its capabilities.

Barclays Bank: The Benefits

Both the Retail and Corporate Risk Management teams learned to utilize the system and in addition, the marketing function of the group was strengthened by the use of the new parallel database for decision support and query technologies.

In terms of risk management, Barclays analysts became able to predict the financial behavior of individual customers over time from a detailed portfolio of information, and assess whether a customer is likely to pay a loan back in full and within the agreed time period. This helps Barclays manage its profitability with greater precision. It can now charge its customers a more appropriate rate of interest based on the results of the risk assessment.

The data warehouse also helps Barclays to manage credit risk by helping them assess the danger of having multiple loans default at the same time. The group can then prevent economic disaster by moving exposures to different industries or geographies.

In Barclays' marketing department, analysts are able to work out which products best suit their customers' individual requirements on a proactive basis. They are able to do this by "mining" customer information in the warehouse, and by identifying trends in historical information they can develop accurate predictive models of the customer's future financial needs. In addition, via a sophisticated customer segmentation system, the warehouse can help the group identify which are its most profitable customers over time—both on a corporate and personal level—and target customers with appropriate financial products. Also, Barclays uses the data warehouse to support its branch strategy planning.

"The improvement that data warehousing has brought to our one-to-one marketing initiatives is highly significant," says Geoff Horn. "Blanket mailing is costly for the business and ultimately annoys our customers, so this ability to relate to our customers on a more personal basis is a drastic improvement in marketing terms."

Barclays' Plans

Going forward, Barclays intends to increase the breadth and depth of the data within the Barclays Information Warehouse. Traditionally, Barclays did not keep detailed historical information on its customers, but rather kept "snapshots" of individuals' account details.

Now, Barclays has gathered up to five years' worth of customer information in some cases, which helps improve the depth and accuracy of analyses carried out by the data warehouse. The goal is to hold detailed historical information on all of Barclays' 10 million customers in the United Kingdom, down to the detail of recording each individual transaction of each customer over time. This information could include details on where each customer's account is held, the locations of the ATMs they use, or how much money they tend to withdraw from an ATM in an average week.

"The data warehouse holds over 350 gigabytes of data at present; I can see this increasing five- or ten-fold over the next couple of years," says Geoff Horn of Barclay's Information Warehouse Team: "The scalability is theoretically limitless, and it can take us where we want to go. We have achieved what seemed like the impossible without resorting to costly application development projects. This is no small feat."

Barclays Bank Results

Barclays can predict the financial behavior of individual customers over time because the data warehouse has been designed to contain a detailed customer portfolio of information, which allows the bank to charge customers a more appropriate rate of interest, based on the results of the risk assessment. The marketing group also can identify trends in historical information to develop predictive models of customers' future needs to proactively develop products.

In 1998, NCR reviewed the banking industry and their uses of information technology to gain customer growth and profitability. An NCVR executive of that time was quoted as saying: "Most banks were found to be sitting on a gold mine. However, many thought it was the gold in their vaults. The real gold was buried, hidden among the reams of transactional data held in their banking computer systems. Fully exploiting this data is the key to enhancing the ways in which banks interact with and manage their customers."

In the increasingly competitive financial services industry, maintaining and nurturing customers is key to survival and growth. Understanding and predicting customers' behavior, motivators, needs, and buying decisions are critical to long-term success.

Many banks have begun to see the value of data warehousing technology in this type of activity. But it is when the technology is leveraged by the business that real bottom-line benefit is achieved. Data mining gives one view to the value of information, but without building the competency of what to do with the information, its value is diminished. Used to its full potential, however, the data warehousing process can be the vital foundation to driving true strategic competitive advantage.

Royal Bank of Canada—Know Your Customer, Know Your Business

The question for bankers today, according to Richard McLaughlin, Vice President of Relationship Marketing at Canada's Royal Bank Financial Group, is how they can create the banking intimacy that was commonplace in the 1950s between manager and client in today's modern era.

Royal Bank made a start in this quest some 20 years ago with a centralized view of its client. It has built on this standpoint with extensive data collection for modeling and decision purposes, driven through a state-of-the-art data mart.

Clients are coded on both a strategic basis (e.g., into categories such as profitability and potential) and by using tactical codes (channel usage, propensity to buy, and so on). The result is that where the bank could once classify its customers into a few micro segments, it now has more than 20,000 segments. "This has allowed us to truly customize product offerings and return us to the stage in the 1950s when my father was a bank manager," says McLaughlin.

But the focus on client needs is just the start of the necessary strategy. The organizational setup needed is equally important. To drive this focus, a bank needs to have cross-functional teams to replicate the view that customers have of the bank—as one unit, not a series of discrete units.

Similarly, cultural change is important; it is vital not to over-complicate procedures in the early stages. "If you do, you will stress systems and people to the breaking point," McLaughlin says. "Yet bankers need to be persuaded that it is acceptable to get an 80% complete solution out of the door. This is counter-culture for many bankers," he adds.

The proof of the system for Royal Bank is in the results it is now enjoying. Through extensive measurement the bank ascertained a 61% improvement in marketing cycle time and a rise in direct response rates, which sometimes were better than 40%.

There has also been an increase in the number of profitable high-value clients and the average return they produce. "Each year for the past three years the amount of revenue per marketing dollar has shown double-digit growth," McLaughlin says.

In October 1999, Royal Bank summarized its journey as one that enables various groups within the bank to use event-driven values of client level profitability in the departments of marketing, products, finance, costing, risk, treasury, service delivery, and network management. This has enabled a **"Client Current Value Measurement"** approach for generating and measuring strategic goals of contributions to the bank's earnings, customer relationships, and market position. The data warehouse also leverages synergies between businesses, increases revenue growth, and maintains cost containment.

Union Bank of Norway—Increases Productivity and Profitability

The early 1990s represented a difficult period for Norwegian banks, with many suffering substantial losses as the result of an economic downturn that saw the failure of a large number of Norwegian businesses. Despite the banking crisis, Union Bank of Norway, the country's largest savings bank group, limited its business losses, while reducing operational costs.

Today, the financial sector is healthy again, although margins for all Norwegian banks continue to shrink.

As a result, Union Bank of Norway is focusing its efforts on improving margins and growing profitability by better targeting services to its customers, directing business to areas that provide the best return on investment, and continuing to manage operational costs.

The Challenge

Initially, the bank needed a better way of gathering and analyzing customer transactions and individual profitability to determine which services could be better marketed, and where.

With 185 branches serving 900,000 consumer and commercial customers, Union Bank of Norway was operating on multiple computer platforms and systems, with disparate data scattered throughout the decentralized branches. The bank could not easily gather and store customer-specific information, which limited its ability to understand individual profitability by customer, product and service.

"Our biggest challenge was finding complete information on our customers and making it actionable," says Geir Bergskaug, general manager and head of direct marketing operations for Union Bank of Norway. "Most of our information was derived from various production systems that contained insufficient customer information. It was an information labyrinth where we didn't know how to get out, how to get the right data, or even how to ask the right questions."

Union Bank of Norway wanted a way to create, store and access customer-specific information in a responsive, easy-to-use format. By tracking customer trends and understanding individual profitability, bank executives reasoned they could improve revenue and margins through cross-selling and increasing customer use of its most profitable products and services.

"We must know as much about our customers as possible in order to boost our own profitability," says Bergskaug.

The Union Bank of Norway's Data Warehouse Solution

Union Bank of Norway decided to build a data warehouse to bring together its disparate data sources and create a repository for customer information.

"To get closer to our customers, the bank's operations are divided into sales districts, with five or six branches per district. The new data warehouse ensures that each branch has a complete profile of its customers," says Bergskaug.

Additionally, the bank utilized outside services, including business and information discovery, technology solution design and integration, database design, and data transformation.

The Benefits

With the new data warehouse, Bergskaug says Union Bank of Norway is able to increase its market share by reacting faster to opportunities in the marketplace.

For example, the bank's marketing management team recently launched a customer loyalty program targeted at the bank's most profitable customers. The response rate, approximately 50%, far exceeded that of traditional direct mail campaigns in the past, typically 2–4%.

"Because of our data warehouse solution, the bank is able to create a complete profile of each customer. Knowing which customers to target saves us time and money," says Bergskaug.

The bank's previous operational systems limited its ability to capture and share customer-specific information between the branches and the central database. As a result, the bank had difficulty analyzing customer transactions and understanding individual profitability.

"With our data warehousing solution, we now are better able to analyze each customer's use of different services, as well as an individual's total net worth to the bank," says Bergskaug. "We can understand the profit and costs associated with each customer, which means better, more customized services for customers and increased profitability for the bank."

In addition, the bank is enhancing teller performance by placing the power of the data warehouse directly at their fingertips. Through their workstations, tellers can instantly call up a complete customer profile, which identifies other services that a particular customer may be interested in. Not only can tellers better serve their customers; they can proactively sell new services.

The data warehouse also has been instrumental in increasing usage of the bank's automated payment services. The bank has used the data warehouse to pinpoint which customers aren't using the payment service best suited to the individual customer's need, and calculate the amount of money each customer loses by not using the service. This information was used to produce a promotion customized for each customer. Not only has use of the automated payment services increased, but the bank more efficiently and cost-effectively serves its customers.

"The data warehouse gives us the ability to store and track information on each individual customer, react to that information and find opportunities for growth. The data warehousing solution helps us increase our market share by giving Union Bank of Norway a strategic edge over our competitors," says Bergskaug.

Today, Union bank of Norway is leading the way in the new century with the implementation of "relationship optimization" software and practices for increased customer satisfaction, customer retention, and customer profitability.

The Manufacturing and Distribution Industries

Western Digital—Takes Quality to the Next Level

To the casual observer, Western Digital makes hard disk drives for the world's leading PC manufacturers, as well as providing replacement and add-on data storage to the consumer market. But a closer examination reveals a company that is intensely focused on quality.

Western Digital is the first U.S.-headquartered, multi-national company to gain company-wide ISO 9001 registration, linking all of its operations with a consistent, global standard for quality processes.

Western Digital began in 1970 as a maker of specialized semiconductors and has evolved into one of the world's leading information storage management companies, with 13,000 employees and a broad array of hard drives for personal and enterprise-wide computing.

Western Digital's Challenge

In an industry with extremely short product life-cycles (product life-cycles shrank 33% in 1999) and a short time to bring products to market, Western Digital's focus on quality and continuous improvement is a must to stay one step ahead of its competition.

Western Digital regularly appears first-to-market and first-to-volume with the greatest capacity per platter in the hard drive industry, and is continually honored by the industry's top trade publications for its products' quality and performance.

But with market share based almost entirely on product quality from the previous quarter, company executives know that past performance doesn't mean a thing. It's all about providing the best products and best support available on the market today and tomorrow.

Any one of Western Digital's hard drives has up to 250 parts, 2,000 product attributes and hundreds of suppliers providing those parts, which can make detecting and correcting errors a monumental task.

"Being able to access detail data on our products is essential to product quality," says Jerry Hill, vice president of Quality Information Systems at Western Digital. "With our information systems, we had the data, but it resided in a variety of data sources that made it difficult to quickly access."

To improve product quality or yield, or perform problem solving, the company had to retrieve data from a number of distributed data silos and manipulate it.

Western Digital stored detailed product information for the entire warranty period on each of the 100,000 hard drives it produced daily. But with disparate information systems and data silos, it lacked the tools to effectively use the stored information to improve product quality.

"We could build 100,000 units a day, but we couldn't get to the data fast enough to improve the product build or accurately detect component defects," says Hill.

Western Digital's Solution

In its computing environment, time wasn't the only issue. Summary data created a false sense of security, says Hill.

"A few defective components could wind up in the end product and then be shipped to the customer. But the defects would escape our summary assessments of the product," says Hill. "Our customers could theoretically have a high percentage of defective products in a small shipment, which is why we simply couldn't measure quality by averages."

The manufacturer realized it needed the ability to drill down into detail data to improve its products and manufacturing process. Western Digital spoke to a number of information systems consulting firms, all of whom recommended that the company build a data warehouse. With no previous data warehousing experience, though, Western Digital looked for a partner with proven experience, and the software and hardware that could scale well beyond its foreseen needs.

Western Digital decided to use the Teradata data warehouse to track the myriad of process and component variables involved in the manufacture of its hard drives.

In only nine months, Western Digital started from scratch in building pilot data marts, then scaling to a fully operational enterprise data warehouse. Users access the data warehouse to perform complex ad hoc queries. With it, the company can quickly detect and correct product defects before being shipped to customers. Through data mining, engineers are beginning to perform "what-if" scenarios to eliminate product defects even before the production process begins.

Within two years from the start of the project, Hill already plans expansion of the data warehouse to scale to over three terabytes of data and plans to support 800 users throughout the entire corporation.

Western Digital's Benefits

Western Digital uses the data warehouse to track all of the process and component variables involved in the manufacture of its hard drives to improve product quality, reduce costs, and improve revenue. The data warehouse provides the company with a single, detailed view of each product as it moves through the production and distribution process.

That single, detailed view gives Western Digital the tools to find defective drives before being shipped to the customer. In the event that defects are discovered during the production and/or distribution process, users can quickly determine which serial numbers have the defective components and identify exactly where each drive is in the process. Prior to building the data warehouse, defective components caused production to grind to a halt as pallets and boxes were hand-sorted to find the faulty drives.

"We can quickly identify where the affected product is, down to the slot in the box on an individual pallet, and then replace those drives without shutting down the manufacturing process," says Hill. "The Teradata Data Warehouse is having a dramatic effect on quality because we know we can find 100% of the drives before they get to the customer, and in a time frame that makes sense." Companies that understand the effective usage of hundreds of high-speed computer chips, combined with the parallel architecture of the advanced data warehouse, have moved their data warehouse to specialized parallel technologies to reduce cost, increase performance, and define vast new arenas of business forecasting, prediction, complex analysis, and uncovering unknown opportunities.

The ability to quickly find defective drives is essential to improving overall quality, but it's still an expensive process at $70 per drive to retrieve, rework and relaunch the product. That's why Western Digital is taking the power of the data warehouse one step further, to engineer better products so costly defects can be avoided prior to production. Through data mining, users can identify the correlation of drive failures to particular testing parameters. By performing sophisticated "what-if" analysis, they can determine where failed drives are likely to appear in the process and determine how to eliminate the failures by tweaking the process.

And that's especially critical as the company's ramp to full production has shrunk 75% in 1999.

"We don't have time to do any fundamental engineering of the product once it's released into production," says Hill. "So we have to use the history of the product that's in the field to develop our future designs. Essentially, we have to do it right the first time, which the data warehouse helps us do."

In the event that drives do fail once in the field, Western Digital retrieves such data as starts and stops, power-on hours, and error-correction history from returned drives. The data is then stored in the data warehouse and used to enhance future designs.

While searching for a solution, Western Digital's executives made it clear to Hill and his team that they did not want the business to be constrained by its information systems. The company needed a solution that would grow if production volumes expanded, if warranty periods were extended, or any other number of factors occurred.

Performance and flexibility were two other key factors in Western Digital's decision. "It is impossible to anticipate the types of complex queries that our engineers will perform. Our solution had to have the power and flexibility to drill down to the atomic detail very efficiently while supporting an ad hoc environment," says Hill.

For another example, see "Excellence in Business Transformation: Hallmark Cards" in Chapter 3.

▶ The Retail Industry

Migros—Optimizing Success in Sales Campaigns and Inventory Levels

The Federation of Migros Cooperatives (FMC), a cooperation of retail outlets, was founded in 1925 and is a Swiss retailer located in Zurich, employing over 50,000 people. Their revenues exceed U.S.$10 billion.

Migros' Challenge

A conservative sales climate, aggressive competition, the expansion of new forms of marketing, and the resulting pressure on prices and margins are typical features of the commercial landscape in Switzerland. Strategists in the FMC have realized for quite a while that new methods would be needed to regulate the product range and marketing to strengthen client relationships and profitability.

Migros decided to use article-specific, final-sale dates, which could be recorded by their check-out scanners. To incorporate this idea, they decided on a comprehensive program to equip more than 500 subsidiaries with check-out scanners. These represent about 90% of the total sales for the Migros co-operative associations.

Technical project leaders and departmental representatives agreed from the beginning of the project that considerable efforts would have to be made in parallel to these high POS investments, in order to ensure a beneficial evaluation of the scanner data.

Migros' Solution

The first rough calculations rapidly showed that several hundred gigabytes of data would be generated with a product range of up to 150,000 articles per distribution warehouse along with the storage of daily sales and deliveries with a history of at least 25 months.

Ernst Walz, project leader at the MFC, had a dilemma: "The data processing specialists wanted the users to provide a choice of the desired evaluations together with the necessary totals exactly specified. However, based on their handling of computer lists and in the absence of any other pre-knowledge, the users required virtually everything that one could theoretically imagine. We believed that this could not be achieved and was incapable of being financed with the existing systems."

At Migros, they started by using a "Data Discovery" using authentic data from Migros on a parallel processing server. Actual Migros scanner and delivery data were used to demonstrate the importance of detailed data per day and article, and per subsidiary.

Following a comprehensive benefit calculation, three Migros co-operative associations decided to build the **Migros Data Discovery**, (MDD) to begin their data warehouse journey. With the data warehouse expanding tremendously in its first two years, the group then added a second massively parallel server using a parallel relational database management system, to accommodate growth.

Christian Biland, food-marketing director in the co-operative association at Aargau/Solothurn, and member of the project team, says several objectives were agreed upon. These were:

- Increase the trading margin
- Reduce the depreciation ratio
- Optimize sales campaigns
- Optimize the selling off of seasonal articles
- Reduce inventory levels
- Use the advertising media more efficiently

Migros' Sales and Inventory Analyses

In the meantime, buyers at the co-operative associations in Aargau/ Solothurn, Bern and Luzern, after having access for almost two years to all product ranges to give day-specific sales, delivery and inventory data, created a new vision for the data warehouse and the use of their data resources. They initiated actions to enable monitoring of various changes in sales and inventory levels over a period of 110 weeks. If, on a particular day, the same article is sold at different prices (this is possible as a result of the pricing policy of Migros), then the sales figures are also stored separately in accordance with prices. A separate examination per weekday of weekly, monthly, quarterly or seasonal values is also now commonly and readily available.

Migros employees usually work from the totals over the groups of products for their area of responsibility down to the individual article. In this way, depending on the task, they can optionally select a purchase-based hierarchy or a sales (demand)-oriented viewpoint. In the geographic dimension, they can analyze the results of the entire co-operative society, individual regions and districts, particular types of location, and each individual subsidiary.

As a result of additional filter adjustments, they can concentrate on defined criteria, such as suppliers' brands or their own brands, models, colors, sizes, or import goods. In addition, differentiation of sales in accordance with normal selling and various sales campaigns for articles that are to be sold can be specified in the query. The average time to respond to such a combined polling query is in the range from 10 seconds to approximately one minute.

Migros—Productivity Gains

Sales changes and inventory changes can be illustrated graphically on the screen of the monitor in a matter of seconds by pressing a button. Without the help of the data warehouse, sales data and delivery data would have to be called up separately from different computers and manually compiled by the technical department.

The most important control programs monitor and manage:

- the degree of sales by the latest selling date
- zero inventory levels
- the inventory level and
- selling at special prices or exceptional prices

For support, Migros developed additional queries that can be initiated by the user, but which also run automatically on specified occasions, usually overnight. Migros has also developed very complex queries and models to assist in the predicting of inventory requirements.

Depending upon the product range, a comparison takes place with parameters that were previously set. Each responsible buyer or managing clerk receives clear instructions for action on steps he or she needs to take for which ranges of products or individual articles in order to prevent zero sales or to reduce excessive inventories. Lists of winners and losers and activity-based costing (ABC) analyses also help him or her to focus on the assignments to yield a high leverage effect.

Migros Benefits

The observation of critical product ranges over an extended period of time shows when and where the consumer reacts to external stimuli. For example, when he or she changed from beef to other products because of negative press reports, Migros was able to quickly identify and promote replacement products, while establishing the consumer's price sensitivity. Consumers returned to beef products when Migros reduced the original price by 50% (despite an unchanged news scenario).

The control of sales campaign articles and a comparison with the "before and after" periods give clear information not only for successful pricing but also for the correct announcement policy. Sales rebates that are announced too early on high value non-food product ranges (for example, TV sets) led to a strong sales decline prior to the sales period and led to a worse overall result. In the future, sales campaigns will be announced with a shorter lead time and the gross profits will be monitored more closely.

The regular optimization of sales ratios and inventory levels is a challenge in each product line. This applies to both seasonal products and standard articles. With the help of automatic functions, Migros can determine where zero inventory levels or excess inventory levels threaten to take place, and it takes such action as timely price reductions, rearranging the selling location of the article or changing the ordering cycles. Appropriate corrections for disposition can be arranged to avoid losing sales. The degree of sales for a seasonal article can be reinforced by a controlled price reduction.

Regarding results, Biland says, "Our data warehouse solution has enabled us to make more uniform ordering decisions over all subsidiaries than when different subsidiary employees were coming to different ordering decisions with the same assumptions."

Migros' Plans

Based upon the results that Migros has obtained from its data warehouse, it plans additional automation steps, which will further intensify the productivity of buyers and managing clerks.

The current integrated data system, which gives a high level of integration with its production plants, makes it easy to link sales data and inventory data for optimizing the future supply of goods. This occurs using the improved basis for short-term supply of goods and for medium-term sales planning.

However, the project team led by Walz is thinking of internal sales, such as the automatic charging of a subsidiary with the actual selling in sales campaigns (without control stock-keeping) and the implementation of a rolling inventory level. Walz also has other challenges in view: Sales campaign effects can be researched even more accurately and new marketing procedures can be planned even better if a sales receipt analysis is compiled alongside a general analysis of the scanner data.

The previously utilized and additionally recognized benefit potential convinced the Migros society of co-operative associations to extend the investment decision for the data warehouse to all co-operative associations in Switzerland. Migros has grown the Teradata database to 420 gigabytes of storage capacity while connecting approximately 500 users in the various co-operative association head offices and also in the subsidiaries.

In Turkey, the local country licensees of Migros stores have created a separate and distinct data warehouse environment to manage the inventory and financial processes. This new data warehouse is a partnership of Migros Turkey with local/country investments of the Koc Family conglomerate. Koc believes in the benefits of data warehousing and has already implemented another data warehouse at one of its financial institutions in Turkey.

The Warehouse—Specialized Retailing in New Zealand

New Zealand retailer *The Warehouse* is improving inventory management and knowing its customers better. Known as much for its employees' distinctive red shirts as it is for its low prices, The Warehouse is New Zealand's largest discount retail chain with 65 stores, 5,000 employees, and annual sales of $700 million. The Warehouse's no-frills approach features bare concrete floors and simple racks to display merchandise, which helps keep costs down to provide customers with the lowest possible prices.

The Warehouse Challenges

With increasing competition from other discount chains, The Warehouse has fought to stay the leader in New Zealand's retail industry. To meet this goal, the retailer focuses on better understanding of its customers and improving its operating efficiencies.

"We need to get to know our customers better to keep the right products in stock and to develop targeted programs that will keep them coming back to The Warehouse," says Neville Brown, general manager of Information Systems at The Warehouse. "We also have to operate as efficiently as we can to drive our costs down, to ensure that we are the low-cost provider in New Zealand."

Disparate information systems made it difficult for The Warehouse to gather and effectively analyze the detailed transaction-by-transaction data it needed to gain a competitive advantage. The company decided it needed to harness the information trapped in its various information systems by building a centralized data warehouse.

The Warehouse: The Solution

The Warehouse purchased the technology and the knowledge necessary to step securely into data warehousing by starting with a departmental warehouse that has the ability to scale as the company's needs grow. The data warehouse solution includes Teradata RDBMS, on an asymmetrical multi-processing server. The system offers record performance levels, exceptional price/performance and industry-leading scalability. The storage is a 168 gigabytes of RAID storage system, and the primary access tool is Information Advantages Decision Suite and Web OLAP.

The system will expand to be used by stores and suppliers, many of whom will access the data through intranet/Internet, with flexible and secure views of their focus areas.

The Warehouse found that its skills in the area of data warehousing could use some enhancement and the experience level was relatively low. So it selected outside consultants to provide a series of proven professional services, including project management, architecture and database design, business information consulting, and system integration services.

Forty users in the company's merchandising department can run standard reports and complex ad hoc queries on the 100-gigabyte system. The Warehouse expects the data warehouse to quickly expand to more than 200 users. As more information, such as census, demographic and weather data, is fed to it, the data warehouse pulls information nightly from point-of-sale, inventory, warehouse management and finance systems.

The Warehouse: The Benefits

During the initial two-week proof-of-concept, The Warehouse discovered that 30% of its customers making a purchase bought only one item. That type of even high-level sales information was previously impossible to obtain with its disparate information systems.

The retailer sees the data warehouse as a tool for providing it with a competitive advantage by allowing the company to identify customers, develop customized marketing programs for customers, and provide information to employees at the point-of-sale so they can better serve customers.

"In order to prosper, a business has to know how it works, what happens internally and who its customers are," says Brown. "With the data warehouse, we are able to understand our business and our customers better than ever before."

As the data warehouse evolves and users begin doing more in-depth analysis, The Warehouse will be able to analyze individual customer purchasing habits to enhance its customer loyalty programs. Initial market-basket analysis efforts have uncovered some interesting trends. In its credit-card business, for instance, The Warehouse discovered that the top five % of its cardholders were more likely to buy higher-priced products.

"The power of the data warehouse lies in its ability to provide us with access to detailed market-basket information," says Brown. "And being able to access and analyze that information will give us a competitive advantage that was previously not possible."

In terms of a quantifiable payback for the system, The Warehouse expects to make major gains in inventory management. With the help of the data warehouse, the retailer plans to reduce inventory costs by 15–20%, while reducing out-of-stock situations by tracking up-to-date individual product information. "Our choice came down to two key criteria—experience and a truly scalable database integrated with a DSS parallel architecture platform."

"We expect the data warehouse to grow rapidly. The hardware and software must provide us with the scalability we need to move forward on the same platform as our data warehouse grows and as our business grows," he says.

An important future application that the retailer is planning will be to provide suppliers access to the data warehouse in order to assist them with inventory planning, another important step in improving its own operating efficiencies.

Sears—Re-inventing Itself

As the United States' third-largest retailer, Sears, Roebuck and Company has been a leader in U.S. retailing for a century. Over the past two decades there has been a well-publicized encroachment by discount mass merchandisers. Sears has accomplished its continuing business successes through embracing data warehousing on a dramatic scale.

Among Sears' most significant initiatives: constructing a single, authoritative sales information data warehouse in less than one year on a parallel DW enterprise server. The massive, 1.7 terabyte data warehouse replaced 18 major databases, each of which previously ran on a separate mainframe or networked server system.

"Analysts say that if there were ever a perfect IT turnaround story in corporate America," wrote Information Week in a 1995 article, "the honor would go to Sears."

Sears continues its success in its industry while competing with its main rivals Wal-Mart, KMart, and JCPenney, who also utilize very extensive data warehousing to remain low-cost and highly competitive.

Sears now tracks sales by individual item and store on a daily basis and fine-tunes its buying, merchandising and marketing strategies with previously unattainable precision. With the addition of inventory and margin data, the data warehouse enables Sears staffers to track profitability daily, by location, by item. Says Mark Manock, merchandise information director for Sears Home businesses, "It will be a near miracle." This is a far cry from Sears' management information systems built throughout the 1980s on its mainframe transaction and accounting systems.

Sears' Business Challenges

Founded in 1886, Sears became synonymous with American retailing over the next century, only to be caught by surprise in the 1980s as shoppers defected to specialty stores and discount mass merchandisers. Sears has responded by introducing its own specialty formats, and now operates 1,950 stores in the United States, including HomeLife Furniture, Sears Hardware, Western Auto, and mall-based Sears department stores. Sears Canada and Sears Mexico, in which Sears, Roebuck and Co. owns majority shares, together operate another 1,600 stores and catalog outlets in those countries.

Sears executives decided that a single data source for its key performance indicators—sales, inventory and margin—was a strategic imperative. The vision: to generate consistent, reliable reporting of sales and other results. Dubbed the Strategic Performance Reporting System, or SPRS (pronounced "spurs"), the system is architected to include comprehensive sales data; information on inventory in stores in transit and in distribution centers; and cost per item, enabling users to determine margin daily by item and location.

Ultimately, "it won't matter if someone is the company president or a replenisher," says Manock. "He or she will be looking at the business the same way." An added benefit of making this information available to a broad base of Sears employees is enhanced business literacy.

Sears also refreshed the merchandise mix units for 810 mall-based stores in the United States. Long viewed as oriented toward male customers, Sears acted decisively when market research revealed that a large portion of buyers for its merchandise, including handling goods, were actually women shopping for their families. The retailer began reconfiguring stores to emphasize women's apparel, simultaneously rolling out the "Softer Side of Sears" advertising campaign, reminding consumers they can pick up, say, new lingerie along with a lawnmower.

That shift has worked very well for Sears. Retailing profits, climbing nearly 20% in both 1994 and 1995, surpassed $1 billion in 1995. These record earnings were achieved on nearly $35 billion in revenue.

Sears' Solution—"Re-invent Sears Itself"

Clearly, Sears needed the right information technology to support its re-invention into a far more agile, responsive store chain. In the early 1990s, Sears operated with 10 to 20-year-old sales information systems packed with redundant, conflicting and sometimes obsolete data. For example, a system set up based on 10 geographic regions didn't reflect closed locations—or Sears' current operations, which are divided into seven regions. Sears' finance, marketing and merchandising departments each had its own systems, which meant a buyer might come up with a different sales figure from the accounting department for the same region.

Even within departments, information was scattered among numerous databases, forcing users to query multiple systems even with relatively simple questions. "The frustration was always in the number of places you needed to go for basic information," says Manock. Data often was summarized, making information difficult to analyze in meaningful detail. What's more, errors were virtually inevitable. "When you're doing calculations based on data from half a dozen systems," says Sears senior systems engineer Douglas Klein, "the chances of those results being flawless are pretty remote."

Sears IS staffers completed a marathon process of consolidating its 18 separate sales, inventory and other systems. Their priority: delivering the sales system (within one year) which was completed in mid-1995. Store and distribution center inventory and ad hoc reporting systems followed, which was followed by a consolidated financial system in 1997.

Sears' Results—Tracks Items Individually and in "Clusters"

SPRS users now have the ability to view each day's sales—nationally, and by region, district, store, line and stock-keeping unit, the equivalent of individual items—on the following morning. Unlike Sears' previous systems, which provided information only daily or weekly, SPRS enables users to specify any starting and ending dates they choose, going back a full 121 weeks. And all information can be accessed via a highly user-friendly, graphical interface.

Sears' staffers now monitor the precise impact of advertising, weather, and other factors on sales of specific items. "We used to know sales were up or down, but we really didn't know which lines or items were driving sales results," says Jonathon Rand, merchandise information director for the Sears' Apparel and Home Fashions group. That means buyers and other specialties can adjust inventory quantities, merchandising, ad frequency and placement, and myriad other variables almost immediately.

"It's a huge plus," says business support administrator Jeffrey Whitehead. "If you have to wait until the end of December to jump on something, it's a little late to catch the Christmas rush."

Significantly, SPRS enables users to group together, or "cluster," widely divergent types of items for the first time. For example, merchandisers can track sales of a store display marked "Gifts under $25" that might include sweatshirts, screwdrivers and other unrelated items. Advertising staffers can follow so-called "Great Items," drawn from vastly different departments that are splashed on the covers of newspaper promotional circulars.

SPRS also provides Sears with the ability to identify the top-selling items in a given category or region, for example. "When you have this many stores and lines to look at, you need to go right to the issues," says Rand. In turn, that capability points to opportunities for staffers to exert the greatest sales leverage. Says Manock, "The data doesn't give you all the answers, but it tells you where to look."

The Sears SPRS data warehouse has over 2,000 users — primarily buyers, replenishers, marketers and strategic planners. Logistics and finance staffers are expected to become users when inventory and financial data is available, and the IS department is currently testing the impact of adding store managers. Response time has dropped from days to minutes for typical information requests. In fact, Sears' biggest SPRS issue involves pacifying users who want more data. "The business people think the system is fabulous," says Rand. "They're yelling, 'Give me inventory!'"

Sears also learned early, in the data warehousing maturation process, to provide standard reports and graphics, which were "expected" by the user management teams and immediately available. This expectation required Sears to be able to provide over 2,500 reporting variations and immediate response times to the previously "mainframe-based" internal cultures. Implementing "internal customer satisfaction and expectation management" is also a key to successful companies, like Sears, that worked closely with their info-structure users to determine the initial and succeeding projects to enhance the original data warehouse deliverables.

The strategic impact of the data warehouse is clear. "This system will get only more valuable," says Manock. "It offers everybody a tool for making better decisions."

How does Sears fit into the arena of customer relationship systems? It is rather simple, but yet complex, based on strategic positioning in the retail markets. If you don't know WHO your customers actually are (by name and address) then you MUST know what they prefer, what they BUY, WHEN they buy it, and be able to predict what they WILL BUY.

Wal-Mart Stores (U.S.A.) Turn Data into Actionable Information

Wal-Mart, with annual revenues of over U.S.$150 billion, realized that it had to make decisions by individual store to meet the needs of its customers, which drove a need for information from store-level detail data. Wal-Mart designed and built a data warehouse solution that buyers, merchandisers, and vendor/supplier partners could access for detailed information to help the retailer get closer to its goal of getting the right products to each store at the right time.

Sam Walton opened his first Wal-Mart store in Rogers, Arkansas, in 1962. Today, this retailer has annual revenues of over $150 billion, and more than 4,000 stores on at least four continents, and over 800,000 employees. Wal-Mart's tremendous growth challenged the way a retail company operated its business. As Wal-Mart expanded into new markets, meeting the needs of an increasingly divergent customer base became more and more difficult. What worked in one store didn't necessarily work for another store.

Wal-Mart's Challenges

"We were looking at the business and asking 'How do we continue to be the best store in town, to be the best at what we do,'" said Randy Mott, former senior vice president and chief information officer at Wal-Mart. Wal-Mart wanted to manage the business one store at a time, which executives knew would be critical to its continued success and growth.

"We were starting to move out of the Midwest, starting to become more national, and we were starting to believe what Sam Walton always believed, that you manage the chain one store and one day at a time," says Charlie McMurtry, Wal-Mart strategy manager at that time. "And we were starting to lose that capability."

Wal-Mart's existing systems, which provided only summary and average data about the business, didn't support its changing needs. "We really needed to change the way we were doing business from the standpoint that we couldn't do things on averages because they may not be representative of any store in the chain," said Mott. "We realized that we had to make decisions by individual store to meet the needs of its customers. We had to merchandise locally, and that drove a need for information in store-level detail." Executives needed a new info-structure of information technology, and began the journey in data warehousing to regain that capability.

Wal-Mart's Solution

Wal-Mart needed a scalable and flexible information info-structure for collection and analysis of its products and activities throughout the entire company. As they developed their data warehousing solution they wanted to be creative and world-class in making the initial and future steps in data warehousing. "We took a different approach than our competitors," said Rick Dalzell, one the key managers (subsequently a Wal-Mart Vice President) of Application Development during the initial data warehouse evolution. "We went to a very detailed, 'I want to know everything that's occurring in a store' type approach." This proved to be highly successful and now Wal-Mart is considered one of the world leaders in using data warehousing to manage their growth and investments, as well as their penchant for providing the lowest possible price to their customers.

Wal-Mart's initial 700-gigabyte data warehouse was stocked with point of sale and shipment data. The system had grown to 7.5 terabytes with the first four years and then proceeded to 24 terabytes. New types of data such as inventory, forecast, demographic, modular, markdowns, returns and market basket were added. The warehouse—which maintains an ongoing rolling 65 weeks of data, kept by item-by-item, also by store, and also by day—runs on multiple NCR World Mark massively parallel servers using NCR Teradata data warehouse databases.

Wal-Mart's buyers, merchandisers, logistics, and forecasting associates, as well as 4,000+ of Wal-Mart's vendor partners, have direct access to the data warehouse. With more than 50 applications running on the system, users can ask virtually any question. The system has handled as many as 40,000+ queries in one week. In 1999, Wal-Mart announced that it had increased the applications, data, number of business and partner users to expand the system to over 101 Terabytes of information. This was the largest known commercial data warehouse in the world during the twentieth century.

Wal-Mart's Benefits

The data warehouse has enabled Wal-Mart to better focus on replenishment at the store level and provide precise information to its buyers and suppliers—moving closer to its goal of getting the right products to each store at the right time. And that helps contribute to Wal-Mart's success at providing everyday low prices and superior customer satisfaction. "Our business strategy depends on detailed data at every level," said Mott. "Every cost, every line item is carefully analyzed, enabling better merchandising decisions to be made on a daily basis."

Through the system, buyers and vendors query information and analyze sales trends by item and by store to make informed decisions on replenishment, look at customer buying trends, analyze seasonal buying trends, make mark-down decisions, and react to merchandise volume and movement at any time.

"The ultimate form of customer service is having what the customer wants when he or she walks into one of our stores to make a purchase decision," stated Mark Glover, development director of decision support for Wal-Mart at that time.

According to Dalzell, since implementing its warehouse and store-level replenishment process, Wal-Mart has improved its in-stock percentage more than 10 points, to over 96%, one of the highest rates in the industry. "Being able to replenish at a store/ item level is a strategic advantage. Our competitors don't do it," said Dalzell, who has moved on to another major merchandising firm.

Mott said that as buyers tie more and more business elements together, they're able to really understand and manage the profitability of a product or category. Buyers across the company give the system high marks, as it has become an invaluable part of their jobs and Wal-Mart's success. "Our buyers can really dissect the business, drill it down to a level that is easy to understand and manage," said Drew Albright, one of the buying managers. "If the data warehouse went away tomorrow, our sales would probably head south and so would our profitability," said Kevin Sullivan, a sporting goods' buyer for Wal-Mart.

Wal-Mart's Results

Wal-Mart's vendor partners can perform their own analyses of buying patterns. Access to this information allows suppliers to work with Wal-Mart buyers in managing their inventory at each store and identifying opportunities for local merchandising. "The best win is when you are able to customize a unique program for Wal-Mart that nobody else in the country has so that it can take a product, run very hard with it and sell a lot of units, meet the needs of its customers and hit its objectives," says Jerry Kihn, business manager for Dow Brands, one of Wal-Mart's vendors.

Sharing information with its vendor partners has benefited Wal-Mart in a number of ways. The company has seen a sharp rise in vendor responsiveness, product costs have decreased, and forecasting has improved significantly.

With the data warehouse, Wal-Mart is able to turn data into actionable information about its business. In turn, Wal-Mart can deliver what its customers want: the right item, at the right store, at the right time and at the right price.

Wal-Mart has utilized its Teradata data warehouse and the entire value chain of information and technology to enhance its ability to provide the lowest cost products to its customers. Wal-Mart has proven its ability to manage supply, inventory, location selection, advertising, pricing, and competitiveness to become the world's leader in retailing, not only in size and number of locations, but also in knowing its customers through the products that they buy.

There is also a wonderful story at Sam's Clubs which provides insight into the use of Wal-Mart's CRM Data Warehouse approach to become a direct marketing organization.

There are many additional case studies and stories that can be told about Wal-Mart's success in the building and use of information and knowledge.

The Airline and Tourism Industries

Continental Airlines—Managing Diverse Operations

Continental Airlines is the fifth largest airline in the United States. In 1999, more than 40 million people flew Continental, which offers more than 2,000 jet and Express departures daily to over 130 domestic and over 50 international destinations.

To win in today's highly competitive skies, Continental has undergone an aggressive expansion which has included the addition of new domestic and international routes, upgrading of certain classes of service and establishment of its value-oriented Continental Express service for shorter flights. Additionally, Continental received the J.D. Powers & Associates airlines industry award for operational performance and on-time performance, further demonstrating the airline's focus on excellence in customer service.

The airline and its competitors continually face a mix of challenges in the areas of efficiency, logistics and consumer marketing that are unique to their industry. In such a hyper-competitive environment, Continental's ability to present information regarding travel patterns throughout many sectors of its organization in various locations has become critical to increasing growth through customer satisfaction.

Continental Airlines' Challenge

In 1995, as its expansion was taking flight, each department at Continental Airlines had its own approach to data management and reporting. The company lacked a corporate data infrastructure which would allow a broad range of employees quick access to key insights about its customers.

Continental determined it would build a new, consolidated decision support solution that would empower its people in areas as diverse as booking, scheduling, customer service, marketing, revenue management, and field operations. They would gain timely, standardized data from which to make faster, more informed decisions. The data warehouse therefore became the focal point of Continental's information technology (IT) planning and implementation efforts.

The airline's initial objective was to enable the accurate forecasting of passenger booking levels. The ability to view travel patterns by the origin and destination of each customer—in essence, getting a complete look at a traveler's itinerary—would provide customer bookings, route scheduling, cargo/baggage operations, and many other internal departments with essential information to further improve results.

"We saw a tremendous need to gain competitive advantage through the better use of information about travel patterns," says Bob Edwards, Continental's senior director of advanced technology. "We wanted to capture, consolidate and analyze information in such a way so that all users could benefit, revenues would be optimized and, most importantly, our customers would be even more satisfied."

The Continental Solution

Built on a framework designed for growth, Continental's data warehouse was designed with industry-standard data access and transformation tools, and a comprehensive use of professional and support services.

The first department to benefit directly from the data warehouse was Continental's Revenue Management Group, which uses the data warehouse to track a customer's travel itinerary from origin to final destination. Previous systems could track only on a segment-by-segment basis.

For example, if a passenger were traveling from Newark to Los Angeles and had to change airplanes in Houston, the previous system recognized the itinerary as two trips—one from Newark to Houston and a second from Houston to Los Angeles. The data warehouse builds a correlation between the two segments to help Continental better understand the customer's actual travel pattern.

Continental Airlines began by building a "Revenue Management System" data warehouse with a parallel processing database. Continental built a system to determine which seats on what routes were generating significant revenue for the airline, and by using external consultants, defined a plan to scale up the system and the collection of data from throughout the airline for the creation of a true *enterprise-wide data warehouse*. This was a significant new approach for them.

"By starting with the Revenue Management Group, we tackled one of our most difficult problems first?," said Edwards. "I believe this approach enabled us to learn the tough lessons early in the project life cycle."

Continental Airlines' Benefits

Continental Airlines has developed its logical database to address several major business questions and present consolidated information to internal clients in diverse areas of the company. Large amounts of historical information about the operation of the airline initially became available to 100 users, with targets of growing to 1,000 users.

Everyone at Continental Airlines benefits from access to more accurate forecasts of passenger demand.

For revenue forecasting, Continental can now tap into historical information and use standard modeling techniques to develop more comprehensive forecasts and improve the revenue and yield for future schedules. This provides much more valuable information than originally planned, and during its maturation process, Continental has moved to include numerous new departments and *subject areas* within its data warehouse.

Continental's marketing-oriented Customer Information group can better associate customers' demographic information with experiences such as special promotions and personal preferences (e.g., who is flying the airline to golf vacations). The operation will use such information to identify trends, helping it build upon relationships, form new ones and fine-tune its marketing promotions. For example, specific travel packages will be offered to certain frequent flyers.

Also under consideration is a "dependent" data mart to present frequent flyer account data and other information to Continental OnePass members via the World Wide Web.

In the plans is Continental's Technical Operations—Continental's field service capability—initiating a new maintenance-related database allowing for the more accurate tracking of parts, including where they are kept and when are they scheduled for forwarding to another location.

Continental's data warehouse is built on a framework designed for growth. For Continental, this meant a reduction in initial investment and minimal risk of system obsolescence:

The value of the data warehouse continues to grow as additional functional areas and applications are added.

"Managing the growth and development of the warehouse will be our greatest challenge in future phases, but the benefit is definitely worth the effort," said Edwards. "I am confident that data warehouse will prove to be our most strategic business development tool."

As part of its in-depth analysis, Continental ran extensive, industry-leading TPC-D benchmarks. The tests were designed to measure a decision-support system's performance in real-world situations with large volumes of data and multiple simultaneous users, as well as to run additional queries specific to the airline industry.

"Many vendors asked Continental to buy their data warehouse solutions on the promise of performance," said Edwards. "Our test results told us where the performance really existed, and that was with the tight coupling of the relational parallel database with massively parallel servers is the only way to go in implementing a real data warehouse environment."

For another example, see "Excellence in Business Transformation: Delta Air Lines Takes Off Using Advanced @ctive Data Warehousing for CRM" in Chapter 11.

Travel Unie's Challenge—Keeping Its Customers Coming Back

How do companies gain and retain competitive advantage? Especially when they are not the largest in size or customer allegiance.

By being the first to arrive. It's an appropriate goal for Travel Unie, the Netherlands' largest tour operator and travel agency. Travel Unie was the first in the Netherlands to use computers to track reservations, first to install a massively parallel processing computer. And Travel Unie soon will be the first Dutch travel agency to provide 24/7 online access to its services.

Travel Unie was formed with the merger of the Netherlands' two largest agencies, Arke Reizen, a company with a history of technological innovation, and Holland International. Travel Unie offers tour packages directly to travelers through 400 branch offices, as well as providing travel package services to more than 1,400 independent travel agents.

Travel Unie's Business Challenges

Travel Unie must be able to provide "on demand" services to each office and agent, or risk losing business to competitors. The travel agency also must be able to capture and use customer data to more easily tailor its tour packages to customer needs.

Meeting these requirements falls directly on Travel Unie's information systems. For years, Arke Reizen implemented successful information technology strategies that helped drive sales growth in excess of 40% in one five-year period and slashed total operating costs per passenger booked by more than 60%.

Travel Unie has worked to adopt Arke Reizen's successful IT strategies company wide. In doing so, Travel Unie wanted to maintain the high levels of availability, flexibility, and price/performance that Arke Reizen enjoyed with its initial massively parallel processing data warehousing computer, which helped them stay ahead in the technology arena.

"We realized the advantages of being first with new technology," says Gerret Goossen, director of information processing for Travel Unie. "Being first is a strategic weapon. Investing in high performance technology enables us to offer the highest quality travel package for the best price, and with superior customer service."

Travel Unie's Solution

To meet its goal of implementing an enterprise-wide computing solution building on Arke Reizen's success, Travel Unie utilized external consultants from Teradata to tap their experience in delivering industry-leading high availability transaction processing and data warehousing solutions.

The Travel Unie data warehouse solution runs on a parallel-processing platform, which enables a large number of users running applications on multiple nodes to access a single data source. Subsequently, Travel Unie implemented additional data warehousing processing nodes for extra reservations application power, and as replacements for some other overloaded systems. Travel Unie designed a flexible online system, including application management services and a single graphical view of the enterprise; and its data warehouse requires and achieves high availability and scalability.

Travel Unie's Benefits

Keeping its mission-critical applications up and running so that customers are properly serviced is only part of the story. The data warehouse system provides deeper analytical and reporting capabilities for marketers and managers. Travel Unie marketers, for example, are able to query the database for specific trend information, which allows them to perform detailed customer profiling, in-depth marketing and advertising analysis. Managers can quickly evaluate tour packages and promotions, and customize or alter them to better fit localized markets or trends.

What about being first in customer service? A travel agent queries the data warehouse and customer profiling applications in less than one second, while system downtime has been virtually eliminated. Both of these practices mean travel agents remain online to provide prompt responses to their customers.

Travel Unie reservationists have immediate access to current detail data from all their transportation, hotel and tour data sources, so they can easily offer real choices and alternatives if one choice isn't available. As a result, customer interaction is more efficient, the customer is more satisfied, and the agent can book more tours.

Travel Unie plans to give its customer service a further boost when it begins storing multimedia objects online in its data warehouse. The data warehouse is planned to store, retrieve, manipulate, and analyze complex objects—such as video, image, audio, graphics, animation, text and other user-defined data types—as well as link them to traditional alphanumeric relational information. Travel Unie utilizes external consulting skills to provide the knowledge and technology for this multimedia database, with project development, user interface development, intranet technology assistance, and software technology. Using the new multimedia features of their data warehouse database, travel agents will be able to take a virtual tour of an intended destination, giving them the ability to search for locations based on almost any customer request.

For instance, if a customer requests only hotels in a given location with walls that are painted yellow, the travel agent can search the database for hotels meeting that requirement. Taking customer service even one step further, Travel Unie plans to offer customers direct, around-the-clock access to the database through self-service kiosks and via the Internet.

Says Goossen. "We are moving closer to offering 24/7 access to our services; having highly available systems becomes even more critical to the success of our operations. The systems ensure unlimited growth possibilities for our company with the ability to maintain excellent price/performance."

Travel Unie's Results

Travel agents have fast and easy access to Travel Unie's reservation system to provide customers with a prompt response. The system also has brought the company closer to its customers. Executives can access detailed information about their customers to analyze trends and create customized tour packages, all of which keep the customers coming back to the Netherlands' premier travel agency.

Kinki Nippon Tourist (Japan)—Driving Toward "One-To-One" Marketing Strategies

In the early 1980s, Kinki Nippon Tourist (KNT) revolutionized the way its Japanese customers purchased travel services by introducing a new marketing channel—newspaper advertising and magazines customized exclusively for its repeat customers. KNT formed a new division, The *Club Tourism*, to develop and implement these types of unique marketing strategies and a new concept of tourism.

To arrange travel prior to KNT's pioneering move, customers had to visit a travel agency. But now, customers can find the trips that interest them through the newspapers and the magazines as new channels to order the trips over the phone (and through the Internet in the future). When the competition followed suit, KNT again took the lead by the strategy of two-way communication with the customers, which allowed them to know their customers well. This reflected the customers' voices and preference to the travel services in a timely manner which fully utilized its customer database.

KNT's unique marketing strategies have helped the company become Japan's second-largest travel agency with annual revenue of $6.7 billion. KNT's Club Tourism division is Japan's largest direct travel service.

KNT's Challenge

A key element of **KNT's Club Travel** business is its *Travel Companions* magazine. The magazine is delivered to all Club Travel customers, twenty times a year, covering as many as 1500 varieties of KNT tours that can be ordered. This on-demand type of service that the catalogue offers is attractive and beneficial to all members.

With the circulation of *Travel Companions* exceeding one million, the division decided to deploy a "one-to-one" marketing strategy to retain core customers and improve customer loyalty by offering the most attractive trips possible for individual needs. That, in turn, would be important to expand its business through word-of-mouth advertising from satisfied customers.

"We want customers to know that we offer, or can offer, any type of group tour to match their interest and pair them with others who share similar interests. The concept we have in tourism is that through these type of group tours, the members can make friends and find new types of tours to promote the quality of their life," says Hideo Takahashi, managing director, KNT.

To implement its "one-to-one strategy," The Club Tourism's marketing personnel needed the ability to analyze customer preferences, behavior, interest areas, expectations, and impressions of tours. Having timely access to such detailed information was critical for Club Tourism to know its customers in order to develop attractive, competitive tours. And it would have to be done quickly to publish in the upcoming magazine or newspaper advertisements.

Operating in a legacy computing environment, requests for information took several days for the IS department to fill. Lack of timeliness wasn't the only issue. Travel and tour designers required more detailed information than the mainframe-based system could provide.

KNT's Solution

KNT's Travel Club division decided to use an open systems architecture to store all customer information and enhance its decision-support capabilities.

Initially, about 100 users accessed the system directly through individual workstations. To implement the solution, KNT also used consulting services for data modeling, data transformation, and client application development. KNT implemented the 1.5 million customer database in only four months.

Successful one-to-one marketing will have to have more detailed and non-transactional data, which enabled forecasting what the customers are going to want. That data will be collected from the customers' conversation with tour conductors, via telephone, or any other opportunity to communicate with the customers.

Therefore the database needs to be flexible to absorb future requirements of the data and to be scalable to ensure the best-cost performance in the future.

KNT—The Benefits

With the customer database, KNT's end users now can quickly and easily access customer information to make proactive decisions.

"The marketing imperative in today's tourism industry is to know our customers. That is the base to deploy one-to-one marketing, which helps us retain our customers by satisfying their needs," says Hideo Takahashi. "We need to study the diversified customer preferences and then develop tours, events, and hospitality in a timely manner. The database helps us do so by providing access to detailed data."

Accessing detailed data led KNT to uncover patterns and information that were previously unattainable in its legacy environment. For example, The Travel Club discovered that customers whose first tour was made by bus were likely to be repeat tour bus customers. The company can now target the appropriate tours to these customers.

KNT can measure the effectiveness of specific advertising efforts by determining which newspaper ads work the best for certain tours and which tours are better to promote through either newspaper or direct mail.

The data warehouse database also incorporates information from customer questionnaires, which users access to analyze customers' preferences in developing tours best suited to their wants and needs.

KNT has improved the efficiency and speed of its direct mailings. The magazine they deliver is customized to fit their targeted customers. The total number of magazines delivered a year is more than 30 million. By accessing the database, marketers can target the customers within defined segments much more accurately and faster than previously possible. The marketers can now print mailing labels for the magazines on the same day they run queries, as opposed to the 3–5 days it took when pulling information from the mainframe.

"One World"—British Airways, American Airlines and Qantas

Creating the Future

It is interesting to note that the next three implementation examples, all airlines, have joined in a common customer-marketing, customer-care, customer-transfer, customer-communications, and customer-rewarding alliance known as "ONE WORLD."

Each of these organizations utilizes the same data warehouse database technology and management system, but still maintains its own data on its own customers; it also shares a multiplicity of information to generate high revenues, high customer satisfaction, and driving resource allocation planning to meet their customers' needs and desires.

Eventually, after cooperation and understanding of the values of customer-centric information, there may be a joining of information resources to ensure outstanding worldwide leadership and differentiation for the benefit of the customers and these airlines.

British Airways

British Airways is held up as a shining example of an airline that encourages its members to fly with it in the hope that they will be promoted to the next customer segmentation tier. Members are more active than with other frequent flyer programs and have proved to be knowledgeable about the rewards and benefits due to them.

British Airways is not resting on its laurels, however. It is using a large data warehouse to discover its customers' preferences with a view to satisfying them on future flights. This may lead to stocking a passenger's favorite drink or meal according to his or her previous request.

This might then lead to cost savings; instead of keeping a large stock of drinks that may or may not be required and then have to be disposed of, all stock can be bought against known demand.

At this level, and because business and first class air passengers are so engaged, airlines are in a position to reach the Holy Grail of one-to-one marketing. The investment is available, because for a small percentage of passengers, the lifetime value of their custom is so large that highly personalized marketing and rewards are possible and profitable.

Airlines of course have another sort of customer—one that they must market to when they cannot find enough human passengers to fill the aircraft. Cargo accounts for an important proportion of airlines' turnover and maximizing loads must be about the ideal mixture of human beings and cargo. The problem here is that the customers divide into entirely different segments with different needs—one consumer, the other commercial—and yet there must be integration of data derived from both segments if aircraft are to fly profitably.

American Airlines

American Airlines has been a long-time user of data warehousing and was an early adopter. American Airlines has continually loaded and grown its detailed data for sales and marketing analysis, *The AAdvantage Frequent Flyer Program* segmentation and reporting, planning and managing incentives (offers to customers) as well as creatively address the loyalty issues through customer "yield management" solutions. Many of American's uses of the data warehouse have been developed by its own The Sabre Group and internal airline statistical groups.

American Airlines also uses Teradata data warehousing for its operations management. American stores data on its purchasing, vendor performance, fixed asset management, asset authorizations, flight traffic analysis, disruption minimization, food and beverage management, computer equipment tracking, and baggage tracking.

American Airlines, through its frequent flyer segmentation, has now built a database of its best customers to ensure long-term retention and increased profitability per customer. In fact, American now telephones its Executive Platinum customers (also known as Emerald Level Customers in the One-World airlines) to discuss the levels of satisfaction and to resolve any problems that the most valuable customers may be experiencing. American is using their systems to define which customers actually have the most revenues/profits (versus the previous method of just using mileage as a determinant of levels).

Their competitors and partners are sometimes performing customer satisfaction activities but do not use the systems to followthrough with measurements on customer retention and re-bookings (after a known problem or dis-satisfaction has occurred within an airline's service).

HINT FOR VALUE (All businesses should consider this in their customer relationships): In discussing the use of customer information and flight historical data, several airlines have not choosen to move forward with the data they already possess. Recently, I advised an airline to consider monitoring and measuring the recency, frequency, and monetary (RFM) value of the top echelon of their customers. RFM is used in retail and many customer contact businesses to determine the value of the customer and actions to be taken to keep them. The airlines could determine which customers had NOT flown their airline within a measurement period (and learn from the historical customer flying patterns for the past three years). This discovery knowledge of how the customers transact with the airline would quickly alert them to contact the customer to determine if there is a problem or issue, then resolve it. The airline would remeasure flights taken to determine if the customer flew again within an appropriate timeframe based on former patterns. This could elevate revenues, resolve customer issues, and alert the airline of when to contact the customer directly. This type of customer *knowledge* has high value and helps retain high-value customers. This customer satisfaction program would also be clearly measurable and would provide additional information for managing customers' satisfaction levels. (By the way, as of early 2000, American Airlines now telephones its top Executive Platinum customers when there are no problems and tries to make sure that everything is going well in the AA and customer relationship.)

Qantas

Qantas of Australia maintains five years of revenues on its data warehouse and can predict future capacities and returns-on-investments as well as any other airline in the world. In the late 1997 and 1998 "Asian Financial Crisis" (sometimes called the Asian FLU), Qantas was able to predict some months in advance the fact that it was not going to achieve the normal loading factors (capacity management) on numerous routes in the North-South Asian-Australian market.

Qantas reallocated numerous aircraft and decided to sign code-sharing agreements with other airlines in order to move its own aircraft to more profitable markets. These types of management analysis and then action have provided Qantas with very high returns on its investment in customer-centric information on the past and future flying patterns of its customers and its loading factors. Prediction of the future through correlation of very detailed data from the historical data warehouse provides high ROI in a competitive environment.

The Ground Transportation Industry

Burlington Northern Santa Fe Railway

Based in Fort Worth, Texas, the Burlington Northern and Santa Fe Railway Company (BNSF) operates one of the largest railroad networks in North America, with more than 35,000 route miles covering 29 states and two Canadian provinces.

BNSF was created in 1995 by the merger of Burlington Northern Incorporated and Santa Fe Pacific Corporations. BNSF knew that it needed to quickly find a way to tightly integrate information from the two companies and thus better understand revenues and profitability, as well as improve operations, and move towards better understanding its customers' future service requirements.

Burlington Northern Santa Fe—The Challenges

To do so, BNSF needed to merge the two companies' separate and distinctly different data warehouse initiatives into an integrated system that would accurately report on and support the newly combined company. In order to build that one central, enterprise-wide data warehouse, BNSF faced a unique challenge because it had to source from two different groups of transaction systems, in different formats, different locations, in different states.

"The former Burlington Northern Railroad and former Santa Fe Railroad each had its own environment, its own transaction systems, and its own reporting systems," said Alonzo Howell, when he was director for systems information at BNSF. "After the merger, we had to quickly get to the point where we could manage our combined company."

The Texas-based railway company recognized early on that the analytical needs of its business users would play a key role in the selection of the right computing platform. Users needed to perform ad hoc queries and access both detailed and summary data—two important factors that led to the BNSF data warehouse solution.

BNSF Solution

BNSF's data warehouse runs a massively parallel processing server and grew data from the original 200 gigabytes to over 900 gigabytes in its first two years. The BNSF warehouse is stocked with very granular-data, extracted from numerous computers running operational applications, as well as financial and human resource data, and utilizes a standard for its query tool.

In addition, BNSF built a custom graphical point-and-click interface tool for users in the field who have limited experience using computers and little time for training. To ensure data quality for all of its users, BNSF updates and refreshes its data nightly with ultra-high speed warehouse load utilities through direct channel connections into two mainframes, which are fed from 20 different source systems.

The over 1,200 BNSF users access more timely and detailed information, resulting in improved decision-making and business management.

Since the BNSF had little initial experience in data warehousing, it chose to utilize outside professional consulting services to build and then maintain consulting personnel on-site for administration of the warehouse environment.

BSNF Benefits—A Better Understanding of Costs and Customers

BNSF has realized a number of benefits from its data warehouse, particularly in the area of data consistency across functional areas. Howell explains that prior to building the data warehouse, BNSF users accessed inconsistent and redundant information from various disparate systems, leading to inaccurate analysis and reporting, inefficient equipment utilization, and poor crew management.

With its data warehouse, BNSF now has a better understanding of its revenue and profitability by customer, product, route, and business unit. Also, understanding the cost of providing a particular service or serving a specific customer allows the giant railway company to more accurately price its services to ensure positive margins.

With all cost and expense information now housed in its data warehouse, BNSF is realizing significant savings by improving expense management of everything from accounts payable to labor and materials. For example, BNSF reduced crew expenses by analyzing work histories to identify problem areas. "The ability to see detailed crew expenses on a daily basis allows BNSF to better utilize crews and control overtime," states Howell. "Within the first few months of implementation, BNSF saved hundreds of thousands of dollars in this area."

The company can now better analyze its cycle times for loading and reloading cargo to improve customer service and asset utilization. In addition, field operations managers, such as train masters, can analyze how their terminal, trains and traffic lanes are performing.

Moreover, with more than 43,000 employees scattered across North America, BNSF's human resources department can more effectively report and comply with such regulatory requirements as the Equal Employment Opportunity (EEO), by analyzing breakdowns of its workforce by age, race, gender, and other demographics.

BNSF management states that the warehouse database allows BNSF users to uniquely perform ad hoc queries and complex interrelated queries without using indices. This is important to them because, "We can concentrate what we need to get out of the data, rather than spend a lot of time trying to identify and define a structure to support predefined queries."

BNSF Results

This railroad is one of many that utilize data warehousing and customer-centric information for managing future resource allocations and deciding on future resource acquisitions (such as expensive locomotives and specialized refrigerator rolling stock/cars, many of which cost millions of dollars).

There have been many articles and presentations documenting the data warehouse successes at Union Pacific Railroad (Omaha) and Union Pacific Technologies (St. Louis), as well as at The French National Railway (SNCF). These organizations are continuing to change their processes and the uses of customer data in becoming more and more customer-centric within their info-infrastructure environments.

The Telecommunications Industry

Israel's Pele-Phone Communications—Maintaining Customers and Gaining Competitive Advantage

Pele-Phone Communications, Ltd., pioneered cellular network services in Israel and is so closely identified with the technology that today many Israelis refer to any cellular phone as a Pele-Phone. The company, which is the largest of Israel's three cellular providers, was established as a joint venture of Motorola and Bezeq, the Israeli Telecommunications Corporation.

With close to one million business and consumer cellular subscribers, Pele-Phone commands approximately 50% of the market share and is well-positioned to continue growing its cellular subscriber base. Among other favorable factors for the company, Israel ranks as one of the world's fastest growing wireless markets. The country's penetration rate of cellular services is 30%, the fifth highest rate in the world. By the year 2000, the penetration rate is expected to reach 50%. Another advantage in providing cellular services in the Israeli market is the length of the average cellular phone call, which exceeds that of most other countries.

Pele-Phone, with corporate headquarters in Tel Aviv, maintains 14 service centers located around Israel to meet local customer needs. Its highly technical and service-oriented work force of nearly 1,000 employees continues to expand its portfolio of cellular services. The company anticipates offering an even broader range of telecommunications services in response to the deregulation of the Israeli telecommunications market in 2000 and beyond.

Pele-Phone determined that it needed to mine the wealth of customer information it collected each day in the face of new and increasingly aggressive competition. Its traditional database technologies used for billing and operational systems, however, could not handle the enormous amount of raw data needed for new marketing initiatives.

The goal was to track customer needs, usage patterns, and network capacity to help develop profitable new services and focused offerings that will build customer loyalty and reduce churn, while increasing overall operating efficiency.

Pele-Phone's Business Challenges

Only two cellular service providers have operated in Israel for many years, and they have developed a fierce rivalry. In 1998 the Ministry of Telecommunications announced the formation of a third provider, resulting in renewed attention for the country's wireless customers. Deregulation of the telecommunications industry further intensified the competition.

In the face of this new and increasingly aggressive competition, Pele-Phone sought ways to launch its own aggressive marketing initiatives. Pele-Phone's marketing executives wanted a solution that would help them build customer loyalty and reduce churn (customers switching to the competition), while increasing product-line profitability. They also wanted a system in place that would help them use customer data to effectively cross-sell evolving service offerings.

Pele-Phone determined that it needed to mine the wealth of customer information it collected each day to increase its competitive advantage.

"We used traditional database technologies for billing and operational systems," says Avshalom Rov, director of application software for Pele-Phone. "But none was capable of handling the enormous volumes of consumer data we needed to store and interrogate in order to identify potential customer needs or determine the profitability of individual products."

Pele-Phone's Data Warehousing Solution

Pele-Phone decided to build a data warehouse to meet its decision-support needs. The cellular provider was interested in marketing initiatives that would require a very large data repository to build customer history.

An enterprise-wide data warehouse strategy was chosen after a seven-month selection process. The process included a business and information discovery analysis that projected a return on investment for about U.S.$6 million, based solely on the system's capability to help reduce churn. After weighing the impact of the raw data needed for its marketing initiatives, Pele-Phone analyzed the capabilities of the various systems, focusing on installations with similar usage requirements. The implementation moved from development to production in six months.

Two classes of users rely on the data warehouse's capabilities. A very sophisticated group of users, which may range from five to 10 people depending on the project, includes market analysts, statisticians, or economists. These users understand how data is structured in the data warehouse and have the ability to write queries to leverage the data for an advantage. Another group of up to 100 users, having far less knowledge of the system, perform predefined queries on call records from the billing system.

Pele-Phone is turning its customer data into a strategic advantage. Mr. Rov attributes the success to the performance and maintenance capabilities of the system. Why is it different from a complex database?

"The data warehouse allows us to do complex queries with multiple joins of very large tables," he explains. "And it provides good performance even with a large number of concurrent users. It's also a low maintenance platform, which is a big advantage. We only have one DBA to support the system. You don't need that much DBA time to reorganize the data, and you can add capacity simply by adding more disks to the system without worrying about how the data is physically distributed."

Pele-Phone began exploring new marketing capabilities shortly after implementation by building a central repository of enterprise information. The first initiatives focused on customer relationship management, marketing segmentation, and call behavior analysis (for customer retention applications).

Based on the customer profile information stored in the data warehouse, Pele-Phone now identifies subscribers' specific needs and targets them with tailored offerings. Customer requirements are also tracked through the data warehouse and used in the development of new products and services. For example, the ability to mine customer data allows Pele-Phone to closely monitor mobile phone usage and the profitability of individual customers. This not only helps to focus marketing efforts, it also helps to develop profitable pricing strategies and evaluate the potential of new marketing initiatives.

"We were considering the idea of promoting car phones with the assumption that they give you better connections and fewer dropped calls," Rov says. "With the data warehouse we were able to go through all the call records and compare the number of dropped calls on car phones to the average number of dropped calls for the handset population. And that told us whether we could justify subsidizing those phones with a big promotion to boost car phone sales, and by how much."

Reducing churn is another benefit resulting from the ability to analyze customer data on a daily basis. By analyzing historical usage patterns, along with other changing market factors, Pele-Phone can pinpoint with greater accuracy those customers who may be considering switching to a competitor. These customers then can be quickly targeted with special promotions or tailored services designed to maintain their interest and loyalty.

One of the calling plans developed with the help of the data warehouse focuses on lower rates for calls made within a specific geographic or home region. According to Rov, the data warehouse was instrumental in both defining the borders of the different regions and in determining optimum pricing. The system's advanced analysis capabilities allowed the service to be priced so that it would be attractive to customers and, at the same time, ensure that it did not cannibalize the regular service.

"We're now able to be a much more customer-focused company," Rov says. "We're segmenting the market and providing each segment with the kind of service and attention that is in line with its needs, and also with its profitability to us. We're able to provide data on customer profitability, including price plan profitability or the profitability of a certain promotion. These are things we were not able to do in the past."

While many of the initial efforts concentrated on marketing, Pele-Phone is investigating several other promising applications for the data warehouse. Work has already begun in the area of fraud management, which is a growing problem for the cellular business. By detecting changes in calling patterns, and performing other sophisticated analyses, the data warehouse helps identify potential areas of fraudulent use. Pele-Phone also intends to use the data warehouse to support engineering applications and to monitor the usage and capacity load of its network infrastructure. This is a significant advantage for any communications supplier anywhere in the world. Significant efficiency gains are expected in this area, as well as further increases in overall profitability. This also drives lower costs and lower prices to customers.

Pele-Phone has gained a clear strategic advantage through the capabilities of its data warehouse. The company now has the ability to operate more competitively and effectively analyze market conditions and potential opportunities.

"I don't think anybody can speculate what the industry will look like three or five years from now." Rov says, "But it's obvious it will be very different from what it is now. Our data warehouse will help us adjust to the change by giving us a better understanding of what our customers want and how they're changing. And it will also help us to change ourselves to satisfy these customer needs in a timely manner and with an unmatched advantage in Israel's cellular market."

Pele-Phone conducted thorough research, conferring with industry analysts, data warehouse experts, and data warehouse users.

"What we needed was real-world experience of delivering successful solutions tailored to the needs of the telecommunications market," says Rov. "We decided to check on reference sites where we could actually see data warehouses in excess of a terabyte running and working. Another important element was professional consulting services, which had the expertise and methodology to help us build the application we wanted that met our quality and schedule requirements."

Pele-Phone, like most of the cases cited here, utilized a methodology to ensure success such as the one described in Chapter 6.

▶ The Health Insurance Industry

DCB Actuaries and Consultants (Czech Republic)—Bringing a New World to the Olde World

DCB Actuaries and Consultants is a Czech consulting and actuarial company offering services to the financial and insurance industries. DCB specializes in the design, development, and offering of techniques to aid strategic decision-making, based on the use of data warehouses. Created in 1991 with 67% Czech capital and 33% American capital, DCB Actuaries and Consultants recently joined the Woodrow Milliman network, which brings together independent actuarial and consulting companies.

The DCB data warehouse—which stores three years of patient care history concerning more than 1.6 million Czech policy-holders, representing several hundred million patient care files—has proven its value to Czech health care, where it has often been requested by the public health organization to carry out detailed performance benchmarks. In preparing to reform the Czech Health Care System in the spring of 1997, for example, the system was used to model the financial impact of the proposed changes on the national budget.

In the private sector, five Czech health insurance organizations use the system to make the most of the masses of information related to each patient care file—defining, clarifying and managing their marketing strategies more effectively. The system, which can be accessed in real time, incorporates a number of high value-added functions. In particular, DCB has found that health insurance companies have shown great interest in the system's ability to underwrite insurance automatically.

DCB pioneered an application for data warehousing which allows public health organizations to better manage their health care strategies, thus delivering more responsive services and more closely controlled medical expenses. In addition, private health insurance organizations may use the DCB system to design and develop new products which better meet the needs of their target markets.

There is an entrepreneurial spirit flowing through Eastern Europe that is producing innovative and exciting solutions to business and organizational problems that are applicable the world over.

Igor Stverka, sales and marketing manager for DCB, commented, "The Czech Republic has undergone a greater number of changes in the last few years than most countries experience in decades. By taking advantage of established technologies in Europe, such as NCR's Teradata, DCB was able to support these changes, particularly in the health care arena. We are now looking to leverage our experience and make our system and services more widely available across Europe."

DCB developed the system with the assistance of actuarial experts from the United States' Milliman Robertson and the United Kingdom's Bacon and Woodrow. The system combines the core NCR Teradata data warehouse with MicroStrategy's Relational OLAP Architecture data mining tools to provide an effective application for browsing and analyzing the high volumes of data and, subsequently, for making best use of the knowledge gained. These volumes require more than 150 gigabytes to be stored on a modular and scalable data warehouse database server platform.

More information on DCB and its services can be found on the World Wide Web at: http://www.dcb.net

Anthem Blue Cross/Blue Shield—The Business Challenges

From its beginnings as a one-product, one-state health insurer in 1944, Indianapolis-based Anthem has grown into a $7.9 billion integrated health care provider with significant market share in two separate regions of the United States.

Anthem Inc. was formed in 1996 by the merger of three former Blue Cross/Blue Shield licensees—The Associated Group (Indianapolis), Community Mutual (Cincinnati) and Southeast Group (Louisville).

Following the merger, which created one of the nation's largest multi-state managed health care companies with more than 6 million policyholders and 350,000 providers, Anthem faced a significant technological challenge: It needed to integrate and manage large amounts of information used to detect fraud among providers, evaluate the insurance risk for new policies, and improve sales and service through better access to information. This need for a strong technology infrastructure and architecture would also be critical to the success of some of the company's strategic objectives, including future growth.

With this growth came a significant challenge in the IT arena: how to integrate several disparate data warehouses into one repository to create a "single version of the truth" for all users. Managing BCBS plans in Ohio, Kentucky, Indiana, and Connecticut, while naturally striving to control costs and maintain premium service, Anthem faced an insatiable need for information about its more than 9 million policyholders and 350,000 providers, the care they provide, and their costs.

To respond to this need, Anthem developed an Integrated Scalable Data Warehouse, which brought together three pre-existing warehouses (from IBM and NCR) into one repository, and provided a one-source solution for multiple business uses in a fraction of the time previously needed to find and analyze information.

Anthem chose to build a single repository system that has significantly improved company-wide access to data. Anthem selected a massively parallel processing (MPP) server to accompany the Teradata RDBMS system as the new common repository for claims, revenue, services provided by hospitals and physicians, and other vital information for Anthem's mid-western business operations. The consolidated data warehouse contained over 2.0 terabytes of data, or enough information to fill 30,000+ four-drawer filing cabinets. And that was just the beginning of a new stage in Anthem's uses of data warehousing.

Anthem's Solutions

The data warehouse helped Anthem better serve existing customers and even win new business. In one instance, Anthem used the data warehouse to design a custom report for a major prospect that showed it how to cut costs in a particular area. The ad hoc reporting capability was something that the competition could not provide, and it proved the difference in Anthem's winning the account. Anthem also has future plans to link external audiences who need detailed data, such as doctors and hospitals, directly to the reporting capabilities of its data warehouse.

Before Anthem's mergers and the construction of an enterprise data warehouse, there was no shortage of data — but there was an acute shortage of accurate answers. Users seeking answers to specific queries were forced to employ data sources from several disparate mainframe environments. This practice proved to be not only daunting and time-consuming, but also a breeding ground for inaccuracies and conflicts of data. Invariably, one department's findings would be different than those of another department. Worst of all, it left little time for data analysis, the lifeblood of the insurance business.

Anthem developed a new data warehouse that provides users with constant access to company-wide information concerning fraud, legal, enrollment, actuarial, underwriting and claims applications. Users are able to perform ad hoc complex queries of the system with reporting consistencies throughout the company on enrollment, utilization, valuation, rate filing, loss ratios, provider profiling, and financial and marketing research. Best of all, with a single version of the truth available for all users at any time, Anthem is able to quickly answer the critical-business questions which are essential to maintain its competitive edge.

Health plan policyholders are concerned with two things: receiving the best treatment possible and saving as much money as possible. With medical costs in the U.S.A escalating ever upward, there is a perception that these two goals are mutually exclusive, and that it is now nearly impossible to obtain quality, or even adequate, health care in this country at a reasonable price.

Fortunately, some health providers are spending the money necessary to ensure that this is not necessarily the case. Anthem Blue Cross/Blue Shield, one of the nation's largest health care management companies, is a particularly encouraging example of this.

"We're moving from an insurance environment, where customers and health care providers submit claims and we pay them, to managing the health care our customers receive by working closely with health care providers," said former Anthem senior vice president William Milnes. "And we've found that you can't manage health care without managing information." (As of mid-1999, Bill is now President of the New Hampshire Blue Cross organization).

This improved access to information helps Anthem to improve the quality and cost of care for its 9 million policyholders by reducing fraud, negotiating lower rates with providers, accurately manage risks and, most importantly, saving lives through increased knowledge of network physicians.

Anthem: Analysis Saves Lives While Saving Money

Anthem has not only accomplished its goal of unifying the disparate parts of a newly merged company but has also realized significant monetary savings and productivity gains, improved the quality and cost of health care for policyholders and improved fraud detection.

Additionally, the time saved on searching for the information allows users more time to analyze the data they have collected. For example, when reviewing the information for one medical procedure, coronary artery bypass surgery, Anthem found that certain providers in their system have superior success rates. By analyzing these success rates, Anthem was able to help save lives by funneling patients to these providers. This new practice was able to reduce the procedure's mortality rate from more than 4% to less than 1% for Anthem policyholders, and reduce costs to employers.

Anthem's Results

In addition to saving lives, Anthem's data warehousing solution has also enabled its negotiating staff to save the company millions of dollars. Armed with detailed data by region, product, procedure, and price, they were able to more negotiate more favorable contracts with its more than 400 provider hospitals.

Anthem's legal department also uses the warehouse for fraud detection. In one instance, an analyst uncovered a $37,000 bogus claims check. A particular provider's pattern of payments didn't meet the norm. Additional research revealed that the health care company had actually paid several times for the same services. The provider was eventually billed for the overpayments.

Anthem's Cures for Today and Plans for the Future

From the beginning, what Anthem wanted from its data warehouse was a system that could grow with it and be poised to meet the challenges of the future.

Designed for enterprise-wide, mission-critical and decision-support applications, the data warehouse incorporates common hardware building blocks across high-end symmetric multiprocessing (SMP), clustered, and massively parallel processing (MPP) systems. Using its Teradata database management system, Anthem plans to easily expand the system to accommodate up to thousands of processors and many terabytes of data. With an anticipated growth rate of approximately 10 times its current size, Anthem is confident to easily scale as its information needs swiftly grow.

The bottom-line? Anthem's integrated data warehouse makes it possible for the company to enhance the quality of patient care and deliver more responsive customer service, while reducing the costs of health care.

More than 250 actuarial, underwriting, legal, sales and marketing personnel have direct access to the data warehouse. Instead of waiting days or weeks for information critical to specific needs, users can quickly perform special purpose, complex queries and analyses never before possible. This access to data helps Anthem reduce fraud, negotiate lower rates with providers, accurately manage risks, improve the quality and cost of care for millions of policyholders—all of which can help save lives.

Anthem believes that the data warehouse info-structure provided the only viable solution to its challenge to handle its enormous information needs, which now provides the organization with a distinct competitive advantage in a very competitive marketplace. Not only does the warehouse handle large amounts of data and give users the ability to analyze this data with complex ad hoc queries, it is also scalable as Anthem's information needs grow—a key consideration for the company's expansion plans.

Anthem is already realizing significant benefits from the new system, including user accessibility, speed and ease of operation, flexibility, and training support.

From a cost/benefit perspective, **Anthem executives estimate an annual return of between five to ten times their investment.** The company has already seen substantial savings in negotiating lower rates with hospitals and in fraud detection.

From a bottom-line perspective, Anthem believes that its data warehouse provides the company with a significant competitive advantage. Most importantly, Anthem is now in a better position than ever to deliver what its policyholders want most: quality care at the lowest possible price.

Now that's really achieving the best of all worlds.

Also read the Wall Street Journal Article about Anthem's data warehouse use, April 22, 1999, "Heart-Care Assessment Finds Reputation And Reality Don't Necessarily Match," by Thomas M. Burton.

The Anthem Executive Interview

In a 1997 videotaped interview by the NCR Corporation, Ms. Cecilia Claudio, Chief Information Officer at that time at Anthem, Inc., stated:

"The data warehouse, very simply stated, allows Anthem to deliver the highest quality care to our members at the lowest cost possible. That's what the data warehouse has really been instrumental in doing for Anthem.

"Anthem is one of the largest health-care corporations in the United States today. We have revenues in excess of six billion dollars and we service a very large population. Our mission is to improve the health of the population we serve.

"Anthem has recognized that without having a very strong technology infrastructure and without having a very strong architecture for how the systems are going to support Anthem going forward, that they probably would not be able to accomplish some of their strategic objectives.

"These are complex structures, complex entities that require an incredible amount of knowledge to be successful. So rely heavily and put a lot of pressure and put your expectations up front on your vendor and then hold their feet to the fire...

"The data warehouse became the critical component of achieving that goal of behaving as one company and operationalizing the merger and bringing together all of the different pieces of information into one central repository. It is a warehouse of data consolidating from hundreds of sources information that has existed throughout the company but that now resides in one single repository. And that in a very simplistic way becomes the sole source for all of the decisions that the company makes day in and day out. So by having one source for claims, one source for membership, one source for providing information, one source for billing, one source for pharmacy data. We can now go straight into that source of information and in a very timely way make decisions. We had to go to six different sources, (and sometimes up to) ten different sources, as they existed prior to the data warehouse... we would not only take a lot longer, but potentially the outcome would not be of the quality that the data warehouse now provides us.

"The data warehouse and the ability to capture information at that level is what is going to continue to appeal to our members and to our constituents and the ability to then translate and tailor all of our products and services to the individual level..."

▶ The Entertainment Industry

Harrah's Entertainment, Inc.

The Company

With 18 casinos in 8 U.S. states, Harrah's Entertainment, Inc., is the most recognized and respected brand name in the casino entertainment industry. Harrah's was founded in 1937, when Bill Harrah opened a bingo parlor in Reno, Nevada. Harrah's grew quickly, building and acquiring properties throughout Nevada and beyond. In 1973, Harrah's became the first casino company to be listed on the New York Stock Exchange.

Today, Harrah's has been recognized by Forbes and Business Week as a market leader, due in large part to its mission to "build lasting relationships" with its customers. Harrah's achieves this mission through operational excellence and technological leadership, which enables Harrah's to manage each customer relationship individually.

The Challenge

In 1997, Harrah's introduced its "Total Gold" system for tracking, retaining, and rewarding its 15 million guests regardless of which casinos they visit over time. For example, a frequent guest at Harrah's Atlantic City, New Jersey, casino will be immediately recognized upon presenting a Total Gold card in the company's Las Vegas casino—and is duly rewarded for his or her repeat business.

"Traditionally, casinos have treated customers as though they belonged to the single property they visited most often. However, we've found that customers who visit more than one of our properties represent a fast-growing segment of our revenue. We want to encourage and reward these customers," said John Boushy, Harrah's Senior Vice President of Information Technology and Marketing Services.

The patented Total Gold program entitles Harrah's repeat customers to free entertainment, vouchers for food and accommodation, and points redeemable for merchandise. These rewards encourage customers to remain loyal to the Harrah's brand across the country, and over time.

Recognized by business publications as a leader in the casino industry, Harrah's has experienced tremendous growth throughout Nevada and beyond during its 60 years of operation.

Harrah's is expanding the Total Gold program which produces more than 20 million customer offers annually. Total Gold and the data warehouse also track each offer to determine when and how offers are redeemed. With the expanded data warehouse, Harrah's can analyze hundreds of customer attributes to determine the likelihood of a visit, predicted spending, opportunities for cross-selling, and determining the "life-time value" of each customer within a short period of time. This allows Harrah's to target promotions and mailings to individual customer preferences. For example, Harrah's might award hotel vouchers to out-of-state guests, while free show tickets would be more appropriate for customers who make day trips to the casino.

Goals

To enhance the casino's reputation for building lasting customer relationships, Harrah's wanted to establish a program to reward individual customers for every visit, regardless of where those visits took place. To achieve this, Harrah's needed to have technology in place that could maintain and analyze large amounts of customer data.

"Many of our customers have an opportunity to visit our properties just once or twice a year. To find important trends and measure repeat business, we must maintain and analyze a large amount of detailed data over a long period of time." Boushy has said.

Total Gold was so successful that Harrah's was ready to expand the program and replace its existing transactional systems database within one year of its installation, to create a new and more powerful data warehouse environment that could store and analyze much higher volumes of detailed data. The data warehouse is now known as the corporate marketing workbench and is available for all departments to search and query the customer database to provide better marketing, service, support, and special requests.

At a Gartner Group conference on CRM in Chicago in September 1999, Tracy Austin highlighted the key areas of benefits and the ROI achieved in the first several years of utilizing the "patron database" and the "marketing workbench" (Data Warehouse). "We have achieved over $74 million in returns during our first few years of utilizing these exciting new tools and CRM processes within our entire organization. Now that a customer is one customer to all of our locations, we are driving higher revenues, profits, and a new ability to utilize the detailed customer data in our databases."

John Boushy, CIO of Harrah's, in a speech at the DCI CRM Conference in Chicago in February 2000, stated: "We are achieving over 50% annual return-on-investment in our data warehousing and patron database activities. This is one of the best investments that we have ever made as a corporation and will prove to forge key new business strategies and opportunities in the future." The title of John Boushy's speech was: "Harrah's Bets on Data Warehousing to Increase Customer Loyalty." The data warehouse is the center focal point of Harrah's information systems architecture and strategies for communicating with its customers. So everybody wins, in the marketing game, every time he or she uses the data warehouse for marketing and customer communications.

Boushy has also stated publicly that his "customer relationship management solution and powerful data warehouse database allow us to keep track of millions of customers' activities and provide Harrah's with the means to analyze, predict, and maximize the value of each customer relationship..."

Knowing Customers Better Differentiates Us from Our Competitors.

▶ Management Considerations

- The goal of successful organizations, using data warehousing and CRM, is to achieve high profitability and competitiveness. This is a constant theme in the cases of successful implementations.
- The data warehouse has enabled all transactional level data to be integrated to provide one "true" picture of the customer.
- If applied correctly, data warehousing can allow flexible, iterative querying of this data on a timely basis. In this way, actionable information can be delivered to those who can use it, when they need it. This itself creates major advantages in a marketplace or competitive environment, especially when servicing customers and/or managing resources that are involved in relationships.
- The ability to act quickly and be maneuverable is critical. To be maneuverable is not easy—yet an organization must find gaps in the market and exploit any opportunity swiftly and effectively.
- The ability to keep competitors guessing is very powerful.
- A solid infrastructure of knowledge and easily accessible, actionable information is required to underpin such flexibility. There is no advantage in being quick if you are working with poor information. Conversely, there is no advantage to being armed with supreme information if it cannot be acted upon quickly and efficiently.

> **Organizations which employ and utilize the power of knowledge discovery and data mining act quickly and efficiently from a position of knowledge.**

- The value is not in looking for the data, it is in finding the information the enterprise doesn't have, interpreting that information and its impact on your business, and then leveraging it to drive a change. This accelerates the capabilities and experiences of the management team and employees who become much more proactive and confident in working with the individual customer or group of customers.
- As you build breakthrough capability, you will drive people and processes to do things differently. For instance, one enterprise in this chapter reaped substantial returns by looking at the transaction patterns across all products for credit card defaulters, and noticing that defaulters displayed specific behavioral traits. They were then able to identify high-risk groups from their

Propensity to Default model, and flag when their behavior began to head down that path. They could then move in quickly to restructure their debts or cancel the cards.

- The key is to recognize that creating cross-unit, customer-centric, resource-identification, and knowledge of the marketplace generates a new level of competence. These actions are a journey; it cannot be bought off the shelf.
- You can start at various points along the road depending on specific needs and objectives. However, the route to the destination may fluctuate due to changing market needs and, therefore, the ability to maneuver and find opportunities is critical to success.

The opportunity is to capitalize on the customer information and turn it into a sustainable competitive advantage.

- Using data warehousing and CRM, customer strategies should add value to the customer as well as to the bottom-line.
- As we have seen, organizations in numerous industries have strived to integrate customer-centric data warehousing for generating new business opportunities, managing present customer retention, increasing their abilities to acquire new customers, and to increase profitability in multiple methods and approaches.
- The key elements of success for these companies appear to be specific management focus on:
  - Defining and solving specific business problems
  - Utilization of a proven process and methodology
  - Outside assistance from highly qualified and experienced consultants for required skills AND thought leadership
- The use of increasingly manageable warehousing technology, large-detailed-historical-data in the database, a customer-centric approach, and creative applications has allowed these companies to successfully accelerate their profitability, flexibility, and competitiveness in their marketplaces.

World leaders are made, not born.

Who is next on the list of successes in using a customer-centric information infrastructure?

Will your organization be cited as a leading case in our next book?

If so, let us know your story by contacting us at: *crmvision@aol.com*

**For more case studies, go to:
www.ncr.com/subscribe**

Studies of Communications Industry Implementations

In this chapter, you will read about a significant study performed in the communications industry to document the various phases and successful implementation strategies achieved.

This study was accomplished by Yancy Oshita, Director of Communications Industry Marketing at NCR Corporation in 1997-99 (Oshita, 1999). Yancy is a special kind of executive who is insightful and thorough in his approaches to customer requirements, customer management issues, and customer services.

▶ The Oshita Research Project—Focus on Knowledge

1. **Definition of** (qualitatively and quantitatively by commercial users) **a "successful," and, conversely, "failed" CRM initiative** or project in which the primary purpose was/is for sales/marketing decision support in the communications industry. To the extent possible, data also will be searched and collected in the retail and financial industries.

2. Provides deeper **understanding of the key issues** (or causal factors) concerning the successful (or failed) application of CRM initiatives or projects. Because the subject applicant is employed in the CRM field, he (as well as others in the field) has gained some anecdotal evidence and intuition concerning these issues. However, the applicant believes very few entities have collected data and provided unbiased analysis of such issues. Hence, such data will either support anecdotal evidence or provide new insights.

▶ Four-Phase Technique for Research in CRM

The project approach is four-phased and involves the following techniques:

Phase 1 (Definition): This phase involved detailed definition of the primary research issue and the definition (both quantitative and qualitative) of a "successful" and "failed" CRM initiative or project. Further, the scope of the issue was defined to research primarily communications companies. Secondary targets were related industries, including financial and insurance. Thus, the exit criteria are a clearly defined research issue and objectives.

Phase 2 (Verification): This phase involved collecting, affinity analysis, and documentation of the assumptions concerning the issues. Secondary research was conducted to verify the key factors concerning the success and failure of CRM initiative/projects for sales/marketing applications. Both secondary research and the professional expertise produce a comprehensive backdrop for the primary data obtained in Phase 3. The exit criteria were a verified list of assumptions that explain the research issue and objectives.

Phase 3 (Design and Research): This phase primarily deployed a retrospective research approach to data collection. A questionnaire was designed to help conduct and collect subject data. There were interviews in-person or by phone/e-mail with 37 end-user professionals from 24 companies. Since CRM is still a discrete application of IT, all of the end-users were selected in advance in order to better reflect the discrete issues. Hence, all end-users were either directly involved in a completed CRM project and/or current CRM project. Fifty-Nine percent of the end-users interviewed were IT professionals and 27% were business professionals, primarily in the marketing/sales activity. Of particular interest is that 14%

of the end-users interviewed were "database marketing" (DBM), a somewhat adjunct function between IT and marketing. Conversations covered CRM key success factors in planning, implementing, and deploying or using CRM technologies.

In addition, longitudinal research was conducted during actual customer engagements. The interviewer participated in the CRM project to plan, implement, and use data mining to solve a specific business problem. Bell South Small Business Markets engaged in a project to use analytic modeling to better predict customers' propensity to buy *BusinessChoice*, a small business offering. Another consultant participated in several customer engagements to explore the business and technical issues surrounding the lack of CRM value. The exit criteria for Phase 3 are collected data and qualitative conclusions.

Phase 4 (Documentation): This phase involved the documentation of the research project's actual approaches and, in particular, research findings concerning the issue. The exit criteria report provides a comprehensive picture of use of CRM relationship technologies in the communications industries. Most importantly, the study provides useful insight for communications companies and other related firms (e.g., insurance, financial) looking to enable building of core CRM capabilities through planning, implementation, and deployment or CRM technologies.

▶ The Communications Industry—A Review

The communications industry can be segmented into specialty (e.g., wireless, Internet) and full service providers, offering a range of products and services to all major customer segments. Migrating from its regulated past, the industry key success factors have been changing from a singular, internal focus on network management to more external customer-focused capabilities.

Today, the desires and needs that their customers have and will pay for are tailored products/services, customized ordering/billing, personalized service, and individualized marketing/sales. Therefore, an explosion of growth of communications firms in all segments are:

1. **Spending an increasingly larger proportion of their IT investments on "CRM" technologies** including data warehousing, applications, customer care, and billing (network investments/

management, while critical to success, are driven increasingly by customer needs).

2. Integrating planning in such investments into business and corporate-level strategy, **heightening the importance of such technologies in terms of solving business problems** and building sustainable competitive advantage.

Although the communications industry is one of the fastest growing in IT investments, the high degree of market instability has created a confusing environment for aligning IT priorities to business strategy. Regardless of these dynamics, communications companies are investing heavily in CRM technologies.

As a good example, Figure 15-1 illustrates a breakdown of the U.S. communications industry, wireline segment by firm. The wireline segment is composed of former Regional Bell Operating Companies (RBOCs), long distance Interexchange Carriers (IXCs), and Competitive Local Exchange Carriers (CLECs). It includes an estimate of total IT investments, total marketing expenses, and a proportion of total IT investments driven by marketing demands. As indicated earlier, while aggregate IT spending is growing at an estimated moderate single-digit percentage, investments in CRM technologies (and services) are growing at over 20%, or an estimated four times the industry. Given rash mergers and acquisitions, many of theses carriers are becoming "integrated" carriers, offering all major products including wireless, Internet, and cable.

Additional segments not reflected below include wireless, Internet, and cable. These segments show similar spending levels in CRM technologies.

▶ RESEARCH FINDINGS

Overall results showed four primary success factors:

- **Strategic impact (25%)**
- **Technology integration (23%)**
- **Strategic partnership (20%)**
- **Technology assimilation (18%)**

Secondary factors were data warehouse technology (8%), technology architecture (4%), user skills (1%), and user desktop (1%).

Company	Tier/Tech	Subscribers	Annual Rev	Revenue Per Subscriber	IT(2% REV) Affordability	Mktng Spend (4% REV)	Mktng Imprvmt (@5%)
							0
AT&T	WL1	100,177,000	51,319,000,000	512	1,026,380,000	2,052,760,000	102,638,000
Bell Atlantic	WL1	39,376,000	30,193,900,000	767	603,878,000	1,207,756,000	60,387,800
Southwestern Bell Telephone Co	WL1	35,070,000	22,370,400,000	638	447,408,000	894,816,000	44,740,800
MCI Communications Corporation	WL1	22,938,000	19,700,000,000	859	394,000,000	788,000,000	39,400,000
BellSouth International	WL1	21,816,000	14,412,560,000	661	288,251,200	576,502,400	28,825,120
GTE Corp.	WL1	20,024,000	23,260,000,000	1,162	465,200,000	930,400,000	46,520,000
Ameritech Communications Inc. (ACI)	WL1	19,704,000	15,998,000,000	812	319,960,000	639,920,000	31,996,000
US West	WL1	15,424,000	9,831,000,000	637	196,620,000	393,240,000	19,662,000
Sprint Corp.	WL1	11,788,000	5,117,300,000	434	102,346,000	204,692,000	10,234,600
SBC Communications Inc.	WL1	5,119,000	17,981,500,000	3,513	359,630,000	719,260,000	35,963,000
WorldCom Inc. (MCI)	WL1	4,297,000	7,351,000,000	1,711	147,020,000	294,040,000	14,702,000
Excel TeleCommunications Inc	WL1	3,792,171	1,090,649,000	288	21,812,980	43,625,960	2,181,298
Southern New England Telecommunications Corporation (SNET)	WL1	2,286,000	1,543,500,000	675	30,870,000	61,740,000	3,087,000
LCI International	WL1	2,244,192	1,103,000,000	491	22,060,000	44,120,000	2,206,000
Alltel Corporation	WL1	1,681,000	1,169,076,000	695	23,381,520	46,763,040	2,338,152
Frontier Corporation (formerly Rochester Telephone Corporation)	WL1	1,500,000	2,352,866,000	1,569	47,057,320	94,114,640	4,705,732
United Telephone of Florida	WL1	1,100,000	1,201,841,000	1,093	24,036,820	48,073,640	2,403,682
Cincinnati Bell Telephone Company	WL2	994,000	650,833,000	655	13,016,660	26,033,320	1,301,666
Citizens Utilities Company	WL2	834,180	752,209,000	902	15,044,180	30,088,360	1,504,418
ICG Communications	WL2	700,000	190,651,000	272	3,813,020	7,626,040	381,302
Aliant Communications (Lincoln Telco)	WL2	560,000	286,328,000	511	5,726,560	11,453,120	572,656
PTI Communications	WL2	559,461	409,015,000	731	8,180,300	16,360,600	818,030
Telephone and Data Systems Inc (TDS)	WL2	550,000	402,629,000	732	8,052,580	16,105,160	805,258
Century Telephone Enterprises Inc	WL2	503,562	273,609,000	543	5,472,180	10,944,360	547,218
Teleport Communications Group (TCG)	WL2	500,000	428,552,000	857	8,571,040	17,142,080	857,104
Contel of California	WL2	360,000			0	0	0
Residential Communications Network (RCN)	WL2	260,000	147,471,000	567	2,949,420	5,898,840	294,942
Long Distance International Inc. (LDI)	WL2	250,000			0	0	0
WilTel	WL2				0	0	0
IXC Communications	WL2		420,700,000		8,414,000	16,828,000	841,400
MFS Communications Inc.	WL2		57,200,000		1,144,000	2,288,000	114,400
Pacific Northwest Bell Telephone Co	WL2				0	0	0
Qwest Communications Inc.	WL2				0	0	0
Shared Technologies Fairchild Inc. (STFI)	WL2				0	0	0
World Telecom Group Inc.	WL2				0	0	0
American Communications Services, Inc.	WL3	6,990,452	6,990,452		139,809	279,618	13,981
USN	WL3	226,024	128,000,000	566	2,560,000	5,120,000	256,000
Commonwealth Telephone Company	WL3	212,000			0	0	0
Tel-Save	WL3	200,000	304,800,000	1,524	6,096,000	12,192,000	609,600
CFW Communications	WL3	190,000	59,010,000	311	1,180,200	2,360,400	118,020
Anchorage Telephone Utility (ATU Telecoms)	WL3	154,792	104,743,000	677	2,094,860	4,189,720	209,486
McLeod USA Inc.	WL3	120,000	282,100,000	2,351	5,642,000	11,284,000	564,200
North State Telephone Company	WL3	109,735	57,947,000	528	1,158,940	2,317,880	115,894
Roseville Telephone Company	WL3	108,336	101,307,000	935	2,026,140	4,052,280	202,614
CT Communications, Inc.	WL3	105,000			0	0	0
Rock Hill Telephone Company	WL3	100,552	70,664,000	703	1,413,280	2,826,560	141,328
Concord Telephone Company	WL3	96,547	55,499,000	575	1,109,980	2,219,960	110,998
Lufkin-Conroe Telephone Exchange Company Inc.	WL3	89,745	76,554,000	853	1,531,080	3,062,160	153,108
Consolidated Communications Inc	WL3	88,229	64,205,000	728	1,284,100	2,568,200	128,410
EnergyOne (PECO Energy Company)	WL3	75,000			0	0	0
Granite State Telephone	WL3	70,000			0	0	0
Conestoga Telephone & Telegraph Company	WL3	67,219	39,219,000	583	784,380	1,568,760	78,438
Horry Telephone Cooperative Inc	WL3	66,147	33,225,000	502	664,500	1,329,000	66,450
North Pittsburgh Telephone Company	WL3	62,086	52,017,000	838	1,040,340	2,080,680	104,034
Standard Telephone Co.	WL3	60,596	52,740,000	870	1,054,800	2,109,600	105,480
East Ascension Telephone Company Inc (EATEL)	WL3	60,000	27,643,000	461	552,860	1,105,720	55,286
Denver and Ephrata Telephone	WL3	52,000	35,229,000	677	704,580	1,409,160	70,458
Pioneer Telephone Cooperative	WL3	50,205	52,016,000	1,036	1,040,320	2,080,640	104,032
S A Telecommunications Inc.	WL3	47,000			0	0	0
Hargray Telephone Cooperative	WL3	43,896	36,564,000	833	731,280	1,462,560	73,128
Matanuska Telephone Association Inc.	WL3	41,194	46,614,000	1,132	932,280	1,864,560	93,228
Gulf Telephone Company	WL3	35,643	33,284,000	934	665,680	1,331,360	66,568
Ben Lomand Rural Telephone Cooperative Inc	WL3	35,000	19,135,000	547	382,700	765,400	38,270
Lynch Corporation	WL3	34,830	42,694,000	1,226	853,880	1,707,760	85,388
Mankato Citizens Telephone Company	WL3	34,789	24,924,000	716	498,480	996,960	49,848
Fairbanks Municipal Utilities	WL3	33,885	25,946,000	766	518,920	1,037,840	51,892
Chillicothe Telecommunications (Horizon PCS)	WL3	33,077	32,441,000	981	648,820	1,297,640	64,882
Coastal Utilities, Inc	WL3	32,904	26,464,000	804	529,280	1,058,560	52,928
Twin Lakes Telephone Cooperative Corporation	WL3	31,440			0	0	0
Mid-Plains Telephone Inc.	WL3	31,034	18,697,000	602	373,940	747,880	37,394
Souris River Telecommunications	WL3	30,244	45,183,000	1,494	903,660	1,807,320	90,366

Figure 15-1 U.S. Communications Industry: Wireline Firms, 1998.

In aggregate, technology factors totaled 12%, consisting of data warehouse technology and technology architecture. Because technology assimilation involves integration to business processes and proper organization structures, user desktop and user skills are believed to be issues within this category. In this case, user information access (via desktop) was a key business requirement to enable a process.

An affinity analysis of the results showed:

- Key success factors are: **strategic impact (25%)**; **technology integration (23%)**; **strategic partnership (20%)**; **technology assimilation (20%)**; **and technology (12%)**. This is shown in Figure 15-2.
- **Non-technology problems** are over seven times more likely to be the chief cause of CRM failures. Of the technology issues, a data warehouse is the chief factor, nearly double the technology architecture.
- **Overall integration,** at the data and business process levels combined, is 40%, validating the new strategy-enabling potential of CRM, unstructured nature, and overall greater complexity relative to operational systems.

An analysis of the aggregate results showed responses varied dramatically by function:

Table 15-1 illustrates the following findings:

- Marketing personnel are much less likely to believe the most important key success factor is a well-defined business problem linked to management/operating processes (strategic impact).

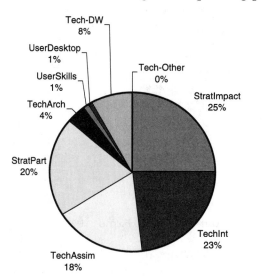

Figure 15-2. Overall distribution of success factors.

Function	Strategic Impact	Technology Integration	Strategic Partnership	Technology Assimilation	Technology
Mktg	16	48	26	10	0
DBM	32	27	7	27	7
IT	27	17	19	21	16
Total	25	23	20	20	12

Table 15-1. Varying responses by organizational position (in %).

- IT personnel are much less likely to believe technology integration is a key factor than their marketing or DBM counterparts.
- Only 7% of DBM personnel (vs. 26% of marketing and 19% of IT) believe a **key success factor is a strategic partnership.**
- Marketing personnel are much less likely to believe a key success factor is technology assimilation, or integrating technologies to business processes, the right structure, skills, and metrics. Database managers are much more likely to believe technology assimilation is critical.

Following are the results within each key success factor and some analysis concerning the overall results and, in particular, results by function.

Strategic Impact

Strategic impact (25%) was considered the most critical factor to successful planning, implementation, and use of CRM technologies. This validates earlier assumptions and verification concerning the inherent difference between operational systems (e.g., billing) and CRM. CRM technologies are aimed at enabling (not necessarily adhering to) new processes. Many of the business problems are unstructured. Hence, many of the CRM systems are reflected in new strategies, often cutting across the enterprise.

The results varied dramatically by two of the three functions. IT respondents as a group showed the same results as the overall. However, only 16% of business or marketing end-users believe strategic impact was critical, while double that, or 32%, of Database Managers (DBM) felt a clearly defined business problem and case (linked to operating/management processes) was critical to CRM success. The most glaring example of this disparity was with a major Incumbent Local Exchange Carrier (ILEC) where interviews were conducted with the customer retention manager, IT manager, and "market information systems" manager (DBM). The customer retention manager responded to the key issue as technology integration, while the DBM manager indicated that past initiatives failed due to lack of strong business cases. Interestingly, in a group meeting, the IT manager indicated that technically what was described was "easy," but that they were not aware of any such requirements from marketing (represented by the DBM function).

Suggestions to this disparity are inherent in the nature and scope of the DBM function. The need and presence of the DBM function reflect more complex issues associated with executing new strategies that cross organizational boundaries, as well as the general lack of ubiquity concerning "technology-enabled marketing." Many of the marketing respondents do not yet have the necessary skills to effectively use these technologies in the same way they use their desktop application. Hence, the need for a database management function.

Most database managers interviewed were considered hybrid functions by their peers in marketing and IT. Database managers act much like a conduit, translating business requirements into IT requirements. Some perform programming (e.g., write SQL) or limited application development work. All reported that they see "both sides" of the issue. In terms of skill profile, Database managers generally reflect the "best of both worlds." They have the knowledge and skills of the marketing processes, as well as the strong technical skills to apply solutions to business problems.

Technology Integration

Technology integration again varied dramatically by function. Business or marketing end-user respondents felt that nearly one-half, or 48%, of the key to success (or reason for failure) was due to the lack of technology integration. The definition of technology integration given by marketing end-user respondents ranged from "can't use the information to improve my selling" to "we spend time marketing to important customers, yet when they call our service centers, our service people don't know who they are or that we have just spoken to them two days ago." DBM respondents were slightly above the overall results.

A marketing end-user executive from a major Australian telco responsible for 4,000 users in 50 sites believes data integration (to call centers) of "marketing intelligence" is critical to improve average selling time (currently 500 seconds; best-in-class is 280 seconds), a strategic business metric. Marketing (on a stand-alone marketing database) that shows which customers cause the highest workloads does profiling. This information is considered valuable by sales agents, but is not "readily-available" in useable form at the "point-of-contact."

Conversely, only 15% of IT respondents believed technology integration was a key success factor. Many respondents felt their project requirements were limited to "departmental use," causing enormous problems at the enterprise level across functions. An example is respondents from a major carrier in Asia—both were involved in a major DW project to enable marketing to become more "data-driven." Yet actual requirements led to a multi-million 10 terabyte DW for specialized business reporting to only a "handful of executives," some of whom are no longer with the company.

A DBM respondent from a major ILEC indicated that technology integration is the biggest bottleneck to achieving the next tier of business benefits to CRM. Getting intelligence data from the warehouse to key operational systems for marketing action is a key pain point. It takes only 2 days to develop a campaign (using the CRM technologies), but the difficulty is in "operationalizing" campaigns. Every time a rate table changes, custom programming work is required, taking weeks (even months) to integrate these changes in provisioning and billing (e.g., rates, offers). Legacy systems still reign supreme because they still work, but are becoming increasingly difficult to use in concert with modern marketing and sales tools like warehouses and analytics.

DBM respondents from a major U.S. "IXC" (International Exchange Carrier) indicated their processes require data inputs from 28 sources and 70 feeds with outputs to 14 sources and 54 feeds to produce "clean lists." The lack of data integration caused enormous quality and time problems to marketing end-users, many of whom went outside to purchase lists to execute their initiatives.

DBM respondents from a major IXC cited integration with service order systems, particularly customer-specific information such as name, address, and so on, and continuously updating (a change in business process of an operational system) accuracy of information upon every customer contact. Failure to integrate and update has led to poor quality data (in the data warehouse) and, subsequently, poor quality marketing campaigns and results.

During a data mining project in which the applicant participated, data was not available in one uniform source. Multiple operation systems, some of which included data that resided on desktop spreadsheets, were extracted. The lack of easy access to clean data for data mining lead to over 75% of time spent pre-processing data, understanding definitions, shipping tapes back and forth, and so on.

An IT representative from a major European telco felt strategic impact, technology integration (data), and technology assimilation (processes/structures/skills/metrics) were critical. In their CRM project they started with a strategic vision, but kept the initial project small and well-defined in scope and business needs. Quality technology integration was a major factor to success because they extracted and transformed data from multiple operational sources including network, billing, and P.O.S. Once the aggregated data is analyzed for the business purpose, it is fed to well-established customer care systems for action. Results are fed back into the CRM infrastructure.

Finally, some IT respondents suggested the difficulty in integrating CRM technologies is inherent in the nature of CRM systems. CRM systems cut across traditional, well-embedded operational systems, both in terms of data collection and application, thereby increasing the challenge of technology integration.

Strategic Partnership

Strategic partnership showed a major difference among DBM participants. DBM respondents were much less likely (7%) to believe a "partnership of constituencies" was critical to success. In fact, DBM respondents rated technology factors as equal to strategic partnership. Many did not feel this was necessary because they were knowledgeable of what was going on from both sides. One explanation to this disparity is that respondents who specialize in either IT or marketing may lack the capabilities for understanding the IT issues in general, the possible strategy impacts, and full breadth of planning, implementing, and deploying CRM technologies or "strategic systems." Hence, they are more likely to suggest a partnership of constituencies, whereas the DBM participants may believe they have this perspective and capabilities. Clearly, as the trend towards client-server use of CRM increases, such capabilities are critical to understanding the IT/IT management issues to exploit the full potential.

Technology Assimilation

Twenty percent of respondents believed technology assimilation (technology alignment to structure/processes/skills/metrics) was a key success factor to planning, implementing, and deploying CRM technologies. The results validate earlier assumptions prior to interviews. CRM technologies enable radically different ways of doing business from traditional mass marketing approaches. Often projects involve more than incremental adjustments. Hence, while proof-of-concepts may show excellent ROI, full-scale implementation and deployment represent a major strategic challenge in terms of structure, processes, skills, and metrics.

A IT respondent who developed analytic models as an initiative from "senior management" indicated the project failed largely due to the fact that the data mining functionality was not imbedded in marketing processes. There also existed a general knowledge gap among senior management and marketing end-users concerning the full potential of such technologies.

A DBM respondent from a major IXC indicated that CRM management and operational processes are still forming. Development and use of a common set of metrics for program performance are critical to gaining acceptance of such technologies. Further, metrics must be limited to a disciplined, consistent review of existing data. Be sure to instill commitment to understand program performance and capture learning about what can be done better next time. Staff with people who know and understand database marketing. Train people or hire the right kind of people who have the skills and know-how to take advantage of these technologies. Spread competency throughout with organization and cross-training, and integrate marketing and CIO.

A DBM respondent from a major IXC indicated that their "multi-terabyte enterprise warehouse is being questioned in terms of economic value." The single biggest problem is lack of deep focus in understanding business problems and integrating/assimilating technology to address the problems. "Far too much time was spent by marketing on evaluating desktop tool features/functions."

Again, the results varied by function, with the largest variance reported by marketing. Only 10% of marketing end-users believed technology assimilation was critical. This compares to 27% of database managers. One explanation is that marketing end-users lack the breadth of IT knowledge to understand that a chief causal factor is an unprepared marketing (and other activity linkages) structure in order to take advantage of the new technologies. Conversely, DBM respondents, unlike their marketing or IT peers, possess broader capabilities and first-hand experience relative to the IT management issues surrounding planning, implementation, and deployment of CRM technologies.

Technology

Although only 12% of respondents said technology was a key success factor, the analysis of the results is interesting and provides potentially useful insights. Marketing end-user respondents did not cite technology as the problem. Both DBM (7%) and IT (16%) respondents felt technology was key. The chief DBM issue was technology architecture: Many of the operational systems imbedded in an ILEC infrastructure are legacy, mainframe-based. To fully exploit CRM technologies and modern client-server applications, they must be integrated into legacy systems. Further adding to the complexity is the unstructured nature of CRM. Many of these systems are domain-specific and the lack of establishment of clear policies concerning data architecture (e.g., independent data mart vs. corporate architecture) has created numerous problems. The lack of evaluating and incorporating such CRM requirements into the main-stream architecture strategy is a major sticking point. Further complicating the issues is the dynamic nature of CRM strategies, requiring architecture flexibility and extensibility.

In terms of DBM respondents, 25% felt technology architecture was the key issue. Many of the respondents reported similar reasons as the DBM respondents. Unique to IT respondents, however, is that fully 75% felt the key technology issue was truly technology. Interestingly, most of these respondents cited a data warehouse foundation, or DSS infra-structure, as critical to successful planning, implementation, and deployment of CRM technologies. Some IT respondents said a "strong technology platform" and "hardware and software to support an environment of complex questions (queries) from many users, a very different environment compared to operational systems."

Another IT respondent believes the biggest problem to executing the company's initiatives was an "underscoped" database. This issue raises some merit in the notion that successful CRM strategies in communications and other related industries require DW technology that scales to support growth. A major bank respondent indicated one marketing initiative alone, marketing a Web site, required feeds from over 40 systems related to 38 million accounts.

In sum, the above technology issues may in fact not be technology issues per se. Lack of appropriate technology architecture to effectively implement CRM technologies or an underpowered database engine may be symptoms to other non-technologies. First, by nature, planning, implementing, and deploying CRM technologies are significantly more complex than operational systems. New information models that cut across the enterprise are often created. Second, because of this complexity, additional emphasis (compared to operational systems) must be given to integrated planning, implementation, and deployment. This requires a strong strategic partnership among IT and business, a corporate champion of change. Hence, the above technology issues may in fact be IT management issues, adding to the importance of the key success factors.

Customer Project

As part of the longitudinal research, the applicant participated directly in a customer project. The project used data mining technologies to predict the propensity of customers to purchase a packaged offering called "*BusinessChoice*." The applicant engaged in the planning, implementation, and deployment of the project. The applicant also collected actual business results obtained to measure the "success" of the project. The campaign results were produced by a campaign management outsourcing service. What follows is a synopsis of project results (due to it's sensitive nature, much of the information is not included in this summary):

Figure 15-3 illustrates the actual list of selections by channel and final count. The list was generated from the scored file of 35,293 Alabama (AL) customers, extracting slightly below the top three deciles for a final count of 8,638.

Marketing Contacts						
Segment	Contacts	Customer Count	Mail Contacts	Telemarketing Contacts	Contacts	Total Contacts
NCR Model						
Strategy#1	DM only	2,879	1	0	1	2,879
Strategy#2	Telemarketing Only	2,879	0	1	1	2,879
Strategy#3	DM and Telemarketing	2,880	1	1	2	5,760
Total		8,638				11,518
Random Selection						
Strategy#1	DM only	3,500	1	0	1	3,500
Strategy#2	Telemarketing Only	3,500	0	1	1	3,500
Strategy#3	DM and Telemarketing	3,500	1	1	2	7,000
Total		10,500				14,000

Figure 15-3. Marketing contacts—an analysis.

It is important to note that, due to the lack of Dun & Bradstreet (D&B) matches, only 38% of the total (92,000) Alabama customers were scored, which may negatively impact results. The generation of the random list is less clear. It is believed the list may have been derived from the total 92,000 Alabama customer base. It is believed the final random list is mutually exclusive, but cannot be confirmed. Further, the random list selection criteria is unknown. In previous campaigns, the customer selected lists based on an intuitive SIC (Standard Industrial Classification) logic. This logic is imbedded in the client's business process. In sum, the list selection is suspect.

The illustration in Figure 15-4 displays the campaign results by products. The purpose of the project was to identify the customers who are most likely to purchase *BusinessChoice*, a value-priced package based on a standard touch-tone business service called "Business Plus", in addition to a flexible menu of calling features such as "RingMaster" and "Three-Way Calling." However, the subject campaign targeted products and features outside *BusinessChoice* such as Voice Mail and Caller ID. According to the customer, the "Summit" or net present value of *BusinessChoice* is $2180 compared to $135 and $180, respectively, for Voice Mail and Caller ID. Further, the campaign did not include the basic Business Plus. Hence, the campaign results are further distorted, as evidenced in Figure 15-5 illustrating the disparity between take rate and return on advertising between NCR and Random approaches.

Sales-Random Selection			

Business Choice - Sales

Total Sales	Units Sold	Summit Value	Total Summit Value
11	12	$2,180	$26,160
19	19	$2,180	$41,420
12	12	$2,180	$26,160
42	43	$2,180	$93,740

Voice Mail Flat Rate - Sales

Total Sales	Units Sold	Segment	Total Summit Value
28	38	$135	$5,130
23	25	$135	$3,375
29	40	$135	$5,400
80	103	$135	$13,905

Voice Fax - Sales

Total Sales	Units Sold	Summit Value	Total Summit Value
-	-	$286	$0
-	-	$286	$0
-	-	$286	$0
-	-	$286	$0

Caller ID - Sales

Total Sales	Units Sold	Summit Value	Total Summit Value
25	28	$180	$5,040
32	39	$180	$7,020
24	27	$180	$4,860
81	94	$180	$16,920

Total Sales

Total Sales	Units Sold	Summit Value	Total Summit Value
64	78	$466	$36,330
74	83	$624	$51,815
65	79	$461	$36,420
203	240	$519	$124,565

Figure 15-4. Campaign results by products.

Sales-NCR Selection				
Business Choice - Sales				
Segment	Total Sales	Units Sold	Summit Value	Total Summit Value
Strategy#1	12	12	$2,180	$26,160
Strategy#2	17	18	$2,180	$39,240
Strategy#3	15	16	$2,180	$34,880
Total	44	46	$2,180	$100,280
Voice Mail Flat Rate - Sales				
Segment	Total Sales	Units Sold	Summit Value	Total Summit Value
Strategy#1	27	27	$135	$3,645
Strategy#2	18	23	$135	$3,105
Strategy#3	25	26	$135	$3,510
Total	70	76	$135	$10,260
Voice Fax - Sales				
Segment	Total Sales	Units Sold	Summit Value	Total Summit Value
Strategy#1	-	-	$286	$0
Strategy#2	-	-	$286	$0
Strategy#3	-	-	$286	$0
Total	-	-	$286	$0
Caller ID - Sales				
Segment	Total Sales	Units Sold	Summit Value	Total Summit Value
Strategy#1	23	25	$180	$4,500
Strategy#2	19	21	$180	$3,780
Strategy#3	26	27	$180	$4,860
Total	68	73	$180	$13,140
Total Sales				
Segment	Total Sales	Units Sold	Summit Value	Total Summit Value
Strategy#1	62	64	$536	$34,305
Strategy#2	54	62	$744	$46,125
Strategy#3	66	69	$627	$43,250
Total	182	195	$634	$123,680

Figure 15-5. Take-rate and return-on-advertising analysis.

NCR results show a 10% increase in take rate, but a 21% improvement in return on advertising as illustrated in Figure 15-6, the Contact Strategy Analysis.

Contact Strategy Analysis		
Segment	Response Rate	ROA
NCR DM Only	2.2%	11.9
Control DM Only	1.8%	10.4
NCR TM Only	1.9%	3.2
Control TM	2.1%	3.0
NCR DM+TM	1.1%	2.5
Control DM+TM	0.9%	1.7
Total	1.5%	3.0
NCR vs Random Selection		
Segment	Response Rate Lift	ROA Lift
DM Only	18%	15%
TM Only	-11%	8%
DM+TM	23%	44%
Total	9%	21%

Figure 15-6. Contact Strategy Analysis.

Now review Figure 15-7 to analyze the campaign results prepared by the campaign management service. As confirmed by the client, the actual results for the random approach, Strategy #2, are overstated due to lack of product clarity. Per discussion with the customer, the result is overstated by at least 12 (74 vs.62) sales, thereby artificially inflating the random results.

In extrapolating the above analysis to consider the effects of the suspect campaign results, the business value scenario is illustrated in Table 15-2:

In comparing NCR results to either random (method undetermined) or prior SIC approach, *it is critical to recognize the following points extracted from the "lessons learned" write-up relative to the subject project*:

- The organization did not produce the original entrance criterion, a file of prescribed variables in a predefined format. Instead, it provided less than 20 of the 165 prescribed variables. Data was simply not available or easily accessible. Many source systems were extracted. Many of the data elements omitted were considered critical ("must have") in determining propensity to buy.

Contact Strategy Analysis

NCR Selection

Segment	Sales	Response Rate	% Lift	Penetration Rate	% Lift	Cost/Mail Package	Total Mail Cost	Cost/Call	Total Telemarketing Cost	Total Cost	Cost/Sale	Total Summit Value	ROA
Strategy#1	62	2.2%		2.2%		$1.00	$2,879		$0	$2,879	$46.44	$34,305	11.92
Strategy#2	54	1.9%	-12.9%	1.9%				$5.00	$14,395	$14,395	$266.57	$46,125	3.20
Strategy#3	66	1.1%	-38.9%	2.3%	6.4%	$1.00	$2,879	$5.00	$14,395	$17,274	$261.73	$43,250	2.50
Total	182	1.6%					$5,758		$28,790	$34,548	$189.82	$123,680	3.58

Random Selection

Segment	Sales	Response Rate	% Lift	Penetration Rate	% Lift	Cost/Mail Package	Total Mail Cost	Cost/Call	Total Telemarketing Cost	Total Cost	Cost/Sale	Total Summit Value	ROA
Strategy#1	64	1.8%		1.8%		$1.00	$3,500		$0	$3,500	$54.69	$36,330	10.38
Strategy#2	74	2.1%	15.6%	2.1%				$5.00	$17,500	$17,500	$236.49	$51,815	2.96
Strategy#3	65	0.9%	-56.1%	1.9%	1.6%	$1.00	$3,500	$5.00	$17,500	$21,000	$323.08	$36,420	1.73
Total	203	1.5%					$7,000		$35,000	$42,000	$206.90	$124,565	2.97

NCR vs Random Selection

Segment	Response Rate Lift	Penetration Rate Lift	Cost/Mail Package	Total Mail Cost	Cost/Call	Total Telemarketing Cost	Total Cost	Cost/Sale	Total Summit Value	ROA
Strategy#1	18%							-15%		15%
Strategy#2	-11%							13%		8%
Strategy#3	23%	23%						-19%		44%
Total	9%							-8%		21%

Figure 15-7. Campaign results analysis.

- Analytic modelers were not as involved early in the process in order to evaluate/"sign-off" on the data before customer files were created, causing time delay and confusion about the data.
- External data (D&B) was delayed due to internal client communication problems. Further, due to the client's manipulation of the data, only 20% was deemed readable, causing time delay and confusion about the data.
- Information concerning the definition of D&B data elements was required for analytic modeling pre-processing/evaluation and modeling, causing additional time delay and confusion.
- Considering the above, there were many questions about the value of the data in terms of solving the business problem. Therefore, if you expect a high quality analytic model, you will have to create much higher quality in the data and database. Then try your best to model the business question.

	NCR take	Random take	NCR Lift to Random	Prior (SIC) Approach take	NCR Lift to Prior	NCR ROA	Random ROA	ROA Change
Random Approach Error Extrapolation	.51%	.29%	179%	.09%	566%			
BusinessChoice Only	.51%	.4%	127%	.09%	566%			
Baseline DiMark	2.1%	1.9%	110%	.09%	2333%	3.58	2.97	21%

Table 15-2. Business value scenario analysis.

In sensitizing the suspect campaign results against the deficiencies in the data, the application of NCR's GrowthADVISOR software showed positive gains compared to the customers' target market approaches. By extrapolating relative campaign effectiveness to the nine-state region with like campaigns, the incremental revenue generated over the average product tenure for a *single* campaign for *BusinessChoice* would range from approximately $1.1 million to $4.4 million.

Because customer bases are dynamic, upside potential exists with the use of such solutions for repeated campaigns on a rolling basis. In sum, despite the problems inherent in a lack of a CRM infrastructure, and the lack of campaign integration, the initial project still showed a measurable "success" in using such technologies.

Further, with the foundational technologies (data warehouse, applications) in place, exponential leverage can be optioned by implementing/integrating additional analytic applications for other products and packages, churn, and customer acquisition, as well as campaign management. As lessons learned, a clearly defined business problem, technology integration, and assimilation are critical.

- CRM technologies have the potential to build significant competitive advantage. As mentioned earlier, sparked by dashed expectations of improving "customer relationship management," sales of data warehoused-enabled CRM technologies and services are growing at an annual clip of 21% (Source: IDC), with the heaviest demands coming from consumer-intensive service industries such as financial, communications, and insurance. The average investment: $1.9 million.
- Yet unlike operational technologies (billing, order entry) where systems have matured and problems are relatively structured, CRM technologies are being applied to enable completely new CRM strategies—strategies that are changing at a dizzying pace. Compounded by the fast growing, high-tech, and competitive

nature of the communications industry, successful full-scale planning, implementation, and deployment of CRM technologies are a complex process. Such new capabilities:

  a. Involve many unstructured business problems.

  b. Involve an underdeveloped or lack of an established system.

  c. Involve building a system that cuts across the enterprise and links to operational systems in terms of both data inputs and outputs.

  d. Involve technology applications to a new constituent of users.

  e. Involve a host of third-order technologies including data warehousing, Internet, data mining, business rules, and object-oriented language.

- Hence, the process of planning, implementing, and deploying CRM technologies creates a host of IT management challenges. As the findings have confirmed, strategic impact, integration (data and business process), and strategic partnerships are critical to success.

- In aggregate, these issues (and opportunities) point to strategy and the firm's overall plan for deploying resources, as the linchpin. Regardless of how the strategy-making process occurs, it involves a "resource-based view of the firm"[1] as a vehicle for decision-making, coordination, and communication.

▶ Understanding Strategic Horizons

The process of strategy making is the basis for aligning major resource commitments to achieve strategic goals. Given the customer-oriented companies moving toward building CRM capabilities, the organizational challenges inherent with CRM IT-based strategies will likely become more complex. In particular, as communications companies and other related firms integrate CRM technologies across the enterprise, each organization embarking on CRM initiatives should consider that the real prizes may very well go to those firms who can best:

- **Innovate new technology-enabled strategies, particularly those aimed at becoming more "customer-oriented."**

---

[1]Robert M. Grant, *Contemporary Strategy Analysis* (1997).

- *Understand and manage the IT management issues associated with planning, implementing, and deploying.*
- Become more knowledgeable about *"relationship technologies."* Unlike the "mainframe era," or the "PC era," today's champions of change must become more knowledgeable of IT and the management issues. In one respect, this study revealed a potentially larger problem (and opportunity). Granted, many executives (middle and workers) may be ill-equipped to fully understand and effectively manage CRM strategies and issues.

  The mere existence of a DBM function and results analysis for DBM respondents strongly suggests the need for deeper and broader knowledge of IT/IT management issues among business and IT personnel. IT professionals must not only revise technical skills, but increase business aptitude. Similarly, marketing personnel need to hone technical skills.
- This gives rise to broader questions worth exploring: What is the relationship between the IT/IT management knowledge of senior managers—particularly those who are directly involved in strategy-making, implementation, and communication—and the success rates of CRM strategies and projects?
- At Capital One, a spin-off of Signet Banking Corp., in 1994 rocketed to the top ten of the largest credit card issuers. Its market value has topped $7.8 billion. Capital One's cofounders were a pair of childhood friends with no previous hands-on experience in banking. Both believe **Capital's "crown jewel" is their capability for innovation** (using information).
- **"Credit cards aren't banking—they're information,"** declares Rich Fairbank, chairman and CEO[2]. The credit-card business has been a grand experiment in using information technology—Capital One uses various CRM technologies (DW, data mining, intelligent agents, CTI, and so on) to figure out what people want to buy and how to sell them—before a caller hears the first ring. Customers who are judged most likely to buy are immediately routed to the most skilled sellers. And, according to Capital One, the system continues to get smarter.

[2]"Marketing Revolution," *Fast Company Magazine,* May 1999, Charles Fishman.

▶ Management Considerations

- The core competency (enabled by CRM technologies) is the basis for competitive advantage, changing the rules of the game, and delivering economic value. What are their skill profiles compared to others in similar "information-intensive" industries? Neither founder had any practical experience in banking, yet both have championed the innovation, planning, and implementation of a "marketing revolution."

- The research shows that when CRM technologies are effectively planned, implemented, and deployed, CRM (and the information within CRM) has helped companies change the way they market/manage to customers. By concurrently managing the technical and organization changes involved in CRM strategies, over one-half of the CRM efforts have been successful in realizing both measurable ROI and competitive advantage.

- Federal Express, which earns up to 400% ROI for marketing programs, states that to achieve such dramatic results, major investments are required in understanding the customer/problem, organization change, and technology infrastructure[3].

- Finally, by judiciously managing technical and organizational issues, CRM efforts can prove to dramatically transform CRM capabilities, delivering solid business value, and competitive advantage.

[3]From Wayne Eckerson, *"How to Architect a Customer Relationship Management Solution,"* Patricia Seybold Group (October 1997).

End Notes and Acknowledgments

▶ Author's End Notes

Special thanks go to the many customers, present associates and partners, former employees and advisors, and experienced business users in CRM, Data Warehousing, Decision Support, Business Intelligence, Executive Information Systems, and interactive marketing systems who participated in interviews and discussions with the author.

These included many seminar on-stage interviews, panels, and business conferences, in dozens of cities throughout the world, and the video studio interview series of 1998 and 1999. In addition, many of the individuals who are listed in the front of this book were also direct contributors of white papers, articles, professional knowledge, ideas, presentations, charts, achievements, processes, and practical approaches.

▶ Chapter 1: Managing Customers

The genesis of this chapter and the book came from professional experiences and mounds of materials created to educate and inform those in business who desire to lead in the use of technology to meet their ever-changing customer marketing and communications needs. As Chris Field, Clive Evans, and Peter Boulter began this journey with me, their thoughts are also included in this first chapter to begin this book and continue to its finalization, which was driven by joint speaking tours and motivation given to me from Don Peppers, Martha Rogers, Regis McKenna, Frederick Reichheld, Scarlett VanDer Muelen, and Carolyn Beauregard-Schinkle. The chapter is also based on sources such as:

The American Way Magazine Articles by Donald Carty (1999), and many articles, presentations, or books published by Inmon (1996), Lea (1197), Haley et al (1998), Harrington (1996-98), Mott (1997), DeBrosse (1996-1999), Watson and Haley (1998), Mc Kean (1999), and Swift (1996-1999, 1998, 1998-1999, 1999).

▶ Chapter 2: The CRM Process

The development of the CRM processes comes from industry professionals, educators, marketers, and those with foresight of what could be. Chris Twogood, Jeff Jones, Dan Harrington, Randy Lea, Mike De Brosse, Jim Donovan, William Wright, David Rocci, Heather Anderson, and others have contributed versions of the CRM Process included here.

Dean Kelly and Peter Hand took the CRM Process and mapped each function to activities and responsibilities, many of which are being used in leading organizations outside of the United States; to create the "future CRM organization."

In addition, ideas and thoughts included in this chapter also come from leading-edge customers who have invested time and resources into changing their world using technology to manage their customers and the relationships. Therefore we included Relationship Technologies and the info-structure to support them within this book.

Avshalom Rov, the Director of Applications (and Data Warehouse) for Israel's Pele-Phone, spent time with me in front of video cameras, in London in 1998, to discuss how he led his company from competitive nightmares in the cellular telephone industry to success. Rov and his team accomplished this by using Relationship Technologies and the processes discussed in this chapter. Therefore, the decision to include their case study: "A New Entrant: Gaining Competitive Advantage."

Rov has also made speeches in the United States and Europe to continually provide updated information to all of us on his journey into the future and the successes achieved along the way. You'll enjoy reading only part of this story, originally coauthored by Katherine Kramer of NCR Dayton, as were many of the case studies that are shared in this book. Some case studies only provide insight into the beginning stages of the company's activities, in order to protect their competitive advantage and also to retain a leading edge in their CRM investments. As author, I plan to provide future updates to these case studies and also to provide ongoing communications on their success.

▶ Chapter 3: The Role of Information Technology

Understanding the role and the move from Information Technology to Relationship Technologies will be important knowledge for the informed business and/or technology manager. The contributors to this chapter include a large number of people who work with me and continually drive to new levels of thinking in the realm of opportunities. This chapter gives you opportunity to think about those roles and what they will be in the near future.

From an interview in 1998 with Tony Marshall of Hallmark Cards, and published materials, you'll find the case study at the end of this chapter most informative and you may want to read more on this subject in Marshall (1998a, 1998b).

▶ Chapter 4: Learning from Information Through Data Mining

In building Chapter 3, there was a major contribution from Ken O'Flaherty of NCR in San Diego and the entire Rancho Bernardo NCR team at the Data Mining Lab. Ken has written excellent foundation white papers describing the basics of many subjects including data mining.

This chapter is of great importance since it is estimated that 80-90% of data mining is spent preparing data; 10-20% is actually spent "mining."

Thus, data warehousing, a process of managing data for the purpose of decision support use, is a prerequisite to data mining and other CRM applications.

Bill Inmon, "father" of data warehousing, says "the data miner fortunate to work on a data warehouse foundation, which offers detailed data that is clean, integrated, and complete, enjoys success that comes from being able to exploit this data as a resource. The data warehouse is integrated so the miner can concentrate on mining rather than on cleansing and integrating data."

Once data is mined, the results can be loaded into a data warehouse for use by business professionals to solve critical business problems such as targeting high value, high risk customers for retention. You will find this information essential as you read Chapters 5-15.

▶ Chapter 5: The Stages of Growth of CRM and Data Warehousing

Each January, I am fortunate to be a speaker at a very interesting and thought-provoking conference which has been sponsored by Dr. Ralph Sprague of The University of Hawaii since the 1960s. The Hawaiian International Conference on Systems Sciences (HICSS) focuses on information technology strategies, research, applications, and analysis at universities and industrial (I/S) companies. HICSS provides opportunities for university graduate students, professors, researchers, and industry practitioners to present both theory and practicality.

During this conference, my good friend Dr. Hugh Watson and I always spend some hours discussing the retrospectives and projections of I/S using the stage theory. We focus on I/S consequences in real life managerial situations, along with the implementations of data warehousing and decision support throughout the world.

Another always interesting meeting is with Dr. Efriam Turban, who has mastered half a dozen books on decision support, expert systems, and the management of information systems. "E.T." continues to seek actual customer case studies that have been presented at conferences (and uses them in his books, articles, and research papers) while also insightfully questioning the value of the processes and uses of the information technologies.

You can read about your competitors maturity in highlighted case studies in books by Hugh Watson, Efriam Turban, Ralph Sprague, Ramon Barquin, and Sean Kelly on the subjects of decision support systems, executive information systems, and data warehousing.

See articles in university management publications or books that discuss definitions of the 1) stages of IT, 2) definitions of decision support, and 3) explanations of the uses of data warehousing.

A special thanks to Dick Nolan (formerly a principle with Nolan and Norton, now back at Harvard University in Cambridge) for being so insightful and also motivating me, so many years ago, to accept a new realm of thinking and visualization of the historical maturation in the uses and purposes of information technology.

The Idea Group Publishing http://www.idea-group.com has published "The Benefits of Data Warehousing at Whirlpool" (1999).

▶ Chapter 6: Data Warehouse Methodology

For more information on the methodology included in this chapter, contact the author at crminsight@aol.com or ron421crm@aol.com or go to http://www.ncr.com and look for information under Data Warehousing professional Services or DW Methodology. It is also reviewed in Chapter 7 in Watson and Gray (1997, in Ch. 7, Pg. 205-236).

▶ Chapter 7: Building the CRM Data Warehouse and Info-Structure

Nothing speaks better than experience. Marcel Bhend contributed several articles to the industry on his insight and also practical activity flows in several journals in the late 1990s. For further reading, see:

Bhend (1999a, 1999b) and Swift (1998).

▶ Chapter 8: Critical Success Factors for CRM

During the late 1970s there were a few champions of industry who developed creative solutions for the widespread management and increasing networking of workstations. As we look back now, these people generated world-class solutions for complex business requirements, and developed management techniques to support the management processes required for success of IT.

During the early 1980s, at IBM, we developed a series of key Critical Success Factors (CSF) for strategic briefings and workshops to drive the thought process to clarity of the CSF from executives to their management teams throughout their organizations.

Some of this work was jointly developed or derived from our associates at the Systems Science Institute and the Information Systems Management Institute (ISMI). These included contributions by Ed Van Schaik, Vic Sassone, Jack Richardson, Reed Thornton, Walt Wojtalak, Perry Free, Don Gilmore, Dave Heim, Don Henderson, Gerry Jacobs, Al Kawamoto, Alan Krull, Charles Lester, Rudy Van Loon, Susan Peabody, and, of course, "Our General," John "Jack" Patton.

My two decades of work at IBM, and subsequently in the consulting arena, and then with AT&T/NCR, has focused a great deal on the CSFs for all types of businesses and governments around the world. My good friend Curt Bynum (formerly of IBM), now a consultant in California, worked with me to assist strategic level executives in their quest for the right CSFs. Along with our team at the Las Colinas' (Williams Square) Executive Briefing Center, under the leadership of Jeanene R. Jenkins, we accomplished this for IT organizations, end-user computing, office systems, departmental computing, and then began the journey into decision support environments.

In the crucial questions area of this chapter, a major contribution was provided by Joe Wenig and Greg Sannik from their white papers on "things to watch out for" or "red flags" developed with professional consulting teams over many years. These should be very helpful to you.

▶ Chapters 9 and 10: Ensuring Confidence and Implementation of Data Privacy

Thanks go to Ken O'Flaherty of San Diego for his white papers on Data Privacy. Under the initial leadership of Bob Henderson, and now of Peter Reid, The NCR Privacy Center has flourished and provides insightful support to numerous organizations. The people involved in this effort are world class and can be proud of their work.

▶ Chapter 11: @ctive Data Warehouse

Dr. Stephen Brobst and I have contributed the materials in this chapter, with vision from my NCR peers in San Diego, and from the many situations we all have experienced in the past.

Stephen Brobst is a highly regarded consultant and visionary on the uses of strategic and tactical decision-support systems. He has provided many articles for technical and managerial staff to gain insight into the high value of the enabling technologies that they are in care of and also have the opportunity to extend through experience and thoughtful maturity. He is a welcome and recent addition to our worldwide team.

▶ Chapter 12: The Economic Value of CRM

None other than Don Peppers and Martha Rogers, along with my visits with executives in 14 industries in 1999, provided the impetus to build and develop this chapter. You will find the ideas and materials to generate more thoughts for discussion on this topic. Contact me for more discussion on your ideas: crminsight@aol.com.

In mid-1999, Curt Hall published "Data Warehousing Issues and Trends: How Organization Worldwide are Adopting and Applying Data Warehousing Technology" (Cutter Consortium, http://www.cutter.com/consortium).

▶ Chapter 13: The Strategic View of DW and CRM

Thanks to Bernie Boar for being gracious to us for sharing his ideas with you here. You should read Boar (1994, 1995).

▶ Chapter 14: How Companies Succeed Using CRM, Data Warehousing, and Relationship Technologies

This and other chapters contain numerous case studies that are the culmination of the work of thousands of people in exciting situations and organizations in many industries around the world.

The materials included originate from: the people interviewed, the consultants and practitioners quoted, interviews with the author, presentations at conferences (in the United States, Canada, Mexico, Europe, Asia, South America, and Australia), articles published in the public domain, Internet case studies available online, press releases in the public domain, from representatives of the companies (with releases to NCR), success stories and white papers provided to the author, or interviews and exchanges with others in the NCR Corporation.

NCR has provided releases to me, the author of this book, and to the publisher, on all materials included in this book and case studies that NCR has published or has releases for from their customers, employees, associates, executives, studies, contractors, and partners.

A special thanks to Ruth Fornell, E.C. Corley, Bill Saylor, Erin Fagan, and Katherine Kramer for their partnership, support, and contributions to this chapter and the whole book.

On a continuing basis you will find case studies and useful information at: http://www.ncr.com/case_study/cs_repository.asp#cdw.

In addition, my monthly articles in *The Relationship Management Report* and *The Data Warehousing Report* can be found at: http://www.ncr.com/subscribe. These publications provide non-technical case studies and are designed to highlight the uses of CRM, Relationship Technologies, and Data Warehousing.

▶ Chapter 15: Study of Implementations Communications Industry CRM

Many thanks to go to Yancy Oshita, former Director of Communications Industry Marketing at NCR Corporation in 1997-99, for his contribution of the study he performed, with the advice and friendship of Dr. Jayesh Prasad at The University of Dayton (prasad@uhura.mis.udayton.edu).

Bibliography/References

Adelman, Leonard. 1992. *Evaluating Decision Support and Expert Systems*. New York: Wiley.

Adelman, Sid. 1995-1999. *Project Management for Data Warehousing*. In Proceedings of Both The DCI Data Warehouse Conferences and The Data Warehouse Institute's Implementation Conferences.

Agosta, Lou. 1999. *The Essential Guide to Data Warehousing*. Upper Saddle River, NJ: Prentice Hall.

Ahrendt, John. 1999. Bank of America, *Re-Engineering the Customer Experience (using CRM)*. In Proceedings of The NCR Partners Conference, October.

Allen, Terry. 1998. *Transforming Data into Revenue Through the Data Warehouse*. In Proceedings of the NCR Partners Conference, San Diego, CA.

Alzheimer, James. 1997. *Improving Compliance Through Technology* (at U.S. IRS). In Proceedings of the NCR Partners Conference, October.

Anahory, Sam and Dennis Murray. 1997. *Data Warehousing in the Real World*. Reading, MA: Addison-Wesley.

Anand, Sarabot S. and Alex G. Buchner. 1998. *Decision Support Using Data Mining*. Atlanta: Pitman.

Anderson, Heather, Randy Lea, Ron Swift, Edward White, Rob Armstrong, et al. 1996–1999. *The Data Warehouse Workshop*, NCR Corp., Seminars of 12 DCI DW Conferences and the NCR Partners Conference. Available at *http://www.ncr.com*.

Anderson, Maribeth. 1998. From First Chicago Mercantile Services, *What? NT Scalable? Solving IT with TOP END*. In Proceedings of the NCR Partners Conference, October.

Anton, John. 1999. *Customer Relationship Management*. Upper Saddle River, NJ: Prentice Hall.

Arikan, Icten. 1999. Kocfinans (Turkey), *Moving Closer to Our Customers—Kocfinans' Journey*. In Proceedings of The NCR Partners Conference, October.

Armstrong, Rob (NCR Corp.), Kevin Bubeck (The Coca-Cola Company), Nancy Colton (Anthem Blue Cross Blue Shield), Sam Burgess (Harburg Associates), Merv Tarde (AT&T Wireless Services). 1997. *Customer Panel: Political and Cultural Issues Within the Data Warehouse*. From a panel at The NCR Partners Conference, October.

Bacon, Terry R. 1999. "Selling to Major Accounts: Tools, Techniques, and Practical Solutions for Sales Managers." *AMACOM*, January.

Baker, Daniel and Stanley Klein. 1995. "Data Warehousing and Decision Support Systems in Telecommunications: A World-wide Survey and Market Analysis of Telecom Buyer Demand and Requirements." U.S.: Technology Research Institute.

Baron, Gerald, R. 1997. *Friendship Marketing: Growing Your Business by Cultivating Strategic Relationships*. Central Point, OR: Oasis Press.

Barquin, Ramon C. 1999. *Data Warehousing Step by Step*. Upper Saddle River, NJ: Prentice Hall.

Barquin, Ramon and Herbert Edelstein, eds. 1997. *Building, Using, and Managing the Data Warehouse*. **Bethesda, Maryland**: Prentice-Hall, May.

Bashein, Barbara J. and M. Lynne Markus. 1999. *Data Warehousing for the Rest of Us*. New York: Financial Executives Research Foundation.

Beckwell, Dawn and Thomas Townsend. 1998. *Mutual of Omaha: Moving the Data Warehouse to a Bigger "Building."* Proceedings of the NCR Partners Conference, October.

Bell, Chip R. 1996. *Customers as Partners: Building Relationships that Last*. San Francisco: Berrett-Koehler.

Berry, Michael and Gordon Linoff. 1999. *Mastering Data Mining: The Art and Science of Customer Relationship Management*. New York: Wiley.

Berson, Alex and Stephen J. Smith. 1998. *Data Warehousing, Data Mining, and OLAP*. New York: McGraw-Hill.

Berson, Alex, Stephen Smith, and Kurt Thearling. 1999. *Building Data Mining Applications for CRM*. New York: McGraw-Hill.

Bhend, Marcel. 1999. "100 Days to Data Warehouse Success." *The Data Warehouse Institute's Journal of Data Warehousing*, September.

Bhend, Marcel. 1999. "Make Your Data Warehouse a Real Success: Start with a Scalable Data Warehouse Pilot Project." *DM Direct Magazine* (1) 17.

Bhote, Keki R. 1996. "Beyond Customer Satisfaction to Customer Loyalty: The Key to Greater Profitability." *AMACOM*, December.

Bieber, Monty. 1998. *CRM in Health and Human Services*, NCR Corp. In Proceedings of the Spring Governmental Conference on I/T, Austin, TX.

Bischoff, Joyce and Ted Alexander. 1997. *Data Warehouse: Practical Advice From the Experts*. Upper Saddle River, NJ: Prentice Hall.

Boar, Bernard H. 1994. *The Art of Strategic Planning for Information Technology*. New York: Wiley.

Boar, Bernard H. 1995. *Practical Steps to Aligning Information Technology With Business Strategies*. New York: Wiley.

Boar, Bernard H. 1996. "Understanding Data Warehouse Strategically." NCR White Paper.

Bodenstab, Charles J. and PSI Research. 1997. *Information Breakthrough: How to Turn Mountains of Confusing Data Into Gems of Useful Information*. Central Point, OR: Oasis Press.

Borschelt, Tom and Susan Woodford. 1999. *Best Practices and Solutions in Automated Database Marketing*. Woodbridge, NJ: NCR Corp.

Brackett, Michael H. 1995. *The Data Warehouse Challenge: Taming Data Chaos*. New York: Wiley.

Brandow, James and Greg Irwin. 1998. *GTE Wireless' Experiences Implementing a Marketing Data Warehouse*. In Proceedings of the NCR Partners Conference, October.

Brobst, Stephen and NCR Corporation. 2000. *Integrating Your Data Warehouse Into the World of E-Business*. In Proceedings of "The Power of One" CRM Conference, Nice, France, May.

Brown, Stanley A. and PriceWaterhouseCoopers. 1999. *The Customer Relationship Management: Linking People, Process, and Technology*. New York: Wiley.

Bulkeley, William, M. 2000. "Data Warehouse Contracts with Web Firms Cracking New Market." NCR. *The Wall Street Journal*, April 17.

Burrows, Cathy. 2000. The Royal Bank of Canada (Canada), *Client Relationship Management—A Journey Not a Destination*. In Proceedings of "The Power of One" CRM Conference, Nice, France, May.

Burrows, Cathy and Brewer, Ted. 1999. The Royal Bank of Canada (Canada), *Client Metrics as a Tool for Organizational Transformation*. In Proceedings of The NCR Partners Conference, October.

Burrows, Cathy and Brewer, Ted, 1998. The Royal Bank of Canada (Canada), *Client Relationship Management at Royal Bank—Realizing Results—Part II*. In Proceedings of The NCR Partners Conference, October.

Business Communications Company Inc., ed. 1997. *Data Warehousing and Storage: Hardware, Software and Applications, Business Communications*. New York: Business Communications.

Campanelli, Melissa, "NCR and MatchLogic Sign Development and Marketing Agreement," *dmnews.com*, April 18, 2000, Available at: *www.dmnews.com/articles/2000-04-17/7821.html*.

Camps, Thomas and Cognos Corporation. 2000. *The Dark Side of E-Business—Decision-Making in the Internet Economy*. In Proceedings of "The Power of One" CRM Conference, Nice, France, May.

Cannon, Casey and Don Meyer. 1997. *Building a Better Data Warehouse*. Upper Saddle River, NJ: Prentice Hall.

Carlisle, John A. and Robert C. Parker. 1990. *Beyond Negotiation: Redeeming Customer-Supplier Relationships*. New York: Wiley.

Carty, Donald J. 1999. "CEO Article," *American Way Magazine*, 15 July.

Cates, Bill. 1996. *Unlimited Referrals: Secrets That Turn Business Relationships Into Gold*. U.S.: Thunder Hill Press.

Cathcart, Jim. 1990. *Relationship Selling: The Key to Getting and Keeping Customers*. Berkeley, California: Berkley Publishing Group.

Chakrovertty, Hari and Philip Ditfurth, and Deutsche Post AG (Germany). 1999. *Data Warehousing and the Privatization of Deutsche Post*. In Proceedings of The NCR Partners Conference, October.

Chapman Hall Staff 1998. *Implementing Systems for Supporting Management Decisions Concepts, Methods and Experiences*. London: Chapman & Hall.

Charles, Cheryl. 1999. *Security, Privacy, and Trust in Financial Services, BITS Financial Services Roundtable*. In Proceedings of the NCR Partners Conference, Orlando, FL, October.

Chen, Zhengxin. 1999. *Computational Intelligence for Decision Support*. Boca Raton, FL: CRC.

Cherkas, Andrew and Tillinghast Towers Perrin (UK). 2000. *The Future and Its Challenges for the Insurance Industry.* In Proceedings of "The Power of One" CRM Conference, Nice, France, May.

Chopra, Henry. 1998. *Managing Customer Relationships in the Financial Industry (Knowledge, Speed, Relevance, Timing, and Execution).* London: NCR Corp.

Christopher, Martin, Adrian Payne, and David Ballantyne. 1993. *Relationship Marketing: Bringing Quality, Customer Service and Marketing Together.* Oxford, U.K.: Butterworth-Heinemann.

Christopher, Martin, Helen Peck, and Moira Clark. 1998. *Relationship Marketing for Competitive Advantage: Winning and Keeping Customers.* Oxford, U.K.: Butterworth-Heinemann.

Church, Nancy W. 1999. *Customer Relationship Management: Solutions for the Insurance Industry.* In Proceedings of the Insurance Industry Roundtable Seminars, New York, Boston, Hartford, and San Diego.

Church, Nancy W. 1999. *Customer Value: Management in the Insurance Industry.* In Proceedings of the Insurance Industry Roundtable, New York.

Church, Nancy W. 1999. *Strategic Uses of Customer Profitability in the Insurance Industry.* In Proceedings of the Insurance Industry Roundtable, New York.

Clinton, William J. and Albert Gore, Jr. 1997. "A Framework for Global Electronic Commerce," July. See *http://iitf.nist.gov/eleccomm/ecomm.htm.*

Continental Airlines. *Revenue Management Using the Teradata Data Warehouse.* 1998. In Proceedings of the NCR Partners Conference, October.

Coucault, Jean-Paul, Michel Croissant, and Chronopost (France). 2000. *Building Valuable Customer Relationships by the Masters of Just-in-Time.* In Proceedings of "The Power of One" CRM Conference, Nice, France, May.

Cox, Steve. 1998. BellSouth Telecommunications, Inc. *Network Infrastructure Warehouse (NIW)—A Tool For Network Management.* In Proceedings of The NCR Partners Conference, October.

Craig, Robert S., Joseph Vivona, and David Bercovich. 1999. *Data Warehousing: Building Distributed Decision Support Systems.* New York: Wiley.

Cranston, Ross, ed. 1993. European Banking Law: *The Banker-Customer Relationship*. Brussels, Belgium: EEC Commission.

Cropper, Steve. 1998. *Enhancing Decision Making in the National Health Service: The Role of Decision Support Systems*. Washington, DC: Taylor & Francis.

Cross, Richard and Janet Smith. 1996. *Customer Bonding: Pathway to Lasting Customer Loyalty*. Chicago, IL:L NTC/Contemporary Publishing.

Curry, Jay. 2000. *The Customer Marketing Method: How to Implement and Profit From Customer Relationship Management*. New York: Simon & Schuster.

Czerniawski, Richard D. and Michael W. Maloney. 1999. "Creating Brand Loyalty: The Management Power of Positioning and Really Great Advertising." *AMACOM*, June.

Dahr, Vasant and Roger Stein. 1996. *Intelligent Decision Support Methods: The Science of Knowledge Work*. Upper Saddle River, NJ: Prentice Hall.

Dawson, Ross. 1999. *Developing Knowledge-Based Client Relationships: The Future of Professional Services*. Oxford, U.K.: Butterworth-Heinemann.

DeBrosse, Michael. 1996–1999. *High Potential Uses of Data Warehouses*, NCR Corp. Conference and Seminar Presentations.

de Bruin, Juliette and ABN AMRO Bank (Netherlands). 1999. *Transformation of a Department*. In Proceedings of The NCR Partners Conference, October.

Decision Support and Knowledge-Based Systems, Proceedings of the Hawaii International Conference on System Sciences (HICSS). University of Hawaii. 1990–1999.

Deviney, David E. and Karen Massetti Miller, eds. 1998. *Outstanding Customer Service: The Key to Customer Loyalty*. New York: American Media.

Devlin, Barry and Lynne Doran Cote, eds. 1996. *Data Warehouse: From Architecture to Implementation*. Reading, MA: Addison-Wesley.

Dietrich, Lothar, Dr., (Germany). 1997. Erbsloh AG: *Enterprise Business Solution SAP/R3 as a Basis for Data Warehouse*. In Proceedings of The NCR Partners Conference, October.

Directive 95/46/EC of the European Parliament and of the Council. 1995. 24 October. See also: *European Union directive on Data protection.* Available at *http://www.odpr.org/restofit/Legislation...les/Directive_Articles.html#anchor3080.*

Direct Marketing Association. 1999. *Customer Relationship Management: A Senior Management Guide to Technology for Creating a Customer-Centric Business.* New York: DMA Publishers.

Doyle, Shaun, Intrinsic and Martyn Pass, from JD Williams Incorporated. 1999. *Exploiting Financial Services: Cross-Sell Opportunities in Mail Order.* In Proceedings of The NCR Partners Conference, October.

D'Silva, Art, 1999. *Royal Bank of Canada: A Shared Infrastructure for Sustainable Data Warehousing.* In Proceedings of The NCR Partners Conference, October.

Dyche, Jill. 2000. *E-Data: Turning Data Into Information With Data Warehousing.* Reading, MA: Addison-Wesley.

Eckerson, Wayne W. 1997. *How to Architect a Customer Relationship Management Solution.* Boston, MA.: Patricia Seybold and Company Publishers.

Eckerson, Wayne W. 1998. *Data Warehousing in Review.* Bethesda, MD: The Data Warehouse Institute Publishers.

Economist Intelligence Unit. 1998. *Managing Customer Relationships: Lessons From Leaders.* London: The Economist Publishers.

Eden, Colin and Jim Radford. 1990. *Tackling Strategic Problems: The Role of Group Decision Support.* Irvine, CA: Sage.

EEC. 1997. *Directive 97/66/EC of the European Parliament and of the Council,* 15 December.

English, Larry P. 1999. *Improving Data Warehouse and Business Information Quality: Methods for Reducing Costs and Increasing Profits.* New York: Wiley.

Engman, Gert and Swedbank (Sweden). 2000. *The Role and Challenges for the Universal Banks in the Internet Economy.* In Proceedings of "The Power of One" CRM Conference, Nice, France, May.

European Union Directive on Data Protection. Available at *http://www.odpr.org/restofit/Legislation...les/Directive_Articles.html#anchor3080.*

Evans, James R. and David L. Olson. 1998. *Introduction to Simulation and Risk Analysis.* Upper Saddle River, NJ: Prentice Hall.

Fechner, Manfred and Mannesmann Mobilfunk (Germany). 1998. *An Enterprise Data Warehouse at Mannesmann Mobilfunk*. In Proceedings of The NCR Partners Conference, October.

Fechner, Manfred and Mannesmann Mobilfunk (Germany). 1998. *OLAP in TeleCommunications*. In Proceedings of "The Power of One" CRM Conference, Nice, France, May.

Ferdinandi, Patricia L. 1998. "Data Warehousing Advice for Managers." *AMACOM*, December.

Field, Leoni, John Andrews, and JD Group (South Africa). 2000. ***Thow JD Group is Managing Customer Relationships Amongst Multiple Retail Brands and Financial Services in a Market that does not yet expect it***. In Proceedings of "The Power of One" CRM Conference, Nice, France, May.

Figallo, Cliff. 1998. *Hosting Web Communities: Building Relationships, Increasing Customer Loyalty, and Maintaining a Competitive Edge*. New York: Wiley.

Finklestein, Clive and Peter Aiken. 2000. *Building Corporate Portals With XML*. New York: McGraw-Hill.

Forseth, Brit Emilie, Telenor 4tel (Norway). 1999. *Rapid Implementation of Data Warehousing in Telenor*. In Proceedings of The NCR Partners Conference, October.

Frachon, Amaud, BNP Global Information Systems (Banque Nationale de Paris, France). 2000. *How Data Warehousing Helps Us to Effectively Manage Our Customer Relationships*. In Proceedings of "The Power of One" CRM Conference, Nice, France, May.

Freemantle, David. 1998. *What Customers Like About You: Adding Emotional Value for Service Excellence and Competitive Advantage*. London: Nicholas Brealey Publishing.

FTC Releases Report on Consumers' Online Privacy. 1998. Report to Congress on Privacy Online, 4 June.

Gamble, Paul, Merlin Stone, and Neil Woodcock. 2000. *Up Close and Personal? Customer Relationship Marketing at Work*. London: Kogan Page.

Gerhard, Ebinger, Gerhard and Mobilkom Austria. 1998. *How Does a Data Warehouse Change Your Organization?* In Proceedings of The NCR Partners Conference, October.

Gentia Software (UK) and PriceWaterhouseCoopers (UK). 2000. *The Use of Balanced Scorecard to Become a CRM-Focused Company*. Special Workshop at "The Power of One" CRM Conference, Nice, France, May.

Gitomer, Jeffrey H. 1998. *Customer Satisfaction is Worthless, Customer Loyalty is Priceless: How to Make Customers Love You, Keep Them Coming Back and Tell Everyone They Know.* Austin, TX: Bard Press.

Gitomer, Jeffrey and Ron Zemke. 1999. "Knock Your Socks Off Selling." *AMACOM*, May.

Glanz, Barbara A. 1994. *Building Customer Loyalty: How You Can Help Keep Customers Returning.* New York: McGraw-Hill.

Godin, Seth. 1999. *Permission Marketing: Turning Strangers Into Friends, and Friends Into Customers (electronic book).* New York: Simon & Schuster.

Goman, Carol Kinsey. 1991. *The Loyalty Factor: Building Trust in Today's Workplace.* New York: Master Media.

Goman, Carol Kinsey and Tony Hicks, eds. 1991. *Managing for Commitment: Building Loyalty Within Organizations.* Menlo Park, CA: Crisp Publications.

Gordon, Ian H. 1998. *Relationship Marketing: New Strategies, Technologies and Techniques to Win the Customers You Want and Keep Them Forever.* New York: Wiley.

Goshi, Tsunayasu, McDonald's Company (Japan), Ltd. 1999. *IT Strategy in the Future.* In Proceedings of The NCR Partners Conference, October.

Govind, Harry, International Air Transport Association (IATA). 2000. *Organizational Impacts in the Airline Culture—From Product to Customer Focus.* In Proceedings of "The Power of One" CRM Conference, Nice, France, May.

Greiner, Donna and Theodore B. Kinni. 1999. *1001 Ways to Keep Customers Coming Back: Wow Ideas That Make Customers Happy and Increase Your Bottom Line.* Boston: Prima Communications.

Griffin, Jill. 1995. *Customer Loyalty: How to Earn It, How to Keep It.* San Francisco: Jossey-Bass.

Griffith, Charles and Bank of America. 1998. *Know Your Customer, Know Your Business.* In Proceedings of The NCR Partners Conference, October.

Groth, Robert. 1997. *Data Mining: A Hands on Approach for Business Professionals.* Upper Saddle River, NJ: Prentice Hall.

Groth, Robert. 2000. *Data Mining: Building Competitive Advantage.* Upper Saddle River, NJ: Prentice Hall.

Gutek, Barbara A. and Theresa Welsh. 1999. "The Brave New Service Strategy: Aligning Customer Relationships, Market Strategies, and Business Structures." *AMACOM*, October.

Hackathorn, Richard D. 1998. *Web Farming for the Data Warehouse*. Orlando, FL: Morgan Kaufmann.

Hackl, Bruno and Post & Telekom Austria AG (Austria). 1998. *Managing the Key Asset for Success: Integrated Enterprise Information Warehouse*. In Proceedings of The NCR Partners Conference, October.

Hackney, Douglas. 1998. *The Seven Deadly Sins of Data Warehousing*. Reading, MA: Addison-Wesley.

Hadden. Earl. 1997. *Modeling Techniques for Successful Data Warehousing and Data Marts*. European Data Warehouse Network, Huntington Beach, CA:Hadden-Kelly Publishing.

Haley, Barbara. 1998. "Implementing Successful Data Warehouses." *Journal of Data Warehousing* (3) 2: 48–51.

Halinen, Aino. 1997. *Relationship Marketing in Professional Services: A Study of Agency-Client Dynamics in the Advertising Sector*. New York: Routledge.

Hall, Curt. 1998. *Data Warehousing Issues and Trends: How Organization Worldwide Are Adopting and Applying Data Warehousing Technology*. New York: Cutter Consortium.

Hallberg, Garth and David Ogilvy. 1995. *All Consumers Are Not Created Equal: The Differential Marketing Strategy for Brand Growth and Profits*. New York: Wiley.

Hammergren, Thomas C. 1996. *Data Warehousing: Building the Corporate Knowledge Base*. London: International Thomson Computer Press.

Hanusa, Rolf, SBC and Rob Armstrong, NCR Corporation, and Thomas Coffing, Coffing DW Consulting, Ohio. 1999. *Data Warehousing in the New Millennium*. In Proceedings of The NCR Partners Conference, October.

Harrington, Daniel. 1998. *Driving Data Warehouse Successes*. In Proceedings of the Prague Conference on Data Warehousing, April.

Hawkins, Gary. 1999. *Building the Customer Specific Retail Enterprise*. Skaneateles, NY: Breezy Heights Publishing.

Hawkins, James. 1997. *AT&T Business Markets Division: Data Warehouse and the Web*. In Proceedings of The NCR Partners Conference, October.

Heil, Gary and Tom Parker. 1999. *One Size Fits One: Building Relationships One Customer and One Employee at a Time.* New York: Wiley.

Heskett, James L., Leonard A. Schlesinger, and W. Earl Sasser. 1997. *The Service Profit Chain: How Leading Companies Link Profit and Growth to Loyalty, Satisfaction, and Value.* New York: Free Press.

Hickman, Brendan. 1997–2000. *Best Practices in Airlines and Transportation Industry Uses of Data Warehousing for Customer Relationships and Higher ROI Through Resource Management.* Los Angeles: NCR Corp.

Hicks, Barry L. 1997. *JC Penney: NCR Teradata Capacity Management.* In Proceedings of The NCR Partners Conference, October.

Hill, Jerry. 1999. *Western Digital Corporation: Exploiting Data Warehousing for a Competitive Advantage.* In Proceedings of The NCR Partners Conference, October.

Hill, Jerry and Lambert, George, 1998. *Western Digital Corporation and KPMG Consulting: Exploiting Data Warehousing for a Competitive Advantage in a Hyper-competitive Marketplace.* In Proceedings of The NCR Partners Conference, October.

Hoeusler, Jacques. 2000. *Building Profits With Lifetime Value, RFM, and Modeling in a Real CRM Environment.* In Proceedings of "The Power of One" CRM Conference, Nice, France, May.

Hootman, John and Boris Zibitsker. 1998. *Kmart's use of Capacity Planning for Internet Workloads on Teradata.* In Proceedings of The NCR Partners Conference, October.

Huesman, Gary. 1999. *TPUMP Unleashed at Anthem Blue Cross Blue Shield.* In Proceedings of The NCR Partners Conference, October.

Humphries, Mark, Michael W. Hawkins, and Michelle Dy. 1998. *Data Warehousing: Architecture and Implementation.* Upper Saddle River, NJ: Prentice Hall.

Hutchins, Joseph. 1998. *Union Pacific Technologies: Enabling Enterprise Meta Data Access Through the Information "Where House."* In Proceedings of The NCR Partners Conference, October.

Hutchins, Joseph. 1997. *Union Pacific Technologies: Data Warehousing: The Business Perspective.* In Proceedings of The NCR Partners Conference, October.

Inmon, William H. 1996. *Building the Data Warehouse.* New York: Wiley.

Inmon, William H. 1998. "Information Management—Charting the Course: Bottom-up Warehouse Development." *DM Review* (February).

Inmon, William H. 1999. *Exploration Warehousing*. New York: Wiley.

Inmon, William H., Claudia Imhoff, and Ryan Sousa. 1998. *Corporate Information Factory*. New York: Wiley.

Inmon, William H. and Richard D. Hackathorn. 1994. *Using the Data Warehouse*. New York: Wiley.

Inmon, William H., Ryan Sousa, W. H. Anmon, and Chris Buss. 1998. *Data Warehouse Performance*. New York: Wiley.

Inmon, William H., J. D. Welch, and Katherine L. Glassey. 1996. *Managing the Data Warehouse*. New York: Wiley.

Inmon, William H., John A. Zachman, and Jonathan G. Geiger. 1998. *Data Stores, Data Warehousing, and the Zachman Framework: Managing Enterprise Knowledge*. New York: McGraw-Hill.

Intelligence Unit Economist, ed. 1997. *Managing Customer Relationships: Lessons from Leaders*. London: Economist Intelligence Unit.

Jarke, Matthias, Maurizio Lenzerini, Yannis Vassiliou, and Panos Vassiliadis. 1999. *Fundamentals of Data Warehouses*. New York: Springer-Verlag.

Jhaveri, Ashutosh. 1999. *MicroStrategy and NCR—Optimized for Maximum ROI*. In Proceedings of The NCR Partners Conference, October.

Johnson, James, The Standish Group, Maribeth Anderson, (First Chicago Corp., and Orlando Sela. Airline Reporting Corp. 1997. *Middleware Customer Panel Discussion: Internet Goes Business Critical*. In Proceedings of The NCR Partners Conference, October.

Kahler, Soren. 1998. *Statoil: Using a Data Warehouse to Support Category Management Implementation*. In Proceedings of The NCR Partners Conference, October.

Kambayashi, Y., ed. 1999. *Advances in Database Technologies: ER 98 Workshops on Data Warehousing and Data Mining, Mobile Data Access, and Collaborative Work Support and Spatio-temporal Data Management*. In Proceedings of the International Conference on Conceptual Modeling. 1998. New York: Springer-Verlag.

Kelly, Dean. 1999. *The Future Marketing Organization*. Presentations by NCR Corp., Sydney, Australia.

Kelly, Sean. 1994. *Data Warehousing: The Route to Mass Customization*. New York: Wiley.

Kelly, Sean. 1997. *Data Warehousing in Action*. New York: Wiley.

Kendall, Kenneth E. 1999. *Emerging Information Technologies: Improving Decisions, Cooperation, and Infrastructure*. Sage.

Kennedy, Siobhan, Excite @ Home's MatchLogic Ditches Oracle for NCR (Teradata Data Warehouse Solution), April 18, 2000 by The 451 Report online located at: *www.the451.com/index/1,1169,sectors-6-564-1,00.html*

Kimball, Ralph, Laura Reeves, Margy Ross, and Warren Thornthwaite. 1998. *The Data Warehouse Lifecycle Toolkit: Expert Methods for Designing, Developing, and Deploying Data Warehouses*. New York: Wiley.

King, Elliot. 1999. *Data Warehousing and Data Mining: Implementing Strategic Knowledge Management*. U.S.: Computer Technology Research Corp.

Klein, Michel R. and Leif B. Methlie. 1995. *Knowledge-based Decision Support Systems: With Applications in Business*. New York: Wiley.

Koved, Michael. 1997. *Bank of America: Web-Based Decision Support and NCR Teradata Access*. In Proceedings of The NCR Partners Conference, October.

Kuntz, Steven. 1999. *Advanced Database Management Systems Using DW for Improving Tax Collection in the State of Texas*. In Proceedings of the Texas Technology Conference, Austin, TX, June.

Larsen, Knut and Skandia/Vesta Insurance (Sweden). 1997. *One-to-One Marketing in the Scandinavian Insurance Industry*. In Proceedings of The NCR Partners Conference, October.

Lautenschlager, Brent and Delta Technology, Inc. (Subsidiary of Delta Air Lines in U.S.). 2000. *The Experience of Delta Air Lines in Enterprise Data Warehousing*. In Proceedings of "The Power of One" CRM Conference, Nice, France, May.

Lautenschlager, Brent and Paul Cummings. 1999. *Delta Air Lines: Integration of Full-Scale ERP With an Enterprise Data Warehouse*. In Proceedings of The NCR Partners Conference, October.

Lawrence, John A. and Barry Alan Pasternak. 1997. *Applied Management Science: A Computer-integrated Approach for Decision Making*. New York: Wiley.

Lea, Randy. 1997. *Building the Successful Data Warehouse*. Presented at DCI Data Warehouse World.

Lenz, Vicki. 1999. *The Saturn Difference: Creating Customer Loyalty in Your Company*. New York: Wiley.

"Life Insurance Industry CEO Survey Report." 1999. New York: Tillinghast-Towers-Perrin Consultants.

Lindelow, Leslie. 1997. *The Sabre Group: Migration to NCR 5100 from Multiple DBCs*. In Proceedings of The NCR Partners Conference, October.

Lipke, Matthew and Anthony Gulbrandsen. 1997. *Air Force Global Weather Service: DBC/1012 to the NCR 5100M WorldMark*. In Proceedings of The NCR Partners Conference, October.

Lockett, A. Geoffrey and G. Islei. 1989. *Improving Decision Making in Organizations*. New York: Springer-Verlag.

Lofti, Vahid and C. Carl Pegels. 1995. *Decision Support Systems for Operations Management and Management Science*. New York: McGraw-Hill.

Lowenstein, Michael W. 1994. *Customer Retention: An Integrated Process for Keeping Your Best Customers*. U.S.: ASQ Quality Press.

Lowenstein, Michael W. 1997. *The Customer Loyalty Pyramid*. New York: Greenwood Publishing Group.

Macavinta, Courtney. 1999. "Data Privacy Policies Fall Short" (a study). *CNET News*, 12 May.

MacStravic, Robin Scott. 1999. *Creating Consumer Loyalty in Healthcare*. U.S.: Health Administration Press.

Major, Grace. 1992. *Take Charge! How to Manage Your Customer Relationships*. New York: Sigma Books.

Marakas, George M. 1998. *Decision Support Systems in the Twenty-first Century*. Upper Saddle River, NJ: Prentice Hall.

Markoff, John. 1998. "U.S. and Europe Clash Over Internet Consumer Privacy." *The New York Times*, 1 July. Available at *http://search.nytimes.com*.

Marshall, Tony. 1998. "Sending Its Best: Hallmark Stays in Touch With Retailers and Customers." *The DW Institute's What Works Magazine* (3).

Marshall, Tony. 1998. "A Data Warehouse Comes of Age." *Teradata Review Magazine*, October/November.

Masagaki, Osamu. 1998. *SDW Implementation at SONY Marketing Japan*. In Proceedings of The NCR Partners Conference, October 1998.

Mattison, Robert M. 1997. *Data Warehousing and Data Mining for Telecommunications*. Norwood, MA: Artech.

Mattison, Rob and Rick Alask, eds. 1998. *Data Warehousing: Strategies, Technologies, and Techniques*. New York: McGraw-Hill.

Mattison, Rob and Brigitte Kilger-Mattison, eds. 1999. *Web Warehousing and Knowledge Management*. New York: McGraw-Hill.

McKean, John. 1999. *Information Masters—Secrets of the Customer Race*. New York: Wiley.

McKenna, Regis. 1993. *Relationship Marketing: Successful Strategies for the Age of the Customer*. Reading, MA: Addison-Wesley.

McKenna, Regis. 1998. *Real Time: Preparing for the Age of the Never Satisfied Customer*. Palo Alto, CA: McKenna Group.

McKenna, Regis. 1999. *Preparing for the Age of the Never Satisfied Customer. Speeches by for NCR Corp*. U.S. and European Seminar Tour with Ron Swift.

McLaughlin, Richard and Ted Brewer. 1998. *A Client Relationship Management Strategy at Royal Bank —Part I*. In Proceedings of The NCR Partners Conference, October.

Merz, Richard. 2000. *The Data Webhouse Toolkit: Building the Web-enabled Data Warehouse*. New York: Wiley.

Middlebrooks, Arthur and Craig Terrill. 1999. *Market Leadership Strategies for Service Companies: Creating Growth, Profits, and Customer Loyalty*. U.S.: NTC Publishing Group.

Miller, James B. and Paul B. Brown. 1994. *The Corporate Coach: How to Build a Team of Loyal Customers and Happy Employees*. New York: HarperBusiness.

Milne, Michael. 1999. *Xerox Canada Ltd.: Achieving an Enterprise View of the Customer*. In Proceedings of The NCR Partners Conference, October.

Monaghan, Glen, USAF Retired, and James Wakefield, NCR Corporation. 1999. *Warlord: How the U.S. Air Force Exploits Data Warehousing*. In Proceedings of The NCR Partners Conference, October.

Morse, Steve and David Isaac. 1997. *Parallel Systems in the Data Warehouse*. Upper Saddle River, NJ: Prentice Hall.

Moss, Larissa. 1998. "The Importance of Entity-Relationship Modeling in a Data Warehouse." *The Navigator*, Summer.

Mott, Randy. 1997. *How Wal*Mart Utilizes Data Warehousing for Enterprise-wide Success*. Keynote speech at DCI Data Warehouse Conference, Orlando, FL, February.

Murphy, Kevin J. 1993. *How to Keep Employees and Customers Faithful to Your Company*. U.S.: Effective Listening Institute.

Musgrave, James and Michael Anniss. 1996. *Relationship Dynamics: Theory and Analysis*. New York: Free Press.

Nadji, Mahvash. 1998. *Continental Airlines Takes Off on Data Warehouse*. In Proceedings of The NCR Partners Conference, October.

Nahshon, Nadav. 1999. *Merck-Medco Managed Care, LLC: Using Metadata Management in a Teradata Environment*. In Proceedings of The NCR Partners Conference, October.

National Golf Foundation, ed. 1998. *Developing Positive Relationships With Members and Customers*. U.S.: National Golf Foundation.

Newell, Frederick. 2000. *Loyalty.com: Customer Relationship Management in the New Era of Internet Marketing*. New York: McGraw-Hill.

Neyt, Phillipe and Corona Verzekeringen Insurance (Belgium). 2000. *Beyond the Corporate Babylonian Confusion of Tongues*. In Proceedings of "The Power of One" CRM Conference, Nice, France, May.

Nolan, Richard L. and Cyrus Gibson. 1974. "The Four Stages of EDP Growth." *Harvard Business Review*, March-April.

Nyberg, Therese. *Directive 95/46/EC on Data Protection*. NCR Paper, April 21, 1998.

O'Dell, Susan M. and Joan A. Pajunen. 1997. *The Butterfly Customer: Capturing the Loyalty of Today's Elusive Consumer*. New York: Wiley.

OECD Guidelines on the Protection of Privacy and Transborder Flows of Personal Data, September 23, 1980. Available at *http://www.oecd.org/dsti/sti/secur/prod/PRIV-EN.htm*.

O'Flaherty, Ken. 1997–1999. *Introduction to Data Mining*. Presentation and White Paper, NCR Corp.

Oikawa, Shigeyoshi Oikawa. 1998. *SDW Strategy at Ryohin Keikaku*. In Proceedings of The NCR Partners Conference, October.

O'Keefe, James. 2000. *Allied Irish Bank—AIB (Ireland): Leveraging the Data Warehouse for Effective Customer Management*. In Proceedings of "The Power of One" CRM Conference, Nice, France, May.

Olovsson, Steve. 2000. *How Telia Business Base (The Corporate Data Warehouse of Telia Communications) Has Helped Telia to Reach Their*

Business Objectives. In Proceedings of "The Power of One" CRM Conference, Nice, France, May.

Olsen, Rene and Telenor Global Services (Norway). 2000. *How Data Warehousing Increased the Profitability of Telenor's Wholesale of International Telephony*. In Proceedings of "The Power of One" CRM Conference, Nice, France, May.

Online Privacy Alliance. 1998. *Letter to President William J. Clinton*, June 3.

Owens, Orv. 1996. *The Psychology of Relationship Selling: Developing Repeat and Referral Business*. New York: Lifetime Books.

Parks, Ronald and AT&T CARM (USA) and Noel Brown, NCR Corporation. 1999. *Data Mining: The Proof Is in Your Data*. In Proceedings of The NCR Partners Conference, October.

Parks, Ronald and AT&T CARM (USA). 1999. *Using Data Warehousing at AT&T to Manage Consumer Risk*. In Proceedings of The NCR Partners Conference, October.

Parson, Chris, NCR Corporation (UK). 2000. *Intelligent E-Business*. Special Workshop at "The Power of One" CRM Conference, Nice, France, May.

Parsons, Emily and Mary Schmidke. 1999. *Whirlpool Corporation (USA): The SAP Data Warehouse: Implementing a Data Warehouse—Sourced from SAP R/3 Data*. In Proceedings of The NCR Partners Conference, October.

Payne, Adrian, Christopher Martin, Helen Peck, and Moira Clark. 1995-1998. *Relationship Marketing for Competitive Advantage: Winning and Keeping Customers*. Oxford, U.K.: Butterworth-Heinemann.

Payne, Sheila. 1997. *Delivering Customer Service: How to Win a Competitive Edge Through Managing Customer Relationships Successfully*. Philadelphia: Trans-Atlantic.

Pearson, Stewart. 1995. *Building Brands Directly: Creating Business Value From Customer Relationships*. New York: New York University Press.

Peppers, Don and Martha Rogers. 1996. *The One-to-One Future: Building Relationships One Customer at a Time*. New York: Doubleday.

Peppers, Don and Martha Rogers. 1997. *Enterprise One-to-One: Tools for Competing in the Interactive Age*. New York: Doubleday.

Peppers, Don and Martha Rogers. 1998. "The One-to-One Report: Customer Strategic Value." *DM Review*, November.

Peppers, Don and Martha Rogers. 1999. *The One-to-One Manager: An Executive's Guide to Customer Relationship Management*. New York: Random House.

Petersen, Glen S. 1999. "Customer Relationship Management Systems: ROI and Results Measurement." *Strategic Sales Performance*, March.

Peterson, John ("JP"). 1999. *AT&T Corporation (USA): Caring for 80 Million Customers—One Customer at a Time*. In Proceedings of The NCR Partners Conference, October.

Phillips, Jay and Lance Mattingly. 1998. *First American National Bank (Nashville, Tennessee): Building Shareholder Value Through Data Warehouse—Part I & Part II*. In Proceedings of The NCR Partners Conference, October.

Poe, Vidette, Stephen Brobst, and Patricia Klauer. 1997. *Building a Data Warehouse for Decision Support*. New York: Simon & Schuster.

Preiss, Kenneth, Steven L. Goldman, and Roger N. Nagel. 1996. *Cooperate to Compete: Building Agile Business Relationships*. New York: Wiley.

"Privacy and the National Information Infrastructure: Principles for Providing and Using Personal Information." 1995. A White Paper of the Privacy Working Group, Information Policy Committee, Information Infrastructure Task Force, June 6. Available at *http://www.iitf.nist.gov/ipc/ipc/ipc-pubs/niiprivprin_final.htm*.

Pyle, D. 1999. *Data Preparation for Data Mining*. Orlando, FL: Morgan Kaufmann.

Reichheld, Frederick F., ed. 1996. *The Quest for Loyalty: Creating Value Through Partnerships*. Cambridge: Harvard Business School Publishing.

Reichheld, Frederick F. and Bain and Company. 1997. *The Loyalty Effect*. Cambridge: Harvard Business School Press.

Reichheld, Frederick F. and Bain and Company. 1998. *Loyalty-Based Management Strategies*. Presentation on U.S. Seminar Tour with Ron Swift.

Richards, Jane and Paul Fuller. 1997. *St. George Bank (Australia): Building a Customer-Focused Strategy for Sustainable Profit Growth*. In Proceedings of The NCR Partners Conference, October.

Ritter, Dwight S. 1993. *Relationship Banking: Cross-Selling the Bank's Products and Services to Meet Your Customer's Every Financial Need*. New York: McGraw-Hill.

Rogissart, Guy. 2000. *Belgacom's Data Warehousing Project*. In Proceedings of "The Power of One" CRM Conference, Nice, France, May.

Romine, Paul. 1997. *Airlines Reporting Corporation: Building a Highly Available Open Systems Solution*. In Proceedings of The NCR Partners Conference, October.

Roth, Pam, ed. 1997. *Data Warehousing and Decision Support: The State of the Art*. Vol. 2. New York: Spiral Books.

Roth, Pam and William Juch, eds. 1996. *Data Warehousing and Decision Support: The State of the Art*. New York: Spiral Books.

Rov, Avshalom. 1999. *Pele-Phone Communications, Ltd.'s (Israel) Data Warehouse—The Unexpected Benefits*. In Proceedings of The NCR Partners Conference, October.

Rov, Avshalom. 2000. *Pele-Phone Communications, Ltd. (Israel): Data Warehouse—A Customer Experience*. In Proceedings of "The Power of One" CRM Conference, Nice, France, May.

Rowe, Alan J. and Sue Anne Davis. 1996. *Intelligent Information Systems: Meeting the Challenge of the Knowledge Era*. New York: Greenwood Publishing Group.

Ruffolo, Michael. 1997. *Empowering the End User: Technology in Action Within NCR*. In Proceedings of The NCR Partners Conference, October.

Rupp, Johannes. 1997. *Mobilkom: Information-Enabled Customer Care*. In Proceedings of The NCR Partners Conference, October.

Ryan, Christel. 1999. *Evaluating and Selecting Data Warehousing Tools*. Upper Saddle River, NJ: Prentice Hall.

Sabin, Steve and Pamela Hudson (IDX / The Huntington Group). 1999. *Columbia/HCA: Health Care Data Warehousing from Conception to Delivery*. In Proceedings of The NCR Partners Conference, October.

Sage, Andrew P. 1991. *Decision Support Systems Engineering*. New York: Wiley.

Sauter, Vicki L. 1997. *Decision Support Systems: An Applied Managerial Approach*. New York: Wiley.

Scheele, Peter and FDB Coop (Denmark). 2000. *Getting Leverage from Your Data Warehouse Investment*. In Proceedings of "The Power of One" CRM Conference, Nice, France, May.

Schwartz, Martin. 1999. *Lufthansa German Airlines (Germany): Creating a Data Warehouse Strategy for an International Airline*. In Proceedings of The NCR Partners Conference, October.

Shabot, M. Michael and Reed M. Gardner. 1993. *Decision Support Systems in Critical Care: Computers and Medicine.* New York: Springer-Verlag.

Shanahan, Kevin and Arkadiusz Harasimiuk (UK). 1998. *Teradata and Windows NT®—A Very Good Match.* In Proceedings of The NCR Partners Conference, October.

Shanham, Liz. 1998–1999. *Customer Relationship Management: Market Trends and Opportunities.* Stamford, CT: Meta Group.

Shore, Patrick. 1999. *The Sprint Story—A 10-Year Lesson in Data Warehousing and Decision Support.* In Proceedings of The NCR Partners Conference, October.

Silverston, Len, William H. Inmon, and Kent Graziano. 1997. *The Data Model Resource Book: A Library of Logical Data Models and Data Warehouse Designs.* New York: Wiley.

Simas, Manuel. 1997. *Micro Compact CAR AG (Germany): IT Support to a Virtual Company.* In Proceedings of The NCR Partners Conference, October.

Simmons, Leroy F. and George Wright. 1990. *Business and Economic Forecasting: Decision Support System Software.* New York: Wiley.

Simon, Alan R. 1997. *Data Warehousing for Dummies.* Foster City, CA: IDG Books Worldwide.

Singh, Harinder S., ed. 1998. *Interactive Data Warehousing Via the Web.* Upper Saddle River, NJ: Prentice Hall.

Singh, Harry S. 1997. *Data Warehousing: Concepts, Technologies, Implementations, and Management.* New York: Simon & Schuster.

Sitruk, Richard. 2000. *ETIS European Telecommunications Informatics Services (EEC), The Customer on the Move—Who will Own Him?* In Proceedings of "The Power of One" CRM Conference, Nice, France, May.

Siu, Brian, Paul K. M. Kwan, Benedict Lam, and Peter de Vries, eds. 1997. *Data Mining, Data Warehousing, & Client/Server Databases.* New York: Springer-Verlag.

Smith, Caroline, Paul Briggs, and Travelocity.com (U.S.). 2000. *Competing at Internet Speed—Converting Lookers to Bookers.* In Proceedings of "The Power of One" CRM Conference, Nice, France, May.

Smith, Charles L. 1998. *Computer-Supported Decision-Making: Meeting the Decision Demands of Modern Organizations.* Norwood, NJ: Ablex.

Smith, Deborah and Flora Khosravi. 1999. *Kmart's Use of Teradata and MicroStrategy: How 1+1 Can Add Up to 3!* In Proceedings of The NCR Partners Conference, October.

Smith, Donald. 1999. *Reliant Energy: The Road to CRM.* In Proceedings of The NCR Partners Conference, October.

Sperley, Eric and Jill Pisoni, eds. 1998. *The Enterprise Data Warehouse: Planning, Building, and Implementation.* Vol. 1. Upper Saddle River, NJ: Prentice Hall.

Sprague, Ralph H. and Hugh J. Watson. 1995. *Decision Support for Management.* New York: Simon & Schuster.

Steermann, Hank (Sears, Roebuck) and Bernadette Boas (NCR Corporation). 1998.*Sears': Creating a Business and IT Liaison: The User Support Group.* In Proceedings of The NCR Partners Conference, October.

Sterne, Jim. 2000. *Customer Service on the Internet: Building Relationships, Increasing Loyalty, and Staying Competitive.* New York: Wiley.

Sterne, Jim and Anthony Priore. 2000. *Building Customer Relationships With Email Marketing.* New York: Wiley.

Sterne, Jim and Anthony Priore. 2000. *Email Marketing: Using Email to Reach Your Target Audience and Build Customer Relationships.* New York: Wiley.

Stokoe, Jeff and Kevin Shanahan. 1999. *Synectics Solutions (UK): Industrial Strength With Teradata on NT.* In Proceedings of The NCR Partners Conference, October.

Stoll, Brian. 1999. *Increasing High-Value Customer Relationships Through CRM Best Practices.* Presentation, The Hartford Commercial Lines Group.

Stone, Merlin and Neil Woodcock. 1989. *Customer Relationship Marketing.* London: Kogan Page.

Stone, Merlin and Neil Woodcock. 1997. *Winning New Customers in Financial Services: Using Relationship Marketing and Information Technology in Consumer Financial Services.* Philadelphia: Trans-Atlantic Publications.

Stowell, Daniel M. 1997. *Sales, Marketing, and Continuous Improvement: Six Best Practices to Achieve Revenue Growth and Increase Customer Loyalty.* San Francisco: Jossey-Bass.

Sunderland, Jeff. 1997. *Principal HealthCare (PHC of USA): Reengineering for Success.* In Proceedings of The NCR Partners Conference, October.

Swift, Ronald S. 2000. *CRM and Data Warehousing Create New Value for Enterprises.* Special Workshop at DCI's CRM and Business Intelligence Conference, Boston, June.

Swift, Ronald S. 2000. *CRM: Increasing Productivity and ROI.* Special Workshop at "The Power of One" CRM Conference, Nice, France, May.

Swift, Ronald S. 2000. *CRM Making it Work for You and Your Customers.* In Proceedings of CRM Conference of the Conference Board, New York, March.

Swift, Ronald S. 2000. *CRM Putting the Theory to Work.* In Proceedings of "European CREDO CRM" Conference, Paris, France, March.

Swift, Ronald S. 2000. *CRM and Data Warehousing Join Forces for High ROI.* In Proceedings of DCI's CRM and Business Intelligence Conferences, USA, February, June, August, and October.

Swift, Ronald S. 1998. *CRM for High Productivity in Telecommunications.* In Proceedings of Conference on Effective DataBase and Management Information Systems Uses, Beijing, China, August.

Swift, Ronald S. 1998. *Customer Relationship Management—High Profitability Through Knowing Your Customers.* In Proceedings of the Partners Conference.

Swift, Ronald S. 1999. *Defining Customer Relationship Management for Competitive Advantage and High Return on Investment.* In Proceedings of the Conference Board's Conference on CRM, Chicago, May.

Swift, Ronald S. 1999. *Defining a New Info-Structure for High Value and Profitability.* In Proceedings of European and Asian Conferences on DW and/or CRM.

Swift, Ronald S. 1999. *Driving (CRM) Value in a Mass Market.* In Proceedings of the IEE Conference, Charlotte, NC.

Swift, Ronald S. 1999. *Generating High Value From Customer Relationships Through CRM.* In Proceedings of the Gobiermo 2000 Conference, Mexico City.

Swift, Ronald S. 1998. *The Future of Data Warehousing.* In Proceedings of DCI DW Conference, August and November.

Swift, Ronald S. 1998–1999. *How Companies Create New Value Through CRM: Putting the Theory to Work.* In Proceedings of Conferences Sponsored by NCR Corp.

Swift, Ronald S. 1999. *How CRM Drives High Customer Retention and Increased Loyalty in Customer Service Businesses and Government.* In Proceedings of European Conference on CRM, London England, June.

Swift, Ronald S. 2000. *Knowledge-based Customer-centric Systems for High ROI*. In Proceedings of DCI CRM Conference, Chicago, February.

Swift, Ronald S. 2000. *Managing Customer Relationships with Data Warehousing*. In Proceedings of the University of Hawaii's International Conference on Systems Sciences (HICSS), Maui, January.

Swift, Ronald S. 1996–1999. *Planning and Architecting a Scalable Data Warehouse*. In Proceedings of DCI Data Warehouse Conferences and The Data Warehouse Institute Conferences.

Swift, Ronald S. 1998–2000. *Putting the CRM Theory to Work*. In Proceedings of DCI CRM Conferences and DCI Data Warehouse World Conferences.

Swift, Ronald S. 1998. "Scalable Data Warehouse Solutions, Decision Support in the Data Warehouse." In *Decision Support in the Data Warehouse* edited by Paul Gray and Hugh J. Watson. Upper Saddle River, NJ: Prentice Hall.

Swift, Ronald S. 2000. *Using Knowledge-based Data Warehousing and Customer Relationship Management to Drive Very High Customer Profitability With Astounding Stock Value Growth*. In Proceedings of CRM and DW Conferences, London, June.

Tan, Joseph K. H. and Samuel Sheps. 1998. *Health Decision Support Systems*. Rockville, MD: Aspen.

Tanler, Richard. 1997. *The Intranet Data Warehouse: Tools and Techniques for Connecting Data Warehouses to Intranets*. New York: Wiley.

Taylor, Steve and NCR Corporation. 2000. *Citizens Are Customers too! Using CRM to Improve the Relationship Between the Government and the Citizen*. In Proceedings of "The Power of One" CRM Conference, Nice, France, May.

Tempelmeier, Horst and Heinrich Kuhn. 1993. *Flexible Manufacturing Systems: Decision Support for Design and Operation*. New York: Wiley.

Terry, Jeff. 2000. *Bank of America (USA): Delivering Risk Management Analysis with Hybrid Data Marts*. In Proceedings of "The Power of One" CRM Conference, Nice, France, May.

Thomson, Alex. 2000. *How the Dixons Group (UK) Leverages a Business-wide View of Data Across Consumer Channels and Multiple Brands without Confusing Customers*. In Proceedings of "The Power of One" CRM Conference, Nice, France, May.

Thomson, Lance. 1999. *SBC Communications, Inc.: Mergers and Acquisitions—The Data Warehouse Integration Challenge.* In Proceedings of The NCR Partners Conference, October.

Timmermans, Harry. 1998. *Design and Decision Support Systems in Architecture and Urban Planning.* Evanston, IL: Routledge.

Townsend, David and Nicholas Radcliffe. 1998. *Barclays (Bank) Information Warehouse Delivers Company-wide Risk and Profitability Measures Using Decisionhouse.* In Proceedings of The NCR Partners Conference, October.

Townsend, Thomas. 1999. *Mutual of Omaha: Customers May Change Their Mind—But Not Your Code!* In Proceedings of The NCR Partners Conference, October.

Townsend, Thomas. 1997. *Mutual of Omaha: Simple Ideas for Maximum Load Performance with Minimal Effort.* In Proceedings of The NCR Partners Conference, October.

Toyofuku, Akihiro. 1999. *Sekisui Chemical Co., Ltd., (Japan): Data Warehouse Implementation at Sekisui Chemical.* In Proceedings of The NCR Partners Conference, October.

Truet, Guy and Mary Joan Roe. 1998. *How CTIRCEAL Uses the Power of Teradata for Decisional and Transactional Support.* In Proceedings of The NCR Partners Conference, October.

Tucker, Jean A. 1997. *General Accident Insurance (U.S.): Tips for a Successful Data Warehouse Environment.* In Proceedings of The NCR Partners Conference, October.

Turner, Steve. 1998. *Does Reuters (U.K.) Have the Most Highly Available Operational 5100 Teradata/UNIX Complex in the World?* In Proceedings of The NCR Partners Conference, October.

Tyson, Monica. 1999. *Converting an Existing Data Warehouse to Teradata.* In Proceedings of The NCR Partners Conference, October.

Unruh, James A. 1996. *Customers Mean Business: Six Steps to Building Relationships That Last.* Reading, MA: Addison-Wesley.

Van de Ven, Saska. 2000. *Anticipating Customer Needs and Individual Customer Communication—How to Get There and How to Get Payback.* In Proceedings of "The Power of One" CRM Conference, Nice, France, May.

Varga, Kenneth J. 1997. *How to Get Customers to Call, Buy, and Beg for More! You Will More Than Double Your Business in Less Than One Year.* New York: World Wide Publishing & Trading.

Vavra, Terry G. 1995. *AfterMarketing: How to Keep Customers for Life Through Relationship Marketing*. New York: McGraw-Hill.

Venerable, Michael and Christopher Adamson, eds. 1998. *Data Warehouse Design Solutions*. New York: Wiley.

Villa, Jean-Paul and Peter W. Turnbull, eds. 1986. *Strategies for International Industrial Marketing: The Management of Customer Relationships in European Industrial Markets*. New York: Viking Penguin.

Von Ditfurth, Philip. 2000. *The Data Warehouse Project at Deutsche Post (Germany)*. In Proceedings of "The Power of One" CRM Conference, Nice, France, May.

Ward, Christopher. 1990. *Company Courtesy: Managing Public and Personal Relations*. Burlington, VT: Ashgate.

Wares, Bruce R. 1996. *Partner$Ell: Creating Lucrative and Lasting Client Relationships*. Dubuque, IA: Kendall/Hunt.

Watson, Hugh J. and Paul Gray. 1997. "Decision Support in the Data Warehouse." In *Special Contributions on Frameworks and Methodologies*, Ronald S. Swift, ed. Upper Saddle River, NJ: Prentice Hall.

Watson, Hugh and Barbara Haley. 1999. "The Benefits of Data Warehousing at Whirlpool Corporation." Annals of Cases on Information Technology Applications and Management in Organizations (1). See also: The Idea Group Publishing at *http://www.idea-group.com*.

Watson, Hugh J. and Barbara J. Haley. 1998. "Managerial Considerations With Data Warehousing." *Communications of the ACM* (41) 9: 32–37.

Watson, Hugh J., George Houdeshel, and R. Kelly Rainer. 1996. *Building Executive Information Systems: And Other Decision Support Applications*. New York: Wiley.

Welbrock, Peter R. 1998. *Strategic Data Warehousing Principles Using Sas, Software*. Cary, NC: SAS Institute.

Whitten, Neal. 1999. "Project Reviews—Looking Inside From Outside." *PM Network*, May.

Wiley, John, Research Team. 1998. *Data Warehousing: Regulatory and Market Intelligence for R&D Organizations*. New York: Wiley.

Williams, Martin. 1998. *Interactive Marketing: Building Customer Loyalty*. Upper Saddle River, NJ: Prentice Hall.

Witten, Ian H. and Eibe Frank. 1999. *Data Mining: Practical Machine Learning Tools and Techniques With Java Implementations*. Orlando, FL: Morgan Kaufmann.

Wixom, Barbara J. (Haley), Hugh J. Watson, and Dale L. Goodhue. 1998. "Data Warehousing at Whirlpool Corporation" (from a study). *Annals of Cases on IT Applications and Management*, 14–25.

Woods, David D., Erik Hollnagel, and Giuseppe Mancini. 1986. *Intelligent Decision Support in Process Environments*. New York: Springer-Verlag.

Woteki, Thomas, and Gregg Hall, and Stephen Conkle. 1998. *Implementing Data Warehousing at the American Red Cross*. In Proceedings of The NCR Partners Conference, October.

Wright, George and F. Bolger. 1992. *Expertise and Decision Support*. Boulder, CO: Perseus Books.

Index

Symbols

@ctive data warehouses, 273-274. *See Also* Active Data Warehouse
  Delta Airlines, 289-293
  first generation implementations, 277-281
  refreshment cycle, 275-277
  strategies, 281-282
  Web-based opportunities, 283-288

A

AAdvantage Frequent Flyer Program, (American Airlines), 2, 379

acceleration, management characteristic, 50

actionable decision support, 273, 277, 281

Active Data Warehouse, 100. *See Also* @ctive data warehouse

activity-based costing, 357

adaptability, 320

administrators, questions to ask CRM providers, 218

advantage classifications, 321-322

affinity analysis, 118-119

aggregated data, 191

airlines
  @ctive data warehouses, 289-292
  American Airlines
    AAdvantage Frequent Flyer program, 2, 379
    CRM example, 378-380
    One World Airline Alliance, 2
  Delta Airlines, 289-293

event-based triggering implementation, 279
successful CRM examples, 339, 378
American Airlines, 378-380
Continental Airlines, 369-371
Qantas, 380

Albright, Drew, 368

Ali, Mohammed, 333

American Airlines
AAdvantage Frequent Flyer program, 2, 379
CRM example, 378-380
One World Airline Alliance, 2

American Express, privacy, 227, 239

analysis, 42, 70

analytic modelers, 58, 418

analytical applications, privacy views, 268

Annals of Cases on Information Technology Applications and Management in Organizations, 148

anonymity, 230

Anonymizing view, 247

Anthem Blue Cross/Blue Shield, 390-395

Reizen, Arke 372

The Art of Strategic Planning for Information Technology, 319

Asian FLU, 380

assets, protection of, 202

Associated Group, The, 390

at-risk customers, 279

attrition fighters, 332, 334

audits, verification of privacy procedures, 271

Automated Data Placement, 166

automated decisions, opt out, 247-248
notice of logic, 248

automated voice response, 343

average return-on-investment (data warehouse study), 25

B

Bank of America, 76, 340-342

banking industry, 76
event-based triggering implementation, 280
successful CRM examples
Bank of America, 76, 340-342
Barclays Bank, 342-347
Royal Bank (of Canada), 347-348
Union Bank of Norway, 348-350

Barclays Bank, CRM success story, 342-347

Barquin, Ramon, 426

Batch window, questions to ask CRM providers, 216

batch-oriented decision support, 275-276

BEA Systems, 285

Belgacom, customer calling analysis, 57

Bell Canada, customer calling analysis, 57

Bell South Small Business Markets, 403

Benefits of DW at Whirlpool, The, 148

Bergskaug, Geir, 349

Bezeq, 58, 384

Bhend, Marcel, 170

Biland, Christian, 355

BIMs (Business Impact Models), 299-300

blocking, 249

Blue Cross/Blue Shield, 390-395

BNSF (Burlington Northern and Santa Fe Railway Company), 381-383

Boar, Bernie, 319

British Airways, 2
  CRM example, 378

Brown, Neville, 359

Burlington Northern and Santa Fe Railway Company (BNSF), 381-383

Business Data Model (BDM), 184

Business Discovery, 158

Business Impact Models. *See* BIMs

Business Choice, 403, 419

businesses. *See Also* individual names of businesses
  @ctive data warehouses.
    See @ctive data warehouses
  business-to-business customers, 4
  business-to-business enterprises, 283
  business-to-business relationships, 49
  business-to-consumer enterprises, 283
  cultural and idea interchanges, 72-73
  data mining. *See* data mining
  data warehouses. *See* data ware-houses
  enabling customer retention, 74

integrating with info-structure, 71-72
large, CRM, 26-27
positioning, 18
small, CRM, 26
users, 147
value
  competitive advantage, 422
  scenario, 417

Bynum, Curt, 124

C

campaign management, 413, 417-420.
  See Also marketing
  Campaign Manager, 54
  data warehouses, 41
  win back, 281

Canada's Royal Bank Financial Group, CRM success story, 347-348

capacity planning, 163

Capital One, innovation, 421

Carrefour, 19

Carty, Donald J., 1

case management, 280

Cathay Pacific, 2

cellular services. *See* communications industry

Chain-Level Management System, 90

change effort (CRM preparations), 49

Change Readiness Assessment, 160

Channel Manager, 55

channels (customers), 4
  analysis, CRM economic value, 313
  Channel Manager, 55

Choice/Consent option, 242

churn, 7

Claudio, Cecilia, 394

clickstreams, 233

Client/Server Application process, 161

Clinton, President William, 231

clustering (data mining), 109

communication management, 200

communications industry, 401
  Oshita Research Project—Focus on
  Knowledge
    customer project, 413-420
    definition, 401
    Four-Phase technique, 402-403
    industry review, 403-404
    research findings, 404-407
    strategic impact, 407-408
    strategic partnerships, 410
    strategy making, 420-422
    technology assimilation, 411-412
    technology integration, 408-410
  Pele-Phone Communications, 58
    business challenges, 58-59, 385
    CRM success story, 384-385
    customer calling analysis, 57
    data warehousing solution, 59-64,
    385-388

Community Mutual, 390

companies. *See* businesses

compliance reports (data warehouses),
  255

Computer Sciences Corp, 124

concurrent users, 210
  questions to ask CRM providers, 215

constancy of purpose (SCA), 320

consumers, 4. *See Also* customers
  recourse mechanisms, 232

Contact Strategy Analysis, 416

Contagion stage, 124

Continental Airlines, CRM example,
  369-371

continual learning, 46-47, 123

contribution to the enterprise, 203

Control stage, 124

Corporate Knowledge Repository, 286

cost benefits, Bank of America, 340

cost justifications, 330

Council of the European Union, 235

credit cards
  information technology, 421
  P3P standard programs, 263

Critical Success Factors. *See* CSFs

CRM (Customer Relationship Management), 7, 13-14, 337. *See Also*
  relationship management
  @ctive data warehouse, 273-274
    Delta Air Lines, 289-290, 292
    first generation implementations,
    277-281
    refreshment cycle, 275-277
    strategy, 281-282
    Web-based opportunities, 283-288
  analytical models, 58
  benefits, 28-29
    continual learning, 46-47
    customer profitability, 42
    customer retention, 42
    predicting future sales, 44-45
    ROI increases, 43
  change preparations, 49-50
  compared to operational
    technologies, 419
  customers
    project, 413-420
    segmentation, 75-77

data mining. *See* data mining
data warehouses, 332-333
    knowledge infrastructure, 333
    ROI, 25-26
    strategic thinking, 334-335
economic value, 295-300, 316-318
    anticipated results, 301-302
    application development, 315
    channel analysis, 313
    competitive advantage, 310
    direct marketing, 310
    failure risks, 302-303
    high returns, 308
    investment payback, 316
    marketing, 312
    payback performance, 309
    payoff, 308
    portfolio management, 311
    productivity increases, 314
    profits, 313
    retention programs, 312, 314
    service assessments, 311-312
    speed, 309-310, 315-316
    success measurements, 312
    success requirements, 303-307
examples of success
    airline industry, 339, 369-371,
        378-380
    banking industry, 340-350
    communications industry,
        384-385
    distribution industry, 338
    entertainment industry, 339,
        395-397
    financial services industry, 338,
        388-389
    ground transportation industry,
        339
    health care industry, 339, 390-395
    manufacturing industry, 338
    PC manufacturers, 351-354
    railroad industry, 381-383
    retail, 339, 354-369
    telecommunications industry, 339

    tourist industry, 375-377
    travel industry, 372-374
flexibility in deploying, 32
goals, 14-17
iterative learning process, 205
large companies, 26-27
management responsibilities, 29-31,
    36
maturity process, 123-125
    6 stages of growth, 125-126,
        140-144, 153, 155
    analytical approach, 126-127
    DSS, 127-135, 137-139
    info-structure, 145-152
organizational responsibilities, 51
    Campaign Manager, 54
    Channel Manager, 55-56
    Marketing Analyst, 52-54
    Marketing VP, 52
    Segment Manager, 54
    structure, 51
privacy views, 265-267
    analytical applications, 268
    audits, 271
    disclosure applications, 270
    names, 268
    opt-ins, 270
    opt-outs, 269-270
    privileged applications, 268
    standard, 267
process, 37-38
    advantages, 39
    analysis and refinement, 42
    customer interaction, 41-42
    knowledge discovery, 39-40
    market planning, 41
providers
    business questions to ask, 208-209
    guidelines for choosing, 205-225
    IT questions to ask, 211-220
    red flags, 221-223
    references, 206-208
    user questions to ask, 220-221
small companies, 26

strategic view, 319, 334-335,
420-422
advantage, 321-322
impact, 407-408
paradox, 327-332
partnerships, 410
rising-tide strategy, 326-327
SCA, 320-322
thinking, 323-326
tactical strategies, 47-48
technologies, 404, 412-413, 419
assimilation, 411-412
integration, 408-410

cross-selling, 9, 33, 282, 341

CSFs (Critical Success Factors),
197-199
application systems, 204-205
customer-centricity, 204-205
enterprises, 199
application strategies, 202-203
asset protection, 202
contribution, 203
enterprise management, 201-202
personnel development, 201-202
relationship strategies, 200-201
resource investments, 202-203
service and communication
management, 200
IT, 199
application strategies, 202-203
application systems, 204-205
asset protection, 202
contribution, 203
customer-centricity, 204-205
enterprise management, 201-202
personnel development, 201-202
relationship strategies, 200-201
resource investments, 202-203
service and communication
management, 200
red flags, 221-223

CSR (customer service representative),
282

cultural interchanges, 72-73

Customer Knowledge Systems. *See*
data warehouses

Customer Proprietary Network Information (CPNI), 240

Customer Relationship Management.
See CRM

customer service representative (CSR),
282

customer-centricity, stages for CRM
growth, 153, 155

customers, 3-4
acquiring, 42
at-risk customers, 279
behavior, 347
business to business, 4
calling analysis, 57
channels, 4
churn, 7
consumers, 4
contact strategy, 342
continual learning, 46-47
data (data warehouses), 76-77
evolving roles, 1-2
individual requirements, 345
infidelity, 49
interaction, 41-42
internal, 4
intimacy, 320
knowing, 5-6, 24, 66-69, 71, 80-81,
342
communications strategies, 33-35
profitability, 25
loyalties, 2-3, 7, 12
marketing, customer-centric, 43-44,
47, 66, 77, 282
ownership, 19

positioning, 23-24
product purchases
  incentives, 13
  Market-Basket Analysis, 9-10
profiles
  information, 255
  P3P standard, 264-265
profitability, 42, 350
  IT role, 74-77
referrals, 19, 43
relationship management. *See* CRM;
  relationship management
relationship optimization, 35
retaining, 42
  CRM economic value, 312-314
  data mining, 116
  IT role, 74-80
satisfaction, 321-322
segmentation, 75-77, 345, 379
target, 345
targeting, 17-22
value of, 8

CVS/Giant Food, data privacy, 227

D

Dalzell, Rick, 366

data
  access, 175
  analysis, 112
  elements, definition information, 418
  informational, 170
  loads, 189
  Market Basket, 91
  marketing, privacy, impacts, 245,
   247-249
  mining. *See* data mining
  modeling, 175, 341
  operational, 171
  privacy. *See* data privacy
  propagation, 147, 174

  replication, 147, 174
  security, 243
  sources, questions to ask CRM
   providers, 216
  transfers, data warehouses, 72
  transformation, 145, 172
  visualization, 108, 113
  warehouses. *See* data warehouses

Data Marts, 173

data mining, 57-58, 93-94, 122, 403,
410
  business applications, 114-115,
   119-120
   affinity analysis, 118-119
   customer retention, 116
   fraud detection, 117-118
   target marketing, 115-116
  classes, 104
  combining with data warehouses,
   100-101
  communication, 101-103
  competitive advantages, 95
   distribution strategies, 95
   restructuring industries, 96-98
  customer projects, 413-420
  discovery-driven data mining, 104
  knowledge deployment, 112
  knowledge discovery, 103-112
  privacy, impact, 245-249
  process, 112-114
  role, 98
  RTs, 98-101
   electronic commerce, 99-100
   data warehouses, 100
  scoring, 247
  selection criteria, 120-121
  taxonomy, 104
   Neural Networks, 106-111
   prediction, 105-106
  verification-driven data mining,
   104-105

Data Preprocessing phase, 112-113

data privacy, 225-228
  blocking, 249
  data marketing, impact, 245-249
  data mining, impact, 245-249
  data warehouses, 239-240, 260
    compliance reports, 255
    customer service interface,
      254-255
    European Union Directive,
      261-262
    general requirements, 240
    global requirements, 240-245
    impact, 245-249
    implementation, 251-255
    privacy views, 252-254
  OECD guidelines, 228-230
  opt-outs. *See* opt-outs
  privacy views, 265-267
    analytical applications, 268
    audits, 271
    disclosure applications, 270
    names, 268
    opt-ins, 270
    opt-outs, 269-270
    privileged applications, 268
    standard, 267
  U.S. Safe Harbor principles, 238-239
  Web commerce, 230
    European legislation, 235-238
    Online Privacy Alliance, 232-233,
      245
    P3P standard, 233-235, 257-265
    U.S. Federal Trade Commission,
      231
    U.S. Self-Regulation Policy, 231

Data Transformation process, 161

Data Warehouse Architecture Design
  process, 159

Data Warehouse Management process,
  162

data warehouses, 34, 71, 337.
  See Also databases
    @ctive data warehouse, 273-274
      Delta Airlines, 289-292
      first generation implementations,
        277-281
      refreshment cycle, 275-277
      strategy, 281-282
      Web-based opportunities, 283-288
  Active Data Warehouse, 100
  average-return-on-investment, 25
  business intelligence, 337
  campaign management, 41
  combining with data mining,
    100-101
  customer knowledge, 66
  customer-centric data, 76-77
  data transfers, 72
  Data Warehouse Audit, 163
  Data Warehouse Framework, 275
  Data Warehouse Tuning, 163
  defining business problems, 82
  examples of success
    airline industry, 339, 369-371,
      378-380
    banking, 340-350
    communications industry,
      384-385
    distribution industry, 338
    entertainment, 339, 395-397
    financial services industry, 338,
      388-389
    ground transportation industry,
      339
    health care industry, 339, 390-395
    manufacturing industry, 338
    PC manufacturers, 351-354
    railroad industry, 381-383
    retail, 354-357, 359, 361-363,
      365-367, 369
    retailing industry, 339

telecommunications industry, 339
tourist industry, 375-377
travel industry, 372-374
failure risks, 302-303
Hallmark Cards, 88-91
identifying need for, 69
Integrated Scalable Data Warehouse,
390
knowledge maturity, 69-70
maneuverability, 332-333
knowledge infrastructure, 333
strategic thinking, 334-335
maturity process, 123-125
6 stages of growth, 125-126,
140-144, 153, 155
analytical approach, 126-127
DSS, 127-139
info-structure, 145-150, 152
methodology, 157, 167
design and implementation
process, 159-162
planning phase, 158-159
scalability, 166
usage, support, and enhancement
phase, 162-165
operationalizing, 100
P3P standards, 234-235, 257-260,
262-263
enhanced personal data, 264
loyalty card/credit card programs,
263
marketing initiatives, 264-265
Pele-Phone Communications, 58-64,
385-388
privacy, 239-240, 260
compliance reports, 255
customer service interface,
254-255
European Union Directive,
261-262
general requirements, 240

global requirements, 240-245
impacts, 245-249
implementation, 251-255
privacy views, 252-254
relationship to high ROI, 25-26
RTs, 83-84
Sam's Direct, 10
scalability, 170
strategic view, 319
advantage, 321-322
paradox, 327-332
rising-tide strategy, 326-327
SCA, 320-322
strategic thinking, 323-326
success requirements, 303-307
Teradata, 91, 367, 389
Wal-Mart Stores, 22

Database Managers (DBMs), 407

Database Optimizer Technologies, 166

databases. *See Also* data warehouses
administrators, 174
questions to ask CRM providers,
218-219
data propagation, 147
data replication, 147
marketing, 141
optimizer, 281
parallel databases, 345
query technologies, 345
relational parallel database, 372
security, 266
single subject systems, 140
views. *See* views

DBMs (Database Managers), 407

DCB Actuaries and Consultants,
388-389

decision support. *See* DSS

decisions
    actionable, 273, 277, 281
    automated, opt out, 247-248
    batch-oriented support, 275-276
    event-based triggering, 278
        airline implementations, 279
        banking implementations, 280
        health care implementations,
        279-280
        insurance implementations,
        280-281
    support. *See* DSS
    tactical, 274
    tree induction, 106

Delta Air Lines, @ctive data
    warehouses, 289-292

DEMAND ANALYSIS, 182

denormalizing, 181

dependent data mart, 173

description (Neural Networks), 108

design and implementation process,
    data warehouse methodology,
    159-162

Differential Marketing, 51

direct marketing
    CRM economic value, 310
    opt-outs, 245-247
        disclosure to third parties, 247
    relationship management, 250

disaster recovery plans, questions to
    ask CRM providers, 219

disclosure
    applications, privacy views, 270
    third party, 247

discovery-driven data mining, 104

distribution industry, successful CRM
    examples, 338

distribution strategies, data mining, 95

distributors, 4

DSS (decision support), 127-128, 172
    applications, 342

DW Methodology, 137-139, 166
    analyzing, 132-133
    predicting the future, 134-137
    reporting, 128-131

E

e-commerce
    @ctive data warehouses, 281-292
    data mining, 99-100
    data privacy, 230
        data warehouses, 260
        European legislation, 235-238
        European Union Directive,
        261-262
        Online Privacy Alliance, 232-233,
        245
        P3P standard, 233-235, 257-260,
        262-265
        U.S. Federal Trade Commission,
        231
    U.S. Self-Regulation Policy, 231

economic value
    anticipated results, 301-302
    CRM, 295-300, 316-318
        application development, 315
        channel analysis, 313
        competitive advantage, 310
        direct marketing, 310
        high returns, 308
        investment payback, 316
        marketing, 312
        payback performance, 309
        payoff, 308
        portfolio management, 311

productivity increases, 314
profits, 313
retention programs, 312, 314
service assessments, 311-312
speed, 309-310, 315-316
success measurements, 312
success requirements, 303-307
failure risks, 302-303

economies of scale, 343

Edelstein, Herb, 121

Education and Support Assessments,
160

Edwards, Bob, 370

EDWs (Enterprise-wide Data
Warehouse), 146

Eggerding, John, 198

EIS (Hallmark Executive Information
System), 90

electronic commerce. *See* e-commerce

eliminating the advantages of
competitors, 321

employee empowerment, 320

encryption, 237

enterprise data warehouses, 173
Enterprise Scalable Data Warehouse,
275
Enterprise System Support, 162
Enterprise-wide Data Warehouse
(EDW), 146

enterprises, CSFs, 199
application strategies, 202-203
asset protection, 202
contribution, 203
enterprise management, 201-202
personnel development, 201-202

relationship strategies, 200-201
resource investments, 202-203
service and communication
management, 200

entertainment industry, successful
CRM examples, 339
Harrah's Entertainment, Inc.,
395-397

European legislation, 235-238

European Union Directive, 261-262

European Union's Data Protection
Directives, 226

event-driven marketing, 51, 86-91

event-based triggering, 278
airline implementations, 279
banking implementations, 280
health care implementations,
279-280
insurance implementations, 280-281

exceptional customer service, 343

excitement actions, 328-330

Executive Platinum, 379

exponential leverage, 419

external data, 418

F

failure risks (data warehouses),
302-303

Fairbank, Rich, 421

Far East Tone, customer calling
analysis, 57

FCC regulations, 240

Federal Express, ROI, 422

Federation of Migros Cooperatives (FMC), CRM success story, 354-359

financial services industry. *See Also* banking industry
    successful CRM examples, 338, 388-389

Finnair, 2

First American Bank of Tennessee, 76

First USA, 80

Five Rings, The, 325

Five Types of Views, 253

Ford, Henry, 2

forecasting, 341

Four Cs, 77

Four P's, 77

Four Stages of EDP Growth, The, 124

France Telecom, customer calling analysis, 57

franchises, 4

fraud detection, 117-118

Frost Bank of Texas, 76

G

Gartner Group, 111

Gates, Bill, 127

generalized insight, 119

Giant Foods, privacy, 239

Gibson, Cyrus, 124

Glover, Mark, 367

Goodhue, Dale, 337

Goossen, Gerret, 373

Graham, Stephen, 25

Grant, Robert M., 420

Griffith, Charles, 341

ground transportation industry, successful CRM examples, 339

Guidelines Governing the Protection of Privacy, 228

H

Haley, Barbara J., 169

Hall, Curt, 301

Hallmark Cards data warehouse, 88-91

Hallmark Executive Information System (EIS), 90

Hand, Peter, 51

Harrah's Entertainment, CRM example, 395-397

Harvard Business Review, 74, 198

Hawaiian International Conference on Systems Sciences, 426

health care industry, 339
    Anthem Blue Cross/Blue Shield, 390-395
    event-based triggering implementation, 279-280

Henderson, Ben, 272

HICSS, 426

Hill, Jerry, 351

Hogan Quality Consultants, 299

Holland International, 372

Hopkins, Bill, 49

Horn, Geoff, 344-345

householding, 5, 8, 343

Howell, Alonzo, 381

Hurd, Mark, 277, 336

Hutaff, Lin, 88

I

Iberia, 2

IBM, 94, 124, 197

IDC (International Data Corporation), 301, 419

idea interchanges, 72-73

inbound marketing communications, 33

incentives, product purchases, 13

Independent Data Marts, 173

index space, questions to ask CRM providers, 212

industry restructuring, data mining, 96-98

info-structures, 67
   CRM maturity process, 145-152
   cultural and idea interchanges, 72-73
   customer-centric, 17, 66
      targeting profitable customers, 17-22
   enabling customer retention, 74
   integrating with business functions, 71-72

relationship management, 3
Sam's Direct Market-Basket Analysis, 10

information access, 147

Information Discovery process, 158

information infra-structures, 338

Information Technology. See IT

Information Week, 362

informational data, 170

infra-structures, information, 338

Initiation stage, 124

innovation, Capital One, 421

insurance industry, event-based triggering implementation, 280-281

Integrated Scalable Data Warehouse, 390

interactive customer interfaces, (data warehouses), 254-255

interactive knowledge, 154

interactive marketing communications, 33

Interexchange Carriers. See IXCs

Interfaces (data warehouses), customer service, 254-255

internal customers, 4

International Data Corporation (IDC), 25, 301

Internet
   @ctive data warehouses, 283-288
   competitiveness, 49

data privacy, 230
  data warehouses, 260
  European legislation, 235-238
  European Union Directive,
    261-262
  Online Privacy Alliance, 232-233,
    245
  P3P standard, 233-235, 257-260,
    262-265
  U.S. Federal Trade Commission,
    231
  U.S. Self-Regulation Policy, 231
electronic commerce. *See* e-commerce

intimacy, customers, 320

banking services, 342

investments
  banking services,342
  CRM economic value, 316

Israeli Telecommunications
  Corporation, 58, 384

IT (Information Technology, 65
  CSFs, 199
    application strategies, 202-203
    application systems, 204-205
    asset protection, 202
    contribution, 203
    customer-centricity, 204-205
    enterprise management, 201-202
    personnel developments, 201-202
    relationship strategies, 200-201
    resource investments, 202-203
    service and communication
      management, 200
  knowledge maturity, 69-70
  priorities, 69
  questions to ask CRM providers,
    211-220
  role, 66-69
    cross-selling, 80-81
    cultural and idea interchanges,
      72-73
    customer-centric marketing, 77
    enabling customer retention,
      74-80
    enabling target marketing, 81-82
    integrating business functions with
      info-structure, 71-72

J-K

JCPenney, 362

Kano Methodology, 328, 330

Kelly, Dean, 51

Kelly, Sean, 170, 426

Kennedy, President John F., 197

Kihn, Jerry, 368

Kinki Nippon Tourist, CRM example,
  375-377

Kinki Nippon Tourist (KNT), 375-377

Klein, Douglas, 363

KMart, 362

Knowledge Capital Group, 49

knowledge deployment, data mining,
  112

knowledge discovery, 39-40, 66-69,
  71, 103-106, 108-112, 147, 380
  Knowledge Discovery Model
    Development, 160

KNT (Kinki Nippon Tourist), 375-377

Koc Family conglomerate, 359

Kotter, John, 49

Kwik-Fit, 19

L

large companies, CRM, 26-27

Lauterborn, Robert, 77

leaderships, change leaders, 50

Learning level (CRM implementation), 317

leveraging data warehousing, 343

Levy, Evan, 120-121

life event triggers, 342

Life-Time Value, 201
  supermarkets/grocery stores, 20

linear logic, 327, 330

Logical Data Marts, 174

Logical Data Model process (LDM), 159, 162, 185

longitudinal research, 403

loyalty of customers, 2-3, 7, 12
  loyalty cards, P3P standard
    programs, 263

M

Machine Learning, 106

Malcom Baldridge Quality Scoring Framework, 300

management
  change leaders, 50
  CRM responsibilities, 29-31, 36

managerial applications, 127

Manasco, Britton, 49

maneuver fighters, 332, 334

Manock, Mark, 362

manufacturing industry, successful CRM examples, 338

Market-Basket Analysis (MBA), 9-10, 91

marketing
  American Airlines AAdvantage
    Frequent Flyer program, 2
  communications strategies, 33-35
  customer specific, 282
  customer-centric, 43-44, 47, 66, 77
  customers. *See* customers
  data, impact of privacy, 245-249

databases, 141
  direct
    CRM economic value, 310
    opt-outs, 245-247
    relationship management, 250
  event driven, 86-91
  evolution, 37-38
  goals, 14, 17, 342
    evolving roles, 1-2
    internal, 4
    knowing, 5, 24
  householding, 5, 8, 343
  market planning, 41
  mass, 37
  models, 342
  one-to-one, 295-300, 345
  profitability, 25
    loyalties, 2-3, 12
    ownership, 19
    positioning, 23-24
    relationship management, 3, 6-7, 9-17
    targeting, 17-22
  target, 45, 115-116
    IT role in enabling, 81-82

Marketing Analyst, 52, 54

Marketing Optimization Solutions, 49

Marketing VP, 52

marketplace state, 332

Marshall, Tony, 88

massively parallel processing (MPP), 390

Mature level (CRM implementation), 317

maturity process, 123

Maturity stage, 124

MBA (Market-Basket Analysis), 9-10, 91

McIntyre, J.M., 78

McKean, John, 65

McLaughlin, Richard, 347

McMurtry, Charlie, 366

Medical claims data, 280

metadata, 175

MicroStrategy, 389

middleware, 175, 285

Migros, 19

Migros Data Discovery (MDD), 355

Milnes, William, 392

mining (customer information). *See* data mining

Model Design, 112

modeling, 175, 341

MOLAP, 105

Motorola, 58, 384

Mott, Randy, 22, 366

MPP (massively parallel processing), 390

multiplier effect (rising-tide strategy), 327

Musashi, Miyamoto, 325

N

names, views, 268

NASA, 197

Nation's Bank, 198

NCDM, (National Council of DataBase Marketing), 33

NCR Corporation, 25

NCR Partners Conference, 341

NCR Privacy Center, 239, 272

Nestle
  Easy Shop, 21
  partnerships, 21

Neural Networks, 106, 108, 110-111

Nolan, Richard L., 124

non-profitable customers, 343

Norton, Nolan, 124

notice of logic, opt-outs, 248

O

O'Flaherty, Ken, 93, 272

ODBC, 175

ODS, 175

OECD (Organization for Economic Cooperation and Development), 228-230

OLAP (On-Line Analytical Processing), 99, 105
  relational architecture, 389
  tools, 194

On-Line Analytical Processing. *See* OLAP

One World, 378
  American Airlines, 2, 379-380
  British Airways, 378
  Qantas, 380

one-to-one marketing, 282, 295-300, 345

one-to-one relationship building, 282

Online Privacy Alliance, 232-233, 245

operational data, 145, 171-172

operational technologies, compared to CR, 419

opt-ins, 229
  P3P standard, 264-265
  privacy views, 270

opt-outs, 229, 242
  automated decisions, 247-248
  direct marketing, 245, 247
  Online Privacy Alliance, 245
  P3P standard, 260, 264
  privacy views, 269-270
  special data categories, 248-249

Organization for Economic Cooperation and Development (OECD), 228-230

organizational responsibilities (CRM), 51
  Campaign Manager, 54
  Channel Manager, 55-56
  Marketing Analyst, 52, 54
  Marketing VP, 52
  Segment Manager, 54
  structure, 51

organizations. *See* businesses

Oshita Research Project—Focus on Knowledge
  communications industry review, 403-404
  customer project, 413-420
  definition, 401
  Four-Phase technique, 402-403
  research findings, 404-407
  strategic impact, 407-408
  strategic partnerships, 410
  strategy making, 420-422
  technology, 408-413

Oshita, Yancy, 401

P

P3P standard, 233-235, 257-260, 262-263
  data warehouses, 234-235, 257-260, 262-263
  enhanced personal data, 264
  loyalty card/credit card programs, 263
  marketing initiatives, 264-265

paradoxes, strategic, 327-332

parallel databases, 345

partnerships, 19
  customer ownership, 19
  Nestle, 21
  strategic, CRM technologies, 410

passive marketing communications, 33

PC manufacturers, Western Digital, 351-354

Pele-Phone Communications, 58
  business challenges, 58-59, 385
  CRM success story, 384-385

customer calling analysis, 57
data warehousing solution, 59-64,
385-388

Peppers and Rogers, 282

performance actions, 328

periodic data transfer, 190

perseverance, 320

personal data, opt-outs, 233, 248-249

personal profiles, 233

personnel
development, 201-202
productivity, 201

Physical Data Model (PDM), 187

Physical Database Design process, 161

Physical Design Review, 162

planning phase, data warehouse
methodology, 158-159

Platform for Privacy Preferences.
See P3P standard

portfolio management, CRM
economic value, 311

positioning, 19
businesses, 18
customers, 23-24

power users, 276

pre-defined queries, 128

pre-defined rules, 342

prediction, 70
data mining taxonomy, 105
DSS/DW, 134-137

predictive maintenance, 149

predictive modeling, 155

premium prices, 43

price, as factor in retaining
customers, 9

privacy, 225-228
blocking, 249
data marketing, impact, 245-249
data mining, impact, 245-249
data warehouses, 239-240, 260
compliance reports, 255
customer service interface,
254-255
European Union Directive,
261-262
general requirements, 240
global requirements, 240-245
impact, 245, 247-249
implementation, 251-255
privacy views, 252-254
OECD guidelines, 228-230
opt-outs. See opt-outs
privacy views, 265-267
analytical applications, 268
audits, 271
disclosure applications, 270
names, 268
opt-ins, 270
opt-outs, 269-270
privileged applications, 268
standard, 267
seal programs, 233
U.S. Safe Harbor principles, 238-239
Web commerce, 230
European legislation, 235-238
Online Privacy Alliance, 232-233,
245
P3P standard, 233-235, 257-260,
262-265
U.S. Federal Trade Commission,
231
U.S. Self-Regulation Policy, 231

privileged applications, privacy views, 268

process control, 320

process cycle, 39

processing environment, CRM providers, 209

productivity
CRM economic value, 314
Federation of Migros Cooperatives, 357-359
personnel, 201

products, purchases, Market-Basket Analysis, 9-10

profiles
customer information, 255
P3P standard, 264-265

profitability
customer knowledge, 25
IT role, 74-77

profits, CRM economic value, 313

propensity to buy, 341

providers, CRM, guidelines for choosing, 205
business questions to ask, 208-209
IT questions to ask, 211-220
red flags, 221-223
references, 206-208
user questions to ask, 220-221

Q

Qantas, 2, 380

queries
pre-defined, 128
technologies, 345

Query tools, 105

questions for CRM providers
business-oriented, 208-209
IT-oriented, 211-220
red flags, 221-223
user-oriented, 220-221

R

railroad industry, Santa Fe Railway, 381-383

Rand, Jonathon, 364

Rasper, 284

RBOCs (Regional Bell Operating Companies), customer calling analysis, 57, 404

RDBMS
Teradata, 390
views, 249, 267

Real Time Marketing, 51

red flags, CSFs, 221-223

references, CRM providers, 206-208

referrals (customer), 19, 43

Reichheld, Fred, 43, 74

relational architecture (OLAP), 389

relational parallel database, 372

relationship management, 6-7, 9, 11.
See Also CRM
benefits, 28-29
business to business relationships, 49
direct marketing, 250
info-structure, 3, 10, 17
one-to-one relationship building, 282
service, 11-14
consistency, 12

relationship optimization, 35, 84-86
event-driven marketing, 86-91

relationship technologies. *See* RTs

relationship value chain, 67

Report templates, 195

reporting, 69-70
DSS/DW, 128-131

research findings, CRM research, 407

resources
investments, 202-203
utilization, 321

retail, successful CRM examples
Federation of Migros Cooperatives,
354-359
Sears, Roebuck and Company,
361-363, 365
The Warehouse, 359-361
Wal-Mart, 365-369

Retail Link, 21

retailing industry, successful CRM
examples, 339

retention of customers
CRM economic value, 312-314
data mining, 116
IT role, 74-80

Return on Investment. *See* ROI

RFM (recency, frequency, and
monetary value), 380

rising-tide strategy, 320, 326-327

risk management, Barclays Bank, 345

risk tolerance, 209

Robert Fair, 285

Robertson, Milliman, 389

Rockart, Dr. John F., 198

Rogers, Martha, 295

ROI (Return on Investment), 17
benefits of CRM, 43
CRM economic value, 308, 316-318
application development, 315
channel analysis, 313
competitive advantage, 310
direct marketing, 310
investment payback, 316
marketing, 312
payback performance, 309
portfolio management, 311
productivity increases, 314
profits, 313
retention programs, 312, 314
service assessments, 311-312
speed, 309-310, 315-316
success measurements, 312
Cutter Consortium Study on ROI in
DW, 301
Federal Express, 422
relationship to data warehouses,
25-26

ROLAP, 105

Rov, Avshalom, 385

Royal Bank (of Canada), CRM success
story, 347-348

RTs (relationship technologies), 82
active data warehouses, 83-84
characteristics, 83
data mining, 98
combining data mining and data
warehouses, 100-101
electronic commerce, 99-100
operationalizing data warehouses,
100
relationship optimization, 84-86
event-driven marketing, 86-91

rule induction, 106

S

Sabre Group, data privacy, 227-228

sales
cross-selling, 9, 33, 80-81, 282, 341
tracking, 341
up-selling, 282

Sam's Direct, Market-Basket Analysis, 9-10

Santa Fe Railway, 381-383

SAs, questions to ask CRM providers, 219

SAS Institute, 94

Sassone, Victor, 299

SCA (Sustainable Competitive Advantage), 320-322

Scalability, data warehouse methodology, 166, 170

Scalable Data Warehouse Methodology, 157

scenario analysis, 320

scoring (data mining), 247, 279-280

Sears, Roebuck and Company, 361-365

security. See Also data privacy
database views, 266
encryption, 237

Segment Manager, 54

segmentation (customer), 75-77, 345, 379

selection criteria, data mining, 120-121

selective inclusion, 279

Sequential Affinity, 110

Sequential Association, 110

service
consistency, 12
CRM economic value, 311-312
management, 200
retaining customers, 11-14

single subject systems, 140

Single Version of the Truth, 143, 147, 202, 343

Six Stages of Growth, 125

small companies, CRM, 26

software, GrowthADVISOR, 419-420

Solution Readiness, 159

Southeast Group, 390

specialized applications, 147

speed, CRM economic value, 315-316

Sprague, Ralph, 426

SPuRS (Strategic Performance Reporting System), 144

SQL, expressions, 267

St. Louis Union Trust Company, 198

Standard Industrial Classification (SIC), 414

standard views, 267

star-schema data models, 181, 192

strategic CRM, 319, 420-422
advantage, 321-322
impact, CRM technologies, 407-408
interest, 322
partnerships, CRM technologies, 410

SCA, 320-322
strategic thinking, 323-326, 334-335
paradox, 327-332
rising-tide strategy, 326-327

Strategic Performance Reporting
System, (SPuRS), 144

strategic thinking, 323-326, 334-335
paradox, 327-332
rising-tide strategy, 326-327

Structured Query Language, 180

Stverka, Igor, 389

success measurements, CRM economic
value, 312

Sullivan, Kevin, 368

summarization, 110

summary data, questions to ask CRM
providers, 212

suppliers, customer knowledge of, 6

sustainable competitive advantage.
See SCA

T

tactical decisions, 274

Takahashi, Hideo, 376

target marketing, 38, 45, 115-116
IT role in enabling, 81-82
targeting customers, 17-19, 345
direct, 20-22

taxonomies, data mining, 104
Neural Networks, 106, 108, 110-111
prediction, 105-106

technology
assimilation, CRM technologies,
411-412
credit card businesses, 421
CRM technologies, 412-413
Information. *See* IT
integration, CRM technologies,
408-410

Telecom Italia, customer calling
analysis, 57

telecommunications industry. *See*
communications industry

Telefonica de Argentina, customer
calling analysis, 57

Telia, customer calling analysis, 57

Teradata
data warehouse, 91, 367, 389
RDBMS, 390

Third normal form, 181

threshold actions, 328

threshold attribute, 330

time
dimension, 326
questions to ask CRM providers, 220

touch points, 56

touch-tone interactions, 343

tourist industry, Kinki Nippon Tourist,
375-377

training, 195
questions to ask CRM providers, 220

Travel Companions (magazine), 376

Travel Unie, CRM example, 372-374

trends, identifying, 345

trust of people, 201

Turban, Dr. Efriam, 426

Tzu, Sun, 333

U

U.S. Federal Trade Commission, 231

U.S. Safe Harbor principles, 238-239

U.S. Self-Regulation Policy, 231

Union Bank of Norway, CRM success story, 348-350

unprofitable customers, 343

up-selling, 282

usage, support, and enhancement phase (data warehouse methodology), 162-165

users, questions to ask CRM providers, 220-221

V

value
customers, 8
enterprise warehouses, 174
retention models, 79

value-chain, 148
Wal-Mart Stores, 22

verification-driven data mining, 104-105

views
privacy, 252-254, 265-267
analytical applications, 268
audits, 271
disclosure applications, 270
names, 268
opt-ins, 270
opt-outs, 269-270
privileged applications, 268
standard, 267
RDBMS, 267

vision, 200

Vodaphone, customer calling analysis, 57

W-X

W3C. *See* World Wide Web Consortium

Wal-Mart Stores, 21, 362, 365-369
data warehouse, 22
value chain, 22

wallet-share expansion, 341

Walton, Sam, 365

Walz, Ernst, 355

warehouses, Enterprise Scalable Data Warehouse, 275

Watson, Dr. Hugh, 169, 426

Web commerce. *See* e-commerce

Web sites, privacy practices, 234

Western Digital, 351-354

Whirlpool Corporation, 148, 337

White House, 226

Whitehead, Jeffrey, 364

win back campaigns, 281

wisdom (knowledge of Enterprise), 70

Wixom, Barbara Haley, 337

World-class level (CRM implementation), 317

World-Wide Web Consortium (W3C), 226, 233

WWW, @ctive data warehouses, 283-288

Y-Z

yield management, 379

About the Author

Ron Swift is an internationally known consultant, author, and strategist in the areas of Customer Relationship Management, Customer Knowledge-Based Information Infrastructures, Data Warehousing, Decision Support, Executive Information Systems, Information Architectures, and the Management of Information Systems Organizations.

Ron Swift has assisted hundreds of clients on six continents to achieve their strategies and goals for over 30 years. For many years, Ron has been one of the most popular and thought provoking speakers at numerous conferences and forums for management of the world's leading corporations and governmental organizations.

He is one of the co-developers of the "IBM Architecture for Managing the Information Systems Business," and also co-developed the process model for NCR's "Data Warehouse Methodology."

Prior to joining NCR in 1996, Ron was a senior partner with an international consulting firm, following a successful career with IBM for over 22 years. Ron now serves as a Vice-President in the area of Customer Relationship Management Solutions and Scalable Data Warehousing with NCR Corporation from his office in Dallas, Texas.

His professional experiences range in industries which include banking, financial services, brokerage, insurance, communications, transportation, and government. Ron's vast consulting and systems implementation experiences also include ten years of teaching in several colleges and universities in graduate, management, and technical professional educational programs.